P9-DHJ-238

Jane's
TANK
RECOGNITION GUIDE

ISBN-10: 0-00-718326-7
ISBN-13: 978-0-00-718326-5

ISBN-10: 0-00-718326-7 (in the United States)
ISBN-13: 978-0-00-718326-5
FIRST U.S. EDITION Published 2006

HarperCollins books may be purchased for educational, business, or sales promotional use. For information in the United States, please write to: Special Markets Department, HarperCollins Publishers, 10 East 53rd Street, New York, NY 10022.

www.janes.com

Printed and bound by Printing Express, Hong Kong

10
9 8 7 6 5 4

Christopher F. Foss

An Imprint of HarperCollins*Publishers*

CONTENTS

7 Introduction

LIGHT TANKS & MAIN BATTLE TANKS

10 TAM (Argentina/Germany)
12 SK 105 (Austria)
14 Type 85-II (China)
16 Type 80 (China)
18 Type 69 (China)
20 Type 59 (China)
22 Type 62 (China)
24 Type 63 (China)
26 Duro Dakovic Degman (Croatia)
28 AMX-13 (France)
30 AMX-30 (France)
32 Leclerc (France)
34 Leopard 2 (Germany)
38 Leopard 1 (Germany)
42 Arjun (India)
44 Zulfiqar (Iran)
46 Merkava (Israel)
48 Ariete (Italy)
50 OF-40 (Italy)
52 Type 90 (Japan)
54 Type 74 (Japan)
56 Al Khalid 2000 (Pakistan)
58 PT-91 (Poland)
60 TM-800 (Romania)
62 T-90 (Russia)
64 T-80B (Russia)
66 T-64 (Russia)
68 T-72 (Russia)
72 T-62 (Russia)
74 T-54/T-55 (Russia)
78 PT-76 (Russia)
80 M-84 (Serbia and Montenegro)
82 ROTEM K1 (South Korea)
84 Challenger 2 (UK)
86 Challenger 1 (UK)
88 Scorpion (UK)
92 Khalid (UK)
94 Chieftain Mk 5 (UK)
96 Vickers Mk 3 (UK)
98 Centurion Mk 13 (UK)
100 T-84 (Ukraine)
102 M1A1/M1A2 Abrams (USA)
106 M60A3 (USA)
110 M48A5 (USA)
114 M41 (USA)
116 Stingray (USA)

TRACKED APCs/WEAPONS CARRIERS

120 Steyr 4K 7FA G 127 (Austria)
122 Saurer 4K 4FA (Austria)
124 BMP-23 (Bulgaria)
126 Type 90 (China)
128 YW 531 H (China)
130 YW 531C (China)
132 Type 77 (China)
134 AMX VCI (France)
136 AMX-10P (France)
138 Marder 1A3 (Germany)
140 Jagdpanzer Jaguar 1 SP (Germany)
142 Wiesel 2 (Germany)
144 Wiesel 1 (Germany)
146 Boraq (Iran)
148 Oto Melara IAFV (Italy)
150 Dardo IFV (Italy)
152 Type 89 (Japan)
154 Type 73 (Japan)
156 Type SU 60 (Japan)
158 Type 60 (Japan)
160 MLI-84 (Romania)
162 MLVM (Romania)
164 MT-LB (Russia)
166 BMP-3 (Russia)
168 BMP-2 (Russia)
170 BMP-1 (Russia)
172 BMD-3 (Russia)
174 BMD-1 (Russia)
176 SO-120 SPH/Mortar (2S9) (Russia)
178 M-60P (Serbia and Montenegro)
180 BVP M80A (Serbia and Montenegro)
182 M-80 (Serbia and Montenegro)

184 Bionix 25 IFV (Singapore)
186 All Terrain Tracked Carrier (S'pore)
188 Korean IFV (South Korea)
190 ASCOD MICV (Spain/Austria)
192 Pbv 302 (Sweden)
194 Combat Vehicle 90 (Sweden)
196 BvS 10 (Sweden)
198 Bv 206S (Sweden)
200 Turkish IFV (Turkey)
202 Warrior (UK)
204 FV432 (UK)
206 Stormer (UK)
208 Spartan (UK)
210 M2A3 Bradley (USA)
212 Armored IFV (USA)
214 M113A2 (USA)
218 M901 Improved TOW Vehicle (USA)
220 LVTP7 AAAV (AAV7A1) (USA)
222 Expeditionary Fighting Vehicle (USA)

4 X 4 VEHICLES

226 Tenix S600 (Australia)
228 ADI Bushmaster (Australia)
230 BDX (Belgium)
232 EE-3 Jararaca (Brazil)
234 RH ALAN LOV (Croatia)
236 Kader Fahd (Egypt)
238 Kader Walid (Egypt)
240 ACMAT (TPK 420 BL) (France)
242 Panhard VBL (France)
244 Panhard M3 (France)
246 Panhard AML (France)
248 Berliet VXB-170 (France)
250 Dingo (Germany)
252 TM 170 (Germany)
254 UR-416 (Germany)
256 Condor (Germany)
258 FUG (Hungary)
260 PSZH-IV (Hungary)
262 RAM AFVs (Israel)
264 Type 6616 (Italy)
266 Puma (Italy)
268 Type 6614 (Italy)
270 Boneschi MAV 5 (Italy)
272 Light Multirole Vehicle (Italy)
274 LBV (Fennek) (Netherlands)
276 Chaimite (Portugal)
278 TABC-79 (Romania)
280 ABI (Romania)
282 BRDM-1 (Russia)
284 BRDM-2 (Russia)
286 BRDM-2 ATGW versions (Russia)
288 BTR-40 (Russia)
290 Aligator (Slovakia)
292 BOV-VP (Slovenia)
294 RG-31 Nyala (South Africa)
296 RG-32M (South Africa)
298 Mamba Mk II (South Africa)
300 Casspir Mk III (South Africa)
302 RG-12 Patrol (South Africa)
304 BLR (Spain)
306 Eagle (Switzerland)
308 Piranha (Switzerland)
310 Roland (Switzerland)
312 Cobra (Turkey)
314 Akrep (Scorpion) (Turkey)
316 Otokar APC (Turkey)
318 Shorland (UK/Australia)
320 Ferret (UK)
322 Fox (UK)
324 Saxon (UK)
326 Shorland S 55 (UK/Australia)
328 Glover Webb APV (UK)
330 Tactica (UK)
332 Simba (UK)
334 Ranger (USA)
336 ASV 150 (USA)
338 LAV-150 (USA)
340 Dragoon (USA)
342 Scout (USA)
344 M1114 (USA)

6 X 6 VEHICLES

348 Pandur (Austria)

CONTENTS

350 SIBMAS (Belgium)
352 EE-11 Urutu (Brazil)
354 EE-9 Cascavel (Brazil)
356 Armoured Vehicle GP (Canada)
358 WZ 523 (China)
360 WZ 551 (China)
362 XA-200 (Finland)
364 ERC 90 F4 Sagaie (France)
366 AMX-10RC (France)
368 VCR (France)
370 VAB (France)
372 Transportpanzer 1 (Fuchs) (Germany)
374 Type 87 (Japan)
376 Type 82 (Japan)
378 BTR-152 (Russia)
380 OMC Ratel 20 (South Africa)
382 BMR-600 IFV (Spain)
384 VEC Cavalry Scout Vehicle (Spain)
386 Saracen (UK)
388 Saladin (UK)
390 LAV-300 (USA)

8 X 8 VEHICLES

394 Bison (Canada)
396 LAV-25 (Canada)
398 OT-64C(1) (SKOT-2A) (Former Czech.)
400 Armoured Modular Vehicle (Finland)
402 VBCI (France)
404 Spähpanzer Luchs (Germany)
406 Boxer MRAV (International)
408 Centauro (Italy)
410 TAB-77 (Romania)
412 TAB-71 (Romania)
414 BTR-90 (Russia)
416 BTR-80 (Russia)
418 BTR-70 (Russia)
420 BTR-60PB (Russia)
422 Rooikat (South Africa)
424 Guardian (Ukraine)

SELF-PROPELLED GUNS

428 155mm PLZ45 (China)
430 152mm Type 83 (China)
432 Type 85 122mm (China)
434 Type 70-1 122mm (China)
436 ZTS Dana 152mm (Former Czech.)
438 SP122 (Egypt/USA)
440 155mm GCT (France)
442 155mm Mk F3 (France)
444 CAESAR 155mm (France)
446 155mm PzH 2000 (Germany)
448 Raad-2 155mm (Iran)
450 Raad-1 122mm (Iran)
452 L-33 155mm (Israel)
454 Palmaria 155mm (Italy)
456 Type 75 155mm (Japan)
458 HSW Krab 155mm (Poland)
460 Model 89 122mm (Romania)
462 240mm SPM M1975 (2S4) (Russia)
464 203mm M1975 (2S7) (Russia)
466 120mm NONA-SVK 2S23 (Russia)
468 152mm 2S19 (Russia)
470 152mm (2S5) (Russia)
472 152mm M1973 (2S3) (Russia)
474 122mm M1974 (2S1) (Russia)
476 Primus 155mm (Singapore)
478 G6 155mm (South Africa)
480 K9 Thunder (South Korea)
482 155mm AS90 (UK)
484 M110 203mm (USA)
486 M107 175mm (USA)
488 M109A2 155mm (USA)
490 M44 155mm (USA)
492 M108 105mm (USA)

494 Glossary

INTRODUCTION

Challenger 2 MBT in Iraq showing extensive stowage and additional armour (MoD/CCR)

The aim of this book is twofold: firstly, to act as a convenient handbook for the reader to identify quickly and accurately almost any modern armoured fighting vehicle (AFV) in service today; secondly, to provide key information on the vehicle.

Some entries are more highly illustrated because there are so many local variants; indeed for some vehicles space limitations have prevented inclusion of every possible variation. A typical example is the M48. This was built with a 90mm gun, but many countries have refitted it with a 105mm gun which has a distinctive bore evacuator mid-way along the barrel; some countries have also added a thermal sleeve. US M48s have never been fitted with skirts, but the South Korean vehicles have skirts.

Recognition features can be further complicated by additional stowage bins and baskets, while the introduction of reactive armour, for example on the Israeli M48, M60 and Centurion tanks and Russian T-62/T-64/T-80 and T-90 series, alters their appearance completely.

Complications can arise from placing a vehicle in one particular section. For example, the Scimitar is used by the British Army as a reconnaissance vehicle, other countries use it as a light tank. As it is one of the few tracked reconnaissance vehicles, we have included it under tanks. 4 x 4, 6 x 6 and 8 x 8 vehicles have all been grouped, as they have in the wheeled armoured personnel carriers section, but some vehicles have been developed for use in a wide range of roles. For example, the Cadillac Gage LAV-150 and the Swiss MOWAG Piranha range of 4 x 4, 6 x 6 and 8 x 8 vehicles can be fitted with weapons ranging from a 7.62mm machine gun to a 105mm gun in the case of the 8 x 8 version.

Although space limitations have prevented all possible versions being included, many of these are mentioned in the text. Each entry has full technical specifications, key recognition features, development notes, list of variants, current status and list of users, manufacturer and, for many entries, a side view drawing and several photographs.

The fourth edition of this book, which has become the standard work of its type in its class, was compiled in late 2004.

Comments and new photographs for future editions should be sent to the author as soon as possible. The author would like to thank the many companies, governments and individuals who have provided information and photographs for the book. Special thanks are due to my wife Sheila for her help and encouragement while the book was being compiled.

Christopher F. Foss

8 x 8 vehicles can be used for many missions and be fitted with different weapon systems. This MOWAG Piranha has a 90mm gun.

LIGHT TANKS & MAIN BATTLE TANKS

TAM Tank (Argentina/Germany)

SPECIFICATIONS

Crew:	4
Armament:	1 x 105mm, 1 x 7.62mm MG (coaxial), 1 x 7.62mm MG (anti-aircraft), 2 x 4 smoke grenade dischargers
Ammunition:	50 x 105mm, 6,000 x 7.62mm
Length gun forwards:	8.23m
Length hull:	6.775m
Width:	3.29m
Height to turret top:	2.43m
Power-to-weight ratio:	24.27hp/tonne
Ground clearance:	0.45m
Weight, combat:	30,000kg
Weight, empty:	28,000kg
Ground pressure:	0.78kg/cm²
Engine:	MTU MB 833 Ka 500 supercharged 6-cylinder diesel developing 720hp at 2,400 rpm
Maximum road speed:	75km/hr
Maximum road range:	590km
Maximum road range with auxiliary tanks:	940km
Fuel capacity:	640 lit
Fording:	1.5m
Fording with preparation:	2.25m
Fording with snorkel:	4m
Vertical obstacle:	1.0m
Trench:	2.5m
Gradient:	60%
Armour:	Classified
Armour type:	Steel
NBC system:	Yes

DEVELOPMENT

In 1974 Thyssen Henschel (today Rheinmetall Landsysteme) was awarded a contract by Argentina for design and development of a new medium tank designated TAM (Tanque Argentino Mediano), as well as infantry combat vehicle VCI (Vehiculo Combate Infanteria) subsequently redesignated VCTP. Three prototypes of each were built and shipped to Argentina. Production commenced at a new factory in Argentina with a requirement for 512 TAMs and VCTPs, but production was stopped after about 350 vehicles for budgetary reasons. Further development by the company has resulted in the R301, which has a number of improvements including a new fire-control system and a more powerful engine.

Driver sits front left of TAM, power pack to his right and turret towards rear. Commander and gunner sit right of turret, loader left. The 105mm gun power-elevates from -7° to +18° and turret traverses through 360°. A 7.62mm MG is mounted coaxial with main armament and there is a similar weapon on the roof for air defence.

To extend its operational range, long range fuel tanks can be fitted at hull rear. Optional equipment for R301 includes additional armour protection.

VARIANTS

VCA 155, lengthened TAM chassis fitted with turret of Italian Palmaria 155mm self-propelled howitzer, developed to meet requirements of Argentinian Army.
VCRT, ARV based on chassis of TAM for Argentinian Army, prototype only.
Rocket launchers, 160mm and 350mm multiple launch rocket systems have been built (chassis is Argentinian with rocket launchers from Israel). In addition many trial versions in Germany.
VC AMUN, ammunition resupply vehicle, trials.

STATUS

Production completed in Argentina. Production yet to commence in Germany. In service with Argentina.

MANUFACTURERS

Rheinmetall Landsysteme, Kassel, Germany; TAMSE, Buenos Aires, Argentina.

KEY RECOGNITION FEATURES

- Hull similar to Marder MICV with well-sloped glacis plate. Driver front left, horizontal hull top with turret towards rear, hull back slopes to rear then inward at mid point

- Turret has flat sides that slope slightly inward, turret bustle extends almost to hull rear, commander's cupola right side of flat roof. 105mm gun mounted in external mantlet, with fume extractor

- Suspension each side has six road wheels, drive sprocket front, idler rear and three track-return rollers. Upper part sometimes covered by skirt

Above left: TAM

Right: TAM

Below: R301

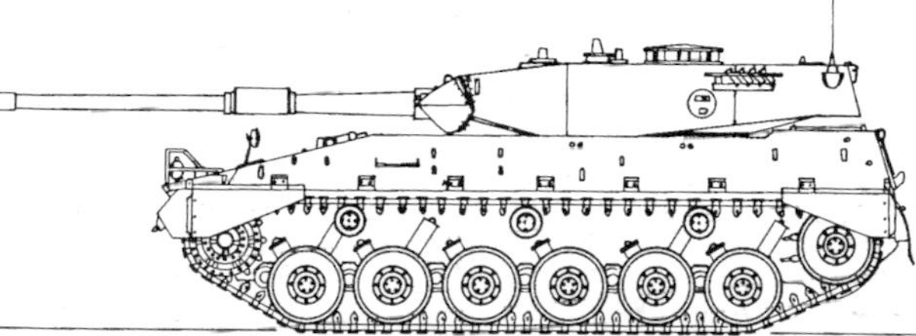

Steyr SK 105 Light Tank (Austria)

SPECIFICATIONS

Crew:	3
Armament:	1 x 105mm, 1 x 7.62mm MG (coaxial), 2 x 3 smoke grenade dischargers
Ammunition:	42 x 105mm, 2,000 x 7.62mm
Length gun forwards:	7.735m
Length hull:	5.582m
Width:	2.5m
Height:	2.529m (commander's cupola)
Ground clearance:	0.4m
Weight, combat:	17,700kg
Power-to-weight ratio:	18.1hp/tonne
Ground pressure:	0.67kg/cm^2
Engine:	Steyr 7FA 6-cylinder liquid-cooled 4-stroke turbocharged diesel developing 320hp at 2,300rpm
Maximum road speed:	70km/hr
Maximum range:	500km
Fuel capacity:	420 lit
Fording:	1m
Vertical obstacle:	0.8m
Trench:	2.41m
Gradient:	75%
Side slope:	40%
Armour:	40mm (maximum)
Armour type:	Steel
NBC system:	Yes
Night vision equipment:	Yes (infra-red for driver and commander)

DEVELOPMENT

SK 105, also known as Kürassier, was developed from 1965 by Saurer-Werke, taken over by Steyr-Daimler-Puch in 1970, to meet the requirements of the Austrian Army for a mobile anti-tank vehicle.

First prototype was completed in 1967 with pre-production vehicles following in 1971.

Driver sits front left, turret centre, engine and transmission rear. Oscillating turret is an improved French Fives-Cail Babcock FL-12 in which 105mm gun is fixed on upper part, commander left, gunner right. The 105mm gun is fed by two revolver-type magazines, each of which holds six rounds. Ammunition fired includes HE, HEAT and smoke, but with modifications SK 105 also fires APFSDS projectiles.

Turret traverse and elevation is powered,

manual controls for emergency use, turret traverse 360°, 105mm gun in upper part of turret elevates from -8° to +12°.

KEY RECOGNITION FEATURES

- Distinctive oscillating turret centre of vehicle, commander's cupola left, large box-shaped infra-red/white searchlight right side of turret roof, laser rangefinder below
- 105mm gun has double baffle muzzle brake and thermal sleeve, overhangs front of vehicle
- Suspension either side has five road wheels, idler front, drive sprocket rear, three track-return rollers

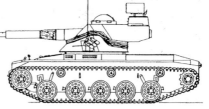

VARIANTS

Steyr SK 105/A2 is upgraded SK 105/A1 with a number of improvements including new FCS and fully automatic ammunition loading system.
Steyr SK 105/A3 is still at prototype stage and has a new oscillating turret with improved armour protection and fitted with 105mm M68 rifled tank gun which can fire standard NATO 105mm ammunition including APFSDS.
Greif armoured recovery vehicle.
Pioneer vehicle is based on ARV.
Driver training vehicle is SK 105 with turret removed and replaced by new superstructure for instructor and other trainee drivers.

STATUS

Production complete. In service with Argentina, Austria, Bolivia, Botswana, Brazil, Morocco and Tunisia.

MANUFACTURER

Steyr-Daimler-Puch AG, Vienna, Austria.

Above right: SK 105

Above left: SK 105

Right: SK 105

Below: SK 105

NORINCO Type 85-II MBT (China)

SPECIFICATIONS

Crew:	3
Armament:	1 x 125mm gun, 1 x 7.62mm MG (coaxial), 1 x 12.7mm (anti-aircraft), 2 x 6 smoke grenade launchers
Ammunition:	40 x 125mm, 2000 x 7.62mm, 500 x 12.7mm
Length gun forwards:	10.28m
Length hull:	7.3m (estimate)
Width:	3.45m
Height:	2.30m (turret top)
Ground clearance:	0.48m
Weight, combat:	41,000kg
Power-to-weight ratio:	18.5 hp/tonne
Engine:	V-12 supercharged diesel developing 730hp
Maximum road speed:	57.25 km/h
Maximum road range:	500km (estimate)
Fuel capacity:	1,000 lit (estimate)
Fording:	1.4m
Vertical obstacle:	0.8m
Trench:	2.7m
Gradient:	60%
Side slope:	40%
Armour:	Classified
Armour type:	Steel/Laminate
NBC:	Yes
Night vision equipment:	Yes

DEVELOPMENT

The Type 85-II MBT is a further development by NORINCO (China North Industries Corporation) of the Type 80 MBT (qv) but has many improvements including a different hull and turret with a significant improvement in armour protection.

The driver is seated in the hull at front left with ammunition to his right with turret in centre. The gunner is seated on the left of the turret and the commander on the right.

Main armament is a 125mm smooth bore gun which is fed by an automatic loader, so enabling the crew to be reduced to three. Ammunition is of the separate loading type (eg. projectile and charge) and is similar to that used in the Russian T-72. MBT Turret traverse is 360 degrees with weapon elevation from -6 to +14°. The main armament is fully stabilised and the computerised fire control system includes a laser rangefinder.

VARIANTS

There are a number of models of the Type 85-II including the **Type 85-IIA** and the **Type 85-IIM** (this may have the Chinese designation Type 88C). The vehicle is also co-produced in Pakistan as the **Type 85-IIAP**. Further development of the Type 85 has resulted in the **Type 85-III** which has many improvements including a 1000 hp diesel engine. **Type 90-II** weighs 48 tonnes and is at present at the prototype stage. This has been developed in association with Pakistan and is also known as the **Khalid, MBT 2000** or **P-90**.

STATUS

In production. In service with China and Pakistan.

MANUFACTURER

Chinese state factories.

KEY RECOGNITION FEATURES

• Well-sloped glacis plate, turret centre and raised engine compartment at rear. 125mm gun has fume extractor mid-way down barrel

• Turret has sloping front with vertical sides with six smoke grenade launchers mounted halfway along turret side, large stowage basket at rear, 12.7mm MG on right side of turret roof

• Suspension either side consists of six road wheels with idler at front, drive sprocket at rear and track return rollers, upper part of suspension covered by skirt with wavy line to lower part

Top left:
Type 85-IIAP MBT (Christopher F Foss)

Right:
Type 85-IIAP

Below:
Type 85-II

NORINCO Type 80 MBT (China)

SPECIFICATIONS

Crew:	4
Armament:	1 x 105mm, 1 x 7.62mm MG (coaxial), 1 x 12.7mm MG (AA), 2 x 4 smoke grenade dischargers
Ammunition:	44 x 105mm, 2,250 x 7.62mm, 500 x 12.7mm
Length gun forwards:	9.328m
Length hull:	6.325m
Height:	2.29m (turret roof), 2.874m (with AA MG)
Width:	3.372m (overall)
Ground clearance:	0.48m
Weight, combat:	38,000kg
Power-to-weight ratio:	19.2hp/tonne
Engine:	V-12 Model VR36 diesel developing 730hp at 2,000 rpm
Maximum road speed:	65km/hr
Maximum road range:	430km
Fuel capacity:	1,400 lit
Fording:	1.4m
Vertical obstacle:	0.8m
Trench:	2.7m
Gradient:	60%
Side slope:	40%
Armour:	Classified
Armour type:	Steel/Composite
NBC system:	Yes
Night vision equipment:	Yes

DEVELOPMENT

Whilst the earlier Type 69 MBT was a further development of the Type 59 MBT, the Type 80 has a number of new features including a brand new hull. The driver is seated at the front left with some ready use 105mm ammunition to his right, the three man turret is in the centre with the commander and gunner on the left and the loader on the right. The powerpack is at the rear.

The 105mm rifled tank gun fires standard NATO ammunition and can be elevated from -4° to +18° under full power control with turret traverse a full 360°, manual controls are provided for emergency use. A 7.62mm machine gun is mounted coaxial with the main armament and a 12.7mm machine gun is mounted on the turret roof for anti-aircraft defence.

A computerised fire control system is fitted and this includes a laser rangefinder for the gunner. One version has the laser rangefinder installed in the gunner's sight while another has the laser rangefinder mounted over the 105mm gun in a similar manner to that of some versions of the NORINCO Type 69 MBT.

For deep fording, a snorkel can be fitted to the vehicle and a fire detection/suppression system is standard. If required a layer of composite armour can be fitted to the glacis plate for improved battlefield survivability.

VARIANTS

Type 80–II is modified Type 80.
Type 80–III is a developmental vehicle.
Type 88 is an upgraded Type 80.
Improved ZTZ-88B is based on Type 80–III.
ZTZ-88B has longer 105mm gun.

STATUS

Production complete. In service with China and Myanmar.

MANUFACTURER

Chinese state factories.

KEY RECOGNITION FEATURES

• Well-sloped glacis plate with splash board running across mid-way up, turret centre and engine compartment at rear. Unlike Type 59 and Type 69 there is no exhaust outlet on left side of hull above last road wheel station. Long-range fuel drum and unditching beam often carried on hull rear

• Circular turret has curved sides with loader's cupola on right side with externally mounted 12.7mm AA MG, 105mm gun barrel has thermal sleeve and fume extractor, cage type stowage basket around sides and rear of turret. Bank of four smoke grenade dischargers either side of the turret

• Suspension either side has six road wheels with gap between 1st/2nd and 2nd/3rd road wheels, idler front, drive sprocket rear, track return rollers, upper part of suspension covered by skirt

***Top left:* Type 80-II MBT**

***Above:* Type 80 MBT**

***Right:* Type 80 MBT**

NORINCO Type 69 MBT (China)

Above: Type 69-II

SPECIFICATIONS

Crew:	4
Armament:	1 x 100mm, 1 x 7.62mm MG (coaxial), 1 x 7.62mm MG (bow), 1 x 12.7mm MG (AA)
Length gun forwards:	8.859m
Length hull:	6.243m
Width over skirts:	3.307m
Width over hull:	3.27m
Height to axis of MG:	2.807m
Ground clearance:	0.425m
Weight, combat:	36,700kg
Power-to-weight ratio:	15.8hp/tonne
Ground pressure:	0.82kg/cm^2
Engine:	Type 12150L-7BW V-12 diesel developing 580hp at 2,000rpm
Maximum road speed:	50km/hr
Maximum road range:	420 to 440km
Fuel capacity:	935 lit
Fording:	1.4m
Vertical obstacle:	0.8m
Trench:	2.7m
Gradient:	60%
Side slope:	40%
Armour:	100mm (maximum) (estimate)
Armour type:	Steel
NBC system:	Yes
Night vision equipment:	Yes (infra-red for commander, gunner and driver)

DEVELOPMENT

Type 69 series is a further development by NORINCO (China North Industries Corporation) of the earlier Type 59 and was first seen in public during 1982. Layout is conventional, with driver front left, some ammunition to his right, turret centre, engine and transmission rear. Commander and gunner sit left of turret, loader right. Both loader and commander have a cupola.

Type 69 I has a smooth bore gun. Type 69 II has a rifled gun. Both have powered elevation from -5° to +18° with turret traverse through 360°. Types of ammunition for Type 69 II include HEAT, HE, APDS and APFSDS. A 7.62mm MG is mounted coaxial with main armament and a similar, driver-operated weapon is fixed in glacis plate firing forwards. The 12.7mm AA MG is manned by loader.

Type 69 lays its own smoke screen by injecting diesel fuel into its exhaust pipe on left side of hull above last road wheel station.

In addition there is also a Type 79 MBT with a 105mm gun which is similar to the Type 59/Type 69.

Some Type 69 MBTs used by China are being upgraded.

VARIANTS

Type 80 self-propelled anti-aircraft gun is Chinese equivalent of Russian ZSU-57-2 but uses Type 69 chassis.
Twin 37mm SPAAG, still at prototype stage, has Type 69 chassis fitted with new two-man turret armed with twin 37mm guns. Two versions of this system have been developed, one with a radar fire control system and the other a clear weather system.
Type 84 AVLB has Type 69 chassis and hydraulic launching mechanism similar in concept to the German Biber AVLB on Leopard 1 chassis, which launches a bridge 18m long.
Type 653 ARV has Type 69 chassis but turret replaced by superstructure, stabiliser/dozer blade front of hull and hydraulic crane right side of hull. In service with Chinese Army. Further development has resulted in the Type 80 and Type 85 MBTs (qv).

STATUS

Production complete. In service with Bangladesh, China, Iran, Myanmar, Pakistan (with local production), Thailand and Zimbabwe.

MANUFACTURER

Chinese state arsenals. Marketing carried out NORINCO (China North Industries Corporation).

KEY RECOGNITION FEATURES

- Well-sloped glacis plate with splash-board across upper part, turret centre, slightly raised engine compartment rear. Unditching beam often carried across vertical hull rear

- Circular turret has curved sides, loader's cupola right side with external 12.7mm MG, long-barrelled 100mm gun with externally mounted laser rangefinder above, large infra-red searchlight above and to right of 100mm gun

- Suspension either side has five road wheels, each of which has five small holes, distinct gap between first and second road wheel, idler front, drive sprocket rear, no track-return rollers, upper part often covered with five-part skirt with saw tooth bottom

Below: Type 69-II MBT

NORINCO Type 59 MBT (China)

Above: Type 59 MBT

SPECIFICATIONS

Crew:	4
Armament:	1 x 100mm, 1 x 7.62mm MG (coaxial), 1 x 7.62mm MG (bow), 1 x 12.7mm MG (AA)
Ammunition:	34 x 100mm, 3,500 x 7.62mm, 200 x 12.7mm
Length gun forwards:	9m
Length hull:	6.04m
Width:	3.27m
Height:	2.59m
Ground clearance:	0.425m
Weight, combat:	36,000kg
Power-to-weight ratio:	14.44hp/tonne
Ground pressure:	0.8kg/cm^2
Engine:	Model 12150L V-12 liquid cooled diesel developing 520hp at 2,000rpm
Maximum road speed:	40 to 50km/hr
Maximum range:	420 to 440km
Fuel capacity:	815 lit
Fording without preparation:	1.4m
Fording with preparation:	5.5m
Vertical obstacle:	0.79m
Trench:	2.7m
Gradient:	60%
Side slope:	40%
Armour:	100mm (maximum)
Armour type:	Steel
NBC system:	None
Night vision equipment:	Yes (infra-red for commander, gunner and driver) (retrofitted)

DEVELOPMENT

In the early 1950s the USSR provided China with a quantity of T-54s and production was subsequently undertaken in China under the designation Type 59.

First production vehicles were identical to the T-54 but had no night vision equipment and no stabiliser for the 100mm gun. Late production Type 59s had a fume extractor for the 100mm gun, weapon stabilisation system and infra-red night vision equipment. More recently, some vehicles have been fitted with a laser rangefinder box mounted externally above the 100mm gun.

Layout is almost identical to the Soviet T-54 but with some internal differences. Driver sits front left with some ammunition 100mm to his right, turret centre, loader right. Both commander and loader have a cupola.

Type 59 is armed with a 100mm rifled gun which power-elevates from -4° to +17° (early vehicles had manual elevation), turret traverses through 360°. Ammunition is similar to Soviet T-54/T-55s and includes AP, APC-T, HE, HE-FRAG, HEAT-FS and HVAPDS-T. A 7.62mm MG is mounted coaxial with main armament and a similar, driver-operated weapon is fixed in glacis plate firing forwards. The 12.7mm AA MG is manned by the loader.

Type 59 lays its own smoke screen by injecting diesel fuel into its exhaust pipe left side of hull above last road wheel. To extend its operational range to 600km long-range fuel drums are mounted on hull rear.

Late production vehicles were called Type 59-I.

VARIANTS

Type 59-I is enhanced Type 59.
Type 59-II has many improvements including 105mm rifled tank gun and new fire control system.
Type 59-III (or Type 59C) is an improved Type 59-II.
Type 59D has a number of improvements including explosive reactive armour and a new fire control system. Another model is Type 59D1.
Type 59 ARV is base line ARV with limited capabilities.
Type 59 – upgrade for trials purposes Type 59 has been fitted with 120mm smooth bore gun.

KEY RECOGNITION FEATURES

• Well-sloped glacis plate with splash board across upper part, turret centre and slightly raised engine compartment rear. Unditching beam and long-range fuel tanks often carried across vertical hull rear.

• Circular turret has curved sides, loader's cupola on right side, externally mounted 12.7mm AA MG, standard 100mm gun with fume extractor to immediate rear of muzzle. Some vehicles have laser rangefinder externally above main armament

• Suspension either side has five road wheels, idler front, drive sprocket rear, no track-return rollers

STATUS

Production complete. In service with Albania, Bangladesh, Bosnia-Herzegovina, Cambodia, China, Democratic Republic of Congo, Iran, North Korea, Pakistan, Sudan, Tanzania, Vietnam, Zambia and Zimbabwe.

MANUFACTURER

Chinese state arsenals.

Below: Type 59 in service with Pakistan and armed with 105mm gun

NORINCO Type 62 Light Tank (China)

SPECIFICATIONS

Crew:	4
Armament:	1 x 85mm gun, 1 x 7.62mm MG (coaxial), 1 x 7.62mm MG (bow), 1 x 12.7mm MG (AA)
Ammunition:	47 x 85mm, 1,750 x 7.62mm, 1,250 x 12.7mm
Length gun forwards:	7.9m
Length hull:	5.55m
Width:	2.86m
Height:	2.25m
Ground clearance:	0.42m
Weight, combat:	21,000kg
Power-to-weight ratio:	20.47hp/tonne
Ground pressure:	0.71kg/cm^2
Engine:	Liquid-cooled diesel developing 430hp at 1,800rpm
Maximum road speed:	60km/hr
Maximum road range:	500km
Fuel capacity:	730 lit
Fording:	1.3m
Vertical obstacle:	0.7m
Trench:	2.55m
Gradient:	60%
Side slope:	40%
NBC system:	None
Night vision equipment:	None

KEY RECOGNITION FEATURES

- Driver's compartment front, rounded turret centre, engine and transmission rear
- 85mm gun overhangs front of chassis, fume extractor rear of muzzle
- Suspension either side has five large road wheels, drive sprocket rear, idler front, no track-return rollers, no skirts

Left: Type 62 light tank

DEVELOPMENT

Type 62 light tank is virtually a scaled-down Type 59 MBT and is used in rugged terrain as found in southern China. It has seen action in both the Far East and Africa.

Layout is identical to Type 59s, with driver seated front left, three-man turret centre, commander and gunner left, loader right, engine and transmission rear.

Main armament comprises 85mm gun, probably identical to that fitted to Type 63 light amphibious tank (qv) which fires AP, APHE, HE, HEAT and smoke projectiles. It has an elevation from -4° to +20° with turret traverse 360°. A 7.62mm MG is mounted coaxial to right of main armament and a similar, driver-operated weapon fixed in glacis plate. A 12.7mm Type 54 MG is mounted on turret roof for anti-aircraft defence.

Type 62 lays its own smoke screen by injecting diesel fuel into the exhaust and, more recently, models have been observed with a laser rangefinder over main armament to improve first round hit probability.

In addition to being used by the Chinese Army it is also used by Chinese Marines.

VARIANTS

It is understood that there are two variants of the Type 62 light tank: armoured recovery and light engineering.

STATUS

Production complete. In service with Albania, Bangladesh, China, Democratic Republic of Congo, North Korea, Mali, Sudan, Tanzania and Vietnam.

MANUFACTURER

Chinese state arsenals.

NORINCO Type 63 Light Amphibious Tank (China)

Above: Type 63 light tank with laser rangefinder over main armament

SPECIFICATIONS

Crew:	4
Armament:	1 x 85mm gun, 1 x 7.62mm MG (coaxial), 1 x 12.7mm MG (anti-aircraft)
Ammunition:	47 x 85mm, 2,000 x 7.62mm, 500 x 12.7mm
Length gun forwards:	8.435m
Length hull:	7.733m
Width:	3.2m
Height:	3.122m (inc AA MG), 2.522m (turret top)
Ground clearance:	0.4m
Weight, combat:	18,400kg
Power-to-weight ratio:	21.74hp/tonne
Engine:	Model 12150-L 12-cylinder water-cooled diesel developing 400hp at 2,000rpm
Maximum road speed:	64km/hr
Maximum water speed:	12km/hr
Maximum range:	370km
Fuel capacity:	403 lit
Fording:	Amphibious
Vertical obstacle:	0.87m
Trench:	2.9m
Gradient:	60%
Side slope:	30%
Armour:	14mm (maximum)
Armour type:	Steel
NBC system:	Yes
Night vision equipment:	Yes (infra-red for driver only)

DEVELOPMENT

Type 63 has a similar hull to the Russian PT-76 light amphibious tank but is based on automotive components of the Chinese Type 77 series APC which is covered in the armoured personnel carriers section. Compared with PT-76 Type 63 has a more powerful engine providing greater road speed and improved power-to-weight ratio.

Main armament comprises an 85mm gun firing AP, APHE, HE, HEAT and smoke projectiles, with elevation of +18° and depression of -4°, and turret traverse 360°. The 7.62mm MG is mounted coaxial to right of 85mm gun and a 12.7mm Type 54 MG is mounted on turret roof for anti-aircraft defence.

The vehicle is fully amphibious, propelled in the water by two water jets mounted rear. Before entering the water bilge pumps are switched on

and trim vane erected on glacis plate. To extend operational range, additional fuel tanks are installed on rear decking.

VARIANTS

A major part of the Chinese Type 63 fleet is being upgraded to Type 63A standard. This includes a new turret with 105mm gun.

STATUS

Production complete. In service with Cambodia, China, Myanmar, North Korea and Vietnam.

MANUFACTURER

Chinese state arsenals.

KEY RECOGNITION FEATURES

- Hull has vertical sides and rear, almost horizontal glacis plate, nose sloping inwards at about 50°
- Rounded turret in centre with 85mm gun overhanging front, fume extractor slightly to rear of muzzle
- Suspension either side has six road wheels, drive sprocket rear, idler front, no track-return rollers or skirt

***Above:* Type 63 Light Tank**

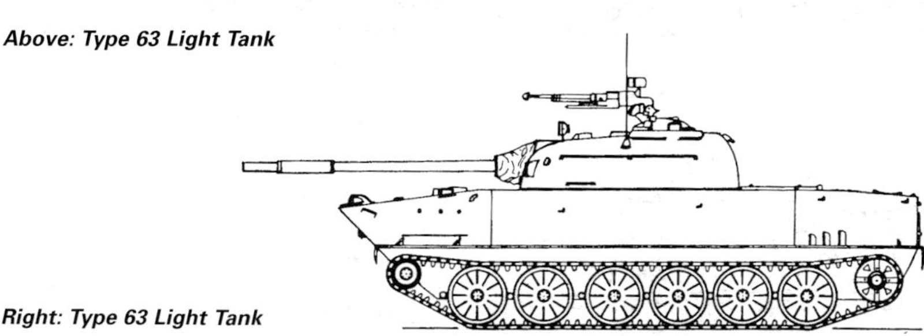

***Right:* Type 63 Light Tank**

Duro Dakovic Degman MBT (Croatia)

Above: Latest Degman MBT complete with new armour array

SPECIFICATIONS

Crew:	3
Armament:	1 x 125mm, 1 x 7.62mm (co-axial), 1 x 12.7mm (anti-aircraft), 2 x 6 smoke grenade launchers
Ammunition:	42 x 125mm, 2,000 x 7.62mm, 360 x 12.7mm
Length gun forwards:	10.14m
Length hull:	6.95m
Width:	3.59m
Height:	2.19m
Ground clearance:	0.428m
Weight combat:	44,500kg
Power-to-weight ratio:	22.47hp/tonne
Ground pressure:	0.95kg/cm²
Engine:	12-cylinder diesel developing 1,000hp (1,200hp optional)
Maximum road speed:	70km/h
Maximum road range:	700km
Fuel capacity:	1,450 litres
Fording:	1.2m (1.8 m with preparation), 5m (with snorkel)
Vertical obstacle:	0.85m
Trench:	2.6 to 2.8m
Gradient:	58%
Side slope:	47%
Armour:	Classified
Armour type:	Steel/Laminate/ERA
NBC system:	Yes
Night vision equipment:	Yes

DEVELOPMENT

The M-84 series MBT (qv) is a further development of the Russian T-72 MBT with many improvements and was manufactured in the former Yugoslavia. Actual assembly took place in the facilities of Duro Dakovic which is now in Croatia.

With the break up of Yugoslavia, Croatia continued development of the M-84 which resulted in the M84A, M84AB and M84A4 which are similar in appearance to the original M-84 but with an improved fire control system.

The latest Degman has a turret and hull of all welded armour to which an additional package of

advanced Explosive Reactive Armour has been fitted which changes its hull and turret appearance.

The layout of the Degman is almost the same as the T-72/M-84 with the driver seated at the front in the centre, two person turret in the centre with gunner on left, commander on right and the powerpack at the rear.

The Degman is fitted with a computerised fire control system that allows stationary and moving targets to be engaged under day and night conditions while the Degman itself is stationary or moving with a high first round hit probability. Degman also has a defensive aids suite which includes a pole type laser detector coupled to the smoke grenade launchers mounted either side of the turret.

VARIANTS

None known. Command versions will probably be developed and there was also an armoured recovery version of the M-84 called the M84ABI which was based on the Polish WZT-3.

STATUS

Development complete. Expected to enter production in the near future.

MANUFACTURER

Duro Dakovic Specijalna Vozila dd, Slavonski Brod, Croatia.

KEY RECOGNITION FEATURES

- Well-sloped glacis plate with driver's position top centre, turret centre of hull, engine and transmission at rear, exhaust outlet on left side of hull above last road wheel station

- Turret is welded armour with an additional armour package. Turret sides are vertical with forward part having a distinct chamfer to the upper part. Gunner's sight on left side of turret roof with commander's cupola with externally mounted 12.7mm machine gun on right. Like M-84, there is a distinctive pole type sensor for the fire control system which is not on the Russian T-72 MBT. Six smoke dischargers either side of turret with snorkel carried on left side of turret towards rear

- Suspension either side has six road wheels, drive sprocket rear, idler front and three track return rollers. Upper part of suspension is covered by skirts with forward skirt being of special armour which is higher than at the rear

Below: Croatian-built M-84AB MBT

GIAT AMX-13 Light Tank (France)

Above: AMX-13 with 90mm gun

SPECIFICATIONS (90MM VERSION)

Crew:	3
Armament:	1 x 90mm, 1 x 7.62mm MG (coaxial), 1 x 7.62mm MG (anti-aircraft) (optional), 2 x 2 smoke grenade dischargers
Ammunition:	32 x 90mm, 3,600 x 7.62mm
Length gun forwards:	6.36m
Length hull:	4.88m
Width:	2.51m
Height to commander's hatch:	2.3m
Ground clearance:	0.37m
Weight, combat:	15,000kg
Weight, empty:	13,000kg
Power-to-weight ratio:	16.66bhp/tonne
Ground pressure:	0.76kg/cm^2
Engine:	SOFAM Model 8Gxb 8-cylinder water-cooled petrol developing 250hp at 3,200rpm
Maximum road speed:	60km/hr
Maximum road range:	350 to 400km
Fuel capacity:	480 lit
Fording:	0.6m
Vertical obstacle:	0.65m
Trench:	1.6m
Gradient:	60%
Side slope:	60%
Armour:	25mm (maximum)
Armour type:	Steel
NBC system:	None
Night vision equipment:	Optional

DEVELOPMENT

Shortly after the Second World War the French Army drew up requirements for three new AFVs including a new light tank. It was subsequently developed by Atelier de Construction d'Issy-les-Moulineaux under the designation AMX-13. First prototypes were completed in the late 1940s, production commencing at Atelier de Construction Roanne in 1952. When production of AMX-30 was underway, production of AMX-13 and its many variants was transferred to Creusot-Loire. Total production of AMX-13 light tank has mounted to over 3,000. (See separate entry for AMX VCI MICV.)

All versions of AMX-13 have similar layout, driver front left, engine to his right and turret to rear. AMX-13 Model 51 was armed with 75mm gun later replaced by 90mm gun with thermal sleeve. A 105mm armed version was built for export. Turret traverses through 360°. Upper part of turret contains main armament, elevates from -5° to +12.5°. FL-10 and FL-12 turrets both

oscillating type, commander sits left, gunner right. Automatic loader mounted in turret bustle includes two revolver type magazines, each of which holds six rounds of ammunition, empty cartridge cases ejected from turret bustle. After 12 rounds, magazines have to be reloaded manually.

Wide range of optional equipment available, including passive night vision equipment, additional armour protection, improved fire-control systems and laser rangefinder. A number of companies have offered upgrade packages for AMX-13, including GIAT Industries (France), GLS (Germany), NIMDA (Israel) and Singapore Technologies Kinetics. AMX-13 can be fitted with other engines including Detroit Diesel, Baudouin and Poyaud.

VARIANTS

Singapore Technologies Kinetics has rebuilt most of the AMX-13 fleet of the Singapore Army to SM1 configuration that includes a new Detroit Deisel engine, new cooling system and new transmission.
Rocket launcher: Venezuela has AMX-13 chassis with Israeli 160mm LAR multiple rocket launcher.
AMX-13 ARV.
AMX-13 AVLB.

KEY RECOGNITION FEATURES

- Well-sloped glacis plate, normally with splash-board on lower part, driver front left, engine to his right, flat roof with turret slightly to rear

- Turret is oscillating type, gun in upper part of turret pivots on lower part with canvas cover joining them, commander's domed hatch cover on left side of turret roof, bustle turret extends to rear

- Suspension either side has five large road wheels, drive sprocket front, idler rear, two or three track-return rollers, no skirts

STATUS

Production complete. No longer marketed. In service with Argentina, Dominican Republic, Ecuador, Indonesia, Ivory Coast, Lebanon, Peru, Singapore and Venezuela.

MANUFACTURERS

Creusot-Loire Industrie at Chalon sur Saône; Atelier de Construction Roanne, Roanne, France. (GIAT Industries has now taken over Creusot-Loire.)

Below: AMX-13 with 75mm gun

GIAT AMX-30 MBT (France)

SPECIFICATIONS

Crew:	4
Armament:	1 x 105mm, 1 x 20mm cannon (coaxial), 1 x 7.62mm MG (AA), 2 x 2 smoke grenade dischargers
Ammunition:	47 x 105mm, 1,050 x 20mm, 2,050 x 7.62mm
Length gun forwards:	9.48m
Length hull:	6.59m
Width:	3.1m
Height including searchlight:	2.86m
Height to turret top:	2.29m
Ground clearance:	0.44m
Weight, combat:	36,000kg
Weight, empty:	34,000kg
Power-to-weight ratio:	20hp/tonne
Ground pressure:	0.77kg/cm^2
Engine:	Hispano-Suiza HS 110 12-cylinder water-cooled supercharged multi-fuel developing 720hp at 2,000rpm
Maximum road speed:	65km/hr
Maximum road range:	500 to 600km
Fuel capacity:	970 lit
Fording:	1.3m
Fording with preparation:	2.2m
Fording with snorkel:	4m
Vertical obstacle:	0.93m
Trench:	2.9m
Gradient:	60%
Side slope:	30%
Armour:	80mm (max)
Armour type:	Steel
NBC system:	Yes
Night vision equipment:	Yes (passive on AMX-30 B2)

DEVELOPMENT

AMX-30 was developed from the mid-1950s by the Atelier de Construction d'Issy-les-Moulineaux to meet the requirements of the French Army. First prototypes were completed in 1960 with production commencing at the Atelier de Construction Roanne (ARE) in 1966; since then over 3,500 AMX-30 MBT and variants have been built for home and export markets. Production of the AMX-30 MBT has been completed and in the French Army it is now being supplemented by GIAT Industries Leclerc MBT.

Driver sits front left with cast turret centre, engine and transmission rear. Commander and gunner sit right of turret, loader left. The 105mm gun power-elevates from -8° to +20°, turret traverses through 360°. Main armament fires APFSDS, HEAT, HE, smoke and illuminating rounds with a 20mm cannon or 12.7mm MG mounted

coaxial to the left. The cannon has independent elevation for engaging low-flying aircraft and helicopters. A 7.62mm MG is mounted right of commander's cupola. Some AMX-30 B2 MBTs of the French Army have been fitted with explosive reactive armour over their frontal arc.

VARIANTS

AMX-30D was developed for desert operations with sand shields for its tracks, engine developing 620hp and reduction in gearbox ratios which limits its speed to 60km/hr.
AMX-30B2: Modifications include a new fire-control system with laser rangefinder and LLTV as well as automotive improvements. In addition to taking delivery of new build AMX-30B2, the French Army also had many earlier vehicles upgraded to this standard.
Modernised AMX-30s: A number of countries and companies have developed modernisation packages for AMX-30 MBT, only one has entered production, in Spain.
AMX-30D ARV.
AMX-30 AVLB.
155mm GCT self-propelled howitzer uses AMX-30 chassis (see SPGs).
AMX-30 driver training tank is AMX-30 with turret replaced by observation cupola.
AMX-30 EBG Combat Engineer Tractor.
Roland anti-aircraft missile system.
Shahine anti-aircraft missile system, built for Saudi Arabia.

KEY RECOGNITION FEATURES

- Well-sloped glacis plate with driver's hatch in upper left part, turret centre, engine rear, hull rear vertical, silencer on track guard above rear drive sprocket

- Cast turret has sides that slope inwards with turret bustle extending over engine deck, stowage basket each side of turret, two smoke grenade dischargers each side at rear, commander's cupola on right side of turret roof. 105mm gun has thermal sleeve, 20mm cannon mounted left of gun

- Suspension each side has five road wheels, drive sprocket rear, idler front, five track-return rollers, no skirts

AMX-30 DCA twin 30mm self-propelled anti-aircraft system. This is only in service with Saudi Arabia.

STATUS

Production complete. In service with Bosnia, Chile, Croatia, Cyprus, France, Qatar, Saudi Arabia, Spain, United Arab Emirates and Venezuela.

MANUFACTURER

GIAT Industries, Roanne, France.

Above left: AMX-30B2

Right: AMX-30B2 fitted with explosive reactive armour

GIAT Leclerc MBT (France)

SPECIFICATIONS

Crew:	3
Armament:	1 x 120mm, 1 x 12.7mm MG (coaxial), 1 x 7.62mm MG (AA), 3 x 9 smoke grenade dischargers
Ammunition:	40 x 120mm
Length gun forwards:	9.87m
Length hull:	6.88m
Width:	3.71m
Height:	2.53m (turret roof)
Ground clearance:	0.5m
Weight, combat:	56,500kg
Power-to-weight ratio:	26.54hp/tonne
Ground pressure:	0.9kg/cm^2
Engine:	SACM V8X 8-cylinder Hyperbar diesel developing 1,500hp
Maximum road speed:	72km/hr (forwards) 38km/hr (reverse)
Maximum road range:	550km
Fuel capacity:	1,300 lit
Fording:	1m
Vertical obstacle:	1.25m
Trench:	3m
Gradient:	60%
Side slope:	30%
Armour:	Classified
Armour type:	Steel/Composite/ Laminate
NBC system:	Yes
Night vision equipment:	Yes (passive)

DEVELOPMENT

The Leclerc MBT was developed by GIAT Industries as the replacement for the French Army's existing fleet of AMX-30 B2 series of MBTs. Development started in 1983 and the first of six prototypes was completed in 1989, these were however preceded by a number of test rig vehicles. The first production Leclerc was completed in December 1991 and delivered to the French Army in 1992. In 1993 the United Arab Emirates ordered a total of 436 Leclerc MBTs, including variants.

The Leclerc turrets are assembled by GIAT's Tarbes facility while the chassis is built at Roanne; the latter also integrate the turret with the chassis and then deliver the complete vehicle to the French Army.

The hull and turret of the Leclerc are of advanced modular armour. The driver is seated at the front of the hull on the left with some 120mm ammunition stowed to his right. The two man power-operated turret is in the centre with the commander being seated on the left and the gunner on the right. No loader is required as a bustle-mounted automatic loader holds a total of 22 rounds of ready use ammunition. Turret

traverse is a full 360° with weapon elevation from -8° to +15° under full power control. A 12.7mm MG is mounted externally on the turret roof and operated by remote control. In either side of the turret are nine dischargers that can also launch a variety of grenades including smoke and decoy.

The suspension system of the Leclerc is of the hydropneumatic type and standard equipment includes a fire detection/suppression system and if required long-range fuel tanks can be fitted at the rear of the hull to increase operational range. United Arab Emirates vehicles have many improvements including different powerpack.

French Army Leclerc MBTs are now being upgraded.

VARIANTS

ARV, in production for France and United Arab Emirates.
AEV, prototype.
AVLB, project.

KEY RECOGNITION FEATURES

- Vertical hull front which then slopes back under front of hull, very well-sloped glacis plate, turret centre, slightly raised engine compartment at rear. Hull rear is vertical with horizontal louvres

- Turret front and sides have vertical lower part with chamfer to upper part, distinctive array of periscopes around upper part of forward part of turret roof. Large periscopic sight on left side of turret roof, externally mounted 7.62mm machine gun

- Suspension has six road wheels either side with idler front, drive sprocket rear and track return rollers. Upper part of suspension is covered by armoured skirts with those above the front two road wheels being thicker

STATUS

Production. In service with France and United Arab Emirates.

MANUFACTURER

GIAT Industries, Satory, France (see text).

Above left: GIAT Leclerc MBT

Right: GIAT Leclerc for UAE

Right: GIAT Leclerc MBT

Krauss-Maffei Wegmann Leopard 2 MBT (Germany)

SPECIFICATIONS

Crew:	4
Armament:	1 x 120mm, 1 x 7.62mm MG (coaxial), 1 x 7.62mm MG (anti-aircraft), 2 x 8 smoke grenade dischargers
Ammunition:	42 x 120mm, 4,750 x 7.62mm
Length gun forwards:	9.668m
Length hull:	7.722m
Width overall:	3.7m
Height to top of commander's periscopes:	2.787m
Height to turret top:	2.48m
Ground clearance:	0.54m (front), 0.49m (rear)
Weight, combat:	55,150kg
Power-to-weight ratio:	27.27hp/tonne
Ground pressure:	0.83kg/cm²
Engine:	MTU MB 873 Ka 501 4-stroke, 12-cylinder multi-fuel, exhaust turbocharged liquid-cooled diesel developing 1,500hp at 2,600rpm
Maximum road speed:	72km/hr
Maximum road range:	550km
Fuel capacity:	1,200 lit
Fording:	1m
Fording with preparation:	2.25m
Fording with snorkel:	4m
Vertical obstacle:	1.1m
Trench:	3m
Gradient:	60%
Side slope:	30%
Armour:	Classified
Armour type:	Laminate/Steel
NBC system:	Yes
Night vision equipment:	Yes (passive for commander, gunner and driver)

DEVELOPMENT

Following cancellation of MBT-70, full-scale development of a new German MBT commenced. First prototypes of this new MBT were completed by Krauss-Maffei (which became Krauss-Maffei Wegmann in 1998) between 1972 and 1974, some armed with a 105mm gun and some with a 120mm. With further improvements it became the Leopard 2, and in 1977 Krauss-Maffei was selected as prime contractor and an order for 1,800 vehicles placed, 810 of which were built by MaK and the remainder by Krauss-Maffei. First production vehicles were completed in 1979 with the last of 2,125 vehicles for the German Army delivered in 1992.

In 1979 the Dutch Army ordered 445 Leopard 2s which were all delivered by 1986, and in 1983

Switzerland selected the Leopard 2 with 35 from Germany and the remaining 345 to be built in Switzerland. More recently, Leopard 2 has been ordered or purchased by Austria, Denmark, Greece, Poland, Spain and Sweden.

Layout is conventional with driver front right, turret centre and engine and transmission rear. Commander sits on right of turret, gunner to his front and loader left. The 120mm smooth bore gun fires APFSDS-T and HEAT multi-purpose rounds and power-elevates from +20° to -9°, with powered traverse through 360°. Main armament is stabilised in both elevation and traverse.

VARIANTS

Buffel armoured recovery vehicle.

Leopard 2A6 is an upgrade of earlier Leopard 2 with many improvements including additional armour over frontal arc. Some Leopard 2s of Germany and Netherlands have been upgraded to this standard. Leopard 2A6 is 2A5 with 120mm L/55 gun. Leopard 2A6EX is the latest export version.

Leopard 2 AVLB - development.

Leopard 2 driver-training vehicle, turret replaced by observation type turret (used by Germany and Netherlands).

Above left: Leopard 2A4 of the German Army

KEY RECOGNITION FEATURES

• Nose slopes back under hull with 45° glacis plate, then horizontal hull. Driver front right, turret centre and raised engine compartment rear. Vertical hull sides and rear, louvres extending full width of vehicle rear

• Turret has vertical front, sides and rear with bustle extending right over engine compartment, commander's low profile cupola on right with periscopic sight to his front, 120mm gun (with thermal sleeve and fume extractor) has large mantlet with gunner's sight in forward part of turret to immediate right of mantlet

• Suspension each side has seven road wheels, drive sprocket rear, idler front and four track-return rollers. Upper part covered by skirting, front idler and first two road wheels also covered by armoured skirts. **Note:** Leopard 2A5 and 2A6 have additional armour to turret with an arrow-head-type appearance

STATUS

In production. In service with Austria, Denmark, Finland, Germany, Greece, Netherlands, Norway, Poland, Spain, Sweden and Switzerland.

MANUFACTURER

Krauss-Maffei Wegmannn, Munich, Germany.

Below: Leopard 2A5 of Netherlands Army (Michael Jerchel)

Krauss-Maffei Wegmann Leopard 2 MBT (Germany)

Above: Leopard 2 Improved (Strv 122) of the Swedish Army

Below: Leopard 2 Improved (Leopard 2A5) of the German Army

Above: Leopard 2 Improved (Strv 122) of the Swedish Army

Below: Latest Leopard 2A6EX

Krauss-Maffei Wegmann Leopard 1 MBT (Germany)

SPECIFICATIONS

Crew:	4
Armament:	1 x 105mm, 1 x 7.62mm MG (coaxial), 1 x 7.62mm MG (anti-aircraft), 2 x 4 smoke grenade dischargers
Ammunition:	60 x 105mm, 5,500 x 7.62mm
Length gun forwards:	9.543m
Length hull:	7.09m
Width without skirts:	3.25m
Height to top of commander's periscope:	2.764m
Ground clearance:	0.44m
Weight, combat:	42,400kg
Weight, empty:	40,400kg
Power-to-weight ratio:	19.57hp/tonne
Ground pressure:	0.88kg/cm^2
Engine:	MTU MB 838 Ca M500, 10-cylinder multi-fuel developing 830hp at 2,200rpm
Maximum road speed:	65km/hr
Maximum road range:	600km
Fuel capacity:	985 lit
Fording:	2.25m
Fording with preparation:	4m
Vertical obstacle:	1.15m
Trench:	3m
Gradient:	60%
Armour:	70mm (maximum)
Armour type:	Steel
NBC system:	Yes
Night vision equipment:	Yes (was infra-red, now replaced by passive in most armies)

DEVELOPMENT

Leopard 1 was developed from the late 1950s and after trials with various prototypes, Krauss-Maffei (now Krauss-Maffei Wegmann) of Munich was selected as prime contractor in 1963, with MaK (today Rheinmetall Landsysteme) responsible for the specialised versions.

First production Leopard 1 was delivered to the

KEY RECOGNITION FEATURES

- Well-sloped glacis plate leads up to horizontal hull top extending right to rear of hull, driver's hatch in right side of roof to immediate rear of glacis plate, turret centre, engine rear, hull rear slopes slightly inwards. Hull sides above suspension slope inwards with horizontal louvres above rear drive sprocket

- Cast turret with sides sloping inwards, external mantlet and 105mm gun with thermal sleeve and fume extractor, infra-red/white light searchlight often mounted above gun mantlet, stowage basket on turret rear, smoke grenade dischargers on turret sides towards rear

- Suspension each side has seven road wheels, idler front, drive sprocket rear, four track-return rollers. Upper part often covered by skirts

German Army in 1965 and production continued, with interruptions, until 1984. Oto Melara produced Leopard 1 for the Italian Army. The Leopard 1 MBT is no longer in front line service with the German Army.

Driver sits front right with NBC pack and some ammunition to his left, turret centre, engine and transmission rear. Commander and gunner sit on right side of turret, loader left.

The 105mm gun is fully stabilised and it power-elevates from -9° to +20° with turret traverse 360°. Types of ammunition include APDS, APFSDS, HEAT and smoke. A 7.62mm MG is mounted coaxial to left of 105mm gun and a similar weapon can be mounted on commander's or loader's hatch.

A wide range of optional equipment is available including additional armour, different fire-control systems, various night vision devices and a dozer blade. Many armies have already upgraded their Leopard 1s to extend their lives into the 21st century.

Above: Leopard 1A5

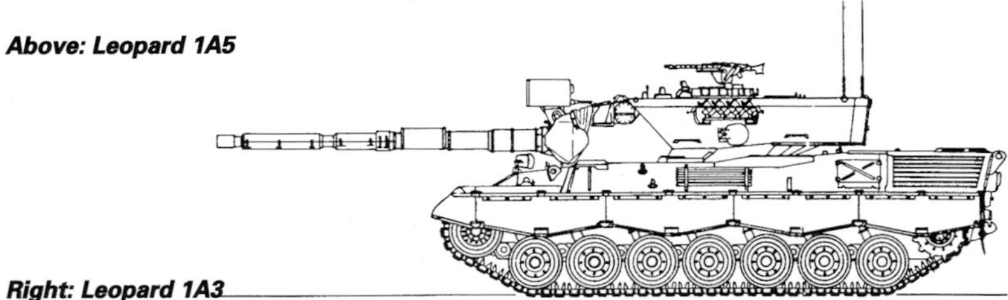

Right: Leopard 1A3

Krauss-Maffei Wegmann Leopard 1 MBT (Germany)

Above: *Leopard 1A5(BE) of the Belgian Army (C R Zwart)*

VARIANTS

Leopard 1A1A1 has a number of improvements including additional armour protection for the turret.

Leopard 1A2 has passive night equipment for commander and driver and improved turret.

Leopard 1A3 has new all-welded turret with improved armour, as well as all the improvements of Leopard 1A2 and 1A3.

Leopard 1A4 was the final model for the German Army and has all-welded turret and integrated fire-control system.

Leopard 1A5 was the upgrade for German Army and has new computerised fire control system and thermal night vision equipment.

Leopard 1 with 105mm Improved Weapon System, trials only.

Leopard 1 AVLB (Biber).

Leopard 1 ARV.

Leopard 1 AEV.

Gepard twin 35mm anti-aircraft system.

Leopard 1 driver training tank has large observation type cupola in place of turret.

Leopard AEV (Norway).

Many countries have their own versions of the Leopard 1, including Brazil (ARV developed in Belgium) and Norway (AVLB).

STATUS

Production complete. In service with Australia, Belgium, Brazil, Canada, Chile, Denmark, Greece, Italy, Norway and Turkey.

MANUFACTURERS

Krauss-Maffei Wegmann, Munich, and Rheinmetall Landsysteme GmbH, Kiel, Germany; Oto Melara, La Spezia, Italy.

Right: Leopard 1 of the Italian Army fitted with applique armour (Richard Stickland)

KFOR

Arjun MBT (India)

SPECIFICATIONS

Crew:	4
Armament:	1 x 120mm gun, 1 x 7.62mm MG (co-axial), 1 x 12.7mm MG (anti aircraft), 2 x 9 smoke grenade launchers
Ammunition:	39 x 120mm, 3,000 x 7.62mm (estimate), 1,000 x 12.7mm (estimate)
Length gun forwards:	10.194m
Length hull:	n/available
Width:	3.847m
Height:	2.32m
Ground clearance:	0.45m
Weight, combat:	58,500kg
Weight, empty:	56,500kg (estimate)
Power-to-weight ratio:	23.93 hp/tonne
Ground pressure:	0.84kg/cm^2
Engine:	MTU 838 Ka 501 12-cylinder liquid-cooled diesel developing 1,400 hp at 2,500 rpm
Maximum road speed:	72 km/h
Maximum road range:	450 km
Fuel capacity:	1,610 lit
Fording:	1m (estimate)
Vertical obstacle:	0.90m
Trench:	2.43m
Gradient:	77%
Side slope:	40%
Armour:	Classified
Armour type:	Steel/Composite
NBC system:	Yes
Night vision equipment:	Yes

DEVELOPMENT

Early in the 1970s, following its experience in licenced production of the 105mm armed Vickers Defence Systems Mk 1 (locally known as the Vijayanta) MBT, a decision was taken to design a new MBT in India which became known as the Arjun.

This was designed by the Combat Vehicle Research and Development Establishment with the assistance of many other facilities in India as well as in the private sector in India and overseas.

The first prototype of the Arjun was completed in 1984 and since then a total of 12 prototypes and 32 pre-production vehicles have been built at the Heavy Vehicles Factory at Avadi where production

of the Vijayanta and, more recently, the Russian T-72M1 (called Ajeya), has been undertaken.

The layout of the Arjun is conventional with the driver's compartment at the front on the right side, turret in centre with commander and gunner on right and loader on left with the powerpack at the rear. The 120mm rifled tank gun is fully stabilised and fires one-piece ammunition. A 7.62mm machine gun is mounted coaxial with the main armament and a 12.7mm machine gun is mounted on the turret roof for air defence purposes.

Standard equipment includes a computerised fire control system, day/night sighting system, NBC system and long range fuel drums mounted at the rear of the hull.

VARIANTS

A number of variants of the Arjun have been projected including armoured recovery vehicle, engineer tank, armoured vehicle launched bridge and air defence platform. For trials purposes the chassis of the Arjun has been fitted with the South African T6 155mm/52 calibre turret with the complete system being called the Bhim by the Indian Army. Early in 2002 India revealed **Tan EX**. This is a T-72M1 series chassis fitted with the complete turret of the Arjun MBT.

KEY RECOGNITION FEATURES

- Well-sloped glacis plate with V-type splash deflector on front of hull leads up to horizontal hull top with raised engine decks at rear

- 120mm gun has thermal sleeve and fume extractor and is mounted in vertical gun mantlet, vertical turret front angled to rear with turret sides also vertical

- Suspension either side consists of seven road wheels with drive sprocket at rear, idler front and track return rollers. Armoured skirt covers upper part of forward hull sides with rubber flap covering remainder

STATUS

Low rate production. Entering service with the Indian Army.

MANUFACTURER

Heavy Vehicles Factory, Avadi, India.

Above left: Arjun MBTs

Below: Arjun MBT

Zulfiqar MBT (Iran)

SPECIFICATIONS

Crew:	3
Armament:	1 x 125mm gun, 1 x 7.62mm MG (co-axial) and probably 1 x 12.7mm MG (anti-aircraft)
Ammunition:	Classified
Length gun forwards:	Classified
Length hull:	Classified
Width without skirts:	Classified
Height:	Classified
Ground clearance:	Classified
Weight, combat:	40,000kg (estimate)
Weight, empty:	38,000kg (estimate)
Power-to-weight ratio:	25 hp/tonne
Ground pressure:	Classified
Engine:	Diesel, 1,000 hp
Maximum road speed:	70km/h
Maximum road range:	500km (estimate)
Fuel capacity:	Classified
Fording with preparation:	Classified
Vertical obstacle:	Classified
Trench:	Classified
Gradient:	60%
Side slope:	30%
Armour:	Classified
Armour type:	Steel/Composite
NBC system:	Yes
Night vision equipment:	Yes

Above: Zulfiqar MBT

DEVELOPMENT

The existence of the Zulfiqar MBT was first revealed in 1994 when it was stated that the vehicle had been developed in Iran by the Islamic Revolutionary Guards Corps. After trials with three different generations of prototype vehicles, production of the Zulfiqar MBT is said to have commenced in 1999.

The layout of the Zufiqar MBT is conventional with the driver's compartment at the front, turret in centre and powerpack at the rear. The 125mm gun and its associated automatic loading system is understood to be from the Russian T-72 MBT which is also manufactured in Iran. The automatic loader has enabled the crew of the vehicle to be reduced to three: commander, gunner and driver.

Standard equipment is said to include a computerised fire control system, day/night sights, NBC system and fire detection and suppression system.

VARIANTS

There are no known variants of the Zulfiqar MBT. Other Iranian MBT projects include local

production/assembly of the Russian T-72 and an upgraded T-54/T-55/Type 59 MBT called the Type 72Z. This features a new powerpack, computerised fire control system, day/night sighting system and the replacement of the existing 100mm rifled tank gun by a NATO standard 105mm L7/M68 rifled tank gun. Another upgraded T-54/T-55 MBT is called the Safir-74. This features the latest generation of explosive reactive armour which provides protection from chemical energy and kinetic energy attack. This explosive reactive armour is installed on the glacis plate, nose, turret front and sides and skirts and is very similar in appearance to the latest Russian explosive reactive armour.

STATUS

Production. In service with Iran.

MANUFACTURER

Defence Industries Organisation, Shahid Dooz Industrial Complex, Iran.

KEY RECOGNITION FEATURES

- Well-sloped glacis plate leads up to horizontal hull top which extends to the rear. Hull rear is vertical with two circular exhaust outlets

- Large turret positioned slightly towards the front of the chassis with front sloping inwards top and bottom, hull sides vertical and basket mounted on vertical turret rear. Main armament has fume extractor mounted mid-way down barrel

- Suspension either side consists of seven road wheels with drive sprocket at rear, idler at front and five track return rollers. No side skirts have been observed so far

***Below:* Iranian Type 72Z is an upgraded T-55 MBT**

Merkava MBT (Israel)

SPECIFICATIONS (MK 1)

Crew:	4
Armament:	1 x 105mm, 1 x 7.62mm MG (coaxial), 2 x 7.62mm MG (anti-aircraft), 1 x 60mm mortar
Ammunition:	62 x 105mm, 10,000 x 7.62mm
Length gun forwards:	8.63m
Length hull:	7.45m
Width:	3.7m
Height to commander's cupola:	2.75m
Height to turret roof:	2.64m
Ground clearance:	0.47m
Power-to-weight ratio:	14.28hp/tonne
Weight, combat:	60,000kg
Weight, empty:	58,000kg
Ground pressure:	0.9kg/cm^2
Engine:	General Dynamics Land Systems AVDS-1790-6A V-12 diesel developing 900hp
Maximum road speed:	46km/hr
Maximum range:	400km
Fuel capacity:	1,250 lit
Gradient:	70%
Side slope:	38%
Armour:	Classified
Fording:	1.38m, 2m (with preparation)
Vertical obstacle:	0.95m
Trench:	3m
Armour type:	Steel/Spaced/Laminate
NBC system:	Yes
Night vision equipment:	Yes

DEVELOPMENT

Merkava was developed from the late 1960s to meet Israeli Army requirements, with particular emphasis on battlefield survivability. First prototype was completed in 1974 with first production vehicles following in 1979. It was used in combat for the first time against Syrian forces in 1982.

Layout is unconventional with engine compartment front, fighting compartment rear and turret above. The commander and gunner sit right of turret, loader left. Main armament comprises a 105mm modified M68 gun which power-elevates from -8.5° to +20° with turret traverse through 360°. A 7.62mm MG is mounted

coaxial to left of main armament and both commander and loader have roof-mounted 7.62mm MG for anti-aircraft or defence suppression. A 60mm mortar is mounted in the turret roof.

The 105mm gun is fully stabilised. Fire-control system includes a ballistic computer and laser rangefinder. Merkava carries a basic load of 62 rounds of 105mm which can be increased to 85 rounds.

VARIANTS

Merkava Mk 2 entered production in 1983 and has several improvements, including improved armour protection and fire-control system.
Merkava Mk 3 has many improvements including a 120mm smooth bore gun, more powerful 1200hp engine coupled to a new transmission, new armour, threat warning system, new suspension and improved fire control system.
Mk 3 Baz has improved armour. Latest version is Mk 4 with further improvements.
The prototype of a 155mm self-propelled artillery system, called the Slammer, has been built but not placed in production. The prototype of an ARV model of the Merkava has been built.

KEY RECOGNITION FEATURES

- Almost vertical hull front, well-sloped glacis plate with distinct bulge in right side for engine. Horizontal hull top extends right to rear, driver's hatch forward of turret on left side

- Turret mounted slightly to rear of vehicle with distinctive pointed front, 105mm gun with thermal sleeve and fume extractor, large turret bustle with stowage rack that extends to hull rear, entry hatch in vertical hull rear

- Suspension each side has six road wheels, drive sprocket front, idler rear and four track-return rollers. Upper part of suspension covered by skirts with wavy bottom

STATUS

In production. In service with Israeli Army.

MANUFACTURER

Israel Ordnance Corps facility, Tel a Shomer, Israel.

Top left: Merkava Mk 3 Baz (Hawk) (IDF)

Right: Latest Merkava Mk 4 (IDF)

Below right: Merkava Mk 1

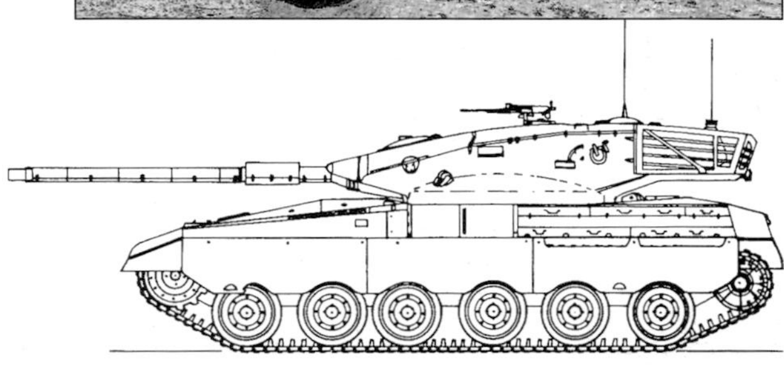

IVECO/OTO MELARA Ariete MBT (Italy)

SPECIFICTIONS

Crew:	4
Armament:	1 x 120mm, 1 x 7.62mm MG (coaxial), 1 x 7.62mm MG (anti-aircraft), 2 x 4 smoke grenade dischargers
Ammunition:	40 x 120mm, 2400 x 7.62mm
Length overall:	9.669m
Length hull:	7.59m
Width overall:	3.601m
Height to turret roof:	2.5m
Ground clearance:	0.48m
Weight, combat:	54,000kg
Power-to-weight ratio:	24hp/tonne
Ground pressure:	0.90kg/cm^2
Engine:	IVECO V-12 MTCA 12-cylinder turbo-charged diesel developing 1300hp at 2,300rpm
Maximum road speed:	65+km/h
Maximum range:	550+km
Fuel capacity:	Not available
Fording:	1.2m (without preparation); 2.1m (with preparation)
Vertical obstacle:	1m
Trench:	3m
Gradient:	60%
Side slope:	30%

Above: Ariete MBT

Below: Ariete MBT

Armour:	Classified
Armour type:	Steel/Composite
NBC system:	Yes
Night vision equipment:	Yes (passive)

DEVELOPMENT

In 1984 the now Oto Melara and IVECO formed a consortium to develop a new family of vehicles for the Italian Army, the Centauro (8x8) tank destroyer (qv), the Ariete MBT and the Dardo infantry fighting vehicle (qv). Oto Melara developed the MBT with IVECO providing the powerpack and other automotive components. The Italian Army has taken delivery of 200 Ariete MBTs built at the Oto Melara facility at La Spezia with IVECO supplying automotive components.

The layout of the Ariete MBT is conventional with the driver at the front right, power operated turret in the centre with commander and gunner on right, loader on left and powerpack at the rear.

The Officine Galileo computerised fire control fire system, which shares many components with the fire control system installed in the Centauro 105mm tank destroyer (in service with Italy and Spain) includes day/night sights and a laser range-finder. The tank commander has a stabilised roof-mounted sight. The 120mm smooth bore gun fires the same ammunition as the Leopard 2 and M1A1/M1A2 MBTs with weapon elevation being from -9° to +20° and turret traverse a full 360°. The main armament is fully stabilised with the ordnance being provided with a fume extractor, muzzle reference system and thermal sleeve. The Ariete Mk 2 MBT is currently under development.

VARIANTS None.

STATUS Production complete. In service with Italian Army.

MANUFACTURER
Oto Melara, La Spezia, Italy (but see text).

KEY RECOGNITION FEATURES

- Turret front slopes well to rear, 120mm gun in internal mantlet, flat roof with commander's cupola on right side with large periscopic sight to front, vertical turret sides with bank of four smoke grenade dischargers either side, ammunition hatch in left side of turret, gunner's sight in forward part of turret roof on right side

- Hull sides vertical, raised engine compartment at back with louvres above each side of last road wheel station

- Suspension either side has seven road wheels, idler front, drive sprocket rear and track return rollers. Upper part of suspension is covered by skirts

Above: Ariete MBT

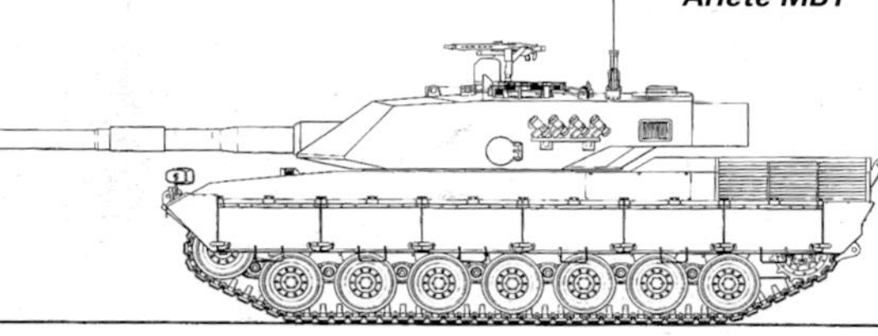

Below: Ariete MBT

OTO MELARA OF-40 MBT (Italy)

Above: OF-40 Mk 2

SPECIFICATIONS

Crew:	4
Armament:	1 x 105mm, 1 x 7.62mm MG (coaxial), 1 x 7.62mm MG (anti-aircraft), 2 x 4 smoke grenade dischargers
Ammunition:	57 x 105mm, 5,700 x 7.62mm
Length gun forwards:	9.222m
Length hull:	6.893m
Width with skirts:	3.51m
Height with sight:	2.68m
Height to turret top:	2.45m
Ground clearance:	0.44m
Weight, combat:	45,500kg
Weight, empty:	43,100kg
Power-to-weight ratio:	18.24hp/tonne
Ground pressure:	0.92kg/cm²
Engine:	MTU MB 838 Ca M500 V10 supercharged diesel developing 830hp at 2,200rpm
Maximum road speed:	60km/hr
Maximum range:	600km
Fuel capacity:	1,000 lit
Fording:	1.2m (without preparation), 2.25m (with preparation), 4m with snorkel
Vertical obstacle:	1.1m
Trench:	3m
Gradient:	60%
Armour:	Classified
Armour type:	Steel
NBC system:	Yes
Night vision equipment:	Optional

DEVELOPMENT

OF-40 was designed as a private venture specifically for the export market from 1977, with Oto Melara responsible for the overall design and production and FIAT for the powerpack. The first prototype was completed in 1980 and in 1981 the United Arab Emirates took delivery of the first of 18 Mk 1s. This was followed by a second order for 18 Mk 2s and three armoured recovery vehicles, all of which have been delivered. The original Mk 1s have now been brought up to Mk 2 standard.

Layout is similar to Leopard 1s with which it shares some components, driver front right, ammunition and NBC pack left, turret centre and engine and transmission rear. Commander and gunner sit right of turret, loader left.

Main armament comprises a 105mm rifled gun that fires standard NATO ammunition and power-elevates from -9° to +20°, with turret traverse 360°. A 7.62mm MG is mounted coaxial left of the main armament and a 7.62mm or 12.7mm MG is mounted on turret roof for anti-aircraft defence. Fire-control system includes laser rangefinder and stabilised day/night roof sight for commander.

KEY RECOGNITION FEATURES

- Well-sloped glacis plate leading up to horizontal hull roof. Driver's position front right, turret centre and slightly raised engine compartment rear

- Turret has wedge-shaped mantlet and 105mm gun with thermal sleeve and fume extractor. Almost vertical turret sides, large bustle rear with stowage basket each side. Commander's cupola right with prominent periscopic sight in front

- Hull sides vertical. Suspension either side has seven road wheels, idler front, drive sprocket rear and five track-return rollers. Upper part of suspension is normally covered by skirts. Exhaust outlets each side at hull rear with horizontal louvres

VARIANTS

OF-40 Mk 2 has the Galileo OG14L2A fire-control system which includes stabilisation system for 105mm gun and an LLTV camera mounted on the turret mantlet and aligned to the 105mm gun.

OF-40 ARV.

OF-40 chassis can be used for other weapons systems, such as the twin 35mm anti-aircraft turret, and with a different engine it is used for the Palmaria 155mm self-propelled howitzer and the OTO 76/62 76mm anti-aircraft tank, which is still at prototype stage. The Palmaria has entered production and details are given in the self-propelled guns and howitzers section.

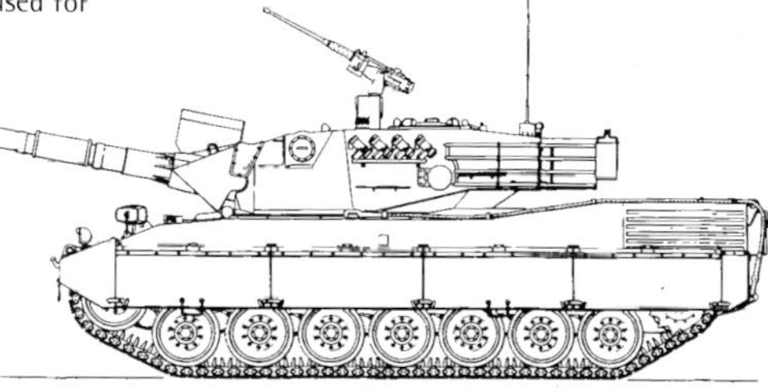

STATUS

Production complete. In service with United Arab Emirates only. The OF-40 MBT is no longer marketed.

MANUFACTURER

Oto Melara, La Spezia, Italy.

Above right: OF-40 Mk 2

Right: OF-40 Mk 2

Mitsubishi Heavy Industries Type 90 MBT (Japan)

Above: Type 90 MBT fitted with dozer blade (Kensuke Ebata)

SPECIFICATIONS

Crew:	3
Armament:	1 x 120mm, 1 x 7.62mm MG (coaxial), 1 x 12.7mm MG (anti-aircraft), 2 x 3 smoke grenade dischargers
Ammunition:	Not available
Length gun forwards:	9.755m
Length hull:	7.5m
Width:	3.43m
Height:	2.34m
Ground clearance:	0.45m (variable)
Weight, combat:	50,000kg
Power-to-weight ratio:	30hp/tonne
Ground pressure:	0.89kg/cm^2
Engine:	Mitsubishi 10ZG 10-cylinder water-cooled diesel engine developing 1,500hp at 2,400rpm
Maximum road speed:	70km/h (forwards); 42km/h (reverse)
Range:	400km (approx)
Fuel capacity:	1,100 lit
Fording:	2m
Vertical obstacle:	1m
Trench:	2.7m
Gradient:	60%
Side slope:	30%
Armour:	Classified
Armour type:	Steel/Composite/Laminate
NBC system:	Yes
Night vision equipment:	Yes (passive)

DEVELOPMENT

In the mid-1970s the Japanese Self-Defence Agency started development work on a new MBT to meet the requirements of the Japanese Ground Self-Defence Force. This was known as the TK-X MBT and the first prototypes were completed in the mid-1980s. This was subsequently accepted for service as the Type 90 MBT with first production vehicles completed in 1992.

Prime contractor is Mitsubishi Heavy Industries, with Japan Steel Works being responsible for the 120mm smooth bore gun which is essentially the German Rheinmetall weapon made under licence with the computerised fire control system being developed by Mitsubishi Electric.

The driver's compartment is at the front, turret in the centre and powerpack at the rear. The commander is seated on the right of the turret with the gunner on the left, no loader is required as an automatic loading system is provided for the 120mm smooth bore gun which fires HEAT-MP and APFSDS-T rounds with a semi-combustible cartridge case.

The computerised fire control system allows either the commander or gunner to aim and fire the main armament whether the Type 90 is moving or stationary with a high probability of a first round hit. A 7.62mm machine gun is mounted coaxial with the main armament with a 12.7mm machine gun being mounted on the roof for anti-aircraft purposes. A laser detector is mounted on the forward part of the roof and a dozer blade can be mounted at the front of the hull.

VARIANTS

Type 90 ARV is based on the chassis of the Type 90 MBT and has a new superstructure with crane mounted at front right, dozer/stabiliser blade at front of hull and hydraulically operated winch.
Type 91 AVLB is based on chassis of Type 90 MBT and has scissors-type bridge.

KEY RECOGNITION FEATURES

- Well-sloped glacis plate which is almost horizontal, hull top horizontal and slightly raised at the rear, hull rear vertical with horizontal louvres

- Turret has vertical sides and rear with distinct chamfer between turret front and sides, commander's cupola on right with large gunner's sight in left side of roof, 120mm gun has thermal sleeve with fume extractor

- Suspension either side has six road wheels, idler front, drive sprocket rear and track return rollers. Upper part of suspension covered by skirts

STATUS

Production. In service with Japanese Ground Self-Defence Force.

MANUFACTURER

Mitsubishi Heavy Industries, Tokyo, Japan.

Below: Type 90 MBT (Paul Beaver)

Mitsubishi Heavy Industries Type 74 MBT (Japan)

Above: Type 74 (Paul Beaver)

SPECIFICATIONS

Crew:	4
Armament:	1 x 105mm, 1 x 7.62mm MG (coaxial), 1 x 12.7mm MG (anti-aircraft), 2 x 3 smoke dischargers
Ammunition:	55 x 105mm, 4,500 x 7.62mm, 660 x 12.7mm
Length gun forwards:	9.42m
Length hull:	6.7m
Width:	3.18m
Height including AA MG:	2.67m
Height to turret top:	2.48m
Ground clearance:	0.2 to 0.65m (adjustable)
Weight, combat:	38,000kg
Weight, empty:	36,300kg
Power-to-weight ratio:	18.94hp/tonne
Ground pressure:	0.86kg/cm^2
Engine:	Mitsubishi 10ZF Type 22 WT 10-cylinder air-cooled diesel developing 720hp at 2,200rpm
Maximum road speed:	60km/h
Maximum range:	400km
Fuel capacity:	950 lit
Fording:	1m
Fording with preparation:	2m
Vertical obstacle:	1m
Trench:	2.7m
Gradient:	60%
Armour:	Classified
Armour type:	Steel
NBC system:	Yes
Night vision equipment:	Yes

DEVELOPMENT

Development of a new MBT to supplement the Type 61 (which is now almost out of service) commenced in the early 1960s with first prototypes completed in 1969. This was followed by a number of further prototypes and first production of Type 74s was completed in 1975. Production of the Type 74 is now complete, after about 870 were built. It was followed in production by the 120mm-armed Type 90 (qv) which was also designed and built by Mitsubishi Heavy Industries.

Layout is conventional with driver front left, turret centre, engine and transmission rear. Commander and gunner sit on turret right, loader left. Commander's cupola is raised above roof line for all-round visibility.

105mm gun is the British L7, made under licence in Japan, which power-elevates from -6° to +12° (-12° to +15° using suspension). The driver can adjust the suspension to suit the type of ground, raise or lower the front or rear, or tilt the tank from side to side.

7.62mm MG is mounted coaxial with main armament and a 12.7mm M2 HB MG is mounted on turret roof for anti-aircraft defence. Some vehicles have been fitted with a dozer blade.

VARIANTS

Type 78 armoured recovery vehicle and Type 87 twin 35mm self-propelled anti-aircraft gun system.

STATUS

Production complete. In service with Japanese Ground Self Defence Force only.

KEY RECOGNITION FEATURES

- Well-sloped glacis plate with driver's hatch upper left side, turret slightly forward of hull centre, engine compartment rear. Hull sides slope inwards with exhaust pipes each side at rear. Vertical hull rear

- 105mm gun has fume extractor but no thermal sleeve, prominent external mantlet, cast turret with well-sloped sides, stowage basket rear, large infra-red searchlight left of main armament

- Suspension either side has five road wheels, drive sprocket rear, idler front, no track-return rollers. Suspension can be raised or lowered to give a ground clearance of 0.2 to 0.65m

MANUFACTURER

Mitsubishi Heavy Industries, Tokyo, Japan.

Above: Type 74 (Kensuke Ebata)

Al Khalid MBT 2000 MBT (Pakistan)

Above: Al Khalid MBT

SPECIFICATIONS

Crew:	3
Armament:	1 x 125mm, 1 x 7.62mm co-axial, 1 x 12.7mm MG anti-aircraft), 2 x 6 smoke grenade launchers
Ammunition:	39 x 125mm, 500 x 12.7mm and 2,000 x 7.62mm
Length gun forwards:	10.067m
Length hull:	6.9m
Width:	3.4m
Height:	2.3m
Ground clearance:	0.45m
Weight, combat:	48,000kg
Weight, empty:	46,000kg estimate)
Power-to-weight ratio:	25hp/tonne
Ground pressure:	n/available
Engine:	8-cylinder, 4 stroke, water-cooled turbocharged diesel developing 1,200hp
Maximum road speed:	70km/h
Maximum road range:	430km
Fuel capacity:	Not available
Fording:	1.40m
Fording with preparation:	5m
Vertical obstacle:	0.85m
Trench:	3m
Gradient:	60%
Side slope:	40%
Armour:	Classified
Armour type:	Steel/Composite
NBC system:	Yes
Night vision equipment:	Yes

DEVELOPMENT

The Al Khalid, also known as MBT 2000, is a joint development between China North Industries Corporation (NORINCO) and Pakistan under an agreement signed in 1988. This covered the upgrading of the existing Type 59 as well as local manufacture of the Type 69-II, Type 85 and finally Al Khalid series of MBT. Following trials with prototype vehicles a pre-production batch of 15 vehicles has now been completed prior to volume production.

The layout of the Al Khalid is conventional with the driver's compartment at the front, fighting compartment in the centre and engine compartment at the rear. The 125mm smooth

bore gun is fed by an automatic loader which first loads the projectile and then the charge. This feature has enabled the crew to be reduced to three: commander, gunner and driver.

Standard equipment includes computerised fire control system, stabilised day/night sighting devices for commander and gunner, NBC system and explosive reactive armour for a higher level of battlefield survivability. A snorkel can be fitted for deep fording.

NORINCO markets a similar vehicle called the Type 90-II MBT which has been developed for the export market.

VARIANTS

There are no known variants of the Al Khalid MBT.

STATUS

In production for Pakistan.

MANUFACTURER

Heavy Industries Taxila, Taxila, Pakistan.

KEY RECOGNITION FEATURES

- Almost horizontal glacis plate, turret centre and slightly raised engine compartment to the rear, 125mm gun has thermal sleeve and fume extractor mid-way down barrel

- Large explosive reactive armour panels are fitted on turret front, sides and rear, glacis plate, nose and side skirts. The suspension either side consists of six road wheels with idler at front, drive sprocket at rear and track return rollers which are covered by skirt

- Turret has sloping front with vertical sides and six smoke grenade launchers either side, stowage basket at rear, 12.7mm MG on right side of turret roof

Below: Al Khalid MBT

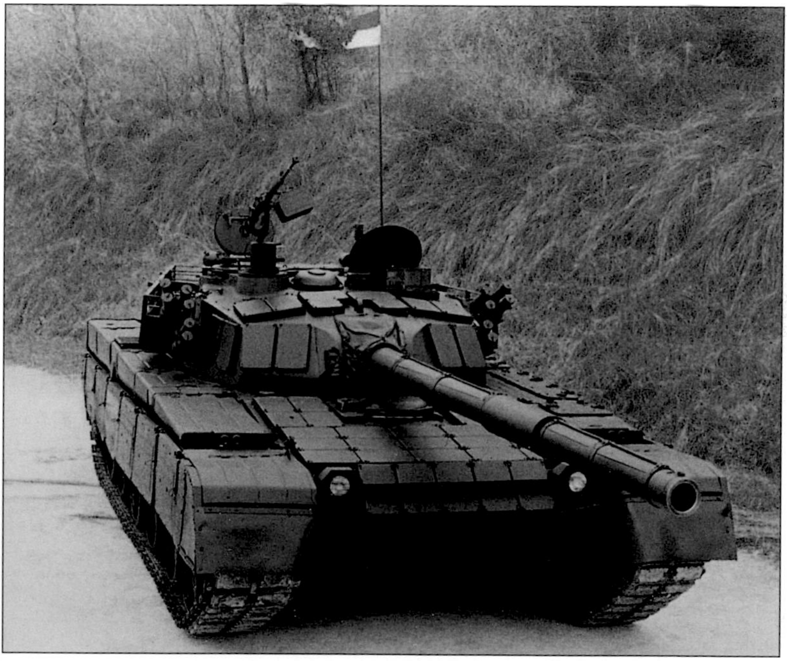

PT-91 MBT (Poland)

SPECIFICATIONS

Crew:	3
Armament:	1 x 125mm, 1 x 7.62mm MG (coaxial), 1 x 12.7mm (anti-aircraft), 2 x 12 smoke grenade launchers
Ammunition:	42 x 125mm, 2000 x 7.62mm, 300 x 12.7mm
Length gun forwards:	9.67m
Length hull:	6.95m
Width:	3.59m
Height:	2.19m (turret top)
Ground clearance:	0.43m
Weight, combat:	45,300kg
Power-to-weight ratio:	18.76hp/t
Engine:	Type S-12U supercharged diesel developing 850 hp at 2300 rpm
Maximum road speed:	60km/h
Maximum road range:	650km
Fuel capacity:	1,000 lit
Fording:	1.4m
Vertical obstacle:	0.85m
Trench:	2.8m
Gradient:	60%
Side slope:	50%
Armour:	Classified
Armour type:	Steel/Laminate/ERA
NBC:	Yes
Night vision equipment:	Yes

Above: Enhanced PT-91 ***Below: PT-91***

DEVELOPMENT

For many years Poland manufactured the Russian T-72M1 series MBT under licence for both the home and export markets. Further development of this resulted in the PT-91 which is also referred to as the *Twardy* (Hard). First prototype was completed in 1992 and over 200 were delivered

to the Polish Army. The layout of the PT-91 is identical to the T-72 MBT with driver front, turret in centre and powerpack at the rear. The gunner is seated on left of turret and commander on right. Turret can be traversed through 360° with weapon elevation from -6° to +13°.

Main improvements over the T-72 include a new Polish-developed explosive reactive armour package to the hull and turret, laser warning system, installation of a computerised fire control system, bank of 12 electically operated smoke grenade launchers either side of the turret, increased protection against mines and more powerful engine.

VARIANTS

Poland also builds a number of variants on the T-72M1 MBT chassis including the T-72M1K commanders tank, WZT-3 armoured recovery vehicle, MID armoured engineer vehicle PMC-90 armoured vehicle launched bridge, and a driver training tank. The PT-91M has been developed for Malaysia and has many improvements including SAGEM fire control system.

STATUS

Production as required. In service with Poland. On order for Malaysia.

MANUFACTURER

Zaklady Mechaniczne Bumar-Labedy SA, Gliwice, Poland.

KEY RECOGNITION FEATURES

- Well-sloped glacis plate with driver's position top centre, turret centre of hull, engine compartment rear, exhaust outlet on left side of hull above last road wheel.

- Hull front, turret front and sides are covered in closely packed explosive reactive armour arrays. Circular turret with raised cupola on right side with externally mounted 12.7mm MG. 125mm main gun has thermal sleeve and fume extractor.

- Suspension each side has six road wheels, drive sprocket rear, idler front and three track return rollers. Upper part of suspension is covered by side skirt with closely packed explosive reactive armour

***Right:* PT-91**

***Below:* PT-91**

TM-800 Medium Tank (Romania)

SPECIFICATIONS

Crew:	4
Armament:	1 x 100mm, 1 x 7.62mm MG (coaxial), 1 x 12.7mm (anti-aircraft), 2 x 5 smoke grenade launchers
Ammunition:	43 x 100mm, 3500 x 7.62mm, 500 x 12.7mm
Length gun forwards:	9.00m
Length hull:	6.74m
Width:	3.30m
Height:	2.35m (turret top)
Ground clearance:	0.425m
Weight, combat:	45,000kg
Power-to-weight ratio:	18.45 hp/tonne
Engine:	diesel developing 830hp
Maximum road speed:	64km/h
Maximum road range:	500km
Fuel capacity:	1,100 lit
Fording:	1.4m
Vertical obstacle:	0.9m
Trench:	2.8m
Gradient:	60%
Side slope:	40%
Armour:	Classified
Armour type:	Steel
NBC:	Yes
Night vision equipment:	Yes

DEVELOPMENT

The Romanian TM-800 MBT is very similar to the Russian T-54/T-55 and has almost same hull and turret, main external difference that it has six smaller road wheels whereas the T-54/T-55 has five larger road wheels. The TM-800 also has side skirts which extend the full length of the vehicle and unlike the Russian T-54/T-55/T-62/T-72 there is no exhaust outlet on the left side of the hull. The driver is seated front left with some ammunition to his right with turret in centre and powerpack at the rear. Commander and gunner are on the left with the loader on the right.

Main armament consists of a 100mm gun which is fitted with a fume extractor near the muzzle. Turret traverse is 360° with weapon elevation from -5° to +17°.

Standard equipment includes infa-red night vision equipment for commander, gunner and driver and a computerised fire control system. A dozer blade and mine clearing system can be mounted at front of the hull.

VARIANTS

TR-85, similar to T-55 but has laser rangefinder above 100mm mantlet, chassis has six road wheels, different rear engine decks and side skirts.
TR-85N, upgraded TR-85.
TR-85M1, latest upgrade with many improvements including additional armour over frontal arc of turret.

KEY RECOGNITION FEATURES

- Well-sloped glacis plate with splash board across upper part with headlamps to right, turret centre and slightly raised engine compartment to the rear. Unditching beam and long range fuel tanks often carried at rear
- Circular turret has curved sides, loader's cupola on right side with externally mounted 12.7mm AA MG, MG ammunition boxes on turret sides
- Suspension has six road wheels each side, idler front, drive sprocket rear, upper part of suspension covered by skirt

***Left:* TM-800** ***Above:* TM-800**

TR-125, was similar to Russian T-72 but only a few were built.
TER-800 is ARV model of TR-800.
TR-580, this is believed to have preceeded the TR-85 and has a similar hull but the six road wheels are spoked, has side skirts fitted.

STATUS

Production complete. In service with Romania, which has upgrade programme for its TR-85 fleet.

MANUFACTURER

Romanian state factories.

***Above:* TR-85M1 upgraded**

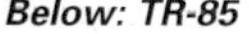

***Below:* TR-85**

T-90 MBT (Russia)

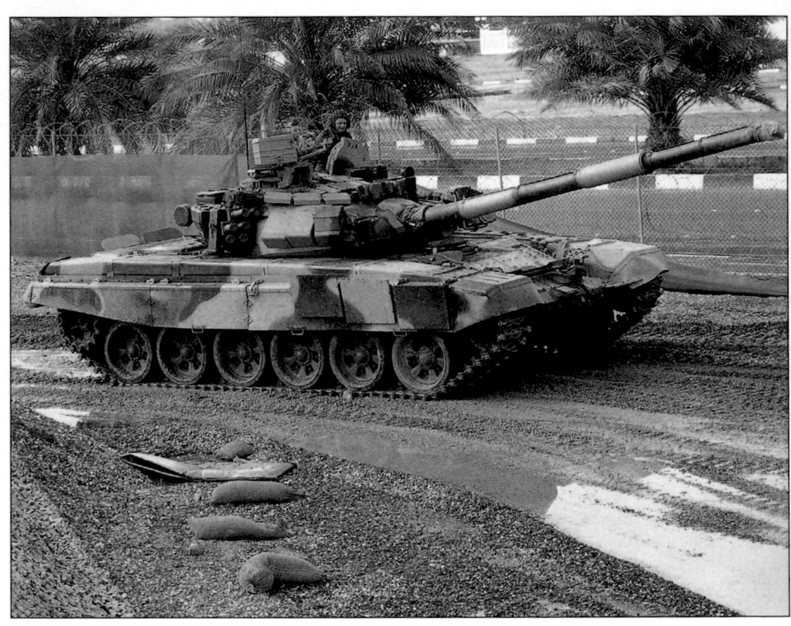

Above: T-90 MBT (Christopher F Foss)

SPECIFICATIONS

Crew:	3
Armament:	1 x 125mm gun/missile launcher, 1 x 7.62mm MG (coaxial), 1 x 12.7mm MG (anti-aircraft), 2 x 6 smoke grenade launchers
Ammunition:	43 x 125mm, 300 x 12.7mm anti-aircraft, 2,000 x 7.62mm (coaxial)
Length gun forwards:	9.53m
Length hull:	6.86m
Width with skirts:	3.78m
Height without 12.7mm MG:	2.226m
Ground clearance:	0.47m
Weight, combat:	46,500kg
Weight, empty:	44,500kg
Power-to-weight ratio:	18.06hp/t
Ground pressure:	0.91kg/cm²
Engine:	Model V-84MS 12-cylinder diesel developing 840 hp
Maximum road speed:	60km/h
Maximum road range:	550km
Fuel capacity:	1,200 lit
Fording with preparation:	5m
Fording without preparation:	1.8 m
Vertical obstacle:	0.85m
Trench:	2.8m
Gradient:	60%
Side slope:	40%
Armour:	Classified
Armour type:	Steel/Composite/ reactive
NBC system:	Yes
Night vision equipment:	Yes (commander, gunner, driver)

DEVELOPMENT

The T-90 MBT is a further development of the T-72 MBT and entered low rate production in 1994. The vehicle incorporates some sub-systems of the T-80 especially in the areas of the defensive aids systems, fire control and latest generation explosive reactive armour which provides protection against kinetic and chemical energy attack.

The overall layout of the T-90 is similar to that of the T-72 with the driver at the front, two man turret in the centre with the gunner on the left and the commander on the right who also operates the roof mounted 12.7mm AA MG. Like the T-72 and earlier T-54/T-55/T-62 MBTs, the T-90 has an exhaust outlet on the left side of the hull towards the rear. Diesel fuel can be injected into the exhaust outlet to lay a smoke screen.

The 125mm smooth bore gun is mounted in a turret with a traverse of 360° and the weapon can elevate from -6° to +14°. The 125mm gun, which is fed by an automatic loader, can also fire a laser guided projectile in addition to HE-FRAG (FS), HEAT-FS and APFSDS-T ammunition types.

The hull front and turret front and sides are fitted with explosive reactive armour and a Shtora-1 defensive aids suite is normally fitted.

KEY RECOGNITION FEATURES

- Well-sloped glacis plate fitted with additional armour, turret centre and engine compartment rear. Long range fuel tanks and unditching beam often carried on hull rear. Exhaust outlet on left side of hull above last road wheel station

- Rounded turret with 12.7mm machine gun mounted on right side of turret roof, smoke grenade launchers mounted either side towards turret rear, either side of 125mm gun is the box type sensor head of the Shtora defensive aids suite

- Suspension either side has six road wheels, idler front, drive sprocket rear with upper part of suspension covered by tracks. Forward part of skirt has additional large square armour panels

VARIANTS

T-90S export model.
T-90M welded turret and more powerful engine.
T-90K/T-90SK command tanks.
IMR-2MA engineer tank.
MTU-90 AVLB.
BRM-3M demining vehicle.

STATUS

Production. In service with India and Russia.

MANUFACTURER

Nizhny Tagil, Russia.

Below: T-90 MBT

T-80B MBT (Russia)

Above: T-80U MBT

SPECIFICATIONS

Crew:	3
Armament:	1 x 125mm gun/missile launcher, 1 x 7.62mm MG (coaxial), 1 x 12.7mm MG (anti-aircraft), smoke grenade dischargers (depends on model)
Ammunition:	36 x 125mm, 1,250 x 7.62mm MG (coaxial), 500 x 12.7mm (anti-aircraft) and 5 AT-8 Songster ATGW
Length gun forwards:	9.9m
Length hull:	7.4m
Width:	3.4m
Height to commander's cupola:	2.202m
Ground clearance:	0.38m
Weight, combat:	42,500kg
Power-to-weight ratio:	25.90hp/tonne
Ground pressure:	0.86kg/cm^2
Engine:	Gas turbine SG-1000 developing 1000hp
Maximum road speed:	70km/hr
Maximum road range:	450km
Fuel capacity:	1,100 lit
Fording:	1.8m
Fording with preparation:	5.0m
Vertical obstacle:	1m
Trench:	2.85m
Gradient:	60%
Side slope:	40%
Armour:	Classified
Armour type:	Steel/Composite/reactive
NBC system:	Yes
Night vision equipment:	Yes (commander, driver and gunner)

DEVELOPMENT

The T-80 MBT was developed in the late 1970s and is believed to have entered production in 1983 with first production MBTs being completed the following year. The most significant features of the T-80 over the earlier T-72 are its gas turbine engine and the ability to fire the Songster AT-8 ATGW from the 125mm gun.

The overall layout of the T-80 is similar to that of other Russian MBTs with the driver at the front, two man turret in centre with the gunner on the left and commander, who also mans the 12.7mm anti-aircraft machine gun, on the right. The powerpack, which includes a gas turbine engine, is at the rear. With the exception of the T-64, all post-Second World War Russian MBTs

had the exhaust outlet on the left side towards the rear. The more recent T-80 has a distinct oblong outlet in the centre of the hull at the rear.

The T-80 has a 125mm smooth bore gun that is fed by an automatic loader which can fire HE-FRAG (FS), HEAT-FS and APFSDS-T rounds, or an AT-8 Songster ATGW. Turret traverse is a full 360° with weapon elevation from -5° to +14°. The gun is fully stabilised.

VARIANTS

T-80, original production model, not built in large numbers.
T-80B, first version produced in large numbers.
T-80BK, command version of T-80B with additional communications equipment.
T-80BV, T-80 with explosive reactive armour, combat weight 42.5 tonnes.
T-80BVK, command version of T-80BV with additional communications equipment.
T-80U, first seen in 1989 and sometimes referred to as M1989 by NATO, has diesel rather than gas turbine engine, different engine decking, new commander's cupola, four smoke grenade dischargers either side of turret, different vision equipment and new armour package that includes armoured side skirts.
T-80UD, has gas turbine replaced by 1100hp diesel engine.
T-80UK, command tank version of T-80U.
T-80UE, T-80UK with command elements removed but retaining Shtora-1 counter measures equipment.
T-80UM, powered by 1250hp gas turbine, new fire control system.
T-80UM1, also called Bars (Snow Leopard) has Shtora-1 countermeasures system and more powerful engine.
T-80UM2, new cast turret.
BREM-80, is armoured recovery vehicle.

KEY RECOGNITION FEATURES

- Well-sloped glacis plate with distinctive V splash board, turret centre and engine compartment rear. Long-range fuel tanks and unditching beam often carried on far rear of hull which also has distinctive rectangular air outlet (not on T-64 series)

- Rounded turret, machine gun ammunition boxes on left, stowage box right, snorkel carried horizontally at rear. Main 125mm gun has thermal sleeve and fume extractor, 12.7mm AA MG on roof and smoke grenade dischargers each side of main armament. Infra-red searchlight on right of main armament

- Suspension each side has six road wheels, idler front, drive sprocket rear and track-return rollers covered by skirts. Unlike T-64 and T-72 there is no exhaust outlet left of engine compartment. Road wheels larger than T-64's with gap between 2nd/3rd and 4th/5th

T-84, further development of T-80 in the Ukraine (qv).

STATUS

Production. In service with Belarus, Cyprus, Pakistan, Russia, South Korea, Ukraine and Uzbekistan.

MANUFACTURERS

Kirov Works (Leningrad), Kharkov (Ukraine) and Omsk.

Right: T-80UK command tank (Christopher F Foss)

T-64 MBT (Russia)

Above: T-64B with ERA

SPECIFICATIONS (T-64B)

Crew:	3
Armament:	1 x 125mm, 1 x 7.62mm MG (coaxial), 1 x 12.7mm MG (AA)
Ammunition:	36 x 125mm, 1250 x 7.62mm, 300 x 12.7mm
Length gun forwards:	9.225m
Length hull:	6.54m
Width without skirts:	3.27m
Width with skirts:	3.415m
Ground clearance:	0.50m
Weight, combat:	39,000kg
Power-to-weight ratio:	17.9hp/tonne
Ground pressure:	0.84kg/cm^2
Engine:	Model 5DTF 5-cylinder opposed diesel developing 700hp
Maximum road speed:	60km/hr
Maximum road range:	500km
Maximum road range with long-range fuel tanks:	700km
Fuel capacity:	1,300 lit
Fording:	1.0m
Fording with preparation:	5.0m
Vertical obstacle:	0.8m
Trench:	2.85m
Gradient:	60%
Side slope:	40%
Armour:	Classified
Armour type:	Laminate/Steel/Reactive
NBC system:	Yes
Night vision equipment:	Yes (infra-red for commander, gunner and driver)

DEVELOPMENT

T-64 entered production in 1966 and was first seen in public in 1970.

T-64 looks similar to T-72 but has infra-red searchlight on left of 125mm gun, different powerpack, narrower track, different suspension and slightly different turret. Layout is similar to T-72 with driver front, turret centre, commander left, gunner right, engine and transmission rear.

Main armament comprises a 125mm smooth bore gun which power-elevates from -6° to 14°, turret traverses 360°. Similar to that installed in the T-72, it has an automatic loader which delivers eight rounds a minute. Three types of

ammunition are fired: APFSDS, HEAT-FRAG and HE-FRAG (FS). A 7.62mm MG is mounted coaxial to right of main armament and a 12.7mm MG is mounted on gunner's cupola for use in the anti-aircraft role.

VARIANTS

T-64, original model, no thermal sleeve for 115mm gun.
T-64A, first production model to be built in quantity, smoke grenade dischargers either side of gun, side skirts.
T-64AK, command vehicle.
T-64B, can fire AT-8 Songster ATGW.
T-64BK, command vehicle.
T-64BM, fitted with 6TD 1,000hp engine
T-64BV, T-64 with explosive reactive armour.
T-64B1, T-64B1K, command version of T-64B1.
T-64BV1K, T-64B with explosive reactive armour and communications equipment for use in command role.
T-64R, believed to be T-64 with gun of T-72/T-80 firing ATGW.
T-64 can be fitted with mineclearing equipment.
BREM-64, ARV on T-64 chassis.
Driver instructor vehicle, T-64 with turret removed and new superstructure.

STATUS

Production complete. In service only with Russia, Ukraine and Uzbekistan. Ukraine has upgraded some of its T-64 to the T-64M2, T-64BV-1 and T-64BV standards.

MANUFACTURER

Russian state arsenals.

KEY RECOGNITION FEATURES

• Well-sloped glacis plate with driver's position top centre, distinctive V splash plate on glacis, turret centre of hull, engine and transmission rear. Unlike T-72, no exhaust outlet on left side of hull

• Circular turret, raised cupola with external 12.7mm MG on right of roof, two stowage boxes right side of turret and one on turret rear (above which is the snorkel), three MG ammunition boxes on left side of turret. Infra-red searchlight to left of 125mm gun with thermal sleeve and fume extractor.

• Suspension each side has six road wheels (much smaller than those on T-72), idler front, drive sprocket rear and four track-return rollers. Side skirts or gill type armour panels often installed over upper part of suspension. Unditching beam and fuel drums often carried rear

***Above:* T-64A**

***Left:* T-64A**

T-72 MBT (Russia)

Above: T-72AV MBT with explosive reactive armour

Right: T-72B1 MBT

SPECIFICATIONS (T-72S)

Crew:	3
Armament:	1 x 125mm, 1 x 7.62mm MG (coaxial), 1 x 12.7mm MG (AA)
Ammunition:	45 x 125mm, 2,000 x 7.62mm, 300 x 12.7mm
Length gun forwards:	9.533m
Length hull:	6.95m
Width without skirts:	3.37m
Width with skirts:	3.59m
Height without AA MG:	2.228m
Ground clearance:	0.49m
Weight, combat:	46,500kg
Power-to-weight ratio:	18.06hp/tonne
Ground pressure:	0.90kg/cm^2
Engine:	V-84 V-12 diesel developing 840hp at 2,000rpm
Maximum road speed:	60km/hr
Maximum road range:	480km, 550km (with long-range tanks)
Fuel capacity:	1,000 lit
Fording:	1.8m (without preparation), 5m (with preparation)
Vertical obstacle:	0.85m
Trench:	2.8m
Gradient:	60%
Side slope:	40%
Armour:	Classified
Armour type:	Composite/Steel
NBC system:	Yes
Night vision equipment:	Yes (infra-red for commander, gunner and driver)

DEVELOPMENT

T-72 entered production in 1971 and was first seen in public in 1977. As well as being produced in the former USSR it has been built under licence in the former Czechoslovakia, India, Iran, Iraq, Poland and former Yugoslavia.

T-72 MBT (Russia)

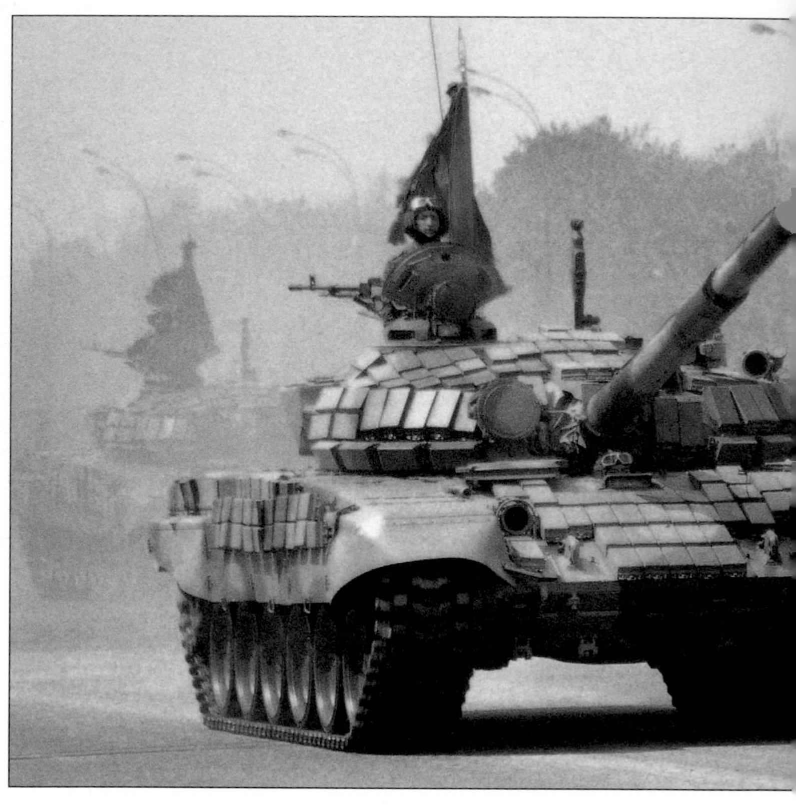

Layout is conventional, with driver front, turret centre, engine and transmission rear. Commander sits right, gunner left. There is no loader as the 125mm smooth bore gun has an automatic carousel loader with charge above and projectiles below. Types of ammunition include HEAT-FS, HE-FRAG (FS) and APFSDS, a normal mix being 12 APFSDS, 21 HE-FRAG (FS) and six HEAT-FS. A 7.62mm MG is mounted coaxial to right of 125mm gun and a 12.7mm AA MG mounted externally on gunner's hatch. Composite armour is used in frontal arc of the turret and the glacis plate.

A dozer blade is mounted under the nose and additional fuel tanks can be placed at the rear to extend operational range.

VARIANTS

The Russians have the following designations for the T-72 series of MBT which differ in some areas from those used by NATO:

T-72, original production model with coincidence rangefinder.

T-72K, command version of above.

T-72A, a number of improvements including laser rangefinder, in the Warsaw Pact was called T-72M with T-72G being export version.

T-72AK, command version of T-72A.

T-72AV, T-72 with explosive reactive armour.

T-72M, export model of T-72A.

T-72M1, modernised T-72M with additional armour.

T-72B, thicker turret armour.

T-72BK, command version of above.

KEY RECOGNITION FEATURES

- Well-sloped glacis plate with driver's position top centre, distinctive V splash plate on glacis, turret centre of hull, engine and transmission rear, exhaust outlet on left side of hull above last road wheel station

- Circular turret, raised cupola with external 12.7mm MG on right of roof, stowage box rear and right, snorkel left side, infra-red searchlight right of 125mm gun which has thermal sleeve and fume extractor. Unditching beam and long-range fuel tanks sometimes fitted rear

- Suspension each side has six road wheels, drive sprocket rear, idler front and three track-return rollers. Upper part often covered by rubber skirt or fold-out armour panels over forward wheel stations

Left: T-72BM MBT (Stefan Marx)

T-72B1, T-72 without capability to launch laser guided anti-tank projectile.
T-72S, export version of T-72B.
T-72S1, export version of T-72B1.
T-72BM, has second generation explosive reactive armour.
T-90, further development of T-72 (qv).
PT-91, Polish version of T-72 (qv).
TR-125, Romanian version of T-72.
M-84, former Yugoslav version of T-84 (qv).
Degman, Croatian version of M-84 (qv).
M84AB, Croatian version of M-84.
T-72 with 155mm turret, for trials purposes. India has fitted French, Slovakian, South African and UK 155mm artillery turrets.
T-72 can be fitted with various types of mineclearing systems.
T-72 with 120mm turret, for trials.
MTU-72 AVLB, similar to MTU-20 but on T-72 chassis.
BREM-1 armoured recovery and repair vehicle.
IMR-2 combat engineer vehicle based on T-72 chassis.
BMR-3M demine vehicle.
BMPT tank support vehicle.

STATUS

In production. In service with Algeria, Angola, Armenia, Azerbaijan, Belarus, Bulgaria, Croatia, Czech Republic, Finland, Georgia, Hungary, India, Iran, Kazakhstan, Kyrgyzstan, Libya, Macedonia, Morocco, Poland, Russia, Serbia and Montenegro, Sierra Leone, Slovakia, Syria, Tajikistan, Turkmenistan, Ukraine, Uzbekistan and Yemen.

MANUFACTURERS

Chelybinsk, Kirov and Nizhnyi Tagil, Russia.
Has also been built under licence, often with modifications, in: former Czechoslovakia, India (T-72M1), Iran (T-72S), Iraq (T-72M1), Poland (T-72M1) and former Yugoslavia (M-84).

T-62 MBT (Russia)

Above: T-62M MBT

SPECIFICATIONS

Crew:	4
Armament:	1 x 115mm, 1 x 7.62mm MG (coaxial), 1 x 12.7mm MG (anti-aircraft)
Ammunition:	40 x 115mm, 2,500 x 7.62mm, 300 x 12.7mm
Length gun forwards:	9.335m
Length hull:	6.63m
Width:	3.3m
Height:	2.395m (without AA MG)
Ground clearance:	0.43m
Weight, combat:	40,000kg
Weight, empty:	38,000kg
Power-to-weight ratio:	14.5hp/tonne
Ground pressure:	0.77kg/cm^2
Engine:	Model V-55-5 V-12 water-cooled diesel developing 580hp at 2,000rpm
Maximum road speed:	50km/hr
Maximum road range:	450km
Maximum road range (with auxiliary tanks):	650km
Fuel capacity:	675 + 285 lit
Vertical obstacle:	0.8m
Trench:	2.85m
Gradient:	60%
Side slope:	30%
Armour:	242mm (maximum)
Armour type:	Steel
NBC system:	Yes
Night vision equipment:	Yes (infra-red for commander, gunner and driver)

DEVELOPMENT

T-62, a further development of T-54/T-55, entered production in 1961, continuing until 1975. A small number were also built in former Czechoslovakia.

Layout is conventional with driver front left, some ammunition stowed to his right, turret centre and engine and transmission rear. Commander and gunner sit left of turret, loader right. Loader also mans roof mounted 12.7mm MG.

115mm smooth bore gun power-elevates from -6° to +16° and powered turret traverses through 360°. The gun fires HE-FRAG(FS), HEAT-FS and APFSDS rounds and empty cartridge cases are

ejected from a trap door in turret rear. A 7.62mm MG is mounted coaxial to right of main armament and a 12.7mm AA MG is mounted on roof. The gun is fully stabilised in both horizontal and vertical planes.

T-62 lays its own smoke screen by injecting diesel fuel into the exhaust, and additional fuel tanks can be fitted at hull rear to extend its operational range. An unditching beam is usually carried rear.

KEY RECOGNITION FEATURES

- Well-sloped glacis plate with splash board mid-way, horizontal hull top with driver's hatch front left, turret centre, engine and transmission rear

- Turret is circular and well-sloped all round, loader's cupola on right normally mounts 12.7mm AA MG, MG ammunition boxes sometimes stowed right side of turret to rear, snorkel left side of turret rear. Main armament has fume extractor about one-third distance from muzzle, infra-red searchlight right of main armament

- Suspension each side has five road wheels, idler front, drive sprocket rear, no track-return rollers, no skirts. Exhaust port on left track guard above fourth/fifth road wheel, flat fuel/oil storage tanks right side of hull above track

VARIANTS

T-62K, K in designation means command.
T-62D, has Drozd anti-tank defensive system, additional armour.
T-62D-1, as above but different engine.
T-62M, can fire laser guided projectile, passive armour and many other improvements.
T-62M-1, similar to above.
T-62M1, passive armour, different engine.
T-62M1-1, upgrade without laser guided projectile capability and passive armour.
T-62M1-2, similar to above.
T-62M1-2-1, similar to above.
T-62MV, upgrade with capability to fire laser guided projectile, also has explosive reactive armour.
T-62 flamethrower (in service), has flame gun mounted coaxial with 115mm gun.
Egyptian T-62s, some of which have two smoke rockets each side of turret.

STATUS

Production complete. In service with Angola, Algeria, Belarus, Cuba, Egypt, Ethiopia (limited numbers), Iran, Kazakhstan, North Korea, Libya, Russia, Syria, Uzbekistan, Vietnam and Yemen.

MANUFACTURERS

Former Czechoslovakian, North Korean and Russian state factories.

Below: T-62M MBT from rear (Christopher F Foss)

T-54/T-55 MBT (Russia)

SPECIFICATIONS (T-54)

Crew:	4
Armament:	1 x 100mm, 1 x 7.62mm MG (coaxial), 1 x 7.62mm (bow), 1 x 12.7mm MG (anti-aircraft)
Ammunition:	34 x 100mm, 3,000 x 7.62mm, 500 x 12.7mm
Length gun forwards:	9m
Length hull:	6.04m
Width:	3.27m
Height without AA MG:	2.4m
Ground clearance:	0.425m
Weight, combat:	36,000kg
Weight, empty:	34,000kg
Power-to-weight ratio:	14.44hp/tonne
Ground pressure:	0.81kg/cm^2
Engine:	Model V-54 V-12 water-cooled diesel, 520hp at 2,000rpm
Maximum road speed:	50km/hr
Maximum road range:	510km
Maximum road range with long range fuel tanks:	720km
Fuel capacity:	812 lit
Fording:	1.4m
Fording with preparation:	5.0m
Vertical obstacle:	0.8m
Trench:	2.7m
Gradient:	60%
Side slope:	40%
Armour:	203mm (maximum)
Armour type:	Steel
NBC system:	None
Night vision equipment:	Yes (infra-red for commander, gunner and driver)

KEY RECOGNITION FEATURES

- Well-sloped glacis plate with splash board mid-way up, horizontal hull top with driver's hatch front left, turret centre, engine compartment rear. Vertical hull rear

- Turret circular and well-sloped all round, loader's cupola on right normally mounts 12.7mm AA MG. 100mm gun has no thermal sleeve but bore evacuator to immediate rear of muzzle. Infra-red night searchlight right of main armament

- Suspension each side has five road wheels, idler front, drive sprocket rear, no track-return rollers or skirts, exhaust pipe on left track guard above fourth/fifth road wheel, distinct gap between first and second road wheels. Flat fuel/oil storage tanks right side of hull above track

Left: Upgraded Slovenian M-55 S1 MBT with 105mm gun

Below: T-55 MBT

T-54/T-55 MBT (Russia)

DEVELOPMENT

T-54 is a further development of T-44 which itself was a development of T-34. First T-54 prototype was completed in 1946 with first production vehicles following in 1947. Production continued in the former USSR as late as 1981 and was also undertaken in China (Type 59 qv), former Czechoslovakia and Poland. Further development resulted in the T-62 with its 115mm gun (qv).

Layout is conventional, with driver front left, some 100mm ammunition stowed to his right, turret centre, engine and transmission rear. Commander and gunner sit on left of turret, loader right. Loader also mans roof mounted 12.7mm AA MG.

Main armament comprises 100mm rifled gun which power-elevates from -5° to +17°, and turret traverses through 360°. The gun fires AP, APC-T, HE, HE-FRAG, HEAT-FS and HVAPDS-T rounds with average rate of fire of four rounds a minute. A 7.62mm MG is mounted coaxial right of main armament and a similar weapon, operated by the driver, is fixed in the glacis plate firing forwards. A 12.7mm AA MG is mounted on the loader's cupola. The T-54 series lays its own smoke screen by injecting diesel fuel into the exhaust outlet on left side of hull. The tank can also be fitted with a dozer blade and various types of mine-clearing system.

VARIANTS

There are countless variants of the T-54/T-55 and listed below is a resumé of those from Soviet sources.

T-54, there are numerous differences between early production T-54 vehicles and later models with some having a wider mantlet and turret undercut at the rear. These are sometimes referred to as the T-54 (1949), T-54 (1951) and T-54 (1953).

T-54A, has fume extractor for 100mm gun, stabilisation system and deep fording equipment.

T-54AK, command tank (Polish model is T-54AD).

T-54M, T-54 upgraded to T-55M standard.

T-54B, first model to have infra-red night vision equipment.

T-55M, 580hp engine, no loader's cupola, stabilised gun, increased ammunition stowage fitted.

T-54 command vehicles have designation of **T-54K, T-54BK** and **T-54MK.** T-55 command vehicles are **T-55K, T55AK, T-55MK** and **T-55MVK.**

T-55, T-54 with new turret and numerous other improvements, late production models have 12.7mm AA MG.

T-55A, radiation shielding added plus 12.7mm AA MG.

T-55K, command versions, eg T-55K1 and T-55K2.

T-55M, T-55 upgrade can fire AT-10 Stabber laser guided ATGW through 100mm gun, plus many other improvements.

T-55M-1, as above but further improvements including passive armour

T-55MV, as T-55M but with explosive reactive armour.

T-55AM-1, T-55A upgrade to fire AT-10 Stabber plus passive armour, also:

Czechoslovakian-built = T-55AM2B
Polish-built = T-55AM2P
Russian-built = T-55AM2PB

T-55AD, T-55M with *Drozd* countermeasure system.
T-55AD-1, as above but with different engine.
There are many variations between production tanks, eg Polish-built vehicles often have large stowage boxes on left side of turret. More recently many have laser rangefinder over 100mm gun.
T-54 ARVs, many versions.
T-54 AVLBs, many versions.
IMR combat engineer vehicle.
Many countries have carried out extensive modifications, including Egypt (105mm gun and new night vision equipment) and Israeli TI-67 (105mm gun, new fire-control system). Romania has upgraded many T-54 vehicles with side skirts, six road wheels and improved engine cooling. Slovenia has upgraded its MBTs to the M-55 S1 standard with new armour and 105mm gun. Some Iraqi T-54/T-55 MBTs have extra passive armour.

STATUS

Production complete. In service with Albania, Algeria, Angola, Armenia, Azerbaijan, Bangladesh, Belarus, Bosnia-Herzegovina, Bulgaria, Cambodia, Central African Republic, Chad, China, Congo, Croatia, Cuba, Czech Republic, Ecuador, Egypt, Eritrea, Ethiopia, Finland, Georgia, Guinea, Hungary, India, Iran, Korea (North), Laos, Latvia, Lebanon, Libya, Macedonia, Malawi, Mauritania, Mongolia, Mozambique, Namibia, Nicaragua, Nigeria, Pakistan, Peru, Poland, Romania, Russia, Rwanda, Serbia and Montenegro, Slovakia, Slovenia, Somalia, Sri Lanka, Sudan, Syria, Tanzania, Togo, Uganda, Ukraine, Uruguay, Uzbekistan, Vietnam, Yemen and Zambia.

MANUFACTURERS

State factories in former Czechoslovakia, Poland, Russia and China as Type 59 (qv).

Below: T-55AM2B with additional armour

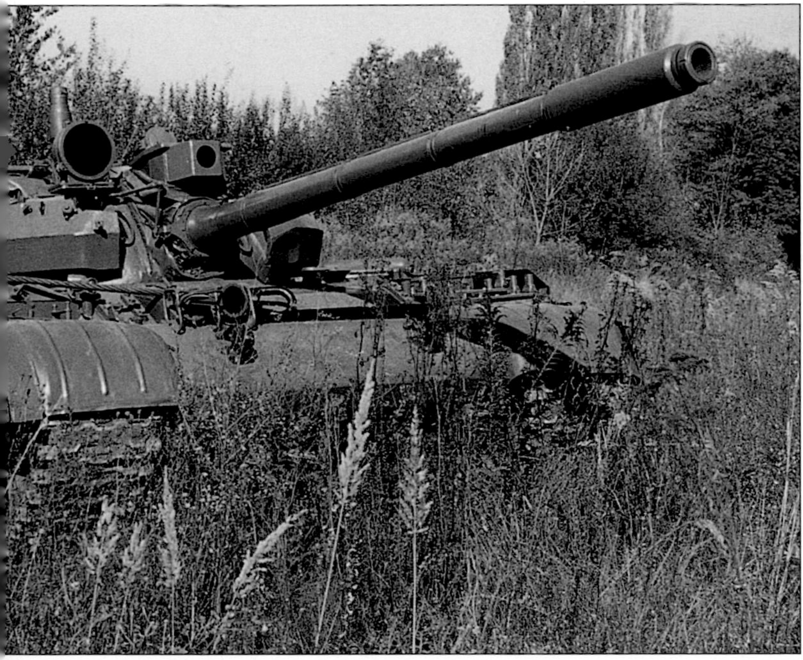

PT-76 Light Amphibious Tank (Russia)

Above: PT-76 (Richard Stickland)

SPECIFICATIONS

Crew:	3
Armament:	1 x 76.2mm (main), 1 x 7.62mm MG (coaxial)
Ammunition:	40 x 76.2mm, 1,000 x 7.62mm
Length gun forwards:	7.625m
Length hull:	6.91m
Width:	3.14m
Height:	2.255m (late model), 2.195m (early model)
Ground clearance:	0.37m
Weight, combat:	14,600kg
Power-to-weight ratio:	16.4hp/tonne
Ground pressure:	0.50kg/cm²
Engine:	Model V-6B 6-cylinder in-line water-cooled diesel developing 240hp at 1,800rpm
Maximum road speed:	44km/hr
Maximum water speed:	8-9km/hr
Road range:	370km
Fuel capacity:	380 lit
Fording:	Amphibious
Vertical obstacle:	1.1m
Trench:	2.8m
Gradient:	70%
Side slope:	35%
Armour:	14mm (maximum)
Armour type:	Steel
NBC system:	No
Night vision equipment:	Yes (infra-red for driver)

DEVELOPMENT

PT-76 was developed shortly after the Second World War with first production vehicles completed in 1950 and production continuing until the late 1960s. In Russian army units PT-76 has been replaced by MBTs or specialised versions of BMP-1/BMP-2.

Many automotive components of PT-76 were subsequently used in the BTR-50P amphibious APC, which has a similar chassis.

Driver sits front, two-man turret centre, engine and transmission rear. It is fully amphibious, propelled in the water by its tracks. Before entering the water the trim vane is erected at front and bilge pumps switched on. To extend the operational range of PT-76 auxiliary fuel tanks can be installed on rear decking; these contain an additional 180 litres and extend road range to 480km.

Main armament comprises a 76.2mm D-56T with elevation from -4° to +30°, turret traverses through 360°. Ammunition fired includes AP-T, API-T, HE-FRAG, HEAT and HVAP-T. Some PT-76s have been fitted with a roof-mounted 12.7mm DShKM MG.

VARIANTS

First production vehicles had D-56T gun with a multi-slotted muzzle brake, but most common version has a double baffle muzzle brake and bore evacuator towards muzzle.

PT-76B has D-56TM fully stabilised gun.

China has produced an improved version of PT-76, Type 63 (qv), which has a new turret with 85mm gun.

Russia has recently developed a new turret for the PT-76 armed with a 57mm gun.

STATUS

Production complete. In service with Benin, Bosnia-Herzegovina, Congo, Croatia, Cuba, Guinea, Guinea-Bissau, India, Indonesia, Laos, Madasgascar, Nicaragua, North Korea, Russia, Uganda, Vietnam and Zambia.

MANUFACTURER

Russian state arsenals.

KEY RECOGNITION FEATURES

- Hull has pointed nose with vertical sides, turret mounted well to front of chassis, rear of driver

- Round turret with sloping sides and flat roof with large oval-shaped roof hatch opening forwards

- Suspension either side has six ribbed road wheels, idler front, drive sprocket rear, no track-return rollers

Below: PT-76 showing amphibious capabilities

M-84 MBT (Serbia and Montenegro)

Above: M-84 MBT

SPECIFICATIONS

Crew:	3
Armament:	1 x 125mm, 1 x 7.62mm (coaxial), 1 x 12.7mm MG (AA), 12 smoke grenade dischargers (one bank of five and one of seven)
Ammunition:	42 x 125mm, 2000 x 7.62mm, 300 x 12.7mm
Length gun forwards:	9.53m
Length hull:	6.86m
Width:	3.57m
Height (turret roof):	2.19m
Ground clearance:	0.426m
Weight, combat:	44,000kg
Power-to-weight ratio:	22.72hp/tonne
Ground pressure:	0.81kg/cm²
Engine:	V-46TK V-12 water-cooled, supercharged diesel developing 780hp at 2,000rpm
Maximum road speed:	65km/hr
Range:	700km
Fuel capacity:	1,450 lit (estimate)
Fording:	1.2m (without preparation), 5m (with snorkel)
Vertical obstacle:	0.85m
Trench:	2.8m
Gradient:	58%
Side slope:	47%
Armour:	Classified
Armour type:	Composite/Steel
NBC system:	Yes
Night vision equipment:	Yes (commander, gunner and driver)

DEVELOPMENT

The M-84 is essentially the Russian T-72 manufactured under licence in Yugoslavia with a number of Yugoslav designed sub-systems, for example the fire control system. The first prototypes of the M-84 were completed in 1982-83 with production commencing in 1983-84 and first production vehicles being completed in 1984. It is estimated that by early 1992 over 600 had been built for the home and export markets. Following the Yugoslav war, production of the M-84 stopped although more recently Croatia has unveiled an MBT called the Degman which is similar to M-84 but has a new armour package.

The layout of the M-84 is identical to that of the T-72 with the driver being seated at the front of the vehicle in the centre, two man turret in the centre of the hull with the gunner on the left and commander on the right with the powerpack at the rear. The M-84 has no loader as the vehicle is fitted with an automatic loader for the 125mm gun, which has an elevation of +13° and a depression of -6° with turret traverse a full 360°; turret controls are powered with manual controls for emergency use. Types of 125mm ammunition fired include HE-FRAG, HEAT-FS and APFSDS-T.

VARIANTS

ARV, has been built in production quantities.
M-84A, latest production model with a number of improvements including a more powerful 1,000hp engine that gives a higher speed and improved power-to-weight ratio. It also has improved armour protection.
M-84AB, version for Kuwait, now built in Slovenia who also builds M84A4 Snajper (Sniper).

STATUS

Production complete. In service with Bosnia-Herzegovina, Croatia, Kuwait, Serbia and Montenegro and Slovenia.

MANUFACTURER

Former Yugoslav state factories.

KEY RECOGNITION FEATURES

• Well-sloped glacis plate with driver's position top centre, distinctive V splash plate on glacis, turret centre of hull, engine and transmission at rear, exhaust outlet on left side hull above last road wheel station

• Circular turret, raised cupola with external 12.7mm MG on right of roof, stowage box rear and right, snorkel left side, infra-red searchlight right of 125mm gun which has thermal sleeve and fume extractor. Unditching beam and long-range fuel drums sometimes fitted at rear. Mounted on forward part of turret roof is distinctive pole type sensor for the fire control system which is not seen on the Russian T-72 MBT

• Suspension each side has six road wheels, drive sprocket rear, idler front and three track return rollers. Upper part usually covered by rubber skirts

Below: Close-up of M-84 MBT turret

ROTEM K1 MBT (South Korea)

SPECIFICATIONS

Crew:	4
Armament:	1 x 105mm, 1 x 7.62mm MG (coaxial), 1 x 7.62mm MG (anti-aircraft), 1 x 12.7mm MG (anti-aircraft), 2 x 6 smoke grenade dischargers
Ammunition:	47 x 105mm, 1,000 x 12.7mm, 8,800 x 7.62mm
Length gun forwards:	9.672m
Length hull:	7.477m
Width:	3.594m
Height to turret top:	2.248m
Ground clearance:	0.46m
Weight, combat:	51,000kg
Power-to-weight ratio:	23.5hp/tonne
Ground pressure:	0.87kg/cm^2
Engine:	MTU 871 Ka-501 diesel developing 1,200hp at 2,600rpm
Maximum road speed:	65km/h
Cruising range:	457km
Fuel capacity:	Not available
Fording without kit:	1.2m
Fording with kit:	2.20m
Vertical obstacle:	1m
Trench:	2.74m
Gradient:	60%
Side slope:	30%
Armour:	Classified
Armour type:	Laminate
NBC system:	Yes
Night vision equipment:	Yes

DEVELOPMENT

The K1 MBT was developed by the now General Dynamic Land Systems Division (who designed and built the M1/M1A1 and M1A2 Abrams series of MBT) to meet the specific operational requirements of the South Korean Army. The first of two prototypes was completed in the United States in 1983 and production commenced by Hyundai Precision & Ind Co Ltd (now ROTEM) at Changwon in 1985/1986 and since then it is estimated that 1,500 (105mm and 120mm) vehicles have been manufactured. Many of the key sub-systems, such as engine, transmission, fire control system and sights were developed overseas.

Layout of the K1 MBT is conventional with the driver at front left, turret in centre and powerpack at the rear. The commander and gunner are seated on the right of the turret with the loader on the left. Turret traverse and weapon elevation is powered with manual controls for emergency use. The 105mm rifled tank gun has an elevation of +20° and a depression of -10° with

turret traverse being a full 360°. An unusual feature of the K1 MBT is its hybrid suspension type which has torsion bars at the centre road wheel stations with hydro-pneumatic units at the front and rear stations, this allows the driver to adjust the suspension to suit the type of terrain being crossed.

The computerised fire control system includes a stabilised sight for the tank commander, digital computer, day/night sights and a laser rangefinder. A fire detection/suppression system is fitted as is a heater.

K1A1 has a number of improvements including 120mm M256 tank gun.

KEY RECOGNITION FEATURES

- Blunt nose with almost horizontal glacis plate, driver's hatch in left side, turret centre, raised engine compartment at rear
- Front of turret slopes slightly to rear, sides slope inwards with turret rear vertical. Stowage basket on either side of turret with bank of smoke grenade dischargers on either side of turret. 7.62mm MG on left side of turret roof with 12.7mm MG on right side
- Suspension either side has six road wheels, idler front, drive sprocket at rear, return rollers with upper part of running gear covered by armoured skirt that extends to rear of vehicle

VARIANTS

AVLB, the bridge and launching system was designed and built by the then Alvis Vickers of the UK in 1990 and integrated on a modified K1 chassis in South Korea. Launches a scissors bridge with a length of 22m when opened out.

ARV, this was developed by the now Rheinmetall Landsysteme and is similar to the Leopard 1 ARV and has a winch, dozer/stabiliser blade and hydraulic crane for changing powerpacks in the field.

STATUS

In production. In service with South Korean Army.

MANUFACTURER

ROTEM Precision & Ind Co Ltd, Changwon, South Korea.

Top left: K1 MBT

Above right: K1 MBT

Right: K1 MBT

Challenger 2 MBT (UK)

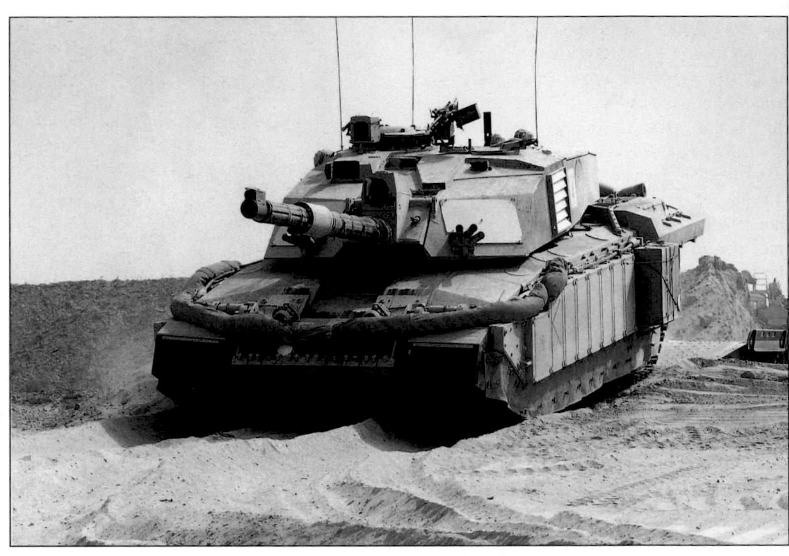

Above: British Army Challenger 2 MBT in Iraq (MoD/CCR)

SPECIFICATIONS

Crew:	4
Armament:	1 x 120mm, 1 x 7.62mm MG (coaxial), 1 x 7.62mm MG (anti-aircraft), 2 x 5 smoke grenade dischargers
Ammunition:	50 x 120mm, 4,000 x 7.62mm
Length gun forwards:	11.55m
Length hull:	8.327m
Width:	3.52m
Height:	2.49m (turret roof)
Ground clearance:	0.50m
Weight, combat:	62,500kg
Power-to-weight ratio:	19.2hp/tonne
Ground pressure:	0.9kg/cm²
Engine:	Perkins Engines Condor V-12 12-cylinder diesel developing 1,200bhp at 2,300rpm
Maximum road speed:	56km/h
Range:	450km
Fuel capacity:	1,592 lit
Fording:	1.07m
Vertical obstacle:	0.9m
Trench:	2.34m
Gradient:	60%
Side slope:	30%
Armour:	Classified
Armour type:	Chobham/Steel
NBC system:	Yes
Night vision equipment:	Yes (passive for commander, gunner and driver)

DEVELOPMENT

The Challenger 2 was originally developed as a private venture by Alvis Vickers and was selected by the British Army in 1991 to meet its requirement for an MBT to replace the Chieftain MBT. A total of 368 were built for the British Army and Oman.

Although the Challenger 2 has some external resemblance to the earlier Challenger 1 MBT it is essentially a new MBT. The new turret is armed with a 120mm L30 rifled tank gun. Turret traverse and gun elevation is all electric and gun is fully stabilised. Turret traverse is a full 360° with

weapon elevation from -10° to +20°. A 7.62mm machine gun is mounted coaxial to the left of the main armament and a 7.62mm machine gun is mounted at the loader's station. The computerised fire control system gives a high first round hit probability against stationary and moving targets with the thermal camera mounted over the 120mm gun mantlet being coupled to the gunner's sight. The commander has a roof mounted 360° stabilised periscopic sight that also includes a laser rangefinder.

The driver is seated at the front of the vehicle, turret in the centre and powerpack at the rear. The commander and gunner are seated on the right side of the turret with the loader on the left. To increase the operational range of the tank additional fuel tanks can be mounted at the rear of the hull. A dozer blade can be mounted at the front of the hull. Additional armour has been provided for the front of the Challenger 2 as well as hull sides.

VARIANTS

Challenger (Oman), improved cooling
Challenger 2E, export model with many improvements.
Driver training tank with no turret.
Titan bridgelayer (under development).
Trojan engineer tank (under development).

KEY RECOGNITION FEATURES

- Front idlers project ahead of nose which slopes back under hull front, well-sloped glacis plate with driver's hatch recessed in centre, slightly raised engine compartment at rear. Hull rear slopes inwards at sharp angle

- Turret has well-sloped front angled to rear, turret sides and rear vertical, gunner's sight on right side of turret roof, raised periscopic sight in front of commander's cupola, 7.62mm machine gun above loader's position

- Suspension either side has six road wheels, idler front, drive sprocket rear, four track-return rollers. Upper part of suspension covered by skirts

STATUS

Production complete. In service with Oman and the UK.

MANUFACTURER

BAE Systems Land Systems, Newcastle-upon-Tyne, UK.

Below: Challenger 2 MBT

Challenger 1 MBT (UK)

Above: Challenger 1

SPECIFICATIONS

Crew:	4
Armament:	1 x 120mm, 1 x 7.62mm MG (coaxial), 1 x 7.62mm MG (anti-aircraft), 2 x 5 smoke grenade dischargers
Ammunition:	64 x 120mm, 4,000 x 7.62mm
Length gun forwards:	11.56m
Length hull:	8.327m
Width overall:	3.518m
Height to top of commander's sight:	2.95m
Height to turret top:	2.5m
Ground clearance:	0.5m
Power-to-weight ratio:	19.35bhp/tonne
Weight, combat:	62,000kg
Weight, empty:	60,000 kg
Ground pressure:	0.97kg/cm^2
Engine:	Perkins Condor 12V 1,200 12-cylinder diesel developing 1,200bhp at 2,300rpm
Maximum road speed:	56km/hr
Maximum range:	450km
Fuel capacity:	1,592 lit
Fording:	1.07m
Gradient:	58%
Side slope:	40%
Armour:	Classified
Armour type:	Chobham/Steel
Vertical obstacle:	0.9m
NBC system:	Yes
Trench:	2.8m
Night vision equipment:	Yes (passive for commander, gunner and driver)

DEVELOPMENT

Challenger 1 is a development of the Shir 2 MBT originally built for Iran. First production tanks were delivered by Royal Ordnance Leeds (taken over by Vickers Defence Systems in 1986) in March 1983 and production continued to 1990 by which time 420 had been built. Further development resulted in the Challenger 2 MBT (qv).

Challenger 1 has Chobham armour in its hull and turret, which gives a high degree of protection against both kinetic and chemical energy attack. Driver sits front, turret centre, engine and transmission rear.

Commander and gunner sit right of turret, loader left. 120mm L11A5 rifled gun is identical to Chieftain's and power-elevates from -10° to +20°, with turret traverse 360°. Ammunition includes APDS-T, APFSDS-T, HESH, smoke and training, all rounds of separate loading type. A 7.62mm MG is mounted coaxial to left of main armament and a second on the commander's cupola. The Improved Fire Control System includes laser rangefinder. Challenger 1s have been fitted with the Barr and Stroud Thermal Observation and Gunnery system. The Challenger 1 was phased out of British Army service in 2000 and most are now being passed on to Jordan who called the vehicle the Al Hussein.

KEY RECOGNITION FEATURES

- Front idlers project ahead of nose which slopes back under hull, well-sloped glacis plate with driver's hatch recessed in centre, turret centre, slightly raised engine compartment rear, hull rear slopes inwards at sharp angle

- Turret has well-sloped front angled to rear, turret sides vertical. Commander's cupola on right side with external 7.62mm MG, opening in right side of turret for TOGS

- Suspension each side has six road wheels, idler front, drive sprocket rear, four track-return rollers. Upper part of road wheels and suspension covered by skirts

VARIANTS

Challenger 1 can be fitted with front mounted dozer blade or mine clearing systems.
Challenger 1s used in Middle East were fitted with additional armour protection.
Challenger Armoured Repair and Recovery Vehicle.
Challenger Driver Training Tank, Challenger 1 with turret replaced by non-rotating turret.

STATUS

Production complete. In service only with Jordan.

MANUFACTURER

Vickers Defence Systems, Leeds, UK (facility now closed).

***Above right:* Jordanian Al Hussein MBT (Christopher F Foss)**

***Right:* Jordanian Al Hussein MBT (Christopher F Foss)**

Scorpion Reconnaissance Vehicle (UK)

Above: Sabre (Richard Stickland)

SPECIFICATIONS

Crew:	3
Armament:	1 x 76mm, 1 x 7.62mm MG (coaxial), 2 x 4 smoke grenade dischargers
Ammunition:	40 x 76mm, 3,000 x 7.62mm
Length:	4.794m
Width:	2.235m
Height:	2.102m
Ground clearance:	0.356m
Weight combat:	8,073kg
Power-to-weight ratio:	23.54bhp/tonne
Ground pressure:	0.36kg/cm²
Engine:	Jaguar J60 4.2 lit 6-cylinder petrol developing 190hp at 4,750rpm (All British Army CVR(T) vehicles have had their patrol engines replaced by a Cummins diesel engine)
Maximum road speed:	80.5km/hr
Maximum range:	644km
Fuel capacity:	423 lit
Fording:	1.067m, amphibious with preparation
Vertical obstacle:	0.5m
Trench:	2.057m
Gradient:	60%
Side slope:	40%
Armour:	Classified
Armour type:	Aluminium
NBC system:	Yes
Night vision equipment:	Yes

DEVELOPMENT

Scorpion (FV101), officially named Combat Vehicle Reconnaissance (Tracked), was developed by Alvis to replace Saladin armoured car. First prototype completed in 1969 and first production vehicles in 1972. By 2004 well over 3,500 had been built for home and export. Driver sits front left with engine to right and two-man turret rear. Turret has commander on left and gunner right. Turret traverse is manual through 360° and 76mm gun elevates from -10° to +35°. Main armament fires HESH, HE and smoke rounds with 7.62mm MG mounted coaxial to left. Flotation screen is carried collapsed round top of hull which when erected makes vehicle fully amphibious, propelled by its tracks. Wide range of optional equipment

available including various fire-control systems, laser rangefinders, diesel engine, 90mm gun, 7.62mm anti-aircraft MG and air-conditioning system. The standard 76mm Scorpion is no longer used by the British Army.

VARIANTS

Scorpion 90, has Belgian Cockerill 90mm MK III gun.
Striker (FV102), ATGW carrier.
Spartan (FV103), APC member of family (see APCs).
Stormer, based on components of CVR(T) (see APCs).
Streaker, high mobility loader carrier, prototypes.
Samson (FV106), ARV member of family.
Samaritan (FV104), armoured ambulance with higher roof.
Sultan (FV105), command post vehicle with higher roof.
Scimitar (FV107), similar to Scorpion, but has 30mm RARDEN cannon in two-man turret.
Sabre, is Scorpion chassis with Fox turret (UK only).

KEY RECOGNITION FEATURES

- Rounded nose with well-sloped glacis plate, driver's hatch in upper left side and louvres to right, horizontal hull top, vertical hull rear with oblong stowage box

- Turret on hull top to rear with short-barrelled 76mm gun, no muzzle brake or fume extractor, sight to right of 76mm gun. Upper part of turret sides slope inwards to roof, lower turret sides slope inwards towards hull roof. Stowage box each side of turret

- Suspension each side has five large road wheels, drive sprocket front, idler rear, no track-return rollers. Original flotation screen round hull top has been removed from British Army vehicles. Long stowage box above rear road wheels

***Below:* Scorpion (90mm)**

Scorpion Reconnaissance Vehicle (UK)

Above: Scimitar (Marc Firmager)

Below: Sultan command post (Richard Stickland)

Right: Samaritan ambulance (Richard Stickland)

STATUS

Production complete. In service with Belgium, Botswana, Brunei, Chile, Honduras, Indonesia, Iran, Ireland, Jordan, Malaysia, Nigeria, Oman, Philippines, Spain, Tanzania, Thailand, Togo, United Arab Emirates, UK and Venezuela.

MANUFACTURER

Alvis Vehicles, Coventry, UK (which has now closed).

Below: Scorpion (76mm)

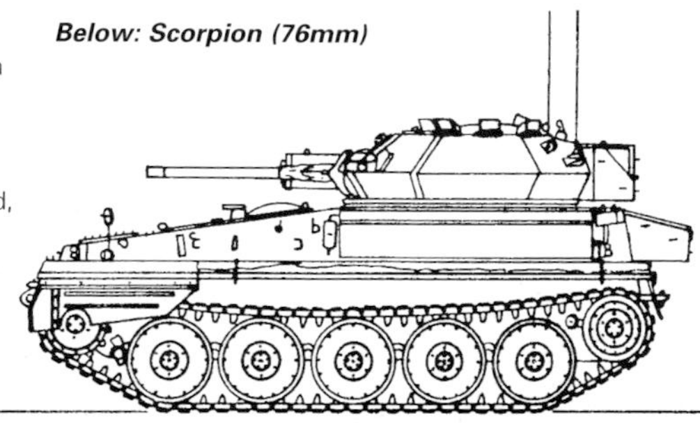

Khalid MBT (UK)

Above: Khalid MBT

SPECIFICATIONS

Crew:	4
Armament:	1 x 120mm, 1 x 7.62mm MG (coaxial), 1 x 7.62mm MG (anti-aircraft), 2 x 6 smoke grenade dischargers
Ammunition:	64 x 120mm, 6,000 x 7.62mm
Length gun forwards:	11.55m
Length hull:	8.39m
Width:	3.518m
Height overall:	2.975m
Ground clearance:	0.508m
Weight, combat:	58,000kg
Weight, empty:	56,500kg
Power-to-weight ratio:	20.68bhp/tonne
Ground pressure:	0.9kg/cm^2
Engine:	Perkins Condor 12V 12-cylinder diesel developing 1,200bhp at 2,300 rpm
Maximum road speed:	56km/hr
Maximum range:	400km
Fuel capacity:	950 lit
Fording:	1.066m
Vertical obstacle:	0.914m
Trench:	3.149m
Gradient:	60%
Side slope:	40%
Armour:	Classified
Armour type:	Steel
NBC system:	Yes
Night vision equipment:	Yes (passive for commander, gunner and driver)

DEVELOPMENT

In 1974 Royal Ordnance Leeds was awarded contracts by the Iranian Government for 125 Shir 1s and 1,225 Shir 2s, but in 1979 the order was cancelled by the new government although Shir 1 production was then under way. In 1979, Jordan ordered 274 slightly modified Shir 1s under the name Khalid, which were delivered from 1981. Khalid is essentially a late production Chieftain with major changes to the fire-control system and powerpack; the latter is the same as Challenger 1 MBT which has now been phased

out of British Army service. Most of these have been passed on to Jordan where they are known as the Al Hussein.

Driver sits front, turret is centre and engine and transmission rear. The 120mm gun has no depression over hull rear. Commander and gunner sit on turret right, loader on left. The 120mm L11A5 rifled gun is identical to that in Chieftain and Challenger 1 and power-elevates from -10° to +20° with turret traverse through 360°. Types of ammunition include APDS-T, APFSDS-T, HESH, smoke and training, all rounds with separate loading. A 7.62mm MG is mounted coaxial to left of main armament and a second is mounted on the commander's cupola.

Khalid has a Thales Optronics Condor commander's day/night sight, former Barr and Stroud laser rangefinder and a former Marconi Improved Fire Control System and all electric gun control and stabilisation system. It is also fitted with the Kidde-Graviner Crew Bay explosion and detection system.

VARIANTS

No variants.

STATUS

Production complete. In service with Jordan.

KEY RECOGNITION FEATURES

- Well-sloped glacis plate with driver's circular hatch in upper part, turret centre and raised engine compartment rear. Vertical sides.

- 120mm gun mounted internally. Turret identical to Chieftain's except for external stowage, commander's cupola on right has tall day/night sight with 7.62mm MG left, no day/night searchlight on left side of turret

- Suspension has six road wheels either side, drive sprocket rear, idler front and three track-return rollers. Upper part of suspension covered by track guards

MANUFACTURER

Royal Ordnance Factory Leeds, UK (this facility has now closed).

Below: Khalid MBT

Chieftain Mk 5 MBT (UK)

Above: Chieftain Mk 5 MBT (MoD/CCR)

SPECIFICATIONS

Crew:	4
Armament:	1 x 120mm gun, 1 x 7.62mm MG (coaxial), 1 x 7.62mm MG (commander's cupola), 1 x 12.7mm RMG (see text), 2 x 6 smoke grenade dischargers
Ammunition:	64 x 120mm, 300 x 12.7mm (see text), 6,000 x 7.62mm
Length gun forwards:	10.795m
Length hull:	7.518m
Width hull:	3.504m
Height overall:	2.895m
Ground clearance:	0.508m
Weight empty:	53,500kg
Weight combat:	55,000kg
Power-to-weight ratio:	13.63hp/tonne
Ground pressure:	0.9kg/cm²
Engine:	Leyland L60, 2-stroke, compression ignition, 6 cylinder (12 opposed pistons) multi-fuel developing 750bhp at 2,100rpm
Maximum road speed:	48km/hr
Maximum range:	400 to 500km
Fuel capacity:	950 lit
Fording:	1.066m
Vertical obstacle:	0.914m
Trench:	3.149m
Gradient:	60%
Side slope:	40%
Armour:	Classified
Armour type:	Steel
NBC system:	Yes
Night vision equipment:	Yes (for commander, gunner and driver)

EVELOPMENT

eveloped from late 1950s with first prototypes ompleted in 1959, first production vehicles ompleted in early 1970s, production continuing ntil 1978. Layout conventional with driver front, urret centre and engine and transmission rear. ommander and gunner sit right of turret with ader left. Main armament consists of 120mm 11 series rifled gun mounted in powered turret ith 360° traverse. Main armament elevates from 10° to +20°. Ammunition is separate loading type g projectile and charge) and ammunition cludes APFSDS, APDS, HESH and smoke. 7.62mm G is mounted coaxial, with similar weapon on ommander's cupola. Original version used 2.7mm ranging MG but was replaced on British rmy vehicles by a Tank Laser Sight (TLS). omputerised fire-control system and main rmament stabilised. The Chieftain MBT was hased out of service with British Army in 1996 ut the ARV, ARRV, AVLB and AVRE will remain in ervice for some time. Chieftain can be fitted with ront-mounted dozer blade and mineclearing ystems.

ARIANTS

Ik 3/3P is Mk 3/3 for Iran.
Ik 5/3P is Mk 5 for Iran.
hir 1 was modified Chieftain for ran but became Khalid (qv).
hieftain ARV and ARRV.
hieftain AVLB.
hieftain AVRE.

TATUS

roduction complete. In service vith Iran and Jordan (ARV only).

MANUFACTURERS

oyal Ordnance, Leeds (taken over by ickers in 1986); Vickers Defence Systems, Iewcastle-upon-Tyne, England, UK (today AE Systems Land Systems).

KEY RECOGNITION FEATURES

- Well-sloped glacis plate with driver's hatch in upper part, splash board across lower part of glacis plate, turret centre, raised engine compartment rear. Long stowage boxes each side of engine compartment
- Cast turret has well-sloped front, 120mm gun mounted in internal mantlet has thermal sleeve and fume extractor. Commander's cupola right side of turret roof, NBC pack on turret rear, stowage basket each side of turret rear
- Suspension each side has six road wheels, drive sprocket rear, idler front and track-return rollers. Upper part normally covered by skirts

Below: Chieftain Mk 5

Below: Chieftain Mk 3

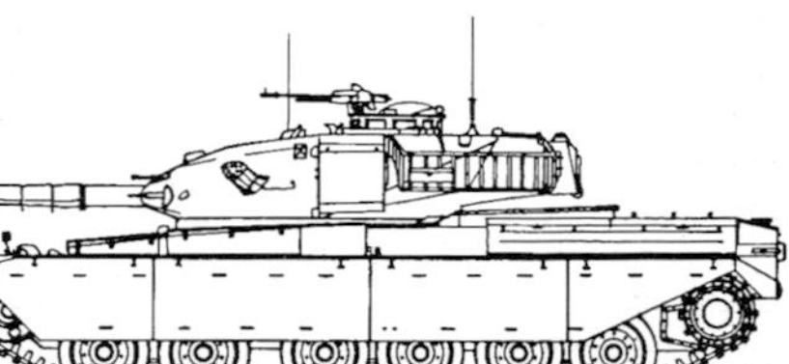

Vickers Mk 3 MBT (UK)

Above: Vickers Mk 3 MBT

SPECIFICATIONS

Crew:	4
Armament:	1 x 105mm, 1 x 7.62mm MG (coaxial), 1 x 7.62mm MG (anti-aircraft), 1 x 12.7mm MG (ranging), 2 x 6 smoke grenade dischargers
Ammunition:	50 x 105mm, 700 x 12.7mm, 2,400 x 7.62mm
Length gun forwards:	9.788m
Length hull:	7.65m
Width:	3.168m
Height to commander's cupola:	3.099m
Height to turret roof:	2.476m
Ground clearance:	0.52m
Weight, combat:	38,700kg
Weight, empty:	36,100kg
Power-to-weight ratio:	18.6bhp/tonne
Ground pressure:	0.88kg/cm²
Engine:	Detroit Diesel 12V-71T turbocharged diesel developing 720bhp at 2,500rpm
Maximum road speed:	50km/hr
Maximum road range:	490km
Fuel capacity:	1,000 lit
Fording:	1.1m
Vertical obstacle:	0.914m
Trench:	2.4m
Gradient:	60%
Side slope:	30%
Armour:	80mm (maximum) (estimate)
Armour type:	Steel
NBC system:	Optional
Night vision equipment:	Optional (passive)

DEVELOPMENT

In 1950 Vickers (which is today BAE Systems Land Systems) designed a new MBT specifically for export which used the standard 105mm L7 rifled tank gun and automotive components of the Chieftain MBT. It was subsequently adopted by the Indian Army with first vehicles, designated Vickers Mk 1 (Vijayanta by India), completed in the UK. Production also began at a new tank plant at Avadi, India. First production vehicles, completed in India in 1965. Production was completed in India in the mid-1980s, by which time about 2,200 had been built. The Vickers Mk 1 differed from the final production Mk 3 in having a Leyland L60 engine (as in Chieftain) and a welded turret. Vickers also built 70 Mk 1s for Kuwait, delivered between 1970 and 1972. These are no longer in service.

Vickers Mk 2 was never built and further development of Mk 1 resulted in Mk 3 which has a new engine and new turret with cast front. Kenya ordered 38 Mk 3s and three ARVs in 1977, with a second order for 38 Mk 3s and four ARVs in 1978. In 1981 Nigeria ordered 36 Mk 3s, five ARVs and six

AVLBs, with a repeat order in 1985. Final deliveries were made late in 1986. In 1990 Vickers Defence Systems received another order from Nigeria with first vehicles being completed late in 1991.

Layout of the Mk 3 is conventional, with driver front right, turret centre, commander and gunner right, loader left, engine and transmission rear. 105mm gun power-elevates from -10° to +20°, turret traverses 360°. Gun fires full range of NATO ammunition including APFSDS, APDS, HESH and smoke. A 7.62mm MG is mounted coaxial with main armament and a 12.7mm ranging MG is installed. Commander's cupola has 7.62mm MG which can be aimed from inside the vehicle.

A wide range of optional equipment was available for the Mk 3, including computerised fire-control system, day/night observation equipment, laser rangefinder, NBC system, deep wading or flotation system, air-conditioning system, automatic fire detection and suppression system, air conditioning system, dozer blade and explosive reactive armour.

KEY RECOGNITION FEATURES

- Well-sloped glacis plate, horizontal hull top with driver's hatch right side to immediate rear of glacis plate, turret centre, slightly raised engine compartment rear, vertical hull rear with projecting track guards

- Turret has cast rounded front and external mantlet for 105mm gun with fume extractor and thermal sleeve, stowage boxes each side to turret rear, stowage basket on turret rear, commander's cupola right side of turret roof with prominent day/night sight in forward part

- Suspension each side has six road wheels, large idler front, drive sprocket rear and three track-return rollers. Upper part of track and suspension normally covered by sheet steel skirts which are ribbed horizontally

VARIANTS

Vickers armoured bridgelayer.
Vickers armoured recovery vehicle.

STATUS

Production of Mk 1 completed. Production of Mk 3 as required. In service with India (Mk 1), Kenya (Mk 3) and Nigeria (Mk 3). Tanzania has a small number of Vickers ARVs.

MANUFACTURERS

BAE Systems Land Systems, Newcastle-upon-Tyne, UK (Mk 1 and Mk 3); Avadi Company, Madras, India (Mk 1).

Below: Vickers Mk 3 MBT

Centurion Mk 13 MBT (UK)

Above: Olifant Mk 1B MBT

SPECIFICATIONS

Crew:	4
Armament:	1 x 105mm, 1 x 12.7mm RMG, 1 x 7.62mm MG (coaxial), 1 x 7.62mm MG (commander's cupola), 2 x 6 smoke grenade dischargers
Ammunition:	64 x 105mm, 600 x 12.7mm, 4,750 x 7.62mm
Length gun forwards:	9.854m
Length hull:	7.823m
Width:	3.39m
Height without AA MG:	3.009m
Ground clearance:	0.51m
Weight combat:	51,820kg
Power-to-weight ratio:	12.54hp/tonne
Ground pressure:	0.95kg/cm^2
Engine:	Rolls-Royce Mk IVB 12-cylinder liquid-cooled petrol developing 650bhp at 2,550rpm
Maximum road speed:	34.6km/hr
Maximum road range:	190km
Fuel capacity:	1,037 lit
Fording:	1.45m
Fording with preparation:	2.74m
Vertical obstacle:	0.914m
Trench:	3.352m
Gradient:	60%
Side slope:	40%
Armour:	152mm (maximum)
Armour type:	Steel
NBC system:	None
Night vision equipment:	Yes (but not always fitted today)

DEVELOPMENT

Centurion was developed towards the end of the Second World War with 4,423 vehicles produced between 1945–46 and 1961–62. First vehicles armed with a 17 Pounder but this was replaced by a 20 Pounder and finally the famous 105mm L7 series gun which has since been adopted by many other countries. Layout of all versions is similar, with driver front right, turret centre, engine and transmission rear. Commander and gunner sit right of turret, loader left. Main armament is stabilised and power-elevates from -10° to +20° with turret traverse 360°. 105mm ammunition includes APFSDS, APDS, HESH and smoke. Main armament on later models is aimed using 12.7mm RMG, 7.62mm MG mounted coaxial with main armament and similar weapon mounted on commander's cupola. To extend operational range a mono-wheel fuel trailer could be towed behind. Can also be fitted with front-mounted dozer blade.

VARIANTS

There were 13 basic versions of Centurion gun tank plus many sub-variants but most countries now use only 105mm armed versions.

Israeli Centurions Israel has a large fleet of upgraded Centurions with 105mm guns but all now converted to specialist roles such as heavily armoured troop carriers.

Jordan Centurions have 105mm gun, computerised fire-control system, new diesel powerpack and new hydropneumatic suspension. These are called the Tariq.

South African Centurions are known as the Olifant (Elephant). Mk1A has many improvements including new powerpack and 105mm gun. Mk1B has upgraded powerpack, new suspension, 105mm gun and new hull and turret armour.

Centurion ARV.

KEY RECOGNITION FEATURES

• Well-sloped glacis leads up to horizontal hull top with driver's hatch in roof to immediate rear of glacis plate on right side, turret centre and raised engine compartment rear. Hull rear slopes slightly inwards. Flat stowage boxes above hull sides with exhaust pipes each side at rear

• 105mm gun has non-concentric fume extractor and is often fitted with thermal sleeve, rectangular external mantlet which is often uncovered. Commander's cupola on right side, large stowage boxes each side of turret and large stowage rack on rear. Circular ammunition resupply hatch lower left side of turret.

• Suspension each side has six road wheels, idler front, drive sprocket rear and return rollers. Upper part of suspension usually covered by skirts

STATUS

Production complete. In service with Jordan (Tariq), Singapore (based in Taiwan for training) and South Africa.

MANUFACTURERS

Leyland Motors, Leyland; Royal Ordnance Factory, Leeds; Vickers, Elswick; Royal Ordnance Factory, Woolwich, UK.

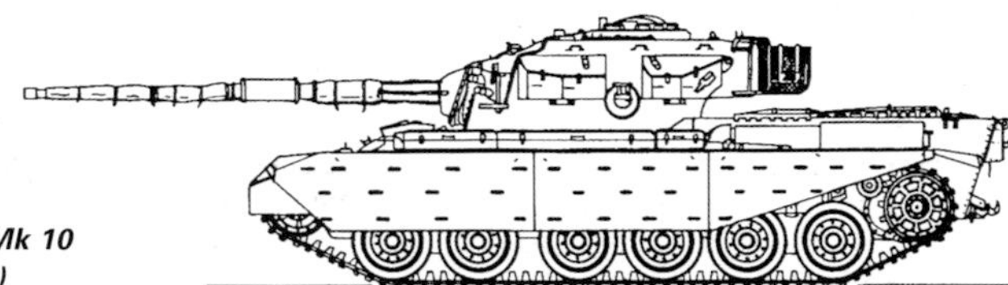

Right: Centurion Mk 10 MBT (105mm gun)

T-84 MBT (Ukraine)

Above: T-84 MBT (Christopher F Foss)

SPECIFICATIONS

Crew:	3
Armament:	1 x 125mm gun/ missile launcher, 1 x 7.62mm MG (coaxial), 1 x 12.7mm MG (anti-aircraft), 2 x 6 smoke grenade launchers
Ammunition:	43 x 125mm, 450 x 12.7mm anti-aircraft, 1,250 x 7.62mm (coaxial)
Length gun forwards:	9.72m
Length hull:	7.085m
Width with skirts:	3.775m
Height with 12.7mm MG:	2.74m
Ground clearance:	0.515m
Weight, combat:	46,000 kg
Weight, empty:	43,500 kg
Power-to-weight ratio:	26.08 hp/t
Ground pressure:	0.93 kg/cm^2
Engine:	Model 6TD-2 6-cylinder diesel developing 1200 hp
Maximum road speed:	65 km/h
Maximum road range:	540 km
Fuel capacity:	1,300 lit
Fording with preparation:	5m
Fording without preparation:	1.8m
Vertical obstacle:	1m
Trench:	2.85m
Gradient:	63%
Side slope:	36%
Armour:	Classified
Armour type:	Steel/Composite/ Reactive
NBC system:	Yes
Night vision equipment:	Yes

DEVELOPMENT

The T-84 MBT was developed by the Kharkov Morozov Design Bureau with production being undertaken by the Malyshev Plant. The T-84 was developed from the T-80UD which has been manufactured at the Malyshev Plant for the home and export markets. Pakistan has taken delivery of 320 T-80UD MBTs from Ukraine and it is understood that late production models

incorporate some components of the T-84.

The overall layout of the T-84 is similar to that of the T-80 and T-90 with the driver at the front, two man turret in the centre with the gunner on the left and the commander on the right who also operates the roof mounted 12.7mm AA MG. Unlike the Russian T-72 and T-90, the T-84 does not have an exhaust outlet on the left side of the hull towards the rear.

The 125mm smooth bore gun is mounted in a turret with a traverse of 360° and the weapon can elevate from -5° to +13°. The 125mm gun, which is fed by an automatic loader, can also fire a laser guided projectile in addition to HE-FRAG (FS), HEAT-FS and APFSDS-T ammunition types.

The hull front and turret front and sides are fitted with explosive reactive armour and a Shtora-1 defensive aids suite is normally fitted.

VARIANTS

T-84-120 Oplot, is export T-84 with NATO standard 120mm smooth bore gun fed by bustle mounted automatic loader.

BTMP-84, heavy infantry fighting vehicle on T-84 chassis.

BREM-84, ARV on T-84 chassis.

T-84 SPAAG, T-84 with ZSU-23-4 turret.

KEY RECOGNITION FEATURES

- Well-sloped glacis plate fitted with blocks of additional armour, turret centre and engine compartment rear. Long range fuel tanks and unditching beam often carried on rear. Upper part of hull has large rectangular exhaust outlet

- Rounded turret with 12.7mm machine gun mounted on right side of turret roof, smoke grenade launchers mounted either side towards turret rear, flaps extend down either side of turret front and on either side of 125mm gun is the box type sensor head of the Shtora defensive aids suite

- Suspension either side has six road wheels, idler front, drive sprocket rear with upper part of suspension covered by tracks. Forward part of skirt has additional armour and a skirt normally hangs down at the front of the hull

STATUS

Production as required. In service with Pakistan and Ukraine.

MANUFACTURER

Malyshev Plant, Kiev, Ukraine.

Above: T-84 MBT

Right: T-84 MBT (Christian Dumont)

General Dynamics, Land Systems, M1A1/M1A2 Abrams MBT (USA)

Above: M1A2 MBT armed with 120mm smooth bore gun

SPECIFICATIONS (M1A2)

Crew:	4
Armament:	1 x 120mm, 1 x 7.62mm MG (coaxial), 1 x 7.62mm MG (AA), 1 x 12.7mm MG (AA), 2 x 6 smoke grenade launchers
Ammunition:	40 x 120mm, 1,000 x 12.7mm, 12,400 x 7.62mm
Length gun forwards:	9.83m
Length hull:	7.92m
Width:	3.657m
Height to turret roof:	2.375m
Height overall:	2.885m
Ground clearance:	0.483m
Weight, combat:	63,086kg
Power-to-weight ratio:	23.77hp/tonne
Engine:	Textron Lycoming AGT1500 gas turbine, developing 1,500hp at 30,000rpm
Maximum road speed:	67.6km/hr
Maximum range:	426km
Fuel capacity:	1,907 lit
Fording:	1.219m, 1.98m with preparation
Vertical obstacle:	1.067m
Trench:	2.743m
Gradient:	60%
Side slope:	40%
Armour:	Classified
Armour type:	Laminate/Steel
NBC system:	Yes
Night vision equipment:	Yes (passive for commander, gunner and driver)

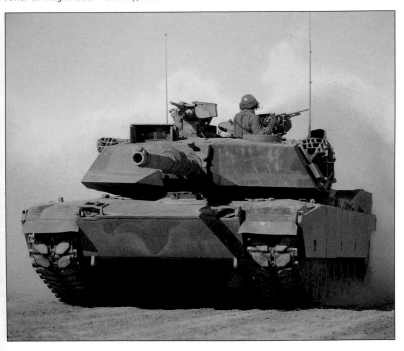

Above: M1A1 MBT armed with 120mm smooth bore gun

General Dynamics, Land Systems, M1A1/M1A2 Abrams MBT (USA)

Above: M1A2

DEVELOPMENT

After trials of XM1 prototypes built by Chrysler (now General Dynamics Land Systems) and General Motors, the tank was further developed and eventually accepted for service as M1 Abrams MBT. The first production M1 was completed in 1980 and production was undertaken at the Lima Army Tank Plant, Ohio and at the Detroit Arsenal Tank Plant, Warren, Michigan, but production is now concentrated at Lima. The M1 was followed in production by the improved M1 and then the M1A1 with 120mm gun and numerous other improvements. Final production model was the M1A2 which has been built for Kuwait, Saudi Arabia and the United States. Some M1s are being upgraded to M1A2 for the US Army.

Layout is conventional with driver front, turret centre and engine and transmission rear. Commander and gunner sit on right of turret, loader on left. Commander mans a roof-mounted 12.7mm MG, loader mans a 7.62mm roof-mounted MG.

The M1A1 and M1A2 are armed with a 120mm M256 smooth bore gun with powered elevation from -9° to +20° and turret traverse through 360°. A 7.62mm MG is mounted coaxial to right of main armament which is stabilised in elevation and traverse.

VARIANTS

M1A1 many improvements, including 120mm smooth bore gun, late production vehicles include heavy armour package.

M1A2, has 120mm gun, new armour, Commanders Independent Thermal Viewer (CITV) and land navigation system.

M1 Heavy Assault Bridge (HAB) is based on modified M1 chassis and is in service with US Army.

M1A1/M1A2 can be fitted with dozer or mine clearing systems at front of hull.

Assault Breacher Vehicle on trials for US Marine Corps.

STATUS

M1, production completed. No longer in service. Many being fitted with new M1A2 turret. M1A1, production complete, in service with Egypt, US Army and Marines. M1A2, production completed 1996, in service with Kuwait, Saudi Arabia and US Army.

MANUFACTURER

General Dynamics Land Systems, Lima Army Tank Plant, Ohio, USA; also assembled in Egypt.

KEY RECOGNITION FEATURES

- Nose slopes back under hull, almost horizontal glacis plate, driver's hatch centre under gun mantlet, turret centre, raised engine compartment rear. Hull rear vertical with air louvres in upper part

- Large turret with almost vertical front that slopes to rear, hull sides slope inwards with bustle extending well to rear, stowage box and basket on each side of turret towards rear. Rectangular gunner's sight on right side of turret roof forward of commander's cupola, which has 12.7mm MG mounted. 120mm gun has fume extractor and muzzle reference system

- Suspension each side has seven road wheels, drive sprocket rear, large idler front, two return rollers. Upper part of suspension, idler and most of drive sprocket covered by armoured skirts

Below: M1A2

General Dynamics Land Systems M60A3 MBT (USA

Above: M60A3

SPECIFICATIONS

Crew:	4
Armament:	1 x 105mm, 1 x 7.62mm MG (coaxial), 1 x 12.7mm MG (anti-aircraft), 2 x 6 smoke grenade dischargers
Ammunition:	63 x 105mm, 900 x 12.7mm, 5,950 x 7.62mm
Length gun forwards:	9.436m
Length hull:	6.946m
Width:	3.631m
Height:	3.27m
Ground clearance:	0.45m
Weight combat:	52,617kg
Weight empty:	48,684kg
Power-to-weight ratio:	14.24bhp/tonne
Ground pressure:	0.87kg/cm^2
Engine:	General Dynamics Land Systems AVDS-1790-2C 12-cylinder air-cooled diesel developing 750bhp at 2,400rpm
Maximum road speed:	48.28km/hr
Maximum road range:	480km
Fuel capacity:	1,420 lit
Fording:	1.22m
Fording with preparation:	2.4m
Vertical obstacle:	0.914m
Trench:	2.59m
Gradient:	60%
Side slope:	30%

Armour:	120mm (maximum) (estimate)
Armour type:	Steel
NBC system:	Yes
Night vision equipment:	Yes (passive)

DEVELOPMENT

M60 MBT series is a further development of M48 series with first prototypes completed in 1958 and first production vehicles completed by Chrysler Corporation, Delaware Defense Plant. From 1960 production was at the Detroit Tank Plant, also operated by Chrysler (later taken over by General Dynamics), and by the time production was completed in 1987 over 15,000 vehicles had been built for home and export markets.

Below: M60A3

KEY RECOGNITION FEATURES

- Well-sloped glacis plate with driver centre, turret centre of hull with slightly raised engine compartment rear, which is almost identical to M48 series

- Main armament has non-concentric fume extractor, usually thermal sleeve, and mounted in large external mantlet with rounded corners. Well-sloped turret sides with wire basket on rear of bustle. Commander's cupola right side of roof

- Suspension each side has six road wheels, idler front, drive sprocket rear and three track-return rollers

General Dynamics Land Systems M60A3 MBT (USA

Layout is conventional with driver front, turret centre and engine and transmission rear. Turret has slightly pointed front with commander and gunner on right and loader left. 105mm gun is stabilised and elevates from -10° to +20° with turret traverse through 360°. Main armament has 105mm gun

which fires APFSDS, APDS, HESH, HEAT and smoke projectiles, 7.62mm MG mounted coaxial to left and 12.7mm AA MG in commander's cupola.

M60A3 has computerised fire-control system, laser rangefinder and thermal night vision equipment. Roller-type mine-clearing devices or dozer blade can be fitted at front of hull.

VARIANTS

M60, first production model, turret similar to M48 series, originally with searchlight over main armament.
M60A1, replaced M60 in production from 1962, has new turret.
M60A2, withdrawn from service.
M60A3, final production model for US Army. Many M60A1s were brought up to M60A3 standard with thermal night vision equipment.
M728, combat engineer vehicle.
M60 AVLB.
In Israel, most M60s fitted with Blazer reactive armour, new commander's cupola with external 7.62mm MG, 7.62mm MG for loader, 12.7mm MG over 105mm gun and smoke grenade dischargers each side of main armament. More recently Israel has developed a further upgraded version of the M60 series called the **MAGACH-7** which has many further improvements including a new passive armour package, Matador computerised fire control system and 908hp diesel engine.
120s. This is modified M60 chassis with complete turret of M1A1 and is for export market.

STATUS

Production complete. In service with Bahrain, Bosnia, Brazil, Egypt, Greece, Iran, Israel, Jordan, Morocco, Oman, Portugal, Saudi Arabia, Spain, Sudan, Taiwan, Thailand, Tunisia, Turkey and Yemen. They are no longer used by the United States.

MANUFACTURER

General Dynamics Land Systems, Detroit, Michigan, USA.

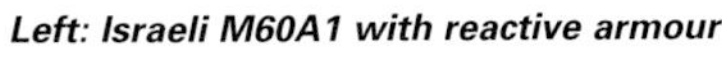

Left: Israeli M60A1 with reactive armour

M48A5 MBT (USA)

Above: M48A2

SPECIFICATIONS

Crew:	4
Armament:	1 x 105mm gun, 1 x 7.62mm MG (coaxial), 1 x 7.62mm MG (commander), 1 x 7.62mm MG (loader), 2 x 6 smoke grenade dischargers
Ammunition:	54 x 105mm, 10,000 x 7.62mm
Length gun forwards:	9.306m
Length hull:	6.419m
Width:	3.63m
Height overall:	3.086m
Power-to-weight ratio:	15.89hp/tonne
Ground pressure:	0.88kg/cm^2
Ground clearance:	0.419m
Weight combat:	48,987kg
Weight empty:	46,287kg
Engine:	General Dynamics Land Systems AVDS-1790-2D diesel developing 750hp at 2,400rpm
Maximum road speed:	48.2km/hr
Maximum road range:	499km
Fuel capacity:	1,420 lit
Fording:	1.219m
Fording with preparation:	2.438m
Vertical obstacle:	0.915m
Trench:	2.59m
Gradient:	60%
Side slope:	40%
Armour:	120mm (maximum)
Armour type:	Steel
NBC system:	None
Night vision equipment:	Yes

KEY RECOGNITION FEATURES

- Well-sloped glacis plate with driver centre, turret centre of hull, slightly raised engine compartment at rear which is almost identical to M60 MBT series

- Main armament has non-concentric fume extractor, no thermal sleeve, mounted in large external mantlet with rounded corners. Large infra-red/white light searchlight often mounted above mantlet. Turret has curved sides and bustle has stowage basket running around rear. Raised commander's cupola on right with external 7.62mm MG with similar weapon for loader on left

- Suspension each side has six road wheels, drive sprocket rear, idler front and five return rollers. US vehicles did not have skirt, South Korean vehicles have

Below: M48A5 of Greek Army with MOLF fire control system with 105mm gun

M48A5 MBT (USA)

DEVELOPMENT

M48 was developed from 1950 with first prototypes completed in 1951 and first production vehicles in 1952. By the time production was completed in 1959, 11,703 vehicles were built. M48 series replaced M47 in US Army and in the mid-1970s many were upgraded to M48A5 standard with 105mm gun and other improvements. Further development of M48 resulted in M60 (qv) series of MBTs. The M48A5 is no longer in front line US Army service. Driver sits front centre, commander and gunner on right side of turret and loader left. 105mm gun is mounted in turret with powered traverse through 360° and powered elevation from -9° to +19°. M48s can also be fitted with dozer blade.

VARIANTS

M48, original model, 90mm gun, petrol engine, commander has external 12.7mm MG, five track-return rollers.
M48C, mild steel hull and turret, training only.
M48A1, 90mm gun, petrol engine, commander has cupola with internally mounted 12.7mm MG.
M48A2/M48A2C, 90mm gun, fuel injection system for petrol engine, five track-return rollers.
M48A3, rebuild of early vehicle with petrol engine replaced by diesel, 90mm gun, vision blocks between commander's cupola and roof, three track-return rollers.
M48A4 was cancelled project.
M48A5, over 2,000 earlier M48s, rebuilt to M48A5 standard from mid-1970s, have many improvements including 105mm gun, new commander's cupola and diesel engine.
Israeli M48s, all have 105mm gun, diesel engine, low profile commander's cupola. Many have explosive reactive armour like Israeli M60 tanks (qv).
South Korean M48s, many brought up to M48A5 standard but also have side skirts.
Spain upgraded many M48s with 105mm gun and many other improvements with M48A5E2 remaining in service.
Taiwan also has model called M48H which is M60A1 chassis and M48A5 type turret with computerised fire control system and laser rangefinder.
Turkish M48s, 170 upgraded to German M48A2GA2 standard but also have MTU diesel engine. Much larger number upgraded with United States' assistance to M48A5 standard (known as M45A5T1 in Turkish Army).
M48 AVLB has scissors bridge.
M48 mine-clearing tank with flails is for German Army.

STATUS

Production complete. In service with Greece, Iran, Israel, Jordan, South Korea, Lebanon, Morocco,

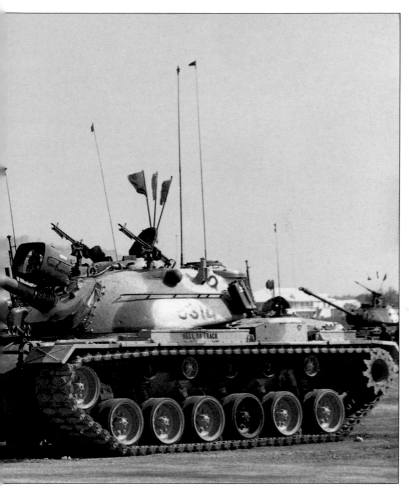

Pakistan, Portugal, Spain, Taiwan, Thailand, Tunisia and Turkey.

MANUFACTURERS

Chrysler Corporation, Delaware; Ford Motor Company, Michigan; Fisher Body Division of General Motors Corporation, Michigan; and Alco Products, Schenectady, New York, USA.

Above: 105mm M48A5 in service with Thailand

M41 Light Tank (USA)

Above: Brazilian Army upgraded M41 light tank (Rinaldo S Olive)

SPECIFICATIONS

Crew:	4
Armament:	1 x 76mm, 1 x 7.62mm MG (coaxial), 1 x 12.7mm MG (AA)
Ammunition:	57 x 76mm, 5,000 x 7.62mm, 2,175 12.7mm
Length gun forwards:	8.212m
Length hull:	5.819m
Height with 12.7mm MG:	3.075m
Height to turret top:	2.726m
Ground clearance:	0.45m
Weight, combat:	23,495kg
Weight, empty:	18,457kg
Power-to-weight ratio:	21.26hp/tonne
Engine:	Continental AOS-895-3, 6-cylinder air-cooled supercharged petrol developing 500bhp at 2,800rpm
Maximum road speed:	72km/hr
Maximum range:	161km
Fuel capacity:	530 lit
Fording:	1.016m
Fording with preparation:	2.44m
Vertical obstacle:	0.711m
Trench:	1.828m
Gradient:	60%
Side slope:	30%
Armour:	31.75mm (maximum)
Armour type:	Steel
NBC system:	None
Night vision equipment:	Optional

DEVELOPMENT

M41 was developed shortly after the Second World War to replace the M24 Chaffee light tank. First production vehicles were completed in mid-1951 and 5,500 vehicles were completed by the late 1950s. In US Army service it was replaced by the M551 Sheridan light tank.

Driver sits front left, turret in centre and engine and transmission rear. Commander sits on turret right with gunner in front and loader on left side of turret.

The 76mm gun power-elevates from -9° to +19° with turret traverse 360°, and fires HE, HEAT, HVAP-DS-T, HVAP-T, HVTP-T, smoke and training rounds. A 7.62mm MG is mounted coaxial to left and a 12.7mm M2 HB MG is mounted on turret roof for anti-aircraft defence.

VARIANTS

M41 was followed in production by the slightly different **M41A1**, **M41A2** and **M41A3**.
Bernardini of Brazil has rebuilt over 400 M41s for the Brazilian Army and Marines, with modifications including new engine, additional armour and gun bored out to 90mm; these are designated **M41/B** or **M41/C**.
Taiwan has upgraded some of its vehicles to M41D standard with many improvements. Some of the vehicles used by Uruguay have new 90mm Cockerill Mk IV gun.

STATUS

Production complete. In service with Brazil, Chile, Dominican Republic, Guatemala, Taiwan, Thailand and Uruguay.

KEY RECOGNITION FEATURES

- Well-sloped glacis plate with horizontal top, driver front left, turret centre, engine rear, exhaust pipe each side of upper hull rear
- Welded turret with sloping sides, bustle overhanging rear, stowage box far rear, commander's cupola on right side, 76mm gun has T-shaped muzzle brake with fume extractor to immediate rear
- Suspension either side has five road wheels, drive sprocket rear, idler front, three return rollers, no skirts

MANUFACTURER

Cadillac Motor Car Division, General Motors Corporation, Cleveland Tank Plant, Ohio, USA.

Below: M41 light tank (US Army)

Cadillac Gage Stingray Light Tank (USA)

Above: Cadillac Gage Stingray II light tank

SPECIFICATIONS

Crew:	4
Armament:	1 x 105mm gun, 1 x 7.62mm MG coaxial, 1 x 12.7mm MG AA, 2 x 4 smoke grenade dischargers
Ammunition:	32 x 105mm, 2,400 x 7.62mm, 1,100 x 12.7mm
Length gun forwards:	9.30m
Length hull:	6.448m
Width:	2.71m
Height overall:	2.55m
Ground clearance:	0.46m
Weight, combat:	21,205kg
Weight, empty:	19,387kg
Power-to-weight ratio:	25.9hp/tonne
Ground pressure:	0.72kg/cm^2
Engine:	Detroit Diesel Model 8V-92TA developing 535hp at 2,300rpm
Maximum road speed:	67km/hr
Maximum range:	483km
Fuel capacity:	757 lit
Fording:	1.07m
Vertical obstacle:	0.76m
Trench:	2.13m
Gradient:	60%
Side slope:	40%
Armour:	Classified
Armour type:	Steel
NBC system:	Yes (optional)
Night vision equipment:	Yes (passive)

DEVELOPMENT

The Stingray light tank was designed by Textron Marine & Land Systems (previously Cadillac Gage Textron) as a private venture with the first prototype being completed in 1985. Following trials in Thailand this country placed an order for a total of 106 Stingray vehicles which were delivered between 1988 and 1990. To reduce procurement and life cycle costs, standard components have been used wherever possible in the design of the vehicle, for example engine, transmission, suspension and tracks.

The driver is seated at the front of the vehicle in the centre with the turret in the centre of the hull and the powerpack at the rear. The commander and gunner are seated on the right of the turret with the loader on the left. Main armament comprises a 105mm Low Recoil Force gun that is fitted with a thermal sleeve, fume extractor and muzzle brake; this can fire the full range of NATO ammunition including APFSDS types. Turret traverse is a full 360° with weapon elevation from -7.5° to +20° under full power control with manual controls being provided for emergency use.

The commander and gunner are provided with day/night sights with the gunner's sight incorporating a laser rangefinder, an HR Textron gun control and stabilisation system is fitted as is a Digital Fire Control System for improved first round hit probability. Various other types of fire

control and night vision equipment can be fitted as can additional armour protection, land navigation system and fire detection and suppression system.

VARIANTS

Chassis can be adopted for other roles. Further development has resulted in Stingray II with a number of improvements including additional armour protection. The first production version of the Stingray is sometimes referred to as the Stingray I. All marketing is now being concentrated on the Stingray II.

STATUS

Production as required. In service with Thailand.

MANUFACTURER

Textron Marine & Land Systems, New Orleans, Louisiana, USA.

KEY RECOGNITION FEATURES

- Well-sloped glacis plate with driver's hatch in upper part, hull top horizontal with two slight steps to raised engine compartment at rear of hull. Sides and rear of hull vertical with exhaust outlet in upper part of hull rear

- Turret in centre of hull with pointed front, sides slope inwards with turret basket at rear, bank of four smoke grenade dischargers on either side of the turret. 12.7mm MG mounted on right side of turret roof

- Suspension either side has six small road wheels with idler front, drive sprocket rear and three track-return rollers, no side skirts

Above: Cadillac Gage Stingray I light tank

Above: Cadillac Gage Stingray I light tank

Below: Cadillac Gage Stingray I light tanks

TRACKED APCs/WEAPONS CARRIERS

Steyr 4K 7FA G 127 APC (Austria)

Above: Steyr 4K 7FA G 127

SPECIFICATIONS

Crew:	2 + 8
Armament:	1 x 12.7mm MG, 4 x smoke grenade dischargers
Ammunition:	500 x 12.7mm (estimate)
Length:	5.87m
Width:	2.5m
Height without MG:	1.611m
Ground clearance:	0.42m
Weight, combat:	14,800kg
Power-to-weight ratio:	21.62hp/tonne
Ground pressure:	0.55kg/cm^2
Engine:	Steyr 7FA 6-cylinder liquid-cooled turbocharged diesel developing 320hp at 2,300rpm
Maximum road speed:	70.6km/hr
Maximum road range:	520km
Fuel capacity:	360 lit
Fording:	1m
Vertical obstacle:	0.8m
Trench:	2.1m
Gradient:	75%
Side slope:	40%
Armour:	25mm (maximum)
Armour type:	Steel
NBC system:	Yes
Night vision equipment:	Yes (passive for driver)

DEVELOPMENT

The Steyr 4K 7FA G 127 is a further development of the earlier 4K 4FA series (see following entry). The first prototype was completed in 1976 and first production vehicles in 1977. Main improvements over earlier Saurer 4K 4FA are better armour protection over frontal arc and improved power-to-weight ratio from more powerful engine. Many automotive components also used in SK 105 tank destroyer.

Driver sits front left, engine compartment to his right, cupola with externally mounted 12.7mm M2 HB MG to his rear. Cupola has front and side armour protection for gunner, rear has bank of four electrically operated smoke grenade dischargers firing to rear. Troop compartment is rear of hull, has roof hatches that open each side and twin doors in rear. Four sockets around top of troop compartment allow quick installation of pintle-mounted MGs.

Standard equipment includes ventilation system and crew compartment heater. Optional

equipment includes passive NVE, NBC system, air conditioning and fire detection/suppression system for engine and crew compartments.

VARIANTS

4K 7FA-KSPz MICV has two ball-type firing ports in each side of troop compartment with periscope for rifle fired from inside.
4K 7FA MICV essentially as above with one-man turret and 12.7mm MG and 7.62mm MG, prototype only.
4K 7FA-F$_s$ command post vehicle has additional communications equipment.
4K 7FA-San is armoured ambulance.
4K 7FA AMC 81 is 81mm mortar carrier.

STATUS

Production complete. In service with Bolivia, Cyprus, Greece, Macedonia and Nigeria.

MANUFACTURERS

Steyr-Daimler-Puch AG, Vienna, Austria; Steyr Hellas SA, Thessaloniki, Greece.

KEY RECOGNITION FEATURES

• Almost identical to 4K 4FA series (qv) with low profile hull, well-sloped glacis plate leading up to horizontal hull top, hull rear slopes sharply inwards, hull sides above tracks slope inwards, horizontal louvres each side of hull front

• Driver front left, engine right, weapon station to his immediate rear (normally cupola with 12.7mm MG)

• Suspension either side with five road wheels which all have small holes between hub and rim, drive sprocket front, idler rear, three track-return rollers, no skirts

Below: Steyr 4K 7FA-San ambulance

Saurer 4K 4FA APC (Austria)

Above: Saurer 4K 4FA-G2 with 20mm cannon

Right: 4F GrW1 81mm mortar (Michael Jerchel)

SPECIFICATIONS

Crew:	2 + 8
Armament:	1 x 20mm cannon or 1 x 12.7mm MG
Length:	5.4m
Width:	2.5m
Height with 12.7mm MG:	2.1m
Height hull top:	1.65m
Ground clearance:	0.42m
Weight, combat (20mm cannon):	15,000kg
Weight, combat (12.7mm MG):	12,500kg
Power-to-weight ratio (20mm model):	16.66hp/tonne
Power-to-weight ratio (12.7mm model):	20hp/tonne
Ground pressure:	$0.52kg/cm^2$
Engine:	Saurer model 4FA 4-stroke 6-cylinder diesel developing 250hp at 2,400rpm
Maximum road speed:	65km/hr
Maximum road range:	370km
Fuel capacity:	184 lit
Fording:	1m
Vertical obstacle:	0.8m
Trench:	2.2m
Gradient:	75%
Side slope:	50%
Armour:	20mm (maximum)
Armour type:	Steel
NBC system:	None
Night vision equipment:	None

DEVELOPMENT

In the mid-1950s Saurer-Werke designed and built a full tracked armoured personnel carrier, further development of which resulted in 4K 4F which entered production for Austrian Army in 1961. Replaced in production by 4K 3FA (230hp engine) and 4K 4FA (250hp engine) with final deliveries in 1968 after about 450 had been built. Further development resulted in the similar 4K 7FA APC (qv).

All vehicles have similar layout with driver front left, engine compartment to his immediate right. Main armament is to rear of driver, troop compartment extending to rear with roof hatches. Troops enter via twin doors in rear.

KEY RECOGNITION FEATURES

- Low profile hull with well-sloped glacis plate leading up to horizontal hull top, hull rear slopes sharply inwards, hull sides above tracks slope slightly inwards, horizontal louvres each side of hull front

- Driver front left, engine right, weapon station to immediate rear (turret with 20mm cannon or 12.7mm MG)

- Suspension either side with five road wheels which all have small holes between hub and rim, drive sprocket front, idler rear, two track-return rollers, no skirts

VARIANTS

4K 4FA-G1 has cupola with 12.7mm MG.
4K 4FA-G2 has a one-man Oerlikon Contraves turret armed with one Oerlikon Contraves 20mm 204GK cannon. Turret traverse is a full 360° with weapon elevation from -12° to +70°.
4K 3FA Fü1 is brigade command post vehicle.
4K 3FA FüA is artillery command post vehicle.
4K 3FA Fü/F1A is anti-aircraft command post vehicle.
4K 3FA-FS is wireless teleprinter vehicle.
4K 4FA-San is armoured ambulance.
4K 4F GrW1 is 81mm mortar carrier.

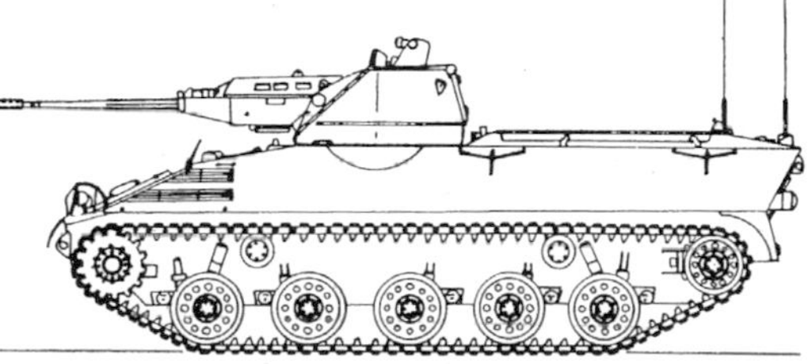

Above: Saurer 4K 4FA-G2 with 20mm cannon

Below: Saurer 4K 3FA with 12.7mm MG (Stefan Marx)

STATUS

Production complete. In service with Austrian Army only. From 2001 this vehicle was supplemented by the Ulan which is the Austrian name for the ASCOD (qv) mechanised infantry combat vehicle.

MANUFACTURER

Saurer-Werke (now Steyr-Daimler-Puch AG), Vienna, Austria.

BMP-23 Infantry Combat Vehicle (Bulgaria)

Right: BMP-30 ICV

SPECIFICATIONS

Crew:	3 + 7
Armament:	1 x 23mm cannon, 1 x 7.62mm MG (coaxial), 1 x AT-3 Sagger ATGW launcher
Ammunition:	600 x 23mm, 2,000 x 7.62mm and 4 x AT-3 Sagger ATGW
Length:	7.285m
Width:	2.85m
Height:	2.53m
Ground clearance:	0.40m
Weight, combat:	15,200kg
Power-to-weight ratio:	20.72hp/tonne
Ground pressure:	0.498kg/cm^2
Engine:	Diesel developing 315hp
Maximum road speed:	61.5km/hr
Maximum road range:	550-600km
Fuel capacity:	500 to 560 lit
Fording:	Amphibious
Vertical obstacle:	0.8m
Trench:	2.5m
Gradient:	60%
Side slope:	30%
Armour:	Classified
Armour type:	Steel
NBC system:	Yes
Night vision equipment:	Yes

DEVELOPMENT

The BMP-23 ICV was developed by the Bulgarian defence industry to meet the requirements of the Bulgarian Army and uses a number of components of the Russian MT-LB multi-purpose armoured vehicle and 2S1 122mm self-propelled artillery system that has been manufactured under licence in Bulgaria.

The driver is seated at the front left with one of the infantrymen on the opposite side of the vehicle with the engine to their rear, the two man turret is in the centre of the vehicle with gunner on the left and commander on the right. The 23mm cannon has a maximum range of 2,000m with the 7.62mm MG being mounted coaxial to the right. The AT-3 ATGW has a maximum range of 3,000m. The infantry compartment is at the rear with three men being seated either side back to back, the infantry enter the BMP-23 via doors in the hull rear. The troop compartment is provided with firing ports, associated vision devices and roof hatches.

The BMP-23 is fully amphibious being propelled in the water by its tracks and before entering the water a trim vane is erected at the front of the hull, which when not required folds back onto the glacis plate. Standard equipment includes heater, fire detection and suppression system and navigation system. It can also lay its own smoke screen by injecting diesel fuel into the exhaust outlet on the right side of the hull.

VARIANTS

BMP-23A, is BMP-23 with three smoke grenade dischargers either side of turret and launcher on roof for AT-4 Spigot ATGW launcher.
BRM-23 is a reconnaissance vehicle with a similar layout and weapon fit but has a five-man crew and additional surveillance equipment.
BMP-30 is essentially BMP-23 fitted with complete turret of Russian BMP-2 ICV which is armed with a 30mm cannon, 7.62mm coaxial machine gun, launcher for AT-4/AT-5 ATGW and a bank of three smoke grenade dischargers mounted either side of the turret.

STATUS

Production as required. In service with Bulgarian Army.

MANUFACTURER

Bulgarian state factories.

KEY RECOGNITION FEATURES

- Chassis has nose sloping back under hull with almost horizontal glacis plate, horizontal hull top, vehicle hull rear and sides are vertical with chamfer between sides and hull top
- Turret mounted in centre of vehicle with sloping front, 23mm cannon has muzzle suppressor and slots. Sagger ATGW mounted externally on left side of turret roof
- Chassis is similar to Russian 2S1 122mm SPG with either side seven road wheels, drive sprockets at front, idler at rear and no track-return rollers

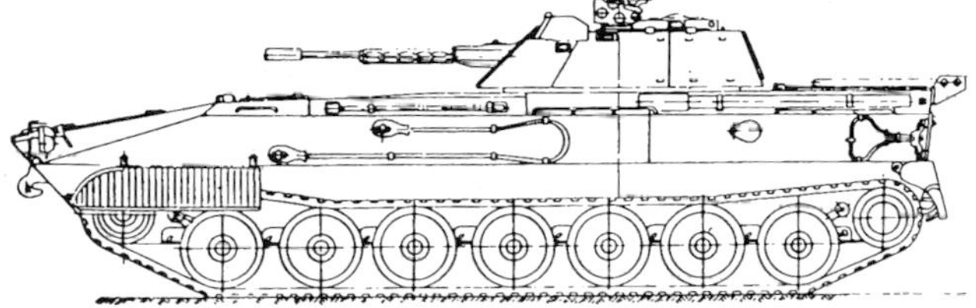

Above: BMR-23 reconnaissance vehicle

Below: BMP-23 ICV

NORINCO Type 90 APC (China)

SPECIFICATIONS

Crew:	2 + 13
Armament:	1 x 12.7mm Type 54 MG
Ammunition:	1,120 x 12.7mm
Length:	6.744m
Width:	3.148m
Height:	(hull top) 1.72m (overall) 2.376m
Ground clearance:	0.42m
Weight, combat:	14,500kg
Power-to-weight ratio:	22hp/tonne
Ground pressure:	0.55kg/cm^2
Engine:	KHD BF8L413F 8-cylinder turbo charged diesel developing 320hp
Maximum road speed:	67km/hr
Maximum road range:	500km
Fuel capacity:	Not available
Fording:	amphibious
Vertical obstacle:	0.7m
Trench:	2.2m
Gradient:	60%
Side slope:	40%
Armour:	12mm (maximum)
Armour type:	Steel
NBC system:	Yes
Night vision equipment:	Yes

Abpve: Type 90 armoured personnel carrier (NORINCO)

DEVELOPMENT

The NORINCO (China Industries Corporation) Type 90 armoured personnel carrier is an evolution of the earlier NORINCO YW 534 family. It has been in service with the Peoples Liberation Army for some years but has yet to be exported.

The layout is similar to the YW 534 with powerpack front right, driver front left with vehicle commander to his rear, both with individual roof hatches. The infantry compartment is at the rear and the infantry enter and leave via a large door in the hull rear.

The 12.7mm machine gun cupola, similar to that fitted to many other Chinese armoured fighting vehicles, provides protection through almost 360 degrees but not to the immediate front or overhead.

There are a total of four roof hatches over the rear troop compartment, two either side. Firing ports are provided in the sides of the rear troop compartment which allow the troops to fire their weapons from within the hull.

The Type 90 is fully amphibious being propelled in the water by its tracks. Before entering the water a trim vane is erected at the

front of the vehicle and the bilge pumps are switched on.

VARIANTS

Infantry fighting vehicle – six road wheels, similar to BMP-2.
ATGW – with roof mounted Red Arrow missiles.
Command post vehicle – extensive communications equipment.
Mortar – two versions, 82mm and 120mm.
Rocket launcher – on roof is 130mm (30 round) multiple rocket launcher.
Ambulance.
Recovery.
Mine layer.
Boraq – this Iranian APC is similar in some respects to the Type 90 but has different road wheels.

STATUS

Production as required. In service with China.

MANUFACTURER

Chinese state factories. Marketed by NORINCO.

KEY RECOGNITION FEATURES

- Well-sloped glacis plate with trim vane on forward part, nose slopes back under front of vehicle, horizontal hull top with 12.7mm machine gun cupola situated in middle

- Hull sides are vertical until mid way up and then slope inwards, periscopes in either side of hull towards rear. Vertical hull rear with large single piece door

- Suspension either side consists of five road wheels with drive sprocket at front, idler at rear and track-return rollers. Upper part of suspension is covered by a horizontal ribbed steel skirt

***Below:* Type 90 armoured personnel carrier**

NORINCO YW 531 H APC (China)

SPECIFICATIONS

Crew:	2 + 13
Armament:	1 x 12.7mm MG
Ammunition:	1,120 x 12.7mm
Length:	6.125m
Width:	3.06m
Height:	2.586m (inc 12.7mm MG), 1.914m (hull roof)
Ground clearance:	0.46m
Weight, combat:	13,600kg
Power-to-weight ratio:	23.5hp/tonne
Ground pressure:	0.546kg/cm²
Engine:	Deutz BF8L 413F air-cooled diesel developing 320hp
Maximum road speed:	65km/hr
Maximum road range:	500km
Fuel capacity:	Not available
Fording:	Amphibious
Vertical obstacle:	0.6m
Trench:	2.2m
Gradient:	60%
Side slope:	40%
Armour:	Classified
Armour type:	Steel
NBC system:	Yes
Night vision equipment:	Yes

DEVELOPMENT

The YW 531 H APC was developed by NORINCO at the same time as the very similar YW 534, the main difference being that the YW 531 H is slightly lighter, shorter, narrower and does not have the bank of four electrically operated smoke grenade dischargers either side of the turret. The driver is seated at the front of the vehicle on the left with another crew member to his rear, to their right is the engine compartment. The troop compartment is to the rear of the hull and is provided with four small roof hatches and a single door in the rear, firing ports and observation devices are provided. On the basic vehicle armament comprises a ring-mounted 12.7mm MG with lateral and side protection. The YW 531 H is fully amphibious being propelled in the water by its tracks and before entering the water the trim vane is erected on the glacis plate and the bilge pumps are switched on. Note: The Peoples Liberation Army normally refers to the Type YW 531H as the Type 85.

VARIANTS

YW 309 ICV with turret of WZ 501 (the Chinese equivalent of the Russian BMP-1).

Type 85 armoured command post vehicle, similar

to basic vehicle but has additional communications equipment, Type 85 armoured command vehicle is almost identical.
Type WZ 751 armoured ambulance, has raised rear compartment.
Type 85 120mm self-propelled mortar.
Type 85 82mm self-propelled mortar.
122mm self-propelled howitzer, uses mount and ordnance of Chinese produced version of the Russian 122mm D-30 howitzer.
Type 85 ARV, fitted with hydraulic crane.
Type 85 maintenance engineering vehicle, has raised hull like **Type 85 ambulance**.

STATUS

Production complete. In service with China, Myanmar, Sri Lanka and Thailand (these have American M2 type 12.7mm MGs in place of Chinese MGs).

MANUFACTURER

Chinese state factories. Marketed by NORINCO.

KEY RECOGNITION FEATURES

- Well-sloped glacis plate with nose sloped back under front of vehicle, horizontal hull top with distinctive domed hatch cover for driver at front left of vehicle, 12.7mm MG on roof provided with lateral and rear protection

- Hull sides slope slightly inwards, vertical hull rear with single large door, either side of which is a large box that protrudes to the rear

- Suspension either side consists of five road wheels with drive sprocket at the front, idler at the rear and track-return rollers, the upper part of which are covered by a light steel skirt with horizontal ribs

Above left: Type YW 531 H APC

Below: Type WZ 751 ambulance

NORINCO YW 531C APC (China)

SPECIFICATIONS

Crew:	2 + 13
Armament:	1 x 12.7mm MG
Ammunition:	1,120 x 12.7mm
Length:	5.476m
Width:	2.978m
Height with MG:	2.85m
Height to hull top:	1.887m
Ground clearance:	0.45m
Weight, combat:	12,600kg
Power-to-weight ratio:	25.39hp/tonne
Ground pressure:	0.57kg/cm²
Engine:	Deutz BF8L 413F 4-cycle turbocharged, V-8 diesel developing 320hp at 2,500rpm
Maximum road speed:	65km/hr
Maximum water speed:	6km/hr
Maximum range:	500km
Fuel capacity:	450 lit
Fording:	Amphibious
Vertical obstacle:	0.6m
Trench:	2m
Gradient:	60%
Side slope:	40%
Armour:	10mm (maximum) (estimate)
Armour type:	Steel
NBC system:	None
Night vision equipment:	None

DEVELOPMENT

The YW 531 series was developed by NORINCO (China North Industries Corporation) in the late 1960s. (It has been referred to as K-63, M1967, M1970 and Type 63 at various times.) Driver sits front left with vehicle commander to rear, another crew member sits front right with engine compartment to rear, 12.7mm MG is mounted in centre of roof, no protection for gunner. Troop compartment at rear of hull with two hatches above, large door in rear and single firing port in each side of hull.

YW 531 is fully amphibious, propelled by its tracks. Before entering the water a trim vane is erected at front of vehicle and bilge pumps switched on.

VARIANTS

YW 531C (modified) has shield for 12.7mm MG.

YW 531C, YW 531D, YW 531E, all have additional communications.

WZ 701 command post vehicle has higher roof line at rear.

YW 750 ambulance is similar to WZ 701.
Type 54-1 122mm self-propelled howitzer uses components of YW 531.
130mm Type 70 self-propelled rocket launcher uses components of YW 531.
YW 304 82mm mortar carrier, mortar can be dismounted.
YW 381 120mm mortar carrier, mortar can be dismounted.
Anti-tank vehicle with turret armed with four Red Arrow 8 ATGWs in ready-to-launch position.
Further development has resulted in the NORINCO Type YW 531H (or Type 85 as it is also referred to) (qv). The NORINCO WZ 501 IFV is essentially a Chinese-built version of the Russian BMP-1 vehicle.

STATUS

Production complete. In service with Albania, China, Democratic Republic of Congo, North Korea, Sudan, Vietnam and Zimbabwe.

MANUFACTURER

Chinese state arsenals.

KEY RECOGNITION FEATURES

- Nose slopes back under forward part of hull, well-sloped glacis plate up to hull top that slopes slightly upwards towards rear. Vertical hull rear with large door that opens right

- Hull sides slope slightly inwards, driver front left, similar hatch cover front right, air inlet louvres in roof on right side, oblong hatches in roof over rear troop compartment

- Suspension each side has four road wheels, idler rear, drive sprocket front, no track-return rollers, upper part of track covered by sheet metal guard

Left: Type YW 701 command post vehicle

Below: Type YW 304 82mm self-propelled mortar

NORINCO Type 77 APC (China)

SPECIFICATIONS

Crew:	2 + 16
Armament:	1 x 12.7mm MG
Ammunition:	500 x 12.7mm
Length:	7.4m
Width:	3.2m
Height:	2.436m
Weight, combat:	15,500kg
Power-to-weight ratio:	25.8hp/tonne
Engine:	Type 12150L-2A 4-cycle, compression ignition, direct injection water-cooled diesel developing 400hp at 2,000rpm
Maximum road speed:	60km/hr
Maximum water speed:	11 to 12km/hr
Maximum road range:	370km
Fuel capacity:	416 lit
Fording:	Amphibious
Vertical obstacle:	0.87m
Trench:	2.9m
Gradient:	60%
Side slope:	40%
Armour:	8mm (maximum) (estimate)
Armour type:	Steel
NBC system:	None
Night vision equipment:	None

DEVELOPMENT

Although very similar to Russian BTR-50PK and Czechoslovak OT-62 APCs, the Chinese Type 77 has a more powerful engine which gives higher road and water speeds and a higher power-to-weight ratio. Many automotive components of Type 77 are also used in the Type 63 APC. Fully enclosed crew and troop compartments are situated at the front, with entry via a door in right side and roof hatches. Engine and transmission are at the rear. Troop compartment has three firing ports, several vision blocks, ventilation system and a white light searchlight for use from inside vehicle.

The Type 77 is fully amphibious, propelled by two waterjets mounted one each side at hull rear. Before entering the water, a trim board is erected at front of vehicle and two bilge pumps switched on. The Type 77 can be used as command post, fuel resupply vehicle, ambulance and load carrier. The Type 77-2 has three loading ramps that can be positioned at rear to carry 85mm Type 56 gun or 122mm Type 54 howitzer. Type 77-2 has no ramps.

VARIANTS

One variant is a lengthened chassis with seven road wheels which is to transport and launch the HQ-2J SAM which is the Chinese equivalent of the Russian SA-2 Guideline SAM system. There is also a recovery vehicle and one carrying an anti-ship missile. Some of the PLA fleet of Type 77 series APCs are being upgraded.

STATUS

Production complete. In service with Chinese Army. Albania may have a small quantity of these vehicles in service.

MANUFACTURER

Chinese state arsenals.

KEY RECOGNITION FEATURES

- Similar in appearance to the Russian BTR-50PK and Czechoslovak OT-62 with high nose sloping back under forward part of hull, almost horizontal glacis plate, forward part of crew compartment slopes rear, half-circular commander's position in right side, hull top horizontal to mid-way along vehicle then drops vertically to engine compartment at rear

- Hull rear and sides vertical, upper part of hull sides slope inwards, door in right side of hull opens forwards

- Suspension each side has six road wheels, idler front, drive sprocket rear, no track-return rollers

***Above left:* Type 77-2 with side door open**

***Below:* Type 77-1 APC from rear with ramps in position**

AMX VCI Infantry Combat Vehicle (France)

Above: AMX VCI

SPECIFICATIONS

Crew:	3 + 10
Armament:	1 x 12.7mm MG
Ammunition:	1,000 x 12.7mm
Length:	5.7m
Width:	2.67m
Height with turret:	2.41m
Height hull top:	2.1m
Ground clearance:	0.48m
Weight, combat:	15,000kg
Weight, empty:	12,500kg
Power-to-weight ratio:	16.67hp/tonne
Engine:	SOFAM model 8Gxb 8-cylinder water-cooled petrol developing 250hp at 3,200rpm
Maximum road speed:	60km/hr
Maximum road range:	350km
Fuel capacity:	410 lit
Fording:	1m
Vertical obstacle:	0.65m
Trench:	1.6m
Gradient:	60%
Side slope:	30%
Armour:	30mm (maximum)
Armour type:	Steel
NBC system:	Optional
Night vision equipment:	Optional

DEVELOPMENT

The AMX VCI (Véhicule de Combat d'Infanterie) was developed in the 1950s and is based on the AMX-13 light tank chassis. First prototype completed in 1955, first production vehicles completed at Atelier de Construction Roanne (ARE) in 1957. Once AMX-30 production was under way at the ARE production of the whole AMX-13 light family was transferred to Creusot Loire, Chalon sur Saône. This vehicle has been replaced in front line French Army service by the GIAT Industries AMX-10P series.

Layout of all versions is similar with driver front left, engine compartment to his right, commander and gunner in raised superstructure to his rear, troop compartment which extends right to rear of vehicle, troop entry via two doors in hull rear. Ten infantry sit five each side back to back, two two-piece hatch covers in each side of troop compartment (lower part of each has two firing ports and folds forwards into horizontal, upper part folds upwards through 180° to rest on troop compartment roof).

Wide range of optional equipment includes NBC system, night vision devices and turrets and cupolas armed with 7.62mm or 12.7mm MGs, 20mm cannon or 60mm breech-loaded mortar. Original petrol engine can be replaced by fuel-efficient Detroit Diesel 6V-71T developing 280hp at 2,800rpm or Baudouin 6F11SRY turbo-charged diesel developing 280hp at 3,200rpm.

KEY RECOGNITION FEATURES

- Well-sloped glacis plate which often has trim vane across front with spare road wheel above, flat hull top to rear of second road wheel station, almost vertical hull front and horizontal roof that extends to rear of vehicle, vertical hull with twin doors

- Armament mounted on left side of forward superstructure with commander to right. Hull sides vertical for first half of troop compartment sides then slope inwards, four firing ports each side

- Suspension each side has five road wheels, drive sprocket front, idler rear, up to four track-return rollers, no skirts

VARIANTS

Ambulance (VTT/TB) transports four seated and three stretcher patients.
Command post vehicle (VTT/PC) has extensive communications equipment.
Cargo (VTT/cargo) with 3,000kg capacity.
Anti-tank, AMX VCI fitted with MILAN or TOW ATGWs.
Fire-control vehicle (VTT/LT), battery command post vehicle for artillery units.
RATAC radar carrier (VTT/RATAC) with RATAC battlefield surveillance radar on roof.
155mm Support Vehicle (VTT/VCA) operates with 155mm Mk F3 self-propelled gun and carries remainder of gun crew and ammunition. Also tows ammunition trailer.
81mm mortar carrier (VTT/PM) has 81mm mortar in rear firing through roof.
120mm mortar carrier (VTT/PM) has 120mm mortar in rear firing through roof.

STATUS

Production complete. In service with Argentina, Cyprus (VTT/VCA and command post), Ecuador, Indonesia, Lebanon, Mexico, Qatar, Sudan, United Arab Emirates and Venezuela.

MANUFACTURER

Creusot-Loire Industrie, Chalon sur Saône, France. This company was subsequently taken over by GIAT Industries.

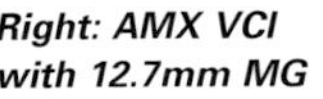

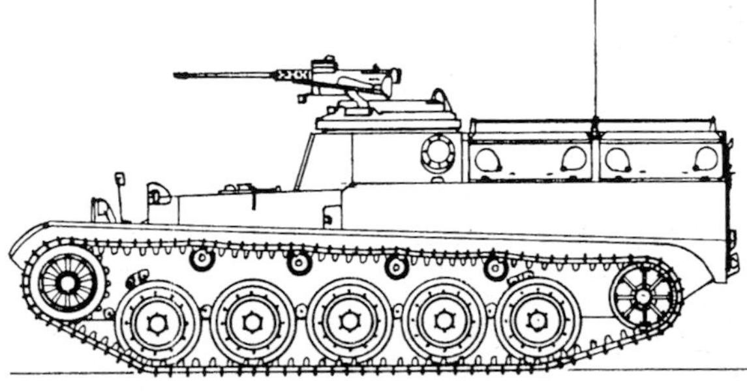

Right: AMX VCI with 12.7mm MG

GIAT AMX-10P Infantry Combat Vehicle (France)

Above: AMX-10P ICV

SPECIFICATIONS

Crew:	3 + 8
Armament:	1 x 20mm cannon, 1 x 7.62mm MG (coaxial), 2 x 2 smoke grenade dischargers
Ammunition:	760 x 20mm, 2,000 x 7.62mm
Length:	5.90m
Width:	2.83m
Height overall:	2.83m
Height hull top:	1.95m
Ground clearance:	0.45m
Weight, combat:	14,500kg
Weight, empty:	12,700kg
Power-to-weight ratio:	17.93hp/tonne
Ground pressure:	0.53kg/cm^2
Engine:	Hispano-Suiza HS-115 V-8 water-cooled supercharged diesel developing 260hp at 3,000rpm
Maximum road speed:	65km/hr
Maximum water speed:	7km/hr
Maximum road range:	500km
Fuel capacity:	528 lit
Fording:	Amphibious
Vertical obstacle:	0.7m
Trench:	2.1m
Gradient:	60%
Side slope:	30%
Armour:	Classified
Armour type:	Aluminium
NBC system:	Yes
Night vision equipment:	Yes (driver, commander and gunner)

DEVELOPMENT

The AMX-10P was developed from 1965 by Atelier de Construction d'Issy-les-Moulineaux to meet requirements of French Army with first prototype completed in 1968 and first production vehicles in 1973. The driver sits front left, with engine compartment to right and troop compartment extending right to rear. A two-man (commander and gunner) power-operated turret is armed with 20mm cannon and 7.62mm coaxial MG. Turret traverses through 360°, weapons elevate from -8° to +50°. Troop compartment has roof hatches and periscopes, two firing ports in rear ramp.

AMX-10P is fully amphibious, propelled by its waterjets, one mounted each side at hull rear.

Before entering the water a trim vane is erected at front of vehicle and bilge pumps switched on.

VARIANTS

AMX-10 ambulance is unarmed.
AMX-10P driver training vehicle has no turret.
AMX-10 ECH repair vehicle has one-man turret and hydraulic crane.
AMX-10P HOT (anti-tank) has turret with four HOT ATGWs.
AMX-10 PC (command vehicle) has additional communications equipment.
AMX-10P with RATAC (radar for field artillery fire) on roof.
AMX-10 SAO (artillery observation vehicle) has turret with 7.62mm MG.
AMX-10 SAT (artillery survey vehicle).
AMX-10 TM (mortar tractor) tows 120mm TDA mortar.
AMX-10 VOA (artillery observer vehicle).
AMX-10Ps used in Atila artillery fire-control system include **AMX-10 VFA, AMX-10 VLA** and **AMX-10 SAF.**
AMX-10P Marine has been developed specifically for amphibious operations. Singapore has vehicle with 90mm TS-90 turret and 25mm Dragar turret while Indonesia has vehicle with TS-90 turret and 12.7mm MG turret.
AMX-10P upgrade, French Army is to upgrade part of its fleet with additional armour and other improvements.

KEY RECOGNITION FEATURES

- Pointed hull front with nose directed back under hull, well-sloped glacis plate with driver's position on upper left side, horizontal roof with hull rear sloping slightly inwards, large power-operated ramp

- Turret mounted centre of roof, 20mm cannon mounted externally with 7.62mm MG to right, two outward-opening roof hatches to rear of turret. Hull sides vertical, no firing ports in sides of rear troop compartment, circular exhaust outlet in right side of hull above second/third roadwheel

- Suspension each side has five road wheels, drive sprocket front, idler rear, three track-return rollers. Upper part of track covered by skirt

STATUS

Production complete. In service with Bosnia-Herzegovina, France, Indonesia (Marines version), Qatar, Saudi Arabia, Singapore (Marines version) and United Arab Emirates.

MANUFACTURER

GIAT Industries, Roanne, France.

Right: AMX-10P Marine with TS-90 turret and trim vane extended

Marder 1A3 Infantry Combat Vehicle (Germany)

Above: Marder 1A3 IFV

SPECIFICATIONS

Crew:	3 + 6
Armament:	1 x 20mm cannon, 1 x 7.62mm MG (coaxial), 6 x smoke grenade dischargers
Ammunition:	1,250 x 20mm, 5,000 x 7.62mm
Length:	6.88m
Width:	3.38m
Height over turret top:	3.015m
Height hull top:	1.9m,
Ground clearance:	0.44m
Weight, combat:	33,500kg
Weight, empty:	29,900kg
Power-to-weight ratio:	18hp/tonne
Ground pressure:	0.94kg/cm^2
Engine:	MTU MB 833 Ea-500 6-cylinder liquid-cooled diesel developing 600hp at 2,200rpm
Maximum road speed:	65km/hr
Maximum road range:	500km
Fuel capacity:	652 lit
Fording:	1.5m, 2m with preparation
Vertical obstacle:	1m
Trench:	2.5m
Gradient:	60%
Side slope:	30%
Armour:	Classified
Armour type:	Steel
NBC system:	Yes
Night vision equipment:	Yes (for commander, gunner and driver) but see text

DEVELOPMENT

In the 1960s development of an infantry combat vehicle to meet requirements of the German Army was undertaken by three companies and after trials with three series of prototypes, pre-production vehicles were completed in 1967/68. In 1969 Rheinstahl was appointed prime contractor for its production vehicle (then known as Marder) with MaK (today known as Rheinmetall Landsysteme) as major sub-contractor.

First production vehicles were delivered to the German Army in December 1970 and production continued until 1975. The chassis remained in production for Roland surface-to-air missile

system until 1983. The driver sits front left, with one infantryman behind him, and the engine compartment to his right. Turret is to rear with commander right and gunner left. 20mm cannon and 7.62mm MG mounted externally above turret, powered elevation from -15° to +65°, traverse 360°. Troop compartment rear with three infantrymen seated each side. Vehicle fords to depth of 2m with preparation and many vehicles have a Euromissile MILAN above commander's hatch on right side of turret.

VARIANTS

Countless trials versions of Marder 1 but only variant in service is Radarpanzer TÜR which is Marder 1 chassis with turret replaced by hydraulically operated arm on which radar scanner is mounted for air defence.

Marder 1 A1(+), double feed for 20mm cannon, image intensification night sight with thermal pointer, new water can racks and flaps for periscopes.

Marder 1 A1(-), as above but prepared for but not fitted with thermal pointer.

Marder 1 A1A, upgraded in all areas except passive night vision equipment.

Marder 1 A2, all Marders upgraded to this standard and includes modified chassis and suspension.

Marder 1 A3, all earlier Marders have upgraded to this standard with improved armour and new roof hatch arrangement.

Marder 1A4 – command post.

Marder 1A5 – has additional mine protection.

Driving Training Tank, has turret replaced by fixed cupola.

KEY RECOGNITION FEATURES

- Well-sloped glacis plate with driver on left leading up to horizontal roof with vertical hull rear, hull sides slope inwards above suspension, power-operated ramp in hull rear

- Large turret with sloping front, sides and rear on roof with externally mounted 20mm cannon and smoke grenade dischargers on left

- Suspension with either side six rubber-tyred road wheels, drive sprocket front, idler rear, three track-return rollers. Upper part of suspension normally covered by track guard

German and Brazilian armies use Marder IFV chassis as basis for their Roland surface-to-air missile system.

Argentina has built an IFV designated VCTP, based on the TAM tank chassis, which is similar to Marder but has simple two-man turret with 20mm cannon.

STATUS

Production complete. In service with German Army only.

MANUFACTURER

Rheinmetall Landsysteme GmbH, Kassel and Kiel, Germany.

Right: Marder 1A3 (Michael Jerchel)

Rheinmetall Landsysteme Jagdpanzer Jaguar 1 SP ATGW Vehicle (Germany)

Above: Jaguar 1 with HOT ATGW launcher extended (Michael Jerchel)

SPECIFICATIONS

Crew:	4
Armament:	1 x HOT ATGW launcher, 1 x 7.62mm coaxial MG, 1 x 7.62mm AA MG, 8 smoke grenade dischargers
Ammunition:	20 HOT ATGW, 3,200 x 7.62mm
Length:	6.61m
Width:	3.12m
Height:	2.54m (including missiles), 1.98m (hull top)
Ground clearance:	0.45m (front), 0.44m (rear)
Weight, combat:	25,500kg
Power-to-weight ratio:	19.6hp/tonne
Ground pressure:	0.7kg/cm^2
Engine:	Daimler Benz MB 837 8-cylinder water-cooled diesel developing 500hp at 2,000rpm
Maximum road speed:	70km/hr
Maximum road range:	400km
Fuel capacity:	470 lit
Fording:	1.2m
Vertical obstacle:	0.75m
Trench:	2m
Gradient:	58%
Side slope:	30%
Armour:	50mm max (estimate)
Armour type:	Steel
NBC system:	Yes
Night vision equipment:	Yes (driver and gunner)

DEVELOPMENT

During 1967/68 370 Jagdpanzer Raketes were built, 185 by Hanomag and 185 by Henschel. They have the same chassis as 90mm Jagdpanzer Kanone (JPZ 4-5) self-propelled anti-tank gun built earlier by the same companies. The 90mm version is no longer in service with Belgian or German armies.

Between 1978 and 1983 316 of the original 370 Raketes were rebuilt and their SS-11 ATGW system replaced by the more advanced and effective Euromissile K3S HOT ATGW system with maximum range of 4,000m. At the same time

applique passive armour was added to glacis plate and fighting compartment sides for increased protection against HEAT attack. The rebuilt vehicles are known as Jaguar 1s.

Mounted in front right side of hull is 7.62mm MG3 bow machine gun with traverse of 15° left and right and elevation from -8° to +15°. A second 7.62mm MG3 is mounted on commander's cupola for use in anti-aircraft role and a bank of eight electrically operated 76mm smoke grenade dischargers is mounted over hull rear firing forwards.

VARIANTS

Jagdpanzer with HOT Compact Turret and four HOT ATGWs in ready-to-launch position (prototype). Jaguar 2 is Jagdpanzer Kanone with 90mm gun removed, applique armour and roof-mounted TOW ATGW launcher. A total of 162 vehicles were converted to the Jaguar 2 configuration with prime contractor now being Rheinmetall Landsysteme, conversions were carried out between 1983 and 1985.

STATUS

Production complete. In service with Austria and Germany. Expected to be phased out of German Army service in 2005.

KEY RECOGNITION FEATURES

- Fighting compartment front with drop-down engine compartment rear, applique armour on front and sides of fighting compartment

- HOT ATGW launcher on left side of fighting compartment roof but can be retracted into vehicle

- Suspension either side has five road wheels, idler front, drive sprocket rear, track-return rollers covered by skirts

MANUFACTURER

Original builders were Henschel and Hanomag but conversion was by Thyssen Henschel (now Rheinmetall Landsysteme GmbH) with Euromissile providing complete HOT ATGW system.

Below: Jaguar 2 with TOW launcher in position (Michael Jerchel)

Rheinmetall Landsysteme Wiesel 2 Airportable Armoured Vehicle (Germany)

Above: Wiesel 2 in command post role (Rheinmetall Landsysteme)

SPECIFICATIONS

Crew:	2 + 5 (depends on version)
Armament:	1 x 7.62mm MG (depends on version)
Ammunition:	varies
Length:	4.20m (depends on version)
Width:	1.852m (depends on version)
Height:	1.7 to 2.11m (depends on version)
Ground clearance:	0.30m
Weight, combat:	4,100kg (depends on version)
Weight, empty:	Depends on version
Power-to-weight ratio:	26.458hp/tonne
Engine:	Audi 4-cylinder TDI diesel developing 109hp
Maximum road speed:	70 km/h
Maximum road range:	550km
Fuel capacity:	Not available
Fording:	0.50m
Vertical obstacle:	0.40m
Trench:	1.50m
Gradient:	60%
Side slope:	40%
Armour:	Classified
Armour type:	Steel
NBC system:	Optional
Night vision equipment:	Optional

DEVELOPMENT

The Wiesel 2 airportable multi-purpose carrier vehicle was originally developed as a private venture by MaK which is now known as Rheinmetall Landsysteme. The first prototype in an armoured personnel carrier configuration was completed in mid-1994.

The layout of the Wiesel 2 is similar to the Wiesel 1 with the engine front left and the driver front right with the troop compartment at the rear. The arrangement of the roof hatches depends on the mission but if used in the armoured personnel carrier role it would be fitted with a roof mounted cupola armed with an externally mounted 7.62mm MG3 machine gun with the troops entering and leaving via two doors in the rear. The vehicle is fully airportable in a CH-53G helicopter as used by the German Army.

The baseline Wiesel 2 chassis was selected as the platform for the Rheinmetall Defence Electronics ATLAS short-range air defence for the German Army which has now taken into service a total of 50 weapon platforms, 10 platoon command posts

and seven battery command posts with first vehicles being delivered in 2001.

These were the first versions of the Wiesel 2 to enter service with the German Army and are normally armed with a 7.62mm MG3 machine gun for local protection and a bank of four electrically operated 76mm smoke grenade launchers are mounted on the lower part of the hull front firing forwards.

The weapon platform has a remote controlled turret with four Stinger fire-and-forget surface-to-air missiles in the ready-to-launch position. The platoon command post has a roof mounted HARD radar system while the battery command post has extensive communications equipment for its specialist role.

VARIANTS

Ambulance – similar hull to command post (in service).

Ammunition – carries ammunition and missiles (prototype).

Command and control vehicle - similar hull to command post (entering production).

Mortar carrier – fitted with a 120mm mortar at the rear (prototype).

Syrano – robotic vehicle for French programme (trials phase).

Engineer reconnaissance (prototype).

ARGUS – airtransportable armoured surveillance and reconnaissance vehicle (prototype).

KEY RECOGNITION FEATURES

• Well-sloped glacis plate with engine louvres on left and drivers hatch on right. Horizontal roof with commanders cupola with externally mounted 7.62mm machine gun on right side. Second circular hatch to rear of gunner's cupola

• Vertical hull sides with distinct gap between suspension and upper part of hull which normally contains stowage. Vertical hull rear which overhangs rear. Personnel enter and leave via twin doors in hull rear

• Suspension either side consists of four small road wheels with a larger road wheel acting as idler and with drive sprocket at front and two track-return rollers

STATUS

In production. In service with German Army.

MANUFACTURER

Rheinmetall Landsysteme GmbH, Kiel, Germany.

Below: Wiesel 2 ambulance from rear (Rheinmetall Landsysteme)

Rheinmetall Landsysteme Wiesel 1 Airportable Armoured Vehicle (Germany)

SPECIFICATIONS (TOW version)

Crew:	3
Armament:	1 x TOW ATGW
Ammunition:	7 x TOW ATGW
Length:	3.31m
Width:	1.82m
Height overall:	1.897m
Height to hull top:	1.352m
Ground clearance:	0.302m
Weight, combat:	2800kg
Power-to-weight ratio:	30.7hp/tonne
Engine:	VW 5-cylinder turbocharged diesel developing 86hp at 4,500rpm
Maximum road speed:	75km/hr
Maximum road range:	300km
Fuel capacity:	80 lit
Vertical obstacle:	0.4m
Trench:	1.2m
Gradient:	60%
Side slope:	30%
Armour:	Classified
Armour type:	Steel
NBC system:	None
Night vision equipment:	Optional

DEVELOPMENT

The Wiesel airportable light armoured vehicle was developed for German airborne units by Porsche but production is undertaken by the now Rheinmetall Landsysteme (at that time MaK) with the first of 345 vehicles being delivered to the German Army late in 1989. The order was 210 with TOW ATGW and 135 with 20mm cannon. Wiesel with TOW, designated TOW A1 by the German Army, has Raytheon Systems Company TOW ATGW launcher in rear with traverse of 45° left and right and a total of seven missiles. The other version selected by the German Army is MK 20 A1 with two-man crew and KUKA turret armed with Rheinmetall 20mm MK 20 Rh 202 cannon with traverse of 110° left and right. It has 160 rounds of ready-use ammunition.

VARIANTS

A total of 16 TOW vehicles has been reconfigured as reconnaissance Wiesel 1s with AOZ sighting system. Some 20mm vehicles have been fitted with a new day/night sight.

Wiesel 2: Further development by Rheinmetall Landsysteme as a private venture resulted in the Wiesel 2, or Extended Base Vehicle as it has also

been referred to. There is a seperate entry for the Wiesel 2 in this section. Wiesel 2 is already in production and service with the German Army.

STATUS

Production complete. In service with the German Army.

MANUFACTURER

Rheinmetall Landsysteme GmbH, Kiel, Germany.

KEY RECOGNITION FEATURES

- Well-sloped glacis plate with engine front left and driver right, TOW ATGW on pedestal mount over open horizontal roof at hull rear

- Suspension each side has three large road wheels, drive sprocket front, large idler and one track-return roller above first and second road wheels

- Hull sides slope inwards to above track guards with air outlet on left side, horizontal louvres with exhaust pipe to immediate rear with gauze-type cover. Right side of hull above tracks has spade

Left: Wiesel with BTM 208 turret

Right: Wiesel with 20mm cannon (MK 20 A1)

Below right: Wiesel with TOW (TOW A1) (Christopher F Foss)

Below: Wiesel with TOW (TOW A1)

Boraq Armoured Personnel Carrier (Iran)

Above: Boraq armoured personnel carrier armed with 12.7mm MG

SPECIFICATIONS

Crew:	3 + 8
Armament:	1 x 12.7mm machine gun
Ammunition:	1000 x 12.7mm
Length hull:	6.65m
Width:	3.25m
Height:	1.75m (hull top)
Ground clearance:	0.45m
Weight, combat:	13,000kg
Weight, empty:	12,000kg (estimate)
Power-to-weight ratio:	25.4hp/tonne
Ground pressure:	0.55kg/cm^2
Engine:	V-8 air-cooled turbocharged diesel developing 330 hp at 2,300rpm
Maximum road speed:	65km/h
Maximum road range:	500km
Fuel capacity:	475 lit
Fording:	Amphibious with preparation
Vertical obstacle:	0.70m
Trench:	2.5m
Gradient:	60%
Side slope:	40%
Armour:	18mm (max estimate)
Armour type:	Steel
NBC system:	Optional
Night vision equipment:	Optional

DEVELOPMENT

The hull of the Boraq armoured personnel carrier is similar in many respects to that of the Russian BMP-2 and its Chinese equivalent the WZ 501 infantry fighting vehicles. The main difference is that the Boraq as currently fielded has a simple 12.7mm machine gun cupola and its road wheels are similar to those of the American United Defense M113 series APC which is used in large numbers by Iran.

The driver is seated at the front of the vehicle on the left side with the powerpack to his right. The commander/machine gunner is seated in the centre of the hull with the troop compartment at the rear. The troops are seated down the centre of the vehicle facing outwards and enter the vehicle

via two doors in the hull rear. Firing ports and associated vision devices allow the troops to fire their weapons from within the hull.

The Boraq is fully amphibious with the minimum of preparation, being propelled in the water by its tracks. Before entering the water a trim vane is erected at the front of the hull and the bilge pumps are switched on.

The vehicle can lay its own smoke screen by injecting diesel fuel into the exhaust outlet at the front of the hull on the right side.

VARIANTS

120mm mortar carrier - prototype.
Fitted with BMP-2 turret - in service.
Fitted with ATGW - believed prototypes only.
Ammunition resupply carrier - prototypes.

STATUS

Production. In service with Iran.

MANUFACTURER

Defence Industries Organisation, Shahid Kolahdooz Industrial Complex, Iran.

KEY RECOGNITION FEATURES

- Pointed nose with almost horizontal ribbed glacis plate, driver front left, engine compartment louvres in roof to right, weapon in centre of roof and troop compartment at rear with two roof hatches, one each side. Vertical hull rear with two bulged doors opening to the rear

- Mounted on the roof is a 12.7mm machine gun with no protection for the gunner although recent production versions have a horseshoe-type armour system for the gunner. Firing ports are provided in hull sides and rear of the troop compartment

- Suspension each side has six road wheels, drive sprocket at front, idler at rear and track-return rollers. Upper part of suspension is covered by a rubber skirt

Below: Boraq APC from the rear

Oto Melara Infantry Armoured Fighting Vehicle (Italy)

SPECIFICATIONS

Crew:	2 + 7
Armament:	1 x 12.7mm MG, 1 x 7.62mm MG
Ammunition:	1,050 x 12.7mm, 1,000 x 7.62mm
Length:	5.041m
Width:	2.686m
Height over MG:	2.552m
Height over commander's cover:	2.032m
Hull to hull top:	1.828m
Ground clearance:	0.406m
Weight, combat:	11,600kg
Power-to-weight ratio:	18.53bhp/tonne
Ground pressure:	0.57kg/cm²
Engine:	Detroit Diesel Model 6V-53 6-cylinder water-cooled diesel developing 215bhp at 2,800rpm
Maximum road speed:	64.4km/hr
Maximum water speed:	5km/hr
Maximum road range:	550km
Fuel capacity:	360 lit
Fording:	Amphibious
Vertical obstacle:	0.61m
Trench:	1.68m
Gradient:	60%
Side slope:	30%
Armour:	Classified
Armour type:	Aluminium with layer of steel
NBC system:	None
Night vision equipment:	Yes (infra-red for driver)

DEVELOPMENT

Infantry Armoured Fighting Vehicle was developed by Automotive Technical Service of the Italian Army and is based on American M113A1, made under licence by Oto Melara. Main improvements over M113A1 are increased firepower, improved armour protection (standard aluminium armour plus layer of steel armour added to hull front, sides and rear), improved seating arrangements, ability for some troops to aim and fire from inside the vehicle using firing ports and vision blocks. Infantry Armoured Fighting Vehicle is also referred to as VCC-1 by the Italian Army. Final deliveries made in 1982.

Engine compartment is front right, 12.7mm MG gunner to rear. Driver sits front left with vehicle commander rear. Infantry compartment is

rear of hull, infantry enter and leave via power-operated ramp. Over top of troop compartment is ring-mounted 7.62mm MG. For operations in Somalia, some vehicles were fitted with Enhanced Applique Armour Kit (EAAK). IAFV is fully amphibious, propelled by its tracks. Before entering water a trim vane is erected at front of vehicle and bilge pumps switched on.

VARIANTS

Saudi Arabia has taken delivery of 224 IAFVs with American Improved TOW system as fitted to M901 Improved TOW Vehicle.

The Italian Army also uses large numbers of M113/M113A1s, some of which have applique armour and firing ports/vision blocks in rear troop compartment (known as VCC-2s). The Italian Army has also used M113A1 as basis for SIDAM 4x25mm self-propelled anti-aircraft gun system.

STATUS

Production complete. In service with Italy and Saudi Arabia.

MANUFACTURER

Oto Melara, La Spezia, Italy.

KEY RECOGNITION FEATURES

- Based on modified M113 hull with well-sloped glacis plate with trim vane, horizontal hull top, hull sides vertical but slope inwards at rear, two firing ports each with observation window above

- Cupola right with external 12.7mm MG, 7.62mm MG on ring mount rear. Hull ramp at rear between two external fuel tanks

- Suspension each side has five road wheels, drive sprocket front, idler rear, no track-return rollers, upper part of track covered by rubber skirt

Left: IAFV fitted with applique armour (Richard Stickland)

Below: IAFV fitted with applique armour (Richard Stickland)

Dardo IFV (Italy)

SPECIFICATIONS

Crew:	2 + 7
Armament:	1 x 25mm cannon, 1 x 7.62mm MG (co-axial), 2 x TOW launchers and 2 x 3 smoke grenade launchers
Length:	6.705m
Width:	3.14m
Height overall:	2.64m
Ground clearance:	0.4m
Weight, loaded:	23,000kg
Weight, empty:	21,500kg
Power-to-weight ratio:	22.6hp/tonne
Ground pressure:	0.70kg/cm^2
Engine:	IVECO 8260 V-6 turbocharged, intercooled diesel developing 520bhp at 2,300rpm
Maximum road speed:	70km/hr
Maximum cruising range:	500km
Fuel capacity:	Not available
Fording:	1.5m
Vertical obstacle:	0.85m
Trench:	2.5m
Gradient:	60%
Side slope:	40%
Armour:	Classified
Armour type:	Aluminium/Steel
NBC system:	Yes
Night vision equipment:	Yes (passive for commander, gunner and driver)

DEVELOPMENT

The Dardo IFV, previously called the VCC-80 IV, has been developed by Consorzio Iveco Oto to meet the requirements of the Italian Army with first production contract being placed late in 1998 for the delivery of 200 vehicles. Hull is all aluminium armour with additional layer of steel for increased protection. Driver sits front left with powerpack to his right, two-man power-operated turret is centre and troop compartment rear. In action the vehicle commander would dismount with the six infrantrymen, five of whom can aim and fire from inside the vehicle using two firing ports/vision blocks in each side of hull and one in

rear ramp. Commander sits on turret left, gunner right. 25mm Oerlikon Contraves KBA cannon power-elevates from -10° to +30° and is stabilised, turret traverses 360°. 7.62mm MG is mounted coaxial to left of 25mm cannon. Fire-control system includes laser rangefinder and thermal image night vision equipment.

VARIANTS

Anti-tank with TOW missile launcher either side of turret.
120mm mortar carrier.
Command post vehicle.
Ambulance.
Fitted with T60/T70 turret system.

STATUS

Production. In service with Italian Army who placed an order for 200 vehicles.

MANUFACTURER

Consorzio Iveco Oto, Rome, Italy..

KEY RECOGNITION FEATURES

- Well-sloped glacis plate with driver's circular hatch in upper left side, horizontal roof, turret centre. Troop compartment rear with a single roof hatch above that opens to the rear

- Hull sides above tracks slope inwards, large horizontal air louvres on forward right side of hull, two spherical firing ports with vision block above in each side troop of troop compartment, hull rear slopes inwards with integral power-operated ramp

- Turret sides slope inwards with commander's cupola on left, periscope sight to his immediate front. Suspension each side has six road wheels, drive sprocket front, idler rear, three track-return rollers. Upper part covered by side skirts

Left: Dardo IFV with TOW

Right: Standard Dardo IFV

Below: Standard Dardo IFVs

Mitsubishi Heavy Industries Type 89 Mechanised Infantry Combat Vehicle (Japan)

SPECIFICATIONS

Crew:	3 + 7
Armament:	1 x 35mm, 1 x 7.62mm MG (coaxial), 2 x ATGW, 2 x 3 smoke grenade dischargers
Length:	6.7m
Width:	3.2m
Height:	2.50m
Ground clearance:	0.45m
Weight, combat:	27,000kg
Power-to-weight ratio:	22.22hp/tonne
Ground pressure:	0.73kg/cm^2
Engine:	Type 6 SY 31 WA diesel developing 600hp
Maximum road speed:	70km/hr (forwards), 42km/hr (reverse)
Maximum road range:	400km
Fuel capacity:	Not available
Fording:	1m
Vertical obstacle:	0.8m
Trench:	2.4m
Gradient:	60%
Side slope:	30%
Armour:	Classified
Armour type:	Steel
NBC system:	Yes
Night vision equipment:	Yes

DEVELOPMENT

Development of a new mechanised infantry combat vehicle started in 1984 and after trials it was classified as the Type 89 with first production vehicles being completed in 1991. Prime contractor is Mitsubishi Heavy Industries with Komatsu being major sub-contractor. The layout of the vehicle is conventional with the driver being seated at the front right with the powerpack to his left, two-man power-operated turret in the centre and the troop compartment at the rear which is provided with entry doors, roof hatches and firing ports.

The commander is seated on the right side of the turret with the gunner on the left with both

crew members being provided with a single piece roof hatch, periscopes for observation and a sight for aiming main armament. Main armament consists of a 35mm Oerlikon Contraves KDE cannon with a 7.62mm machine gun mounted coaxial and a Jyu-MAT medium range wire-guided anti-tank missile being mounted either side of the turret. Once these have been launched new missiles have to be reloaded manually.

VARIANTS

As far as it is known there are no variants of the Type 89 MICV although the vehicle can be fitted with mine clearing equipment at the front of the hull.

STATUS

In production. In service with the Japanese Ground Self Defence Force.

MANUFACTURER

Mitsubishi Heavy Industries, Tokyo, Japan.

KEY RECOGNITION FEATURES

- Well-sloped glacis plate with driver front right, turret centre, troop compartment rear with two-part roof hatch opening left and right and three firing ports in each side

- Turret has vertical sides with ATGW mounted externally each side, 35mm cannon in forward part of turret with night sight right

- Suspension each side has six road wheels, drive sprocket front, idler rear, three track-return rollers, skirts

***Far left:* Type 89 MICV (Paul Beaver)**

***Below:* Type 89 MICV (Kensuke Ebata)**

Mitsubishi Heavy Industries Type 73 APC (Japan)

SPECIFICATIONS

Crew:	3 + 9
Armament:	1 x 12.7mm MG (main), 1 x 7.62mm MG (bow), 2x3 smoke grenade dischargers
Length:	5.8m
Width:	2.8m
Height including MG:	2.2m
Height, hull top:	1.7m
Ground clearance:	0.4m
Weight, combat:	13,300kg
Power-to-weight ratio:	22.6hp/tonne
Engine:	Mitsubishi 4ZF air-cooled 2-stroke V4 diesel developing 300hp at 2,200rpm
Maximum road speed:	70km/hr
Maximum water speed:	7km/hr
Maximum road range:	300km
Fuel capacity:	450 lit
Fording:	Amphibious (with kit)
Vertical obstacle:	0.7m
Trench:	2m
Gradient:	60%
Side slope:	30%
Armour:	Classified
Armour type:	Aluminium
NBC system:	Yes
Night vision equipment:	Yes (infra-red for driver)

DEVELOPMENT

Development of a new APC to succeed Type SU 60 in Japanese Ground Self Defence Force commenced in 1967. After extensive trials with competing designs, Mitsubishi vehicle was accepted for service as Type 73 APC with first production vehicles completed in 1974. Production was completed after 225 had been built. It was followed by the Mitsubishi Heavy Industries Type 89 mechanised infantry combat vehicle (qv).

Bow 7.62mm MG gunner sits front left with driver front right and vehicle commander slightly to right and rear of bow MG gunner. Engine compartment to rear of driver with 12.7mm MG cupola on right side of hull roof. 12.7mm MG can

be aimed and fired from inside vehicle, elevation from -10° to +60°, turret traverse 360°. Roof hatches over troop compartment and six T-shaped firing ports, two in each side of hull and two in rear, allowing some troops to fire from inside.

The Type 73 is fully amphibious with the aid of a kit which includes trim vane on glacis plate, buoyancy aids for wheels, skirts over tracks and protection for air inlet and air outlet louvres on roof.

VARIANTS

Only variant in service is command post vehicle with higher roof at rear. Automotive components of Type 73 are used in Type 75 self-propelled ground wind-measuring system and used with Type 75 130mm self-propelled rocket launcher. Components of the Type 73 APC are also used in the Type 92 Japanese mineclearing vehicle.

STATUS

Production complete. In service with Japanese Ground Self Defence Force only.

Left: Type 73 APC

KEY RECOGNITION FEATURES

- Low profile hull with glacis plate at 45°, horizontal hull top, vertical rear with two doors, vertical hull sides

- Flotation screen on glacis plate, 7.62mm MG in left side of glacis plate, 12.7mm MG on raised cupola on right side of hull top, 2x3 smoke grenade dischargers at hull rear above twin doors

- Suspension each side has five road wheels, drive sprocket front, idler rear, no return rollers or skirt

MANUFACTURER

Mitsubishi Heavy Industries, Tokyo, Japan.

Below: Type 73 APC (Ryuta Watanabe)

Mitsubishi Heavy Industries Type SU 60 APC (Japan)

Above: Type SU 60 APC

SPECIFICATIONS

Crew:	4 + 6
Armament:	1 x 12.7mm MG, 1 x 7.62mm MG (bow)
Length:	4.85m
Width:	2.4m
Height including 12.7mm MG:	2.31m
Height hull top:	1.7m
Ground clearance:	0.4m
Weight, combat:	11,800kg
Weight, empty:	10,600kg
Power-to-weight ratio:	18.64hp/tonne
Engine:	Mitsubishi Model 8 HA 21 WT, V-8 air-cooled 4-cycle diesel developing 220hp at 2,400rpm
Maximum road speed:	45km/hr
Maximum road range:	300km
Fuel capacity:	Not available
Fording:	1m
Vertical obstacle:	0.6m
Trench:	1.82m
Gradient:	60%
Side slope:	30%
Armour:	Classified
Armour type:	Steel
NBC system:	None
Night vision equipment:	None

DEVELOPMENT

In the mid-1950s Japanese Ground Self Defence Force issued a requirement for a full tracked APC and after trials with various prototypes one was accepted for service as Type SU 60. Production subsequently undertaken by Komatsu and Mitsubishi from 1959 through to the early 1970s, an estimated 430 being built. As its successor, Type 73 has been built in smaller numbers. Type SU 60 will remain in service in declining numbers until well into the next decade.

Driver sits front right with bow machine gunner on left side, vehicle commander between them, 12.7mm M2 HB MG complete with shield on right side of roof to rear of commander. Troop compartment at hull rear with twin doors rear and roof hatches above. No provision for weapon-firing from inside.

VARIANTS

Type SX 60 81mm mortar carrier has 81mm mortar mounted in hull rear which can also be deployed away from vehicle. Only 18 built.

Type SX 60 4.2 inch (107mm) mortar carrier has 107mm (4.2 inch) mortar mounted in rear which can also be deployed away from vehicle. Only 18 built. 107mm mortar carrier can be distinguished from 81mm version by distinct chamfer to top of hull rear.

SU 60 dozer, only two in service, front-mounted dozer blade.

NBC detection vehicle has device at rear for taking soil samples.

Anti-tank vehicle, a few Type SU 60s have been fitted with two KAM-3D anti-tank guided missiles on hull roof at rear.

For training, a few SU 60s have been modified to resemble Russian BMD-1 airborne combat vehicles.

STATUS

Production complete. In service with Japanese Ground Self Defence Force only.

KEY RECOGNITION FEATURES

- Glacis plate at about 60° with 7.62mm MG ball mounted on left side, horizontal roof, engine compartment on left side to rear of bow MG operator and commander, troop compartment rear with roof hatches opening left and right

- Vertical hull sides and rear, twin doors in rear open outwards

- Suspension either side has five road wheels, drive sprocket front, idler rear, three track-return rollers, no skirts

MANUFACTURER

Mitsubishi Heavy Industries, Tokyo; Komatsu Manufacturing Corporation, Minato-ku, Tokyo, Japan.

Below: Type SX 60 4.2 inch (107mm) mortar carrier

Komatsu Type 60 106mm SP Recoilless Gun (Japan)

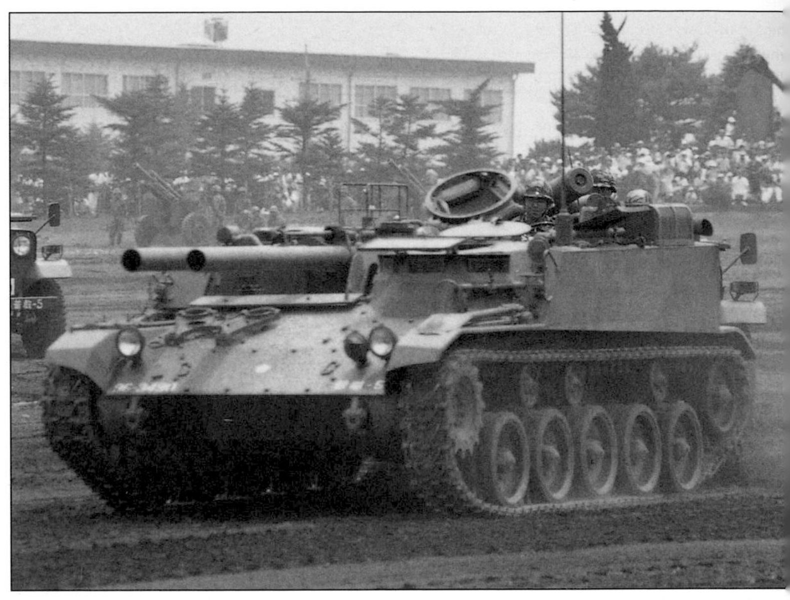

SPECIFICATIONS

Crew:	3
Armament:	2 x 106mm recoilless rifles, 1 x 12.7mm MG
Ammunition:	8 x 106mm
Length:	4.3m
Width:	2.23m
Height:	1.59m
Ground clearance:	0.35m
Weight, combat:	8,000kg
Weight, empty:	7,600kg
Power-to-weight ratio:	18hp/tonne (150hp engine)
Ground pressure:	0.67kg/cm^2
Engine:	Komatsu Model 6T 120-2 air-cooled, 6-cylinder diesel developing 120hp at 2,400rpm (late production vehicles have 150hp engine)
Maximum road speed:	45km/hr (early production model), 55km/hr (late production model)
Maximum road range:	250 + km
Fuel capacity:	140 lit
Fording:	0.7m
Vertical obstacle:	0.60m
Trench:	1.8m
Gradient:	60%
Side slope:	30%
Armour:	12mm max (estimate)
Armour type:	Steel
NBC system:	No
Night vision equipment:	IR night sight (optional)

DEVELOPMENT

Type 60 twin 106mm was developed from the 1950s to meet requirements of Japanese Ground Self Defence Force with production under way in 1960. Three versions were built, the final Model C having more powerful engine. Production completed in 1979 after 223 had been built. By 2004 about 150 of these remained in service.

Main armament comprises two 106mm recoilless rifles in right side of hull with traverse of 10° left and right and elevation from -5° to + 10°. The two rifles and mount can be raised with

ıe aid of powered controls above roof of vehicle, ʋhen they have traverse of 30° left and right, ɩevation from -20° to + 15°. Mounted over right ɛcoilless rifle is 12.7mm ranging machine gun. ɦe effectiveness of these 106mm recoilless rifles ɡainst the more modern armours is questionable. ɔr improved mobility in snow, extra wide tracks ɑn be fitted.

The recoilless rifles fire fixed HEAT and HE ɱmunition. A rangefinder is carried on the ɐhicle and some vehicles have been fitted with ıfra-red night vision equipment.

'ARIANTS

ıo variants.

TATUS

roduction complete. In service with Japanese ɪround Self Defence Force only.

ɅANUFACTURER

omatsu Seisakujyo, Tokyo, Japan.

.eft: Type 60 106mm with weapons owered (Keiichi Nogi)

ʒelow: Type 60 106mm

KEY RECOGNITION FEATURES

- Low profile hull with two 106mm recoilless rifles in right side with travelling lock on hull front

- Suspension has five road wheels, drive sprocket front, idler rear, three track-return rollers

Above: Type 60 106mm from rear with weapons lowered (Kensuke Ebata)

MLI-84 Infantry Combat Vehicle (Romania)

Above: Standard MLI-84 IFV

SPECIFICATIONS

Crew:	2 + 9
Armament:	1 x 73mm, 1 x 7.62mm MG (co-axial), 1 x 12.7mm MG (anti-aircraft), 2 x Sagger (ATGW launcher)
Ammunition:	40 x 73mm, 2,000 x 7.62mm, 500 x 12.7mm, 4 x Sagger ATGW
Length:	7.32m
Width:	3.15m
Height:	1.975m
Ground clearance:	0.40m
Weight, combat:	16,600kg
Weight, empty:	15,400kg
Power-to-weight ratio:	21.68hp/tonne
Ground pressure:	0.7kg/cm^2
Engine:	Model 8V-1240 DT-S supercharged diesel developing 360hp
Maximum road speed:	65km/h
Maximum water speed:	7km/h
Maximum road range:	600km
Fuel capacity:	460 lit
Fording:	Amphibious
Vertical obstacle:	0.8m
Trench:	2.2m
Gradient:	60%
Side slope:	30%
Armour type:	Steel
NBC system:	Yes
Night vision equipment:	Yes

DEVELOPMENT

The Romanian MLI-84 is essentially a Romanian produced version of the Russian Kurgan Machine Construction Plant BMP-1 IFV but is heavier, has a different powerpack and is fitted with a 12.7mm DShKM machine gun over the left rear circular roof hatch. It is understood that a total of 184 MLI-84 vehicles were built for the Romanian Army. It was not exported.

In MLI-84 the driver sits front left with the vehicle commander to the rear with both having circular roof hatches. The powerpack is to the right with the one person power operated turret in the centre.

Turret can be traversed through a full 360° and the 73mm 2A28 gun and 7.62mm PKT coaxial machine gun can be elevated from -4° to +30°. These weapons are not stabilised. Mounted over the 73mm gun is a launcher for the AT-3 Sagger

wire-guided ATGW which has a maximum range of 3,000m.

The troop compartment is at the rear with eight infantry seated four each side back to back. In each side of the troop compartment are four firing ports and in each of the rear doors is a firing port and periscope.

MLI-84 is fully amphibious being propelled in the water by its tracks. Before entering the water a trim vane is erected at the front of the vehicle and the bilge pumps are switched on.

KEY RECOGNITION FEATURES

- Pointed nose with almost horizontal ribbed glacis plate, driver front left, engine compartment louvres in roof to right, commander's position to rear of driver, turret slightly to rear of vehicle, troop compartment at rear with four roof hatches, two each side. Vertical hull rear with two bulged doors opening rear. Similar in appearance to Russian BMP-1

- Circular turret with well-sloped sides has 73mm gun with launcher above for Sagger ATGW (not always fitted in peacetime), single gunner's hatch on left side of roof. Four firing ports each side of rear hull troop compartment

- Suspension each side has six road wheels, drive sprocket at front, idler rear and three track return rollers. Upper part of track is normally covered by skirts

VARIANTS

MLI-84M upgrade – Romania has started to upgrade its fleet of vehicles to the enhanced MLI-84M standard which includes the installation of a new Perkins C9 diesel developing 400hp, new final drives, upgraded suspension and new communications equipment.

The existing turret is removed and replaced by a RAFAEL Overhead Weapon Station (OWS) armed with an Oerlikon Contraves 25mm KBA cannon, 7.62mm PKT coaxial machine gun and two locally produced AT-3 Sagger ATGW. The latter are expected to be replaced by the RAFAEL Spike ATGW.

STATUS

Production complete. In service only with Romania. Upgrade programme underway.

MANUFACTURER

ROMARM SA, Bucharest, Romania.

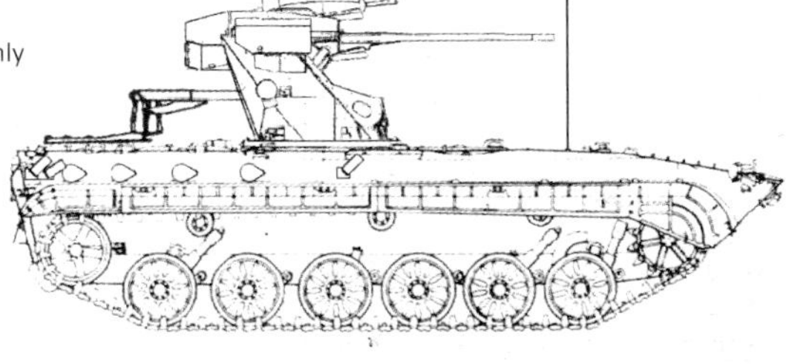

Right: Upgraded MLI-84M IFV

Right: Standard MLI-84 IFV

MLVM Mountaineers Combat Vehicle (Romania)

Above: MLVM Mountaineers Combat Vehicle (Paul Beaver)

SPECIFICATIONS

Crew:	2 + 7
Armament:	1 x 14.5mm MG, 1 x 7.62mm MG (coaxial)
Ammunition:	600 x 14.5mm, 2,500 x 7.62mm
Length:	5.85m
Width:	2.714m
Height:	1.95m (turret roof), 1.55m (hull top)
Ground clearance:	0.38m
Weight, combat:	9,000kg
Power-to-weight ratio:	17.11hp/tonne
Ground pressure:	0.47kg/cm^2
Engine:	Model 798-05M2 4-stroke supercharged diesel developing 153hp
Maximum road speed:	48km/hr
Range:	370/400km (cross-country), 680/740km (road)
Fuel capacity:	480 lit
Fording:	0.6m
Vertical obstacle:	0.6m
Trench:	1.5m
Gradient:	60%
Side slope:	30%
Armour:	Classified
Armour type:	Steel
NBC system:	Yes
Night vision equipment:	Yes (infra-red)

DEVELOPMENT

The MLVM Mountaineers Combat Vehicle was developed to meet the specific operational requirements of the Romanian Army for a vehicle capable of operating in mountainous terrain. The driver is seated at the front left with the vehicle commander to his rear and the powerpack to their right. The troop compartment is at the rear with the troops entering via two doors in the hull

rear. The troop compartment is provided with firing ports and vision devices and each of the rear doors contains an integral fuel tank.

VARIANTS

MLVM AR, this has a modified rear hull and is fitted with a 120mm mortar.

ABAL armoured vehicle for combat supply.

Ambulance, this is similar to the ABAL armoured vehicle for combat supply.

STATUS

Production complete. In service with Romania.

MANUFACTURER

ROMARM SA, Bucharest, Romania.

KEY RECOGNITION FEATURES

- Large box type hull with well-sloped glacis plate, nose slopes back under front of vehicle, hull sides slope slightly inwards with chamfer either side of hull at front, vertical hull rear with two doors

- Suspension either side consists of six spoked road wheels, drive sprocket at front, idler at rear and three track-return rollers, upper part of track covered by shallow skirt

- Turret in centre of hull roof with flat top and conical sides, distinctive sight is on left of turret and is protected by a distinctive wire cage

Below: MLVM Mountaineers Combat Vehicle

MT-LB Multi-Purpose Tracked Vehicle (Russia)

Above: MT-LB

SPECIFICATIONS

Crew:	2 + 11
Armament:	1 x 7.62mm MG
Ammunition:	2,500 x 7.62mm
Length:	6.454m
Width:	2.86m
Height:	1.865m
Ground clearance:	0.4m
Weight, combat:	11,900kg
Weight, empty:	9,700kg
Power-to-weight ratio:	20.16hp/tonne
Ground pressure:	0.46kg/cm^2
Engine:	YaMZ 238 V, V-8 diesel developing 240hp at 2,100rpm
Maximum road speed:	61.5km/hr
Maximum water speed:	4-5km/hr
Maximum road range:	500km
Fuel capacity:	450 lit
Fording:	Amphibious
Vertical obstacle:	0.61m
Trench:	2.41m
Gradient:	60%
Side slope:	30%
Armour:	3-10mm
Armour type:	Steel
NBC system:	Yes
Night vision equipment:	Yes (infra-red for commander and driver)

DEVELOPMENT

The MT-LB was developed in the late 1960s to replace the AT-P armoured tracked artillery tractor which is no longer in front-line service. It is based on MT-L unarmoured tracked amphibious carrier. Typical roles include carrying 11 fully equipped troops, towing 122mm D-30 howitzers or 100mm T-12 anti-tank guns, command and radio vehicle, artillery fire-control vehicle, cargo carrier and many specialised versions.

The vehicle is fully amphibious, propelled by its tracks. Basic version normally has 350mm wide tracks which give ground pressure of 0.46kg/cm^2, but these can be replaced by much wider 565mm tracks which lower ground pressure to 0.27/ 0.28kg/cm^2, giving vehicle improved mobility in snow or swamp. Turret is manned by commander and has single 7.62mm PKT MG with manual elevation from -5° to + 30° and manual traverse through 360°. No roof hatch.

VARIANTS

MT-LBV is standard MT-LB with 565mm wide tracks.

MT-LB artillery tractor normally has fully enclosed box over troop compartment for gun equipment.

MT-LBU command has additional radios, enerator, land navigation system and canvas over that extends to rear for additional space.
MT-LBU with Big Fred artillery/mortar locating adar mounted on roof; when travelling antenna olds forward. Russian designation is TT-LB.
MTP-LB repair vehicle has no turret, A-frame, towage on vehicle roof, winch, tools and other pecialised equipment.
MT-LB ambulance has stretchers in rear troop ompartment.
MT-LB engineer vehicle has stowage box on roof nd hydraulically operated blade at hull rear.
SA-13 Gopher SAM system is based on MT-LB hassis.
MT-LB with AT-6 ATGW, has launcher which is aised when required.
MT-LBs are used for a variety of artillery and air lefence fire control vehicles.
RKhM chemical reconnaissance vehicle is based on MT-LB components.
There are numerous **Polish variants** of MT-LB.
There are numerous **Bulgarian variants** of MT-LB.
MT-LB mortar, includes 82mm Vasilek and 120mm.
MT-LB with WAT turret, used by Poland, has turret of OT-64C (2) (SKOT-2AP) turret.

KEY RECOGNITION FEATURES

- Commander's and driver's compartment to immediate rear of glacis plate, small flat-topped turret right of driver
- Troop compartment extends from crew compartment to rear of vehicle, almost vertical sides with chamfered top, twin rear doors, single firing port in left hull side
- Six equally spaced ribbed road wheels, drive sprocket front, idler rear, no track-return rollers

STATUS

Production complete. In service with Armenia, Azerbaijan, Bangladesh, Belarus, Bulgaria, Finland, Georgia, Hungary, Kazakhstan, Lithuania, Moldova, Nigeria, Russia, Sweden, Ukraine, Uruguay and Yugoslavia.

MANUFACTURER

Kharkov Tractor Plant, Kharkhov, Ukraine; also made in Bulgaria and Poland.

Below: MT-LB with Big Fred (SNAR-10) radar (Michael Jerchel)

BMP-3 Infantry Combat Vehicle (Russia)

SPECIFICATIONS

Crew:	3 + 7
Armament:	1 x 100mm, 1 x 30mm cannon (coaxial), 1 x 7.62mm MG (coaxial), 2 x 7.62mm (hull front, one either side), 2 x 3 smoke grenade dischargers
Ammunition:	40 x 100mm, 500 x 30mm, 6,000 x 7.62mm, 6 x ATGW
Length:	7.14m
Width:	3.15m
Height:	2.30m (turret roof)
Ground clearance:	510mm (see text)
Weight, combat:	18,700kg
Power-to-weight ratio:	26.73hp/tonne
Ground pressure:	0.61kg/cm^2
Engine:	Type UTD-29M developing 500hp
Maximum road speed:	70km/hr
Maximum water speed:	10km/hr
Maximum road range:	600km
Fuel capacity:	Not available
Fording:	Amphibious
Vertical obstacle:	0.8m
Trench:	2.5m
Gradient:	60%
Side slope:	30%
Armour:	Classified
Armour type:	Steel
NBC system:	Yes
Night vision equipment:	Yes (commander, gunner and driver)

DEVELOPMENT

The BMP-3 was developed to meet the requirements of the Russian Army and was first seen in public during a parade held in Moscow in 1990.

The driver is seated at the front of the vehicle in centre with an additional crew member to his left and right, all three being provided with a single piece hatch cover. The two man turret is in the centre of the hull with the commander being seated on the right and the gunner on the left, both with a roof hatch. Main armament consists of a 100mm rifled gun that in addition to firing conventional ammunition also fires a laser guided ATGW which has the NATO designation of the AT-10. Mounted to the right of this is a 30mm cannon that is attached to the 100mm gun. In addition there is a 7.62mm machine gun mounted to the right of the 30mm cannon with another 7.62mm machine gun being mounted either side at front of hull firing forwards. A total of seven infantrymen are carried, one either side of the driver with the remainder being seated to the sides and rear of the turret.

The engine is located at the rear of the vehicle on the right side with the fuel tanks being under the floor of the vehicle. The small troop compartment at the rear of the BMP-3 is provided with roof hatches and two doors in the rear that open outwards. As the floor of the troop compartment is so high from the ground, steps unfold as the rear doors are opened.

The vehicle is fully amphibious being propelled in the water by two waterjets mounted at the rear of the hull and before entering the water the trim vane is erected at the front of the vehicle and the bilge pumps are switched on. The suspension is of the adjustable type and the driver can adjust the suspension to suit the type of ground being crossed.

VARIANTS

BMMP Marines fighting vehicle has same turret as BMP-2.
BMP-3F, marine version.
BMP-3 plus ERA, for export.
BMP-3 reconnaissance, called BRM, or Rys (Lynx).
BMP-3 driver training vehicle.
BMP-3 recovery vehicle (BREM-L).
BMP-3K command vehicle.
BMP-3M, latest model for export.
120mm 2S31 Vena artillery system is based on BMP-3 chassis (prototype).
BMP-3 Kornet-E ATGW system (prototype).
BMP-3 Krizantema ATGW system (prototype).

KEY RECOGNITION FEATURES

- Large box type hull with almost horizontal glacis plate, nose slopes back under front of hull, vertical hull sides rear with two small doors in hull rear. Mounted in either side of hull front is a 7.62mm MG firing forwards

- Circular turret in centre of hull with two hatches, over frontal 180° of the turret is another layer of armour, long-barrelled 100mm gun with 30mm cannon mounted coaxial to right, distinctive box over rear of main armament

- Suspension either side has six road wheels with idler at front, drive sprocket at rear and three track-return rollers, upper part of track covered by light steel cover similar to that on BMP-1 and BMP-2

STATUS

In production. In service with Azerbaijan, Cyprus, South Korea, Kuwait, Russia, Ukraine and United Arab Emirates (Abu Dhabi).

MANUFACTURER

Kurgan Machine Construction Plant, Kurgan, Russia.

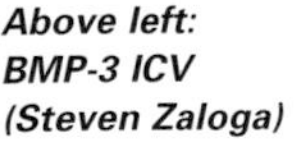

***Above left:* BMP-3 ICV (Steven Zaloga)**

***Right:* BMP-3 ICV**

BMP-2 Infantry Fighting Vehicle (Russia)

Above: BMP-2

SPECIFICATIONS

Crew:	3 + 7
Armament:	1 x 30mm cannon, 1 x 7.62mm MG (coaxial), 1 x Spandrel ATGW launcher, 2 x 3 smoke grenade dischargers
Ammunition:	500 x 30mm, 2,000 x 7.62mm, 4 x Spandrel ATGW
Length:	6.735m
Width:	3.15m
Height:	2.45m
Ground clearance:	0.42m
Weight, combat:	14,300kg
Power-to-weight ratio:	20.30hp/tonne
Engine:	Model UTD-20 6-cylinder diesel developing 300hp at 2,600rpm
Maximum road speed:	65km/hr
Maximum water speed:	7km/hr
Maximum road range:	600km
Fuel capacity:	462 lit
Fording:	Amphibious
Vertical obstacle:	0.7m
Trench:	2.5m
Gradient:	60%
Side slope:	30%
Armour:	Classified
Armour type:	Steel
NBC system:	Yes
Night vision equipment:	Yes (commander, gunner and driver)

DEVELOPMENT

The BMP-2 IFV is a further development of BMP-1 and was first seen in public during a Moscow parade in 1982. In addition to a more powerful engine BMP-2 has a new two-man turret with different weapons. Driver sits front left with one of the seven infantrymen to his rear, engine compartment to his right. Turret is slightly to rear with troop compartment far rear. Six infantrymen sit three each side back to back, each man with firing port in side of hull and periscope above. Two-man turret has commander on right, gunner on left, new 30mm cannon with powered elevation up to +75° for use against helicopters and slow-flying aircraft, turret traverse 360° and 30mm cannon fully stabilised. 7.62mm MG is mounted coaxial to left of 30mm cannon.

Mounted on turret roof rear is launcher for AT-5 Spandrel ATGW which has maximum range of 4,000m. Some vehicles have launcher for 2500m AT-4 Spigot instead. Some BMP-2s have applique armour on turrets and hulls. BMP-2 is

ully amphibious, propelled by its tracks. Before ntering the water a trim vane is erected at front f hull and bilge pumps switched on.

ARIANTS

MP-2D, late production vehicle with applique rmour and provision for fitting mine clearing quipment under nose of vehicle.

MP-2K, command version with additional ommunications equipment.

VP-2, Czechoslovakian designation for BMP-2.

 number of upgrades are available including the liver turret and another with standard turret but vith new sights and 30mm grenade launcher.

TATUS

roduction complete. In service with Algeria, ngola, Armenia, Azerbaijan, Belarus, Czech epublic, Finland, Georgia, India, Indonesia, ran, Jordan, Kazakhstan, Kyrgyzstan, Kuwait, lacedonia, Russia, Sierra Leone, Slovakia, ri Lanka, Sudan, Syria, Tajikistan, Togo, urkmenistan, Ukraine, Uzbekistan and Yemen.

MANUFACTURER

ussian state arsenals. Manufactured under icence in former Czechoslovakia and India. The atter country calls it the Sarath and has eveloped numerous variants.

KEY RECOGNITION FEATURES

- Pointed nose with almost horizontal ribbed glacis plate, driver front left, engine compartment louvres in roof to right, turret slightly to rear of vehicle, troop compartment rear with two roof hatches. Vertical hull rear with two bulged doors opening rear. Similar in appearance to BMP-1 but with different turret and wider hull

- Turret has long-barrelled 30mm cannon with muzzle brake, three forward-firing smoke dischargers each side of turret, ATGW launcher in centre of turret at rear. Four firing ports in left side of hull and three in right plus one in each rear door

- Suspension each side has six road wheels, drive sprocket front, idler rear, track-return rollers covered by skirts with horizontal ribs

Right: BMP-2

Below: BMP-2

BMP-1 Infantry Combat Vehicle (Russia)

SPECIFICATIONS

Crew:	3 + 8
Armament:	1 x 73mm, 1 x 7.62mm MG (coaxial), 1 x Sagger ATGW launcher
Ammunition:	40 x 73mm, 2,000 x 7.62mm, 1 x 4 Sagger ATGW
Length:	6.74m
Width:	2.94m
Height over searchlight:	2.15m
Ground clearance:	0.39m
Weight, combat:	13,500kg
Weight, empty:	12,500kg
Power-to-weight ratio:	22.22hp/tonne
Ground pressure:	0.6kg/cm^2
Engine:	Type UTD-20 6-cylinder in-line water-cooled diesel developing 300hp at 2,000rpm
Maximum road speed:	65km/hr
Maximum water speed:	7km/hr
Maximum road range:	600km
Fuel capacity:	460 lit
Fording:	Amphibious
Vertical obstacle:	0.8m
Trench:	2.2m
Gradient:	60%
Side slope:	30%
Armour:	33mm (maximum)
Armour type:	Steel
NBC system:	Yes
Night vision equipment:	Yes (infra-red for commander, gunner and driver)

DEVELOPMENT

BMP-1 was developed in the early 1960s to replace BTR-50P series tracked APCs and was first seen in public during 1967. It was replaced in production by BMP-2 ICV (previous entry) which, although similar in appearance, has slightly different layout and new turret and weapon system.

In the BMP-1, driver sits front left with vehicle commander to rear, engine compartment is to right of driver with one-man turret centre and troop compartment rear. Turret power-traverses through 360° and 73mm gun elevates from -4° to +33° and fires HEAT or HE-FRAG rounds. 7.62mm MG is mounted coaxial to right of 73mm gun and mounted over gun is launcher for AT-3 Sagger wire-guided ATGW which has maximum range of 3,000m.

Troop compartment is at rear with eight infantry seated four each side back to back. In each side of troop compartment are four firing ports with periscope above, and in each of two rear doors is a further firing port and periscope.

BMP-1 is fully amphibious, propelled by its tracks. Before entering the water a trim vane is erected at front of vehicle and bilge pumps switched on.

As BMP-1 was produced for some 20 years there are minor detailed differences between production models.

VARIANTS

BMP-1F, reconnaissance model used by Hungary.
BMP-1K, BMP-1 commander's model.
BMP-1K3, BMP-1 commander's model.
BMP-1P, BMP-1 with no Sagger and roof-mounted AT-4 ATGW fitted.
BMP-1PK, BMP-1P commander's model.
BRM-1K, BRM-1 basic reconnaissance - armoured cavalry.
BREM-1 and BREM-4, recovery vehicles.
BMP-1KShM, unarmed command version of BMP-1.
BWP, Polish version of BMP-1.
Czech BMP-1, many variants including OT-90 (BMP-1 with turret of OT-64C(1)).
Egyptian BMP-1, have new French diesel engine.
BMP-1 can be fitted with mine clearing equipment.
BMP-1 has been fitted with 30mm grenade launcher.
BRM and BRM-1 reconnaissance vehicles, new two-man turret.
PRP-3 Radar, two-man turret in radar in roof.
IRM, Amphibious reconnaissance vehicle.
BMP-POO, Mobile Training Centre, no turret, raised roof.
BMP-1G, for export, no Sagger, roof-mounted Spandrel ATGW plus 30mm grenade launcher.
Pbv 501, Swedish version of BMP-1.

STATUS

Production complete. In service with Algeria, Angola, Armenia, Azerbaijan, Belarus, Bulgaria, Cuba, Czech Republic, Egypt, Eritrea, Ethiopia, Finland, Georgia, Greece, Hungary, India, Iran, Kazakhstan, Korea (North), Kyrgyzstan, Libya, Mongolia, Mozambique, Poland, Romania, Russia, Slovakia, Sri Lanka, Sweden, Syria, Taijikistan, Turkmenistan, Ukraine, Uruguay, Vietnam and Yemen.

KEY RECOGNITION FEATURES

- Pointed nose with almost horizontal ribbed glacis plate, driver front left, engine compartment louvres in roof to right, turret slightly to rear of vehicle, troop compartment rear with four roof hatches, two each side. Vertical hull rear with two bulged doors opening rear. Similar in appearance to BMP-2 but with different turret with long-barrelled 30mm cannon and wider hull

- Circular turret with well-sloped sides has 73mm gun with launcher above for Sagger ATGW (not always installed in peacetime), single gunner's hatch on left side of roof. Four firing ports each side of hull

- Suspension each side has six road wheels, drive sprocket at front, idler rear and three track-return rollers. Upper part of track covered by skirts

MANUFACTURER

Former Czechoslovakian and Russian state arsenals. China builds a version of BMP-1 designated WZ 501.

Top left: BMP-1 (Richard Stickland)

Right: BMP-1 (Richard Stickland)

BMD-3 Airborne Combat Vehicle (Russia)

Above: BMD-3

SPECIFICATIONS

Crew:	3 + 4
Armament:	1 x 30mm cannon, 1 x 7.62mm MG (coaxial), 1 x AT-4/ AT-5 ATGW launcher, 1 x 40mm grenade launcher (bow), 1 x 5.45mm MG (bow)
Ammunition:	860 x 30mm, 2000 x 7.62mm, 2160 x 5.45mm, 551 x 30mm grenade, 4 x ATGW, 2 x 3 smoke grenade launchers
Length:	6.36m
Width:	3.134m
Height:	2.170m
Ground clearance:	0.15 to 0.53m
Weight, combat:	13 200kg
Power-to-weight ratio:	34 hp/tonne
Engine:	2V-06 water-cooled diesel developing 450hp
Maximum road speed:	71km/h
Maximum road range:	500km
Fuel capacity:	450 lit
Fording:	Amphibious
Vertical obstacle:	0.8m (estimate)
Trench:	1.8m (estimate)
Gradient:	60%
Side slope:	30%
Armour:	Classified
Armour type:	Aluminium
NBC:	Yes
Night vision equipment:	Yes

DEVELOPMENT

The BMD-3 has been developed as the follow-on to the earlier BMD-1 and BMD-2 airborne combat vehicles with the BMD-3 being larger and much heavier. Production commenced in 1989 and so far it has been identified only in service with Russian airborne units.

The driver is seated in the front of the hull in the centre with another person either side. Mounted in the left side of the hull is a 30mm AG-17 automatic grenade launcher while in the right side is mounted a 5.45mm RPKS machine gun.

The two man power operated turret is mounted in the centre of the forward part of the hull and is the same as that fitted to the BMP-2 ICV and armed with a 30mm 2A42 cannon with a 7.62mm machine gun mounted coaxial. Turret traverse is 360° with weapon elevation from -5°

to +75°. Mounted on the turret roof is a launcher for the AT-4 or AT-5 ATGW.

An unusual feature of the BMD-3 is its hydropneumatic suspension system which allows the ground clearance to be varied from 150mm to 530mm, normal ground clearance is 450mm. The standard tracks are 320mm wide but these can be replaced by wider 480mm tracks.

The BMD-3 is fully amphibious being propelled in the water at a speed of 10km/h by two waterjets mounted at the rear of the hull. Before entering the water a trim vain is erected at the front of the hull and the bilge pumps are switched on.

KEY RECOGNITION FEATURES

- Pointed nose with horizontal hull top extending to rear of hull, three hatches in hull top at the front, turret (as fitted to BMP-2) in the centre, louvres in hull top either side, vertical hull rear

- Turret has long barreled 30mm cannon that overhangs front of vehicle, hull sides are almost vertical

- Suspension either side consists of five road wheels with idler at the front, drive sprocket at the rear and four track-return rollers

VARIANTS

BMD-3M has new turret like BMP-3 ICV.

RKhM-5 is NBC recce vehicle.
BTR is a multi-purpose carrier.
125mm 2S25 self-propelled anti-tank gun uses components of the BMD-3 but remains at the prototype stage.

STATUS

In production. In service only with Russia.

MANUFACTURER

Volgograd Tractor Plant, Volgograd, Russia.

Left: BMD-3 (Steven Zaloga)

Below: BMD-3

BMD-1 Airborne Combat Vehicle (Russia)

Above: BMD-2 which has new turret armed with 30mm cannon (Steven Zaloga)

SPECIFICATIONS (BMD-1)

Crew:	3 + 4
Armament:	1 x 73mm (main), 1 x 7.62mm MG (coaxial), 1 x AT-3 Sagger launcher, 2 x 7.62mm forward-firing MG
Ammunition:	40 x 73mm, 2,000 x 7.62mm, 3 x Sagger
Length:	5.4m
Width:	2.63m
Height:	1.62m to 1.97m
Ground clearance:	0.1 to 0.45m
Weight, combat:	7,500kg
Power-to-weight ratio:	32hp/tonne
Ground pressure:	0.57kg/cm^2
Maximum road speed:	70km/hr
Maximum water speed:	10km/hr
Maximum road range:	320km
Fuel capacity:	300 lit
Fording:	Amphibious
Vertical obstacle:	0.8m
Trench:	1.6m
Gradient:	60%
Side slope:	30%
Armour:	15mm (max hull), 23mm (max turret)
Armour type:	Aluminium
NBC system:	Yes
Night vision equipment:	Yes (commander, gunner and driver, infra-red)

DEVELOPMENT

The BMD-1 Airborne Combat Vehicle was developed to meet requirements of the Russian Airborne forces and was first seen in public in 1973. Driver sits front centre, commander to his left and bow machine gunner to his right. Turret is identical to BMP-1 ICV's and has 73mm 2A28 smooth bore gun fed by automatic loader with 7.62mm PKT MG mounted coaxially to right. Guns power-elevate from -4° to +30°, turret traverses through 360°. Mounted over 73mm gun is an AT-3 Sagger wire-guided ATGW and in each corner of bow is a 7.62mm MG. To rear of turret sit remaining three crew members, engine is far rear of hull.

The vehicle is fully amphibious, propelled by two waterjets mounted at rear and is fitted with smoke generating equipment and engine pre-

heater. Hydropneumatic suspension allows height adjustment.

VARIANTS

BMD-1P, BMD-1 with Sagger removed and fitted with pintle-mounted AT-4 Spigot ATGW on turret roof.
BMD-2, new turret armed with 30mm cannon as used in BMP-2, 7.62mm coaxial MG and pintle mount on roof for AT-4 Spigot or AT-5 Spandrel ATGW. Only one bow-mounted 7.62mm MG.
82mm mortar carrier, BMD-1 with 82mm mortar in rear, probably field expedient for Afghanistan.
BTR-RD Robot, is anti-tank version with ATGW.
BTR-D APC, longer chassis with no turret, six road wheels, higher roof.
BMD-KShM, command version of above.
BMD-OOB, communications vehicle
BRehM-D, repair and recovery vehicle.
1V118, BMD artillery observation post vehicle.
1V119, BMD artillery fire direction centre vehicle.
BMD-1 with RPV, BMD-KShM is used as launcher for Shmel RPV.
BREM-D, BMD ARV.
BTR-ZD, BTR-D towing or carrying ZU-23 LAAG.
SO-120, BMD chassis is used as basis for SO-120 (or 2S9) 120mm self-propelled howitzer/mortar. covered in Self-propelled Guns and Howitzers section.

STATUS

Production complete. In service with Angola, Armenia, Azerbaijan, Belarus, India, Moldova, Russia, Ukraine and Uzbekistan.

MANUFACTURER

Russian state arsenals, possibly Izhevsk.

KEY RECOGNITION FEATURES

- Same turret as BMP-1 ICV mounted on forward part of hull roof with Sagger ATGW over 73mm gun

- Suspension each side has five small road wheels, drive sprocket rear, idler front, four track-return rollers (first and fourth support inside of track only)

- Pointed nose with trim vane on glacis plate, hull sides vertical with slight chamfer along two-thirds of hull side

Below: BMD-1 Airborne Combat Vehicle (Michael Jerchel)

120mm SO-120 SPH/Mortar (2S9) (Russia)

SPECIFICATIONS

Crew:	4
Armament:	1 x 120mm mortar
Ammunition:	25 x 120mm
Length:	6.02m
Width:	2.63m
Height:	2.3m (with max ground clearance)
Ground clearance (variable):	0.1 to 0.45m
Weight, combat:	8,700kg
Power-to-weight ratio:	27.58hp.tonne
Ground pressure:	0.5kg/cm²
Engine:	Model 5D20 diesel developing 240hp
Maximum road speed:	60km/hr
Maximum water speed:	9km/hr
Maximum road range:	500km
Fuel capacity:	400 lit
Fording:	Amphibious
Vertical obstacle:	0.8m
Trench:	1.8m
Gradient:	60%
Side slope:	33%
Armour:	15mm (max) (hull)
Armour type:	Aluminium
NBC system:	Yes
Night vision equipment:	Yes (infra-red for driver)

DEVELOPMENT

The 120mm SO-120 (industrial number 2S9) Anona (Anemone) self-propelled howitzer/mortar was developed in the early 1980s and first seen in public in 1985. It was originally developed for use by the then Soviet air assault divisions, but has since been deployed with other units.

It is essentially a modified BTR-D air assault transporter, which was itself developed from the BMD-1 airborne combat vehicle, with a modified hull and fitted with a new fully enclosed turret armed with a 120mm 2A51 breech-loaded mortar. Turret traverse is 35° left and right with weapon elevation from -4° to +80°, maximum range of the mortar is 8,855m.

An automatic rammer is fitted which enables a rate of fire of six to eight rounds a minute to be fired and after the breech opens when a round is fired the rammer bleeds compressed air into the chamber to force firing fumes from the muzzle.

The driver is seated at the front of the SO-120 in the centre with the commander being seated to the left, the turret is in the centre with the engine and transmission at the rear. The hydropneumatic suspension system can be adjusted to give a ground clearance from 100 to 450mm. It is also fully amphibious being propelled in the water by two waterjets mounted at the rear of the hull. Before entering the water,

bilge pumps are switched on and two splash vanes are erected to the immediate front of the driver's position.

VARIANTS

There are no known variants of the 2S9 although its turret, in a slightly modified version, is installed on the 2S23 (8x8) self-propelled howitzer/mortar (qv).

The 1V118 artillery observation post vehicle and the 1V119 artillery fire detection vehicle used with the 2S9 are based on chassis of BMD-1 vehicle.

STATUS

Production complete. In service with Azerbaijan, Belarus, Kyrgyzstan, Moldova, Russia, Turkmenistan, Ukraine, Uzbekistan and Vietnam (unconfirmed user).

MANUFACTURER

Russian state factories.

Above left: 120mm SO-120 SPH/mortar (2S9) (Michael Jerchel)

Below: 120mm SO-120 SPH/mortar (2S9)

KEY RECOGNITION FEATURES

- Hull similar to BMD-1 airborne combat vehicle but fitted with larger turret with sloped front, sides curve round to rear, 120mm weapon level with front of hull

- Well-sloped glacis plate, horizontal hull top with driver's hatch in centre, second hatch to his left, turret in centre of hull

- Vertical hull sides and rear with six road wheels either side idler front, drive sprocket rear, five track-return rollers

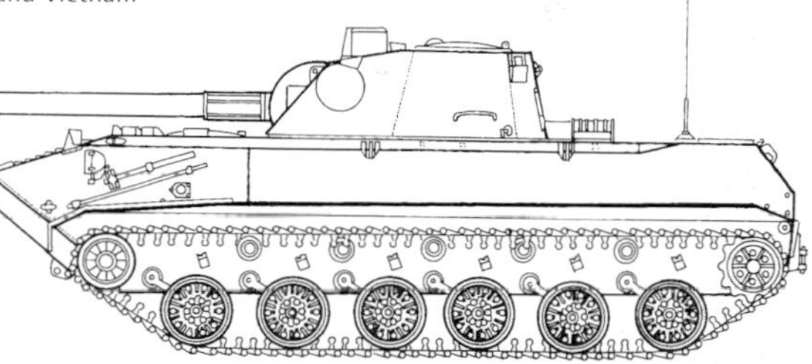

Above: 120mm SO-120 SPH/mortar (2S9) (Steven Zaloga)

M-60P APC (Serbia and Montenegro)

Left: M-60P with 12.7mm MG

Left: Infantry dismount from M-60P

SPECIFICATIONS

Crew:	3 + 10
Armament:	1 x 12.7mm MG (AA), 1 x 7.92mm MG (bow)
Length:	5.02m
Width:	2.77m
Height:	2.385m (with 12.7mm MG), 1.86m (without armament)
Ground clearance:	0.4m
Weight, combat:	11,000kg
Power-to-weight ratio:	12.73hp/tonne
Ground pressure:	0.7kg/cm^2
Engine:	FAMOS 6-cylinder in-line water-cooled diesel developing 140hp
Maximum road speed:	45km/hr
Maximum road range:	400km
Fuel capacity:	150 lit
Fording:	1.35m (still water), 1.25m (running water)
Vertical obstacle:	0.6m
Trench:	2m
Gradient:	60%
Side slope:	40%
Armour:	25mm (maximum)
Armour type:	Steel
NBC system:	None
Night vision equipment:	Yes (infra-red for driver)

DEVELOPMENT

M-60P was developed to meet requirements of Yugoslav Army in late 1960s and made first appearance during parade in 1965. For a short period it was also referred to as M-590. Driver sits

front left with co-driver to his right (who also operates bow mounted 7.92mm MG), engine and transmission below. Commander's cupola is to rear of driver and protrudes slightly over left side of hull, with similar machine gunner's cupola on opposite side. 12.7mm M2 HB MG can be used both in anti-aircraft and ground-to-ground roles, no provision for firing from inside vehicle. 12.7mm M2 HB MG can be dismounted and used in ground role.

The troop compartment is at the rear and infantry enter and leave via two doors in rear, each of which has firing/observation port. Three firing/observation ports in each side of troop compartment. M-60P has no amphibious capability but board mounted on glacis plate deflects water rushing up glacis plate when fording.

KEY RECOGNITION FEATURES

- Well-sloped glacis plate with hatches for driver and assistant driver in upper part, cupola with externally mounted 12.7mm M2 HB MG on right side of hull, commander's cupola opposite

- Troop compartment has vertical sides with top half sloping inwards, vertical hull rear with two doors

- Suspension extends each side of hull with five road wheels, drive sprocket front, idler rear, three track-return rollers. Upper part of track covered by skirt

VARIANTS

Only known variant is M-60PB anti-tank which has twin 82mm recoilless rifles mounted on top left or top right of hull at rear, elevation of +6°, depression of -4°, traverse and elevation both manual. Ten 82mm HEAT projectiles are carried.

Other versions of M-60P are probably in service, such as ambulance, command and radio vehicles.

MANUFACTURERS

Croatian and Yugoslavia state factories.

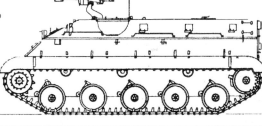

Below: M-60P with 12.7mm MG

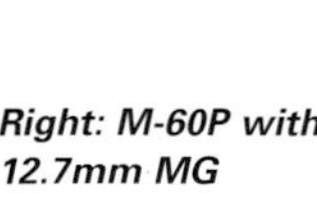

STATUS

Production complete. In service with Bosnia, Croatia and Serbia and Montenegro.

Right: M-60P with 12.7mm MG

BVP M80A Infantry Combat Vehicle

(Serbia and Montenegro)

Above: BVP M80AK which has 30mm cannon

SPECIFICATIONS

Crew:	3 + 7
Armament:	1 x 20mm cannon, 1 x 7.62mm MG (coaxial), 2 x Sagger ATGW
Ammunition:	1,400 x 20mm, 2,000 x 7.62mm, 4 Sagger ATGW
Length:	6.42m
Width:	2.995m
Height:	2.67m (with ATGW)
Ground clearance:	0.4m
Weight, combat:	14,000kg
Power-to-weight ratio:	22.5hp/tonne
Ground pressure:	0.67kg/cm^2
Engine:	FAMOS 10V003 4-stroke 10-cylinder direct-injection diesel developing 315hp at 2,500rpm
Maximum road speed:	64km/hr
Maximum water speed:	7.8km/hr
Maximum road range:	500km
Fuel capacity:	510 lit
Fording:	Amphibious
Vertical obstacle:	0.8m
Trench:	2.4m
Gradient:	66%
Side slope:	55%
Armour:	Classified
Armour type:	Steel
NBC system:	Yes
Night vision equipment:	Yes (commander, gunner and driver)

DEVELOPMENT

The BVP M80A is a further development of M-80 and was seen in public for the first time during a military exhibition in Cairo in late 1984. Main improvement over M-80 is a more powerful diesel engine which gives slightly higher speed and higher power-to-weight ratio.

Overall layout is very similar to earlier M-80 with driver front left, vehicle commander to his rear, engine compartment front right, turret centre and infantry compartment rear. Infantry sit back to back along centre of vehicle, enter and leave via two doors in hull rear each of which has firing port and vision block. In each side of personnel compartment are a further three firing

ports with periscope above for aiming. Over top of troop compartment are two oval roof hatches. One-man turret traverses through 360°. 20mm cannon and 7.62mm MG mounted coaxially right elevate from -5° to +75° under power control, with manual controls provided for emergency use. Twin launcher for Sagger-type wire-guided anti-tank missiles mounted on turret rear (launched from inside turret).

The BVP M80A is fully amphibious, propelled by its tracks. Before entering the water a trim vane is erected on glacis plate and bilge pumps switched on. Engine compartment fire suppression system fitted as standard. Vehicle lays its own smoke screen by injecting diesel fuel into exhaust.

KEY RECOGNITION FEATURES

- Well-sloped glacis plate leads up to hull top which is horizontal all way to rear, vertical back with hull sides above track sloping inwards, two doors in hull rear
- Circular turret with sloping sides slightly to rear of vehicle centre, 20mm cannon in front and twin launcher for Sagger ATGW externally at rear
- Suspension either side has five road wheels, drive sprocket front, idler rear, two track-return rollers. Rollers and upper part of track covered by sheet metal skirt

VARIANTS

BVP M80AK, new one-man turret armed with 30mm cannon, 7.62mm coaxial MG and twin launcher for locally manufactured Sagger ATGW.
BVP M80A1, two-man turret armed with twin 30mm anti-aircraft cannon, prototype only.
BVP M80A KC, company commander's vehicle.
BVP M80A KB, battalion commander's vehicle.
BVP M80A LT anti-tank, new turret with six Sagger ATGW in ready-to-launch position.
BVP M80A Sn, ambulance, has no turret.
SAVA low altitude SAM system.

STATUS

Production complete. In service with Bosnia, Croatia, Macedonia, Serbia and Montenegro and Slovenia.

MANUFACTURERS

Former Yugoslavian state factories.

Below: BVP M80K ICV

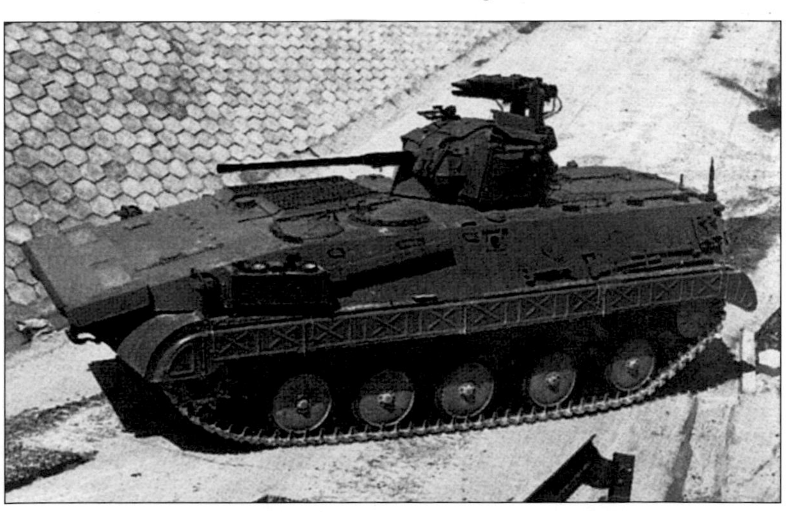

M-80 Mechanised ICV (Serbia and Montenegro)

SPECIFICATIONS

Crew:	3 + 7
Armament:	1 x 20mm, 1 x 7.62mm MG (coaxial), twin launcher for Sagger ATGW
Ammunition:	400 x 20mm, 2,250 x 7.62mm, 4 x Sagger ATGW
Length:	6.4m
Width:	2.59m
Height over ATGW:	2.5m
Height over turret:	2.3m
Height hull roof:	1.8m
Ground clearance:	0.4m
Weight, combat:	13,700kg
Weight, empty:	11,700kg
Power-to-weight ratio:	18.97hp/tonne
Ground pressure:	0.64kg/cm^2
Engine:	HS 115-2 V-8 water-cooled turbo diesel developing 260hp at 3,000rpm
Maximum road speed:	60km/hr
Maximum water speed:	7.5km/hr
Maximum road range:	500km
Fuel capacity:	Not available
Fording:	Amphibious
Vertical obstacle:	0.8m
Trench:	2.2m
Gradient:	60%
Side slope:	30%
Armour:	30mm (maximum) (estimate)
Armour type:	Steel
NBC system:	Yes
Night vision equipment:	Yes (infra-red for commander, gunner, driver)

DEVELOPMENT

M-80 was developed in the early 1970s and seen in public for the first time in May 1975. The vehicle was originally referred to by the Yugoslavs as the M-980, but this was subsequently changed to the M-80. Driver sits front left with commander to his rear, engine compartment to right. Turret is in centre with 20mm cannon and 7.62mm coaxial MG which elevates from -5° to +75°, turret traverses 360°. Mounted externally on right side of turret at rear is launcher with two Sagger-type wire-guided ATGWs which have maximum range of 3,000m. Troop compartment is at rear, three men sit each side back to back, each with firing port and periscope above. Two roof hatches above troop compartment with periscope above. Over top of troop compartment are two roof hatches hinged in centre. M-80 is fully amphibious, propelled by its tracks. Before entering the water the trim vane is erected and bilge pumps switched on.

VARIANTS

No known variants. There is a separate entry for the very similar M80A.

STATUS

Production complete. In service with Bosnia, Croatia, Macedonia, Serbia and Montenegro and Slovenia.

MANUFACTURERS

Former Yugoslavian state arsenals.

KEY RECOGNITION FEATURES

- Well-sloped glacis plate with trim vane folded back on lower part, horizontal hull top to rear, hull rear slopes slightly inwards with two doors that open on outside

- Circular turret with sloping sides slightly to rear of vehicle centre with 20mm cannon in front, 7.62mm MG coaxial to right, twin launcher for Sagger ATGW right rear

- Suspension either side has five road wheels, drive sprocket front, idler rear, two track-return rollers. Rollers and upper part of track covered by sheet metal skirt. Hull sides at rear slope inwards, firing ports in sides and periscopes above

Left & below: M-80 (Roderick de Normann)

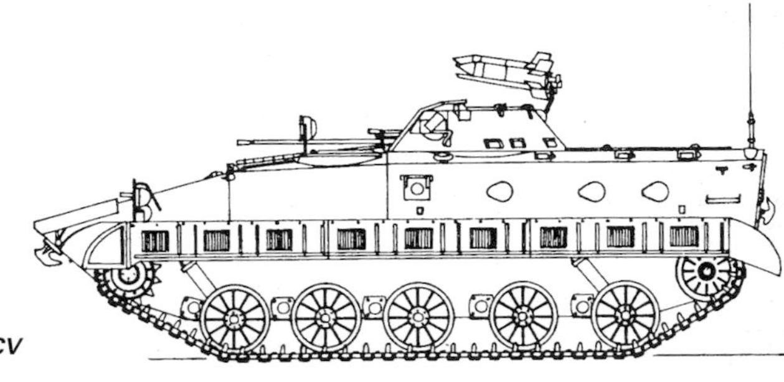

Right: M-80 MICV

Singapore Technologies Kinetics Bionix 25 IFV (Singapore)

SPECIFICATIONS

Crew:	3 + 7
Armament:	1 x 25mm cannon, 1 x 7.62mm MG (co-axial), 1 x 7.62mm MG (anti-aircraft), 2 x 3 smoke grenade launchers
Ammunition:	Classified
Length hull:	5.92m
Width:	2.70m
Height:	2.57m
Ground clearance:	0.475m
Weight, combat:	23,000kg
Weight, empty:	21,000kg
Power-to-weight ratio:	20 hp/tonne
Ground pressure:	0.76 kg/cm²
Engine:	Detroit Diesel Model 6V-92TA diesel developing 475 hp at 2,400 rpm
Maximum road speed:	70km/h
Maximum road range:	415km
Fuel capacity:	527 lit
Fording:	1m
Vertical obstacle:	0.60m
Trench:	2.0m
Gradient:	60%
Side slope:	30%
Armour:	Classified
Armour type:	Steel plus applique
NBC system:	No
Night vision equipment:	Yes

DEVELOPMENT

The Bionix 25 IFV (infantry fighting vehicle) was developed to meet the operational requirements of the Singapore Armed Forces by Singapore Technologies Kinetics. Following trials with prototypes and pre-production vehicles it was accepted for service and first production vehicles were completed in 1997.

The driver is seated towards the front of the hull on the left side with the engine compartment to his right, turret in the centre and troop compartment at the rear.

The power operated turret is armed with The ATK Gun Systems Company stabilised 25mm M242 cannon with a 7.62machine gun being mounted coaxial. Turret traverse is 360 degrees with the gunner being provided with a day/thermal sight. A 7.62mm machine gun is mounted on the turret roof for air defence purposes.

The infantry enter and leave via a power

operated ramp in the hull rear and a 7.62mm machine gun can be mounted over the top of the troop compartment.

KEY RECOGNITION FEATURES

- Well-sloped glacis plate with driver on left side leads up to horizontal hull top that extends to the rear. Large turret with pointed front and sloping sides in centre of hull. To rear of turret is roof hatch that opens to rear

- Vertical hull rear with ramp, hull sides vertical with each side having six road wheels with drive sprocket at front, idler at rear and return rollers

VARIANTS

Singapore Armed Forces also use the **Bionix 40/50** which is fitted with a locally developed one person cupola armed with a locally developed 40mm grenade launcher and 12.7mm machine gun. This cupola is also fitted to some of the upgraded M113 series APCs used by Singapore.
AVLB – in service.
ARV – in service.
Low profile APC – prototype.

STATUS

Production. In service with Singapore.

MANUFACTURER

Singapore Technologies Kinetics.

Left: Bionix 40/50 IFV

Right: Bionix 25 IFV

Below: Bionix 25 IFV (Terry J Gander)

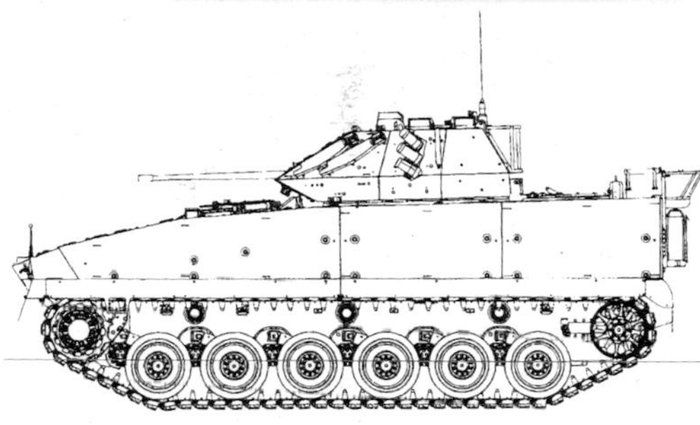

Singapore Technologies Kinetics All Terrain Tracked Carrier (Singapore)

Above: All Terrain Tracked Carrier in APC role (STK)

SPECIFICATIONS

Crew:	6 + 10
Armament:	1 x 7.62mm MG (optional)
Ammunition:	1,000 x 7.62mm
Length hull:	8.6m
Width:	2.3m
Height:	2.2m
Ground clearance:	Not available
Weight, combat:	16,000kg
Weight, empty:	11,400kg
Power-to-weight ratio:	21.87hp/tonne
Ground pressure:	Not available
Engine:	Caterpillar 3126B turbo-charged and charged air cooled diesel developing 350bhp at 2,400rpm
Maximum road speed:	60km/h
Maximum water speed:	5km/h
Range:	Not available
Fuel capacity:	Not available
Fording:	Amphibious
Vertical obstacle:	0.60m
Trench:	1.5m
Gradient:	60%
Side slope:	30%
Armour:	Classified
Armour type:	Steel
NBC system:	Optional
Night vision equipment:	Optional

DEVELOPMENT

The All Terrain Tracked Carrier (ATTC), also called the Bronco, was developed by Singapore Technologies Kinetics to meet the operational requirements of the Singapore Armed Forces for a vehicle with armour protection and increased payload over the current in service Bv 206 vehicles.

Development of the ATTC commenced in the mid-1990s and the first automotive test bed was completed in 1997 with two pre-production vehicles following in 1999. One of these was in the APC role and the other in the cargo carrying role. First production vehicles were delivered to the Singapore Armed Forces in 2001.

The ATTC consists of two full tracked units which are joined together by a special hydraulic

articulated joint. The units are made of all welded steel to which a special passive armour package developed by IBD of Germany can be fitted. The front unit has seats for six people including the driver while the rear unit has seats for 10 people.

The vehicle is fully amphibious being propelled in the water by its tracks. The only preperation required is to activate the two electrically operated bilge pumps installed in the front and rear units. Maximum payload of the front unit is 1,200kg while for the rear unit it is 3,000kg. It is fully air transportable in a Lockheed Martin C-130 Hercules transport aircraft.

Standard equipment for the ATTC includes an air conditioning system in the front and rear units and there is numerous optional equipment as well as various weapon stations such as roof mounted 7.62mm machine gun and grenade launchers.

VARIANTS

In addition to the APC version, the Singapore Armed Forces have procured at least three variants of the ATTC, armoured engineer, ambulance and resupply.The latter version is fitted with a mechanical handling system that can carry pods of fuel or cargo. Also used as a test bed for a 120mm mortar and a new rapid coupling concept.

STATUS

Production. In service with Singapore.

KEY RECOGNITION FEATURES

• Similar in appearance to the Swedish Hägglunds BvS 10 and Bv 206S armoured personnel carriers (APC) (qv) which also consists of two full tracked units joined togther by a special articulated joint

• The front unit has six road wheels with the last being the idler and has the drive sprocket at the front and return rollers that support inside of the track only. The rear unit also has six road wheels with the drive sprocket at the front and return rollers that support inside of track only

• Vertical hull front with bonnet sloping up to two piece windscreen. Two forward opening doors in either side with rectangular window in upper part. Horizontal roof with hatches and vertical hull rear. Rear unit has vertical sides and rear in which is a large door that opens to the right and also has roof hatches

MANUFACTURER

Singapore Technologies Kinetics, Singapore.

Below: All Terrain Tracked Carrier in cargo role (STK)

Daewoo Korean Infantry Fighting Vehicle (South Korea

SPECIFICATIONS

Crew:	3 + 9
Armament:	1 x 12.7mm MG, 1 x 7.62mm MG, 1 x 6 smoke grenade dischargers
Length:	5.486m (overall)
Width:	2.846m
Height:	1.93m (hull top), 2.518m (MG shield)
Ground clearance:	0.41m
Weight, combat:	12,900kg
Weight, empty:	10,700kg
Power-to-weight ratio:	21.70hp/tonne
Ground pressure:	0.63kg/cm^2
Engine:	MAN D-2848T V-8 diesel developing 280hp at 2,300rpm
Maximum road speed:	74km/hr
Maximum water speed:	6km/hr
Maximum cruising range:	480km
Fuel capacity:	400 lit
Fording:	Amphibious
Vertical obstacle:	0.64m
Trench:	1.68m
Gradient:	60%
Side slope:	30%
Armour:	Classified
Armour type:	Aluminium and steel
NBC system:	Yes
Night vision equipment:	Yes (passive for commander and driver)

DEVELOPMENT

Korean Infantry Fighting Vehicle was developed to meet requirements of South Korean Army by Special Products Division of Daewoo Heavy Industries with hull very similar to American Armored Infantry Fighting Vehicle. KIFV has MAN engine, British David Brown Engineering T-300 fully automatic transmission and different roof arrangement.

Commander has pintle-mounted 7.62mm M60 MG which cannot be fired from inside vehicle, gunner has full front, side and rear protection for 12.7mm M2 HB MG. Mounted on glacis plate is bank of six electrically operated smoke grenade dischargers firing forwards. KIFV is fully amphibious. Late production vehicles are known as K200A1 series and have different powerpack.

VARIANTS

More recently Daewoo has offered an improved version of the KIFV with a new powerpack consisting of the D2848T turbocharged diesel

eveloping 350hp coupled to an Allison X-200-5D eries fully automatic transmission.

:0mm SPAAG, basic KIFV fitted with locally roduced Vulcan 20mm anti-aircraft gun system hat is made in South Korea.

Aortar carrier, two versions, 81mm and 107mm.

Recovery, fitted with roof-mounted hydraulic rane and a winch for recovery operations.

OW anti-tank, can be fitted with various TOW nti-tank systems including the Norwegian one-nan turret with two TOW ATGW in ready-to-aunch position.

IBC reconnaissance, no weapons stations and itted with a complete range of NBC detection ystems.

:ommand, would have higher roof similar to that f the American M577 vehicle.

KEY RECOGNITION FEATURES

- Well-sloped glacis plate with trim vane, driver front left, commander's cupola with external 7.62mm MG to rear of driver, gunner's cupola with shield, 12.7mm MG right

- Troop compartment rear with single roof hatch, ramp in hull rear, two firing ports with vision block in each side of troop compartment

- Suspension either side has five road wheels, drive sprocket front, idler rear, no track-return rollers

JEW GENERATION

n 1992 the company unveiled a new family of ehicles with a new and more powerful owerpack. These include an ammunition esupply vehicle and a twin 30mm self-ropelled anti-aircraft gun system. hese are both in volume production nd have a larger and different hassis than the KIFV.

STATUS

Production complete. In service with outh Korean Army and Malaysia.

MANUFACTURER

Daewoo Heavy Industries, Seoul, South Korea.

Above: Korean Infantry Fighting Vehicle without armament

Top left: Korean Infantry Fighting Vehicle

Right: Recovery version of Korean Infantry Fighting Vehicle

ASCOD MICV (Spain/Austria)

SPECIFICATIONS

Crew:	3 + 8
Armament:	1 x 25mm cannon, 1 x 7.62mm MG, 2 x 6 smoke grenade launchers
Ammunition:	402 x 25mm, 2,900 x 7.62mm
Length:	6.986m
Width:	3.15m
Height:	1.775m (hull top), 2.653m (overall)
Ground clearance:	0.45m
Weight, combat:	28,000kg
Power-to-weight ratio:	21.8hp/tonne
Engine:	MTU 8V 183 TE22 8 V-90 V-8 diesel developing 600 hp at 2300rpm
Maximum road speed:	70km/h
Maximum road range:	600km
Fuel capacity:	860 lit
Fording:	1.2m
Vertical obstacle:	0.95m
Trench:	2.50m
Gradient:	75%
Side slope:	40%
Armour:	Classified
Armour type:	Steel
NBC:	Yes
Night vision equipment:	Yes

DEVELOPMENT

The ASCOD (Austrian Spanish Co-Operative Development) mechanised infantry combat vehicle has been jointly developed by Steyr-Daimler-Puch of Austria and Santa Barbara Sistemas of Spain with the latter country placing the first production order for a total of 144 vehicles under the local name of Pizarro early in 1996. Austrian Army placed an order for 112 vehicles under name Ulan with first four vehicles being delivered in mid-2002.

The driver is seated at front left with the powerpack to his right, turret in the centre and the troop compartment at the rear. The infantry enter and leave via a large door in the hull rear that opens to the right.

The two man power operated turret is armed with a stabilised Mauser 30mm MK 30-2 cannon with a 7.62mm machine gun being mounted co-axial to the left. Turret traverse is through a full 360° with weapon elevation from -10 to +50°.

Standard equipment includes a NBC protection system, heater, applique armour and a computerised day/night fire control system.

ARIANTS

lone of these is currently in production.)
izarro with ERA – Spanish Army only.
nti-tank with various ATGW.
rmoured recovery and repair vehicle.
rmoured command vehicle.
rmoured engineer vehicle.
rmoured mortar carrier.
ICV, various alternative weapon fits.
ght tank with 105mm gun.
AM system.
PAAG.

TATUS

roduction. In service with Austria (Ulan) nd Spain (Pizarro).

IANUFACTURERS

teyr-Daimler-Puch, Vienna, Austria; anta Barbara Sistemas, Madrid, pain.

KEY RECOGNITION FEATURES

- Hull has vertical sides with well-sloped glacis plate leading up to horizontal hull top which extends right to rear of vehicle. Hull rear vertical but large stowage bin either side of rear door
- Driver front left with powerpack to right, turret in centre of hull and offset to right
- Suspension either side consists of seven road wheels, drive sprocket front, idler rear and track return rollers, upper part of suspension covered by wavy skirt

op left: Ulan MICV

ight: Pizarro MICV

elow right: Pizarro MICV

elow: Pizarro MICV

Hägglunds Vehicle Pbv 302 APC (Sweden)

Above: Pbv 302 APC (Richard Stickland)

SPECIFICATIONS

Crew:	2 + 10
Armament:	1 x 20mm cannon, 1 x 6 smoke grenade dischargers, 2 x Lyran launchers
Ammunition:	505 x 20mm
Length:	5.35m
Width:	2.86m
Height:	2.5m (turret top), 1.9m (hull top)
Ground clearance:	0.4m
Weight, combat:	13,500kg
Power-to-weight ratio:	20.74hp/tonne
Ground pressure:	0.6kg/cm²
Engine:	Volvo-Penta model THD 100B horizontal 4-stroke turbocharged diesel developing 280hp at 2,200rpm
Maximum road speed:	66km/hr
Maximum water speed:	8km/hr
Maximum road range:	300km
Fuel capacity:	285 lit
Fording:	Amphibious
Vertical obstacle:	0.61m
Trench:	1.8m
Gradient:	60%
Side slope:	40%
Armour:	Classified
Armour type:	Steel
NBC system:	None
Night vision equipment:	None

DEVELOPMENT

Pbv 302 (Pansarbandvagn 302) was developed by the then Hägglund and Söner to meet requirements of Swedish Army with prototype completed in 1962 and production from 1965 to 1971. Hull is all-welded steel armour with spaced armour in the sides for increased protection. Engine is mounted under floor of vehicle with crew compartment front and infantry compartment rear. Ten infantrymen sit five each side facing, and enter and leave via two doors in rear. They can fire small arms via roof hatches.

Turret is manually operated and armed with 20mm cannon with elevation of +50° and

epression of -10°, turret traverses 360°, cannon an be fed by belt containing 135 rounds of HE mmunition or box magazine holding 10 rounds f AP ammunition. Pbv 302 is fully amphibious, ropelled by its tracks. Before entering the water rim vanes are erected at front of vehicle and ilge pumps switched on.

Further development resulted in the Pbv 302 lk 2 and the Product Improved Pb 302, but none f these entered production. Hägglunds and Söner s now known as BAE Systems Land Systems weden – Hägglunds. For operations in the former ugoslavia, some Pbv 302s were fitted with dditional passive armour protection.

ARIANTS

tripbv 3021 armoured command vehicle has our radio antennas compared to Pbv 302's two, nd additional communications equipment.
pbv 3022 is an armoured observation post ehicle and has commander's hatch replaced by upola with rangefinding devices, three radio ntennas, additional buoyancy aids on trim vanes.
plpbv 3023 is armoured fire direction post ehicle with four antennas and fire-control/communications equipment inside.
lpbv 3024 – radio relay station.

KEY RECOGNITION FEATURES

- Hull front slopes to rear and curves to join vertical sides, hull rear also vertical and curves to join sides, twin doors rear, hatches over rear troop compartment
- Driver's cupola at front with commander's cupola right and large 20mm gun turret left
- Suspension either side has five large road wheels, drive sprocket front, idler rear, no track-return rollers

STATUS

Production complete. In service with Swedish Army only.

MANUFACTURER

BAE Systems Land Systems – Hägglunds AB, Örnsköldsvik, Sweden.

Below: Pbv 302 APC with applique armour added to hull and turret (Michael Jerchel)

Combat Vehicle 90 (Stridsfordon 90) (Sweden)

Above: CV 9030CH

SPECIFICATIONS (CV 9040)

Crew:	3 + 8
Armament:	1 x 40mm, 1 x 7.62mm MG (coaxial), 2 x 3 smoke grenade dischargers
Length:	6.471m
Width:	3.003m
Height:	2.5m (turret roof), 1.73m (hull top)
Ground clearance:	0.45m
Weight, combat:	22,800kg
Power-to-weight ratio:	24.12hp/tonne
Ground pressure:	0.53kg/cm^2
Engine:	Scania DS14 diesel developing 550hp
Maximum road speed:	70km/hr
Maximum road range:	600km
Fuel capacity:	525 lit
Fording:	1.40m
Vertical obstacle:	1.0m
Trench:	2.4m
Gradient:	60%
Side slope:	40%
Armour:	Classified
Armour type:	Steel
NBC system:	Yes
Night vision equipment:	Yes (passive)

DEVELOPMENT

In 1985 HB Utveckling, a small holding company jointly established by Bofors Defence and Hägglunds and Söner (now BAE Systems Land Systems – Hägglunds) was awarded a contract by the Swedish Defence Material Administration for the construction of five prototypes of the Stridsfordon 90 (or Combat Vehicle 90) family of armoured vehicles for the Swedish Army. Before this, under separate contracts, an automotive test rig and a two-man 40mm turret had been funded. In 1986 a further contract was awarded for four two-man turrets, three with the 40mm cannon and one with a 25mm cannon.

Early in 1991 the first production order was placed for the Combat Vehicle 90 (CV 9040) with first production vehicles delivered in October 1993. Hägglunds built chassis which were then sent to the now Bofors Defence which built the 40mm turrets and integrated this with the chassis and then delivered the complete system to the Swedish Army.

The driver is seated at the front of the vehicle on the left side with the powerpack to his right, the two-man turret is in the centre with the troop compartment at the rear. The infantry are seated either side facing inwards and enter and leave via a door in the rear. Roof hatches are also provided but there is no provision for the infantry to use their weapons from within the vehicle.

The 40mm gun has an elevation of +35° and a depression of -8° with turret traverse a full 360°, the CV 9040 has fully powered traverse and elevation with manual controls for emergency use. Some Swedish CV 9040s have been fitted with additional armour.

VARIANTS

CV 9025 IFV, two man turret, 25mm cannon, prototype only.
TriAD 40mm self-propelled anti-aircraft gun, Swedish Army.
CV 90 Forward Command Vehicle, Swedish Army.
CV 90 Forward Observation Vehicle, Swedish Army.
CV 90 Armoured Recovery Vehicle, Swedish Army.
CV 90 anti-tank, concept.
CV 9030N, two man 30mm turret, for Norway.
CV 9030FIN, for Finland.
CV 9030CH, for Switzerland.
CV 90120-T, 120mm light tank, trials only.
CV 90 AMOS, twin 120mm mortar, trials only.

STATUS

Production. In service with Finland (30mm), Norway (30mm), Sweden (40mm) and Switzerland (30mm).

MANUFACTURER

Swedish vehicles were built by Bofors and Hägglunds while all export vehicles have been built by Hägglunds.

KEY RECOGNITION FEATURES

- Hull has well-sloped glacis plate with turret in centre that is offset slightly to left of hull. The sides and rear of hull are vertical with large door in hull rear

- Suspension either side consists of seven road wheels very close together, drive sprocket front, idler rear and upper part of suspension covered by skirt with wavy bottom

- Turret of 40mm version has sloped front, vertical sides and rear, 40mm cannon has distinctive muzzle with large gunner's sight in the right of turret roof

Above right: CV 9040 IFV with extra armour

Right: TriAD 40mm SPAAG

Hägglunds BvS 10 APC (Sweden)

Above: BvS 10 armed with 7.62mm MG in service with Royal Marines (MoD/CCR)

SPECIFICATIONS

Crew:	4 + 10
Armament:	1 x 7.62mm MG (see text)
Ammunition:	1000 x 7.62mm
Length gun forwards:	not applicable
Length hull:	7.55m
Width:	2.19m
Height:	2.20m
Ground clearance:	0.35m
Weight, combat:	10,500 to 11,500kg
Weight, empty:	7,760kg
Power-to-weight ratio:	23.80hp/tonne
Ground pressure:	Not available
Engine:	Cummins 5.9-litre 6-cylinder in-line diesel developing 250hp with growth potential to 300hp
Maximum road speed:	65km/h
Maximum road range:	300km
Fuel capacity:	Not available
Fording:	Amphibious
Vertical obstacle:	Not available
Trench:	Not available
Gradient:	100%
Side slope:	40%
Armour:	Steel
Armour type:	Classified
NBC system:	Optional
Night vision equipment:	Optional

DEVELOPMENT

The BvS 10 articulated armoured personnel carried was developed as a private venture by Hägglunds based on their experience in the design, development and production of the earlier and smaller Bv 206S articulated tracked all terrain vehicle.

The main advantage of the BvS 10 is its larger size which enables it to carry out more battlefield roles as well as having an increased payload.

The vehicle was shown for the first time in 1998 and in 1999 it was selected by the UK Royal Marines to meet its requirement for an All-Terrain Vehicle (Protected). Three versions have been acquired: Troop Carrier Vehicle (TCV), Command Post Vehicle (CPV) and Recovery Vehicle (RV).

The BvS 10 consists of two units coupled together by a special articulation system. The powerpack is installed in the front unit which has

as seats for the driver and three passengers. The ear powered unit has 10m³ of cargo space and an carry up to 10 people and their equipment.

The baseline vehicle provides the occupants ith protection from 7.62mm armour-piercing ttack but higher levels of protection are vailable.

The BvS 10 is fully amphibious being propelled 1 the water by its tracks and a wide range of ptional equipment is available including winch, ir conditioning system, power take off, 300 hp ngine and engine pre-heater. A 7.62mm or 2.7mm machine gun can be mounted on the oof of the front unit if required. Prime ontractor is the now BAE Systems Land Systems · Hägglunds.

VARIANTS

'he BvS 10 is of modular construction enabling it o underake a wide range of battlefield missions ind unit can be modified to accept a wide range of specialist bodies.

STATUS

n production. In service with UK Royal Marines.

MANUFACTURER

3AE Systems Land System – Hägglunds AB, Örnsköldsvik, Sweden.

KEY RECOGNITION FEATURES

- The BvS 10 is similiar in appearance to the older Hägglunds Bv 206S APC covered in the following entry but is larger

- It consists of two full-tracked units joined together with both units having wide rubber band type tracks. Front unit has six road wheels with last road wheel acting as idler, drive sprocket at front and track return rollers. Rear unit also has six road wheels with return rollers

- Front unit has almost vertical hull front and bonnet that slopes up to the two part windscreen, horizontal roof, vertical sides with two doors in each side, forward one has window in upper part

- Rear unit has vertical front, sides and rear with horizontal roof with one large single door in rear

Below: BvS 10 (Christopher F Foss)

Hägglunds Bv 206S APC (Sweden)

SPECIFICATIONS

Crew:	4 + 8
Armament:	1 x 12.7mm MG (typical)
Length:	6.92m
Width:	2m
Height:	2.1m without armament
Ground clearance:	0.35m
Weight, combat:	7,000kg
Weight, empty:	5,330kg
Power-to-weight ratio:	19.42hp/tonne
Engine:	Steyr M16 6-cylinder in-line diesel developing 186hp at 4,300rpm
Maximum road speed:	52km/hr
Maximum road range:	300km
Fording:	Amphibious
Vertical obstacle:	Not available
Trench:	Not available
Gradient:	100%
Side slope:	60%
Armour:	Classified
Armour type:	Steel
NBC system:	Optional
Night vision equipment:	Optional

DEVELOPMENT

The Bv 206S is the Hägglunds Bv 206 all terrain vehicle (of which over 11,000 have been made) fitted with two new all-welded steel bodies to protect the occupants from small arms fire and shell splinters.

The front unit has the engine at the front and seats for the commander and driver in the centre, plus two for passengers in the back. The rear unit has seats for eight people, four down either side. The units are linked by a steering unit. Steering is accomplished by two hydraulic cylinders, servo-controlled from a conventional steering wheel.

The Bv 206S is fully amphibious, propelled in the water by its tracks. Before entering the water, a trim vane is erected. A wide range of equipment can be fitted, including an NBC system, winch and night vision aids. A ring-mounted machine gun can be carried on the front unit's roof.

VARIANTS

The Bv 206S can be adapted for use as an ambulance, command post or weapons carrier.

STATUS

In production. In service with France, Germany, Italy, Spain and Sweden.

MANUFACTURER

BAE Systems Land Systems – Hägglunds, Örnsköldsvik, Sweden

KEY RECOGNITION FEATURES

- Unique vehicle consisting of two fully-tracked units joined together. Both units have wide rubber band type tracks
- Front unit has vertical hull front and bonnet that slopes up to the two-part windscreen.
- Front unit has single side door with window above in each side, smaller window to rear. Rear unit normally has two rectangular windows with large door at the back.

Left: Bv 206S

Below: Bv 206S

Bottom: Bv 206S in ambulance role

FNSS Savunma Sistemleri Turkish Infantry Fighting Vehicle (Turkey)

SPECIFICATIONS

Crew:	2 + 11
Armament:	1 x 25mm cannon, 1 x 7.62mm MG, 2 x 3 smoke grenade dischargers
Ammunition:	230 x 30mm, 1610 x 7.62mm
Length:	5.26m
Width:	2.82m
Height:	2.01m (turret roof), 2.62m (hull roof)
Ground clearance:	0.43m
Weight, combat:	13,687kg
Power-to-weight ratio:	21.91bhp/tonne
Ground pressure:	0.67kg/cm^2
Engine:	Detroit Diesel Model 6V-53T developing 300 hp
Maximum road speed:	65km/hr
Maximum water speed:	6.3km/hr
Maximum road range:	490km
Fuel capacity:	416 lit
Fording:	Amphibious
Vertical obstacle:	0.74m
Trench:	1.83m
Gradient:	60%
Side slope:	30%
Armour:	Classified
Armour type:	Aluminium/Steel
NBC system:	Optional
Night vision equipment:	Optional

DEVELOPMENT

The Turkish Infantry Fighting Vehicle has been developed by FNSS Savunma Sistemleri as a joint venture for the Turkish army. It is based on the United Defense Armored Infantry Fighting Vehicle (qv). A total of 1998 vehicles were initially built, of which 650 were the AIFV version fitted with a one-man power-operated turret with a 25mm cannon and 7.62mm coaxial machine gun. The vehicle is fully amphibious, propelled in the water by its tracks. One version of AIFV has French Dragar 25mm turret while other has United Defense 25mm turret.

VARIANTS

AAPC (Advanced Armored Personnel Carrier) with 12.7mm machine gun turret.

81mm mortar carrier.

120mm mortar carrier (private venture from TDA of France).

ATGW carrier (two TOWs in launch position).

JAE has upgraded versions including engineering squad vehicle, repair/recovery and artillery upport.
Armoured Combat Vehicle – Stretched, has six road wheels either side.

STATUS

Production. Malaysia (10 variants including 25mm), Turkey and United Arab Emirates (various models).

MANUFACTURER

FNSS Savunma Sistemleri AS, Ankara, Turkey.

Left: AIFV

Below: UAE vehicle with external storage

Bottom left: Mortar carrier version

Bottom right: ATGW carrier as used by Malaysia

KEY RECOGNITION FEATURES

- Glacis plate with trim vane at 45°, hull roof horizontal at rear, angled downwards with hull rear sloping inwards

- Driver front left, commander rear, with engine compartment on right. Turret has vertical sides and rear, offset to right of hull. Large ramp in hull rear

- Hull sides vertical with curve to top, upper part of rear troop compartment slopes inwards, two firing ports with vision block above in each side. Suspension has five road wheels, drive sprocket at front, idler in rear. No track-return rollers.

Warrior Mechanised Combat Vehicle (UK)

Above: Warrior MCV with applique armour

SPECIFICATIONS

Crew:	3 + 7
Armament:	1 x 30mm cannon, 1 x 7.62mm MG, 2 x 4 smoke grenade dischargers
Ammunition:	250 x 30mm, 2,000 x 7.62mm
Length:	6.34m
Width:	3.034m
Height:	2.791m (turret roof), 1.93m (hull roof)
Ground clearance:	0.49m
Weight, combat:	28,000kg
Power-to-weight ratio:	19.6bhp/tonne
Ground pressure:	0.65kg/cm^2
Engine:	Perkins CV8 TCA V-8 diesel developing 550hp at 2,300rpm
Maximum road speed:	75km/hr
Maximum road range:	660km
Fuel capacity:	770 lit
Fording:	1.3m
Vertical obstacle:	0.75m
Trench:	2.5m
Gradient:	60%
Side slope:	40%
Armour:	Classified
Armour type:	Aluminium (hull), steel (turret)
NBC system:	Yes
Night vision equipment:	Yes (passive for commander, gunner and driver)

DEVELOPMENT

Warrior (previously known as MCV-80) was developed from mid-1970s by GKN Defence (today BAE Systems Land Systems) for the British Army. Following prototype trials it was accepted for service in November 1984 with first production vehicles completed in December 1986. The British Army took delivery of 789 Warrior MCV and variants with final deliveries in 1995.

In 1993 Kuwait placed an order for 254 Desert Warrior vehicles and variants with the first of these being completed in 1994. Desert Warrior has American turret armed with 25mm cannon, 7.62mm coaxial machine gun and a launcher for TOW ATGW either side of turret. It also has a different armour package and an air conditioning

ystem. Kuwaiti variants include command ehicles, repair and recovery and high mobility railers. For operations in the Middle East the Varrior was fitted with additional passive armour rotection.

Driver sits front left with engine to right, two-nan turret in centre and troop compartment rear.

'ARIANTS

he British Army has following versions: section ehicle with two-man turret armed with 30mm RARDEN cannon and 7.62mm coaxial MG, ommand vehicle (three versions, platoon, ompany and battalion all with same turret as ection vehicle but with different ommunications equipment), Warrior Repair and Recovery Vehicle, Warrior Combat Repair Vehicle, Varrior Mechanised Artillery Observation Vehicle, Battery Command Vehicle (for Royal Artillery) and MILAN ATGW carrier. Export models include: Desert Fighting Vehicle with firing ports, 81mm nortar carrier, fitted with various anti-tank nissile systems, anti-aircraft, load carrier and itted with other turrets such as 25mm or 90mm. Varrior 2000 is latest export model with 30mm urret fitted.

STATUS

Production complete. In service with Kuwait Desert Warrior) and UK.

MANUFACTURER

BAE Systems Land Systems, Telford, Shropshire, JK.

KEY RECOGNITION FEATURES

- High hull with well-sloped glacis plate, driver's hatch in upper left side and louvres to right, horizontal hull top with turret centre, vertical hull rear with stowage boxes each side of single door. No firing ports

- Turret has vertical sides with long barrel 30mm RARDEN cannon with flash eliminator and mounted in external mantlet. Commander and gunner have hatches opening to rear and distinctive roof-mounted periscopes to their front, stowage basket on turret rear

- Troop compartment at rear has chamfered sides with stowage basket above. Suspension each side has six road wheels, drive sprocket front, idler rear and three track-return rollers covered by skirt

Above: Desert Warrior

Above: Warrior MAOV

Above: Warrior MCV (Richard Stickland)

FV432 APC (UK)

Above: FV432 in armoured personnel carrier configuration (Christopher F Foss)

SPECIFICATIONS

Crew:	2 + 10
Armament:	1 x 7.62mm MG, 2 x 3 smoke grenade dischargers
Ammunition:	1,600 x 7.62mm
Length:	5.251m
Width:	2.8m
Height including MG:	2.286m
Height hull top:	1.879m
Ground clearance:	0.406m
Weight, combat:	15,280kg
Weight, empty:	13,740kg
Power-to-weight ratio:	15.7bhp/tonne
Ground pressure:	0.78kg/cm^2
Engine:	Rolls-Royce K60 No 4 Mk 4F 2-stroke 6-cylinder multi-fuel developing 240bhp at 3,750rpm
Maximum road speed:	52.2km/hr
Maximum road range:	480km
Fuel capacity:	454 lit
Fording:	1.066m
Vertical obstacle:	0.609m
Trench:	2.05m
Gradient:	60%
Side slope:	30%
Armour:	12mm (maximum)
Armour type:	Steel
NBC system:	Yes
Night vision equipment:	Yes (passive for driver)

DEVELOPMENT

FV432 series was developed to meet requirements of British Army in the late 1950s with first prototype completed in 1961. Production undertaken by Sankey from 1962 with first production vehicles completed in 1963 and over 3,000 built by production completion in 1972. The FV432 has now been supplemented by the Warrior MCV although the FV432 is expected to remain in service in specialised roles such as mortar, ambulance and signals for many years.

FV432 is all-welded steel with engine front left, driver front right and hatch to his rear, 7.62mm GPMG is normally mounted on roof. Troops sit on bench seats, five each side facing, and enter via large door in rear. Four-part circular roof hatch over top of troop compartment.

VARIANTS

Ambulance model is unarmed and carries both seated and stretcher patients.
Command, has extensive communications equipment and optional tent erected at rear.
Maintenance carrier (FV434) has different hull and crane for removing powerpacks in field.
Mortar carrier has turntable-mounted 81mm mortar in rear firing through roof.
Minelayer, tows Bar minelayer rear.
Recovery, has winch mounted in vehicle rear.
Artillery command has Battlefield Artillery Target Engagement System (BATES). Royal Artillery also uses it with sound ranging system.
FV432 with Fox turret, training role.
FV439 is specialised Royal Signals vehicle. Some of the FV438 Swingfire ATGW vehicles were converted into Wavell electronics carriers.

STATUS

Production complete. In service with UK.

MANUFACTURER

The FV432 was originally built by Sankey which has been taken over or merged numerous times. The facility where it was built in Telford, Shropshire, is now part of BAE Systems Land Systems.

KEY RECOGNITION FEATURES

- Glacis plate slopes at about 60° with horizontal hull roof extending to rear, vertical hull rear with large door opening left

- Driver front right, engine to his left and machine gunner to his rear, troop compartment rear with four-part circular roof hatch above, two parts opening left and right. Vertical hull sides with exhaust pipe on left side and NBC pack protruding on right side

- Suspension each side has five road wheels, drive sprocket front, idler rear, two track-return rollers. Upper part sometimes covered by skirt

Below: FV432 with BATES (Richard Stickland)

Alvis Stormer APC (UK)

SPECIFICATIONS

Crew:	3 + 8
Armament:	See text
Ammunition:	Depends on above
Length:	5.27m
Width:	2.4m
Width over stowage boxes:	2.764m
Height with 7.62mm MG:	2.49m
Ground clearance:	0.40m
Weight, combat:	12,700kg
Power-to-weight ratio:	19.68bhp/tonne
Ground pressure:	0.46kg/cm²
Engine:	Perkins T6/3544 water-cooled 6-cylinder turbocharged diesel developing 250bhp at 2,600rpm
Maximum road speed:	80km/hr
Maximum water speed (tracks):	5km/hr
Maximum road range:	650km
Fuel capacity:	405 lit
Fording:	1.1m, amphibious with preparation
Vertical obstacle:	0.6m
Trench:	1.75m
Gradient:	60%
Side slope:	35%
Armour:	Classified
Armour type:	Aluminium
NBC system:	Optional
Night vision equipment:	Optional

Above: Stormer command post vehicle from rear

DEVELOPMENT

In the 1970s a British Government research and development establishment built FV4333 armoured personnel carrier prototype using components of Alvis Scorpion CVR(T) range. Further development by Alvis resulted in Stormer which entered production in 1981 for export with 25 sold to Malaysia, 12 of which had FVT900 turret, 20mm Oerlikon Contraves cannon and 7.62mm MG and remaining vehicles had TH-1 turret with twin 7.62mm MG. Late in 1986 British Army selected Stormer to mount Starstreak High Velocity Missile (HVM) system. This has an unmanned turret with a total of eight Starstreak SAM in ready to launch position, four either side.

All versions have similar layout with driver front left, engine compartment right, troop compartment extending right to rear. Wide range

Above: Stormer High Velocity Missile System

KEY RECOGNITION FEATURES

- Blunt nose with sloping glacis plate, driver's position on left side, engine to right, horizontal hull top with vertical hull rear, large door opening right. Sides vertical, chamfer between sides and roof

- Weapon station normally on forward part of roof with hatches to immediate rear

- Suspension each side has six road wheels with drive sprocket front, idler rear, track return rollers which are sometimes covered by skirt

of weapon stations for hull top including turrets with 7.62mm and 12.7mm MG, 20mm, 25mm or 30mm cannon up to 76mm or 90mm guns. Wide range of optional equipment including NBC system, night vision devices, flotation screen, firing ports/vision blocks, automatic transmission, land navigation system.

VARIANTS

Alvis has proposed wide range of roles for Stormer including air defence (with guns or missiles), engineer vehicle, recovery vehicle, ambulance, minelayer, 81mm or 120mm mortar carrier and command/control.

For Operation Desert Storm, Alvis designed and built a flatbed version of the Stormer to carry the GIAT Minotaur mine scattering system. New version with ATK Volcano is called the Shielder.

STATUS

Production as required. In service with Indonesia, Malaysia, Oman and the UK. Indonesian variants include command post, armoured personnel carrier, bridgelayer, flatbed cargo carrier and ambulance.

MANUFACTURER

BAE Systems Land Systems (previously Alvis Vickers/Alvis), Telford, UK.

Left: Stormer armoured personnel carrier

Alvis Spartan APC (UK)

SPECIFICATIONS

Crew:	3 + 4
Armament:	1 x 7.62mm MG, 2 x 4 smoke grenade dischargers
Ammunition:	3,000 x 7.62mm
Length hull:	5.125m
Width:	2.242m
Height overall:	2.26m
Ground clearance:	0.356m
Weight, combat:	8,172kg
Power-to-weight ratio:	23.25bhp/tonne
Ground pressure:	0.338kg/cm^2
Engine:	Jaguar J60 No1 Mk 100B 4.2 litre 6-cylinder petrol developing 190hp at 4,750rpm (British Army Spartan vehicles have been upgraded with Jaguar petrol engine being replaced by a more fuel efficient Cummins diesel engine)
Maximum road speed:	80.5km/hr
Maximum road range:	483km
Fuel capacity:	386 lit
Fording:	1.067m, amphibious with preparation
Vertical obstacle:	0.5m
Trench:	2.057m
Gradient:	60%
Side slope:	35%
Armour:	Classified
Armour type:	Aluminium
NBC system:	Yes
Night vision equipment:	Yes (passive)

DEVELOPMENT

Alvis Spartan (FV103) is a member of Scorpion CVR(T) family and entered service with British Army in 1978 for specialised roles such as carrying Javelin SAM or Royal Engineer assault teams. It is not replacement for FV432 APC (qv).

Driver sits front left, engine compartment to right, vehicle commander/7.62mm MG gunner to his rear and section commander, who dismounts with four infantry, right of vehicle commander. Troops in rear with two-part roof hatch opening left and right, no firing ports. Flotation screen can be fitted round top of hull which, when erected, makes Spartan fully amphibious, propelled by its tracks.

New production vehicles have a number of improvements including upgraded suspension and the option of the more fuel efficient Perkins diesel engine which has already been installed in some export Scorpions. Production was undertaken at Coventry so any future production would be at another facility.

KEY RECOGNITION FEATURES

- Similar to Stormer but has narrower hull, blunt nose with sloping glacis plate, driver's position on left side with engine right, horizontal hull top with vertical hull rear, larger door opening right. Hull sides vertical, chamfer between sides and roof
- Cupola on hull top to rear of driver's position, 7.62mm MG on left side manned by vehicle commander, troop section commander has hatch to right which is flush with roof, two outward-opening roof hatches rear
- Suspension each side has five road wheels, drive sprocket front, idler rear, no return rollers, no skirts

VARIANTS

Spartan can be adopted to take a wide range of other weapons including anti-tank guided missiles and various air defence weapons.

STATUS

Production as required. In service with Belgium, Jordan, Oman and the UK.

MANUFACTURER

Alvis (today BAE Systems Land Systems), Telford, Shropshire, UK.

***Left:* British Army Spartan APC (Richard Stickland)**

***Right:* Spartan APC**

***Below:* Spartan APC (Richard Stickland)**

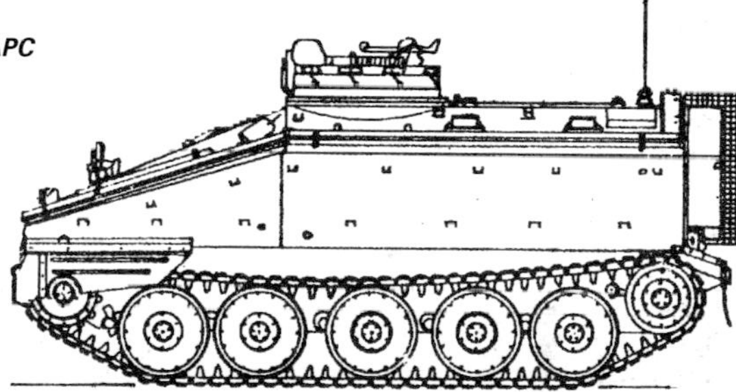

United Defense M2A3 Bradley IFV (USA)

Above: M7 Bradley Fire Support Team Vehicle

SPECIFICATIONS

Crew:	3 + 7
Armament:	1 x 25mm cannon, 1 x 7.62mm MG (coaxial), 2 x TOW ATGW launcher, 2 x 4 smoke grenade dischargers
Ammunition:	900 x 25mm, 4000 x 7.62mm, 7 x TOW ATGW
Length:	6.55m
Width:	3.28m
Height:	3.38m
Height turret roof:	2.565m
Ground clearance:	0.46m
Weight, combat:	36,659kg
Power-to-weight ratio:	16.7hp/tonne
Ground pressure:	0.82kg/cm^2
Engine:	Cummins VTA-903T turbocharged 8-cylinder diesel, 600hp at 2,600rpm
Maximum road speed:	61km/hr
Maximum water speed:	6.4km/hr
Maximum cruising range:	400km
Fuel capacity:	662 lit
Fording:	Amphibious with preparation
Vertical obstacle:	0.914m
Trench:	2.54m
Gradient:	60%
Side slope:	40%
Armour:	Classified
Armour type:	Aluminium/Laminate/ Steel
NBC system:	Yes
Night vision equipment:	Yes (passive for commander, gunner and driver)

DEVELOPMENT

M2 Bradley is the culmination of an early 1960s programme to provide the US Army with a supplement for M113 APC. First two prototypes of XM2 were completed by FMC Corporation (now United Defense LP) in 1978. After trials it was standardised as M2 in 1980 with first production vehicles in 1981, when it was named Bradley IFV.

Hull is welded aluminium with additional layer of spaced laminated armour for increased

protection. Driver sits front left, engine to his right, troop compartment extending right to rear. Two-man power-operated turret armed with 25mm M242 Chain Gun, 7.62mm M240 MG mounted coaxial to right, turret traverse 360°, weapon elevation from -10° to +60°. Mounted on left side of turret is twin launcher for Raytheon TOW ATGW with range of 3,750m. M2 Bradley is fully amphibious with flotation screen erected (carried collapsed round top of hull).

Later production vehicles are M2A1/M2A2 and M3A1/M3A2 which have many improvements with the A3 models having increased armour protection and upgraded powerpack. Some Bradley vehicles have been fitted with explosive reactive armour to their turrets and hulls for increased battlefield survivability.

KEY RECOGNITION FEATURES

- High hull line with well-sloped glacis plate, driver's hatch left side, horizontal hull top, turret centre of roof. Large ramp at hull rear, hatch above rear troop compartment

- Turret has twin TOW ATGW launcher on left side, extensive external stowage with 25mm cannon front and 7.62mm MG right

- Suspension each side has six road wheels, drive sprocket front, idler rear, two track-return rollers. Upper part of track and hull sides has applique armour

VARIANTS

M3 Cavalry Fighting Vehicle (CFV) is similar to M2 but has no firing ports, five-man crew and more ammunition.
M7 Bradley FIST, Fire Support Team Vehicle.
M6 Bradley Linebacker, TOW ATGW replaced by four Stinger SAM.
Ambulance, modified Bradley chassis, no turret (prototype).
MLRS, based on Bradley chassis with new cabs.
M4, Command and Control Vehicle (MLRS chassis).

STATUS

Production complete. In service with Saudi Arabia and USA.

MANUFACTURER

United Defense LP, Ground Systems Division, San José, California, USA.

Below: Bradley A3 with applique armour and Commander's Independent Viewer

United Defense, LP, Armored IFV (USA)

Above: Armored Infantry Fighting Vehicle

SPECIFICATIONS

Crew:	3 + 7
Armament:	1 x 25mm cannon, 1 x 7.62mm MG (coaxial), 1 x 6 smoke grenade dischargers
Ammunition:	324 x 25mm, 1,840 x 7.62mm
Length:	5.258m
Width:	2.819m
Height to top of periscope:	2.794m
Height to hull top:	2.007m
Ground clearance:	0.432m
Weight, combat:	13,687kg
Weight, empty:	11,405kg
Power-to-weight ratio:	19.29hp/tonne
Ground pressure:	0.67kg/cm^2
Engine:	Detroit Diesel 6V-53T V-6 liquid cooled diesel developing 264hp at 2,800rpm
Maximum road speed:	61.2km/hr
Maximum water speed:	6.3km/hr
Maximum road range:	490km
Fuel capacity:	416 lit
Fording:	Amphibious with preparation
Vertical obstacle:	0.635m
Trench:	1.625m
Gradient:	60%
Side slope:	30%
Armour:	Classified
Armour type:	Aluminium/laminate
NBC system:	Optional
Night vision equipment:	Yes (gunner and driver)

DEVELOPMENT

Armored Infantry Fighting Vehicle was developed as a private venture by former FMC Corporation in the late 1960s, originally named Product Improved M113A1. With further improvements it was renamed AIFV, Netherlands placing initial order for 880 in 1975, followed by Philippines. In 1979 Belgium ordered 514 AIFVs and 525 M113A2s which were produced under licence in Belgium. It is now being manufactured in Turkey for home and export markets by FNSS Savunma Sistemleri (qv).

The AIFV has many improvements over M113 series including improved firepower, mobility and armour protection. One-man power-operated turret armed with 25mm KBA cannon, 7.62mm FM MG coaxial to left, turret traverse 360°, weapon elevation from -10° to +50°. AIFV is fully

amphibious, propelled by its tracks. Before entering the water a trim vane is erected at front of vehicle.

VARIANTS

Basic vehicle is designated YPR 765 PRI by Netherlands Army and variants in service include YPR 765 PRCO-B command vehicle, YPR 765 PRCO-C1 to C5 command vehicles, YPR 765 PRRDR radar vehicle, YPR 765 PRRDR-C radar command vehicle, YPR 765 PRGWT ambulance, YPR 765 PRI/I squad vehicle with 12.7mm MG, YPR 765 PRMR mortar tractor towing 120mm mortar, YPR 765 PRVR-A and PRVR-B cargo vehicles, YPR 765 PRAT anti-tank vehicle twin TOW launcher as fitted to American M901 Improved TOW Vehicle and YPR 806 PRBRG armoured recovery vehicle.
Taiwan also produces a similar vehicle to the AIFV with various weapon installations.
Philippines models are similar to Dutch AIFV but have 12.7mm MG in place of 25mm KBA cannon.
Belgian versions include AIFV-B which is similar to Dutch vehicles.
AIFV with 12.7mm cupola weapon station.
AIFV-B-CP command post vehicle.
Turkey, there is a separate entry for these vehicles.

Below: AIFV of Dutch Army 120mm mortar role (Richard Stickland)

KEY RECOGNITION FEATURES

- Glacis plate with trim vane at 45°, hull roof horizontal to hull at rear, angled downwards at 45°, hull rear sloping inwards

- Driver front left, commander rear, engine compartment right, turret with vertical sides and rear offset right of hull. Troop compartment rear with hatch above, large ramp in hull rear

- Hull sides vertical with curve to top, upper part of rear troop compartment slopes inwards, two firing ports with vision block above in each side. Suspension either side has five road wheels, drive sprocket front, idler rear, no track-return rollers

STATUS

Production complete. In service with Bahrain, Belgium, Egypt, Malaysia (Turkish built), Netherlands, Turkey (Turkish built) and United Arab Emirates (Turkish built).

MANUFACTURER

United Defense LP, San José, California, USA; Belgian Mechanical Fabrication SA, Grace-Hollogne, Belgium; FNSS Savunma Sistemleri AS, Ankara, Turkey.

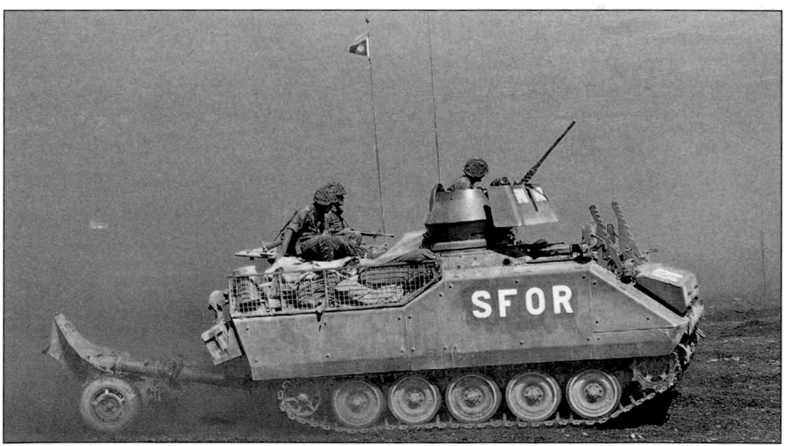

United Defense M113A2 APC (USA)

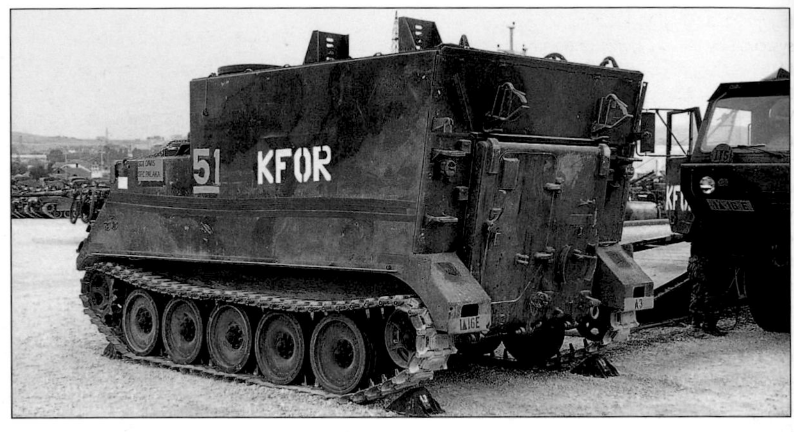

Above: M577A1 command post (Richard Stickland)

SPECIFICATIONS (M113A2)

Crew:	2 + 11
Armament:	1 x 12.7mm MG
Ammunition:	2,000 x 12.7mm
Length:	4.863m
Width:	2.686m
Height overall:	2.52m
Height to hull top:	1.85m
Ground clearance:	0.43m
Weight, combat:	11,253kg
Weight, empty:	9,957kg
Power-to-weight ratio:	18.51hp/tonne
Ground pressure:	0.55kg/cm^2
Engine:	Detroit Diesel Model 6V-53, 6-cylinder water-cooled diesel developing 212bhp at 2,800rpm
Maximum road speed:	60.7km/hr
Maximum water speed:	5.8km/hr
Maximum cruising range:	480km
Fuel capacity:	360 lit
Fording:	Amphibious
Vertical obstacle:	0.61m
Trench:	1.68m
Gradient:	60%
Side slope:	40%
Armour:	44mm (maximum)
Armour type:	Aluminium
NBC system:	Optional
Night vision equipment:	Yes (passive or infra-red for driver)

DEVELOPMENT

M113 series full tracked APC was developed in late 1950s and first vehicles completed in 1960, powered by petrol engine. M113 was replaced in production by diesel-powered M113A1 in 1964 which in turn was replaced by M113A2 with a number of automotive improvements. Latest model is M113A3 which entered service in 1987 and has many improvements including more powerful engine, spall liners and optional applique armour. Over 76,000 M113s and its variants were built, including about 4,500 built in Italy by Oto Melara. Basic vehicle is fully amphibious, propelled in the water by its tracks. Before entering the water a trim vane is erected at front of hull and bilge pumps switched on.

VARIANTS

There are countless local modifications of M113, for example Israeli vehicles have additional armour protection and German vehicles have smoke grenade dischargers on hull front and 7.62mm MG in place of standard 12.7mm M2 HB MG. The following list is by no means exhaustive (see separate entries in this section for United Defense Armored Infantry Fighting Vehicle (AIFV) and Italian Infantry Fighting Vehicle:

M113 with dozer blade, M106 107mm mortar carrier, M125 81mm mortar carrier, M113 A/A

(Egypt 2 x 23mm), M163 20mm Vulcan air defence system, M548 unarmoured cargo carrier, M577/ M1068A3 command post vehicle with higher roof, M113 series recovery vehicle, M901 Improved TOW Vehicle, M981 Fire Support Team Vehicle, M113 with Green Archer radar (Germany).

The Norwegian Army has a number of specialised versions of the M113 series including the NM135 which has a one-man turret armed with a 20mm cannon and a 7.62mm MG and the NM142 which has a one-man Armoured Launching Turret with two TOW ATGW in the ready to launch position. Italy has the SIDAM 4 x 25mm SPAAG on M113 series chassis.

Chassis is also used as basis for ADATS air defence system.

M548 used for many specialised vehicles including Chapparral air defence missile system, minelayer (Germany) and electronic warfare carrier.

A number of countries have fitted applique armour to hull front, sides and rear.

STATUS

In production. In service with Argentina, Australia, Bahrain, Belgium, Bolivia, Bosnia, Brazil, Cambodia, Canada, Chile, Colombia, Congo, Denmark, Ecuador, Egypt, Ethiopia, Germany, Greece, Guatemala, Iran, Iraq, Israel, Italy, Jordan, South Korea, Kuwait, Lebanon, Libya, Lithuania, Macedonia, Morocco, New Zealand, Norway, Pakistan, Peru, Philippines, Portugal, Saudi Arabia, Singapore, Somalia, Spain, Sudan, Switzerland, Taiwan, Thailand, Tunisia, Turkey, USA, Uruguay, Vietnam and Yemen.

KEY RECOGNITION FEATURES

- Box-shaped hull with front sloping at 60° to rear, horizontal roof, vertical hull rear with large power-operated ramp, vertical hull sides with no firing ports or vision devices

- Driver's circular hatch front left with air louvres to right, commander's cupola with externally mounted 12.7mm M2 HB MG in centre of roof with rectangular hatch to rear. External box-type fuel tanks each side of ramp on hull rear

- Suspension each side has five road wheels, drive sprocket front, idler rear, no track-return rollers, upper part of track normally covered by rubber skirt

MANUFACTURER

United Defense LP Ground Systems Division, San José, California, USA. Also built by Oto Melara in La Spezia, Italy and by BMF in Belgium for Belgian Army.

Below: Israeli M113 with extra armour

United Defense M113A2 APC (USA)

Above: M113A2 with applique armour and external fuel tanks on either side of rear ramp

Above: M113A3 of the Greek Army (Richard Stickland)

Above: Italian Army M113 with firing ports (Richard Stickland)

Above: Norwegian NM135 APC with 20mm cannon

Above: M1064 120mm self-propelled mortar (US Army)

Above: M113 engineer vehicle used by Canada

Above: M113 series APC of the Italian Army (Michael Jerchel)

M901 Improved TOW Vehicle (USA)

Above: M901 ITV

SPECIFICATIONS

Crew:	4 or 5
Armament:	1 x twin TOW ATGW launcher, 1 x 7.62mm MG, 2 x 4 smoke grenade dischargers
Ammunition:	2 + 10 TOW ATGW, 1,000 x 7.62mm
Length:	4.83m
Width:	2.686m
Height, launcher erected:	3.35m
Height, travelling:	2.91m
Weight, combat:	11,794kg
Power-to-weight ratio:	18.22hp/tonne
Ground pressure:	0.58kg/cm^2
Engine:	Detroit Diesel Model 6V-53, 6-cylinder water-cooled developing 215bhp at 2,800rpm
Maximum road speed:	67.59km/hr
Maximum water speed:	5.8km/hr
Maximum cruising range:	483km
Fuel capacity:	360 lit
Fording:	Amphibious
Vertical obstacle:	0.61m
Trench:	1.68m
Gradient:	60%
Side slope:	30%
Armour:	38mm (maximum)
Armour type:	Aluminium
NBC system:	None
Night vision equipment:	Optional (passive for gunner and driver)

DEVELOPMENT

Following trials with prototype systems submitted by three manufacturers, Emerson (now known as Systems & Electronics Inc) was awarded low rate initial contract in 1976 for M901 Improved TOW Vehicle and by 1995 well over 3,200 had been built for home and export markets. M901 Improved TOW Vehicle (ITV) is essentially M113A2 APC with roof-mounted launcher for two Raytheon Systems Company TOW ATGWs. Further 10 missiles carried in reserve which are manually loaded via roof hatch to rear of launcher. Latest version of ITV launches all three versions of TOW, Basic TOW, Improved TOW I-TOW and TOW 2; TOW 2 has range of 3,750m. Actual launcher has powered traverse through 360°, elevates from -30° to +34° and can be fitted to wide range of

vehicles including Armored Infantry Fighting Vehicle (adopted by Dutch Army), Italian VCC-2 (adopted by Saudi Arabia).

VARIANTS

Fire Support Team Vehicle (FISTV) is M901 but used to locate and designate targets instead of anti-tank capability. Equipment includes AN/TVQ-2 GLLD with north-seeking gyro and line-of-sight sub-system, AN/TAS-4 sight, land navigation system and extensive communications equipment.

FISTV is designated M981 and entered service with US Army in 1984.

Egyptian version of FISTV is called the Artillery Target Location Vehicle.

STATUS

Production complete. In service with Egypt (and AIFV chassis), Greece, Jordan, Kuwait, Netherlands (on AIFV chassis), Pakistan, Saudi Arabia (VCC-2 chassis) and Thailand. No longer in service with US Army, US Marine Corps uses same launcher on General Dynamics Land Systems Canada LAV (8 x 8) chassis.

MANUFACTURER

United Defense LP, San José, California, USA (chassis); Systems & Electronics Inc, St Louis, Missouri, USA (turret).

KEY RECOGNITION FEATURES

• M113 APC with elevating launcher for two TOW ATGWs on hull roof; when travelling it folds flat on hull top with launcher to rear, when elevated to launch TOWs it has T-shaped profile

• Glacis slopes at 45° with trim vane hinged at bottom, flat hull roof with vertical hull sides and rear, hull has ramp with external fuel tanks each side (did not appear on early vehicles)

• Suspension each side has five road wheels, drive sprocket front, idler rear, no track-return rollers. Upper part of suspension normally covered by rubber skirt

Below: M981 FISTV in operating configuration

United Defense LVTP7 AAAV (USA) (now designated AAV7A1 by US Marine Corps)

SPECIFICATIONS

Crew:	3 + 25
Armament:	1 x 12.7mm MG*
Ammunition:	1,000 x 12.7mm*
Length:	8.16m
Width:	3.27m
Height:	3.31m (overall)
Ground clearance:	0.406m
Weight, combat:	22,838kg
Weight, empty:	17,441kg
Power-to-weight ratio:	17.51hp/tonne
Engine:	Detroit Diesel model 8V-53T, 8-cylinder, water-cooled, turbocharged diesel developing 400hp at 2,800rpm
Maximum road speed:	64km/hr
Maximum water speed:	13.5km/hr (waterjets), 7.2km/hr (tracks)
Maximum road range:	482km
Fuel capacity:	681 lit
Fording:	Amphibious
Vertical obstacle:	0.914m
Trench:	2.438m
Gradient:	60%
Side slope:	60%
Armour:	45mm (maximum)
Armour type:	Aluminium
NBC system:	None
Night vision equipment:	Yes (for driver only)

* American vehicles have new turrets with 40mm grenade launcher and 12.7mm MG

DEVELOPMENT

In the mid-1960s FMC Corporation (now United Defense, LP) was awarded a contract to design and build prototypes of a new armoured amphibious assault vehicle to replace the then current LVTP5 series. First prototypes were completed in September 1967 under the designation LVTPX12 and after trials it was accepted for service as LVTP7 (Landing Vehicle, Tracked, Personnel, Model 7). First production models completed in 1971 and final deliveries in late 1974.

Hull is all-welded aluminium, engine compartment to front right and MG turret to rear. Turret traverses through 360° and 12.7mm MG elevates from -15° to +60°. Driver sits front left with periscope that extends through roof of cupola, commander sits to rear. Troop compartment extends to hull rear with normal means of entry and exit via power-operated ramp in rear, troops

nd supplies can be loaded via overhead hatches /hen alongside ship. LVTP7 is fully amphibious, ropelled by its tracks or via two waterjets, one ach side of hull above idler. Specialised kits ıclude stretcher, navigation, visor and /interisation.

'ARIANTS (excluding prototypes)
VTC7 (Landing Vehicle, Tracked, Command, Aodel 7), no MG cupola but extensive ommunications equipment.
VTR7 (Landing Vehicle, Tracked, Recovery, Model), no MG turret but specialised equipment ıcluding winch and crane.
VTP7A1 with mine-clearing kit, basic LVTP7A1 /ith mine-clearance kit inside troop compartment /hich is raised when required, fires rockets over ront of vehicle into minefield.
.VTP7A1 with 40mm/12.7mm turret. From 986/87 many vehicles have been fitted with a ıew turret called the Upgunned Weapons Station /hich is armed with a 40mm grenade launcher ınd a 12.7mm machine gun.
.VTP7A1 is LVTP7 rebuilt, improvements including ıew Cummins engine, smoke generating capability, assive night vision equipment and improved :lectric weapon station under Service Life :xtension Program (SLEP). In addition to SLEP new /ehicles were built to LVTP7A1 standard with final leliveries in 1986 to US Marine Corps and some :xport customers.
.VTP7A1 with applique armour, some US Marine :orps vehicles have been fitted with the Enhanced Applique Armor Kit (EAAK) as the replacement for the earlier P900 armour kit. Part of the USMC fleet now being upgraded under RAM/RS programme.

KEY RECOGNITION FEATURES

- Boat-shaped hull, nose sloping under forward part of hull to tracks, vertical front with glacis almost horizontal, hull sides vertical to rear of commander's cupola then slope inwards at an angle to troop compartment roof, large ramp at rear

- Suspension either side has six road wheels, drive sprocket front, idler rear, no track-return rollers, skirt over upper forward part of track

- Driver's cupola front left with commander's cupola rear, MG cupola on right side of hull to rear of engine compartment

STATUS

Production complete. In service with Argentina, Brazil, Italy, South Korea, Spain, Thailand, Venezuela and USA. In US Marine Corps service this will be replaced by the General Dynamics Expeditionary Fighting Vehicle (previously called the Advanced Amphibious Assault Vehicle).

MANUFACTURER

United Defense LP, San José, California, USA.

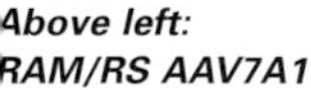

Above left: RAM/RS AAV7A1

Right: AAV7A1 with Upgunned Weapons Station and RAFAEL applique armour

General Dynamics Amphibious Systems Expeditionary Fighting Vehicle (USA)

Above: Expeditionary Fighting Vehicle showing its amphibious capabilities (General Dynamics)

SPECIFICATIONS

Crew:	3 + 17
Amament:	1 x 30mm/40mm MK 44 cannon, 1 x 7.62mm MG
Ammunition:	405 x 30mm, 1,400 x 7.62mm
Length:	(overall land) 9.33m (overall water) 10.67m
Width:	3.66m
Height:	3.28m (turret roof)
Ground clearance:	0.406m
Weight, combat:	34,473kg
Weight, empty:	28,712kg
Power-to-weight ratio:	34.476hp/tonne
Ground pressure:	0.625 kg/cm²
Engine:	MTU MT 883 Ka-523 diesel developing 2,702hp in water mode and 850hp in land mode
Maximum road speed:	72.41km/h
Max water speed:	37 to 46km/h
Maximum range:	Land 523km; water 120km
Fuel capacity:	1,226 lit
Fording:	Amphibious
Vertical obstacle:	Not available
Trench:	Not available
Gradient:	60%
Side slope:	30%
Armour:	Classified
Armour type:	Cteel/Composite
NBC system:	Yes
Night vision equipment:	Yes

DEVELOPMENT

In June 1996, following a competition, General Dynamics Land Systems was awarded the Program Defenition and Risk Reduction contract for the Expeditionary Fighting Vehicle (then called the Advanced Amphibious Assault Vehicle) to replace the current AAV7A1 series of vehicles. To handle this contract General Dynamics Amphibious Systems was established and a total of three prototypes were built.

In 2001 the company was awarded the Systems Development and Demonstration contract which covers the construction of nine prototypes, eight in the troop carrier configuration and one in the command and control configuration.

Low rate production is expected to start in 2007 and under current plans the Marine Corps expects to purchase a total of 1,013 vehicles of which 935 will be in the personnel carrier mode and 78 in command and control configuration.

The hull of the EFV is of welded aluminium with an applique layer of modular ceramic armour. The driver is seated front left with another crew position to the front right.

Mounted on the forward part of the roof is the General Dynamics Armament Systems MK 46 two person power operated turret armed with a 30mm/40mm MK 44 dual feed stabilised cannon with a 7.62mm M240 coaxial machine gun. This is coupled to a computerised fire control system with a day/thermal sighting system which enables stationary and moving targets to be engaged while the vehicle is on land or water.

The troop compartment is at the rear and the troops enter and leave via a large power operated ramp in the hull rear, in addition there are hatches over the troop compartment.

The vehicle is fully amphibious being propelled in the water by two powerful water jets mounted one either side of the vehicle at the rear. The hydropneumatic suspension system is retracted during amphibious operations and a prow plate extends outwards to extend the planing surface. At the rear two flaps open to expose the water jets.

VARIANTS

At the present time there is only one variant of the EFV and that is the command and control vehicle.

KEY RECOGNITION FEATURES

- Nose slopes back under hull with well-sloped glacis plate leading up to almost horizontal roof that extends to rear. Trim vane folds back under forward part of vehicle when not in use. Large power-operated ramp at hull rear with covered water jets either side

- Large turret mounted on forward part of hull roof with single roof hatch in right rear. Additional crew stations and hatches are at front right and left of vehicle

- Vertical hull sides with skirts covering almost all of the suspension that consists of seven road wheels with drive sprocket at front, idler at rear and track-return rollers

STATUS

Under development for US Marine Corps.

MANUFACTURER

General Dynamics Amphibious Systems, USA.

Below: Expeditionary Fighting Vehicle In land mode

4 x 4 VEHICLES

Tenix S600 APC (Australia)

Above: Tenix S600 fitted with obstacle clearing blade

SPECIFICATIONS

Crew:	1 + 11
Armament:	1 x 12.7mm MG (typical)
Ammunition:	1000 x 12.7mm MG (typical)
Length hull:	5.76m
Width:	2.95m
Height:	2.70m
Ground clearance:	0.44m
Weight, combat:	12,500kg
Power-to-weight ratio:	17.1hp/tonne
Ground pressure:	Not available
Engine:	Mercedes-Benz 6-cylinder in-line turbo-charged and inter-cooled diesel developing 214hp at 2,600rpm
Maximum road speed:	110km/h
Maximum road range:	1,000km
Fuel capacity:	320 lit
Fording:	1.20m
Vertical obstacle:	0.5m
Trench:	Not available
Gradient:	75%
Side slope:	58%
Armour:	Classified
Armour type:	Steel
NBC system:	No
Night vision equipment:	Optional

DEVELOPMENT

The S600 was originally developed by Shorts of Northern Ireland and was first revealed in September 1995. The design, sales and marketing rights were subsequently sold to British Aerospace Australia which eventually sold its complete range of 4 x 4 light armoured vehicles, including the S600, to Tenix Defence Systems, also of Australia.

The first customer for the S600 was the Kuwait National Guard who ordered 22 vehicles which were delivered between 1998 and 1999. In early 2001 Belgium placed an order for the S600 for use in the IS role.

The S600 is based on a Mercedes-Benz Unimog (4 x 4) truck chassis for which parts are available all over the world. The body provides the occupants with protection from small arms fire, shell splinters and small mines.

The powerpack is at the front of the vehicle

vith the remainder being taken up by the troop ompartment. The commander and driver are eated at the front with the troops being seated n bench seats that run down either side of the ull at the rear. Various types of light weapons an be mounted on the roof such as 7.62mm or 2.7mm machine guns or a 40mm automatic renade launcher.

A wide range of optional equipment can be rovided such as front mounted winch, applique rmour, grenade launchers, land navigation ystem, central tyre pressure regulation system, eater, fire detection and suppression system and ight vision equipment. Different roof hatches nd seating arrangements are also possible.

VARIANTS

Barricade removal vehicle, ambulance, 81mm nortar, command post, surveillance vehicle and irport security vehicle.

STATUS

Production as required. In service with Belgium and Kuwait.

MANUFACTURER

Tenix Defence Systems, Bandlana, Victoria, Australia.

KEY RECOGNITION FEATURES

- Vertical hull front with bonnet sloping upwards to two part windscreen which slopes slightly to the rear. Horizontal roof and vertical rear with two part hatch; the upper part opens upwards and the lower part opens downwards to form a step

- The upper and lower parts of the hull sides slope inwards with the wheels being at either end of the vehicle. In each side of the hull is a large window to the front and a single side door, the upper part opens upwards and the lower part opens downwards to form a step

- Two spare wheels are normally carried one either side at the rear and a 7.62mm or 12.7mm machine gun can be mounted on the roof. There is a distinct air intake tube on the front right side of the hull

Below: Tenix S600 APC without armament

ADI Bushmaster APC (Australia)

Above: Bushmaster IMV

Below: Bushmaster IMV

SPECIFICATIONS

Crew:	2 + 8
Armament:	1 x 7.62mm MG (typical)
Ammunition:	1000 rounds (typical)
Length:	7.087m
Width:	2.50m
Height:	2.65m
Ground clearance:	0.47m
Weight, combat:	15,000kg
Weight, empty:	12,300kg
Power-to-weight ratio:	21.42hp/tonne
Ground pressure:	Not available
Engine:	Caterpillar 3126 ATAAC 6-cylinder diesel developing 300hp at 2,400rpm
Maximum road speed:	120km/h
Maximum road range:	1000km
Fuel capacity:	385 lit
Fording:	1.20m
Vertical obstacle:	0.44m
Trench:	Not available
Gradient:	60%
Side slope:	40%
Armour:	Classified
Armour type:	Steel
NBC system:	No
Night vision equipment:	No

DEVELOPMENT

Following an international competition, in early 1999 the Australian Army placed a contract with ADI for the supply of 320 Infantry Mobility Vehicles (IMV). Following trials with early vehicles a number of problems were encountered but

these were resolved and first low rate production vehicles were completed in 2003.

The hull of the Bushmaster is of all welded steel armour which provides the occupants with protection from small arms fire, shell splinters and mines. The powerpack, consisting of a diesel engine coupled to a fully automatic transmission, is mounted at the front of the vehicle with the driver and commander to the rear.

The infantry are seated on individual seats that run down each side of the hull rear facing inwards. Entry is via a large door in the hull rear. The troop compartment is provided with seven large bullet proof windows, three each side and one in the rear door, each of these windows has a firing port.

Standard equipment includes power steering, air conditioning system, cooled water supply system and hydraulically operated 10 tonne winch. A 7.62mm or 5.56mm machine gun can be mounted on the roof of the vehicle above the commander's and driver's positions.

KEY RECOGNITION FEATURES

- Box shaped hull with vertical front with horizontal louvres, bonnet slopes gently up to large one piece windscreen which slopes well to rear, horizontal roof extends to vertical hull rear

- Hull sides are vertical with distinct step above road wheels. Large side window towards front and three smaller ones to rear. Mounted on either side of hull at rear is a replacement wheel and tyre

- Single circular roof hatch over forward part of roof on which a 7.62mm MG or similar weapon can be mounted, four rectangular roof hatches over rear troop compartment

VARIANTS

Ambulance.
Command post.
Mortar carrier.
Direct fire weapons.
Engineer (assault pioneer).
FireKing is bush fire fighting vehicle now in production.

STATUS

In production for Australian Army and Air Force.

MANUFACTURER

ADI Limited, Bendigo, Australia.

***Above right:* Bushmaster IMV**

***Right:* Bushmaster IMV**

BDX APC (Belgium)

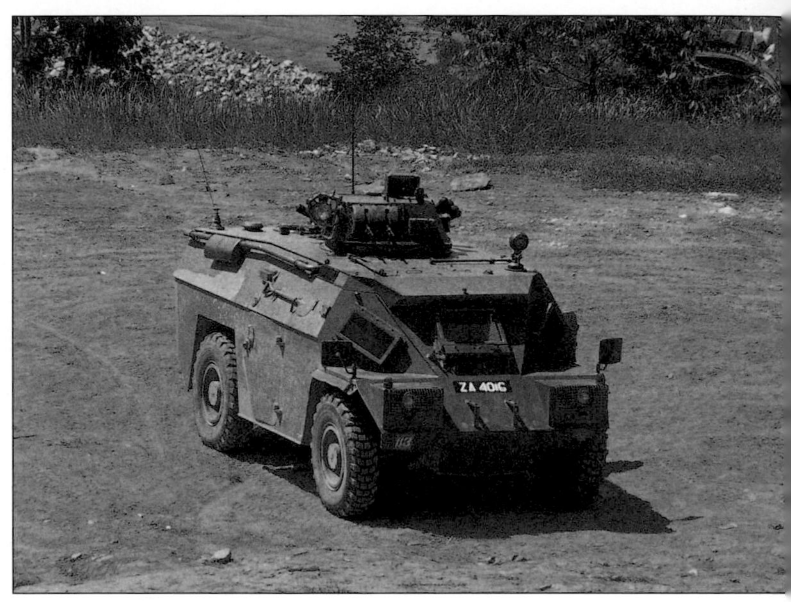

SPECIFICATIONS

Crew:	2 + 10
Configuration:	4 x 4
Armament:	See text
Length:	5.05m
Width:	2.5m
Height with turret:	2.84m
Height to hull top:	2.06m
Ground clearance:	0.4m
Wheelbase:	3.003m
Weight, combat:	10,700kg
Weight, unloaded:	9,750kg
Power-to-weight ratio:	16.82hp/tonne
Engine:	Chrysler V-8 water-cooled petrol developing 180bhp at 4,000rpm
Maximum road speed:	100km/hr
Maximum road range:	500 to 900km
Fuel capacity:	248 lit
Fording:	Amphibious
Vertical obstacle:	0.4m
Trench:	Not applicable
Gradient:	60%
Side slope:	40%

Above: BDX with twin 7.62mm MG turret

Armour type:	Steel
Armour:	12.7mm (maximum)
NBC system:	Optional
Night vision equipment:	Optional

DEVELOPMENT

In 1976 the Engineering Division of Beherman Demoen obtained a licence to produce an improved version of the Irish Timoney (4 x 4) APC. In 1977 the Belgian Government ordered 123 vehicles, 43 for the Belgian Air Force for airfield protection and 80 for the Belgian gendarmerie, delivered between 1978 and 1981. Five vehicles were also delivered to Argentina, and more recently most of the Belgian vehicles have been transferred to Mexico.

The driver sits far front with engine to rear. Behind this is troop compartment with entry doors sides and rear. Variety of weapons can be mounted on roof including turret with twin 7.62mm MGs or turret with twin MILAN ATGWs in ready-to-launch position.

The BDX is fully amphibious, propelled by its wheels. Waterjets, NBC system, smoke grenade dischargers, air-conditioning system and front-mounted dozer blade were originally available as optional extras. As an option the petrol engine fitted to all production vehicles could be replaced by the more fuel efficient Detroit Diesel Model V-53T developing 180hp at 2,800rpm.

VARIANTS

Gendarmerie order comprised 41 APCs without turret, 26 with dozer blade and 13 81mm mortar carriers.

Technology Investments built 10 Timoney APCs for Irish Army, five Mk 4s and five Mk 6s. (no longer in service).

STATUS

Production complete. In service with Argentina and Mexico.

MANUFACTURER

Beherman Demoen Engineering (BDX), Mechelen, Belgium. (No longer involved in armoured vehicles.)

***Right:* BDX with twin 7.62mm turret**

***Below:* BDX without armament**

KEY RECOGNITION FEATURES

- Box-type hull, sloping glacis plate with large bullet-proof window in front of driver with smaller window each side

- Lower hull sides vertical with door between roadwheels, upper part of hull slopes inwards, vertical hull rear with door opening to right

- Horizontal roof with armament mounted centre, exhaust pipe and silencer mounted on each side of upper part of hull sides which extend to rear of vehicle

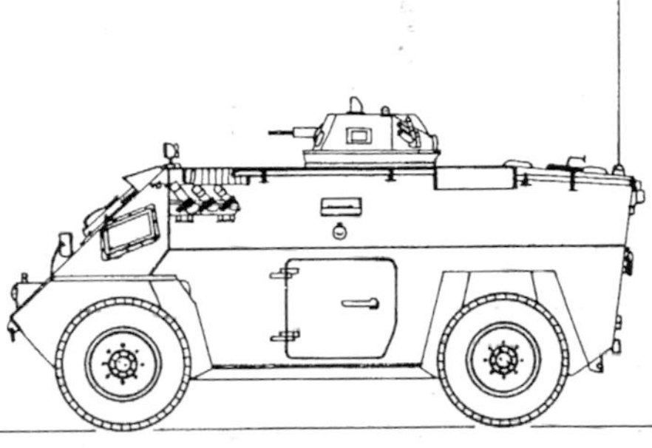

ENGESA EE-3 Jararaca Scout Car (Brazil)

Above: ENGESA EE-3 armed with 12.7mm M2 MG

SPECIFICATIONS

Crew:	3
Configuration:	4 x 4
Armament:	1 x 12.7mm MG
Ammunition:	1000 x 12.7mm
Length:	4.163m
Width:	2.235m
Height (top of 12.7mm mount):	2.3m
Height (hull top):	1.56m
Ground clearance:	0.335m
Wheelbase:	2.6m
Weight, combat:	5,800kg
Power-to-weight ratio:	20.7hp/tonne
Engine:	Mercedes-Benz OM 314A turbocharged, 4-cylinder water-cooled diesel developing 120hp at 2,800rpm
Maximum road speed:	100km/hr
Maximum road range:	700km
Fuel capacity:	140 lit
Fording:	0.6m
Vertical obstacle:	0.4m
Trench:	Not applicable
Gradient:	60%
Side slope:	30%
Armour:	Classified
Armour type:	Steel (2 layers)
NBC system:	Optional
Night vision equipment:	Optional

DEVELOPMENT

EE-3 Jararaca (4 x 4) was designed by ENGESA to complement its EE-9 (6 x 6) Cascavel armoured car and EE-11 Urutu (6 x 6) armoured personnel carrier. Like other ENGESA wheeled armoured vehicles the Jararaca has proven and common automotive components wherever possible. The driver sits front with machine gunner to his right rear and vehicle

ommander, who also operates communications quipment, to left rear. All three crew members ave roof hatches and there is a large forward-pening door in the right side of the hull. Standard quipment included central tyre pressure egulation system that allows driver to adjust tyre ressure to suit ground, and run-flat tyres. ptional equipment includes smoke grenade lischargers, passive night vision equipment, NBC ystem, radios and intercom.

A wide range of armament could be installed n the roof including a pintle-mounted uromissile MILAN ATGW system, and the tandard 12.7mm M2 HB MG can be replaced by a .62mm MG or a 20mm cannon. Other armament nstallations marketed by ENGESA included a 0mm breech-loaded mortar, ENGESA ET-MD ne-man turret armed with one 20mm cannon nd one 7.62mm MG

KEY RECOGNITION FEATURES

- Nose slopes back under hull front headlamps recessed, well-sloped glacis plate with horizontal roof line, driver's position protruding from roof line over glacis plate

- Armament normally mounted on top of hull in centre (offset to right), engine rear, air louvres in vertical hull rear

- Vertical hull sides with chamfer between hull sides and roof, door in right hull side on late production models, two road wheels each side at extreme ends of vehicle

VARIANTS

Apart from the different armament options the only known production variant is the NBC reconnaissance version with raised roof and NBC monitoring equipment.

STATUS

Production complete. In service with Cyprus, Equador, Gabon and Uruguay.

MANUFACTURER

ENGESA, São José dos Campos, Brazil. This company is no longer in existence.

Above right: EE-3 armed with MILAN ATGW system

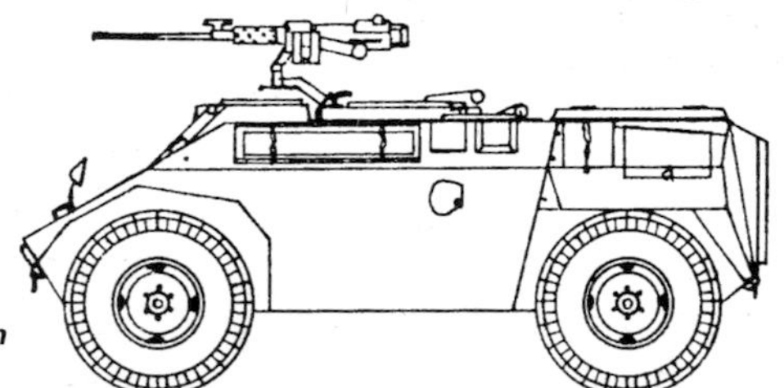

Right: EE-3 armed with 12.7mm M2 MG

RH ALAN LOV APC (Croatia)

SPECIFICATIONS

Crew:	2 + 10
Armament:	1 x 12.7mm MG
Ammunition:	1,000 x 12.7mm
Length:	5.89m
Width:	2.39m
Height:	1.98m (hull top)
Ground clearance:	0.315m
Weight, combat:	8,200kg
Weight, empty:	7,200kg
Power-to-weight ratio:	15.85hp/tonne
Ground pressure:	Not available
Engine:	Deutz BT6L 912S turbocharged diesel developing 130 hp at 2650rpm
Maximum road speed:	110km/h
Maximum road range:	500/700km
Fuel capacity:	170 litres
Fording:	1m
Vertical obstacle:	0.50m
Trench:	Not available
Gradient:	65%
Side slope:	35%
Armour:	Classified
Armour type:	Steel
NBC system:	Optional
Night vision equipment:	Optional

DEVELOPMENT

The LOV family of 4 x 4 vehicles was developed from 1992 by the Torpedo company to meet the requirements of the Croatian Army for a basic armoured personnel carrier which could be adopted for a wide range of operational roles.

The LOV is based on the locally produced Torpedo TK - 130 T-7 (4 x 4) truck chassis to which an all welded steel body has been fitted which provides the occupants with protection from small arms fire and shell splinters.

The driver is seated at the front left with the commander front right with the powerpack installed towards the front of the vehicle. The troop compartment is at the rear and entry via two doors.

The basic APC is fitted with a roof mounted 12.7mm M2 machine gun with the gunner being provided with side and rear protection.

Standard equipment includes a central tyre pressure regulation system that allows the driver to adjust the tyre pressure to suit the terrain being crossed. Run flat tyre devices are also fitted as standard on the LOV.

Optional equipment includes air conditioning system, communications equipment, night vision equipment, electric winch and auxiliary power unit.

VARIANTS

LOV-IZV reconnaissance.
LOV-Z command post.
LOV-ABK NBC reconnaissance.
LOV-RAKL 24/128mm rocket launcher.
LOV-ED electronic warfare.

STATUS

Production as required. In service with Croatia.

MANUFACTURER

RH ALAN, Rijeka, Croatia.

KEY RECOGNITION FEATURES

• Boxed-shaped hull with radiator louvres under nose of vehicle with glacis plate sloping up to horizontal roof that extends to the rear. Raised drivers compartment at front left with window to front and small window to sides

• Weapon station normally mounted in centre of hull roof with two roof hatches to rear. Vertical hull rear which often has a spare wheel and tyre fitted

• Upper part of hull sides slope inwards as does lower part of hull with wheels at ends of vehicle. There is a forward opening door in each side of the hull just forward of the front road wheel

Left: LOV-IZV with 12.7mm MG

Below LOV-AP APC with 12.7mm MG

Kader Fahd APC (Egypt)

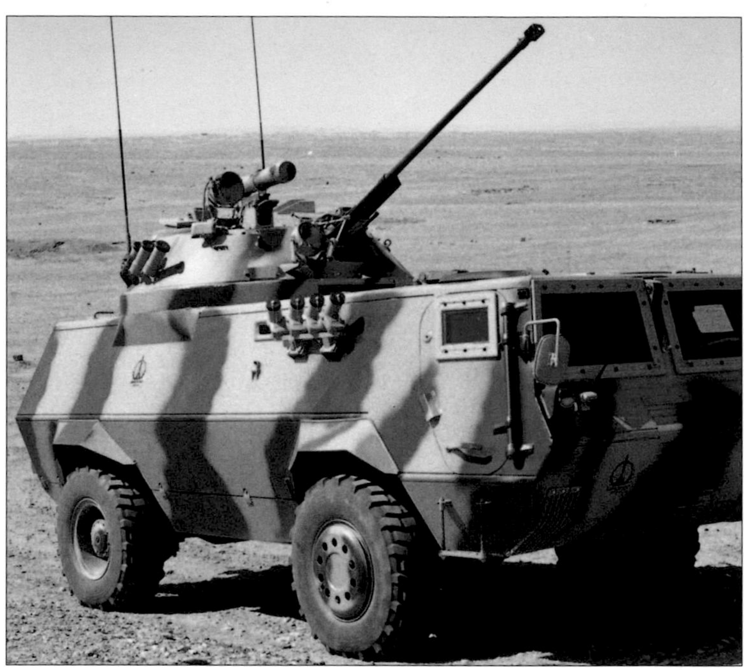

Above: Fahd 30 (4 x 4) APC has turret of Russian BMP-2

SPECIFICATIONS

Crew:	2 + 10
Configuration:	4 x 4
Armament:	1 x 7.62mm MG (see text), 2 x 4 smoke grenade dischargers
Ammunition:	1,000 x 7.62mm (estimate)
Length:	6m
Width:	2.45m
Height:	2.1m (hull top)
Ground clearance:	0.31 to 0.37m
Wheelbase:	3.2m
Weight, combat:	10,900kg
Weight, empty:	9,100kg
Power-to-weight ratio:	15.4hp/tonne
Engine:	Mercedes-Benz OM-352 A 6-cylinder direct injection water-cooled turbocharged diesel developing 168hp at 2,800rpm
Maximum road speed:	90km/hr
Maximum road range:	800km
Fording:	0.7m
Vertical obstacle:	0.5m
Trench:	0.9m
Gradient:	70%
Side slope:	30%
Armour:	10mm (maximum) (estimate)
Armour type:	Steel
NBC system:	Optional
Night vision equipment:	Optional

DEVELOPMENT

Fahd (4 x 4) was designed by the now Rheinmetall Landsysteme (at that time Henschel Wehrtechnik), Germany, under the designation TH 390 to meet requirements of the Egyptian Army. Production commenced in 1985, first deliveries in 1986. It consists of a modified Mercedes-Benz 4 x 4 truck chassis with an armoured body that provides complete protection from attack by 7.62 x 54mm armour-piercing projectiles and shell splinters.

Commander and driver sit front, engine below and between, troop compartment rear, normal means of entry and exit for 10 troops via two-part hatch in rear, top part opens upwards and lower part folds downwards to form step. Firing ports with vision block above in each side of troop compartment, another each side of rear entry hatch. Hatches in roof.

Standard equipment includes central tyre pressure regulation system allowing driver to adjust tyre pressure to suit ground, power-assisted steering. Options include NBC system, front-mounted winch, ventilation system, night vision equipment and smoke grenade dischargers.

Fahd 30 was shown for the first time in 1991 and is essentially the Fahd fitted with the complete turret of the Russian BMP-2 IFV armed with 30mm cannon, 7.62mm coaxial machine gun and roof-mounted ATGW.

VARIANTS

Fahd can be fitted with wide range of armaments ranging from pintle-mounted 7.62mm MG up to 20mm cannon. Variants suggested by manufacturer include ambulance, command post, multiple rocket launcher, recovery, minelayer and internal security. Latest production vehicles are powered by the Mercedes-Benz OM 366 LA 6-cylinder diesel developing 240hp at 2,600rpm.

KEY RECOGNITION FEATURES

- Fully enclosed hull with front, sides and rear slightly sloping inwards

- Commander and driver sit front, each with large side door and large windscreen to immediate front which can be covered by armoured shutter hinged at top

- Radiator grille low down in nose of vehicle, firing ports in rear troop compartment, two-part rear entry hatch

STATUS

Production as required. In service with Algeria, Democratic Republic of Congo, Egypt, Kuwait, Oman and Sudan.

MANUFACTURER

Kader Factory for Developed Industries, Heliopolis, Egypt.

Below: Fahd (4 x 4) without armament

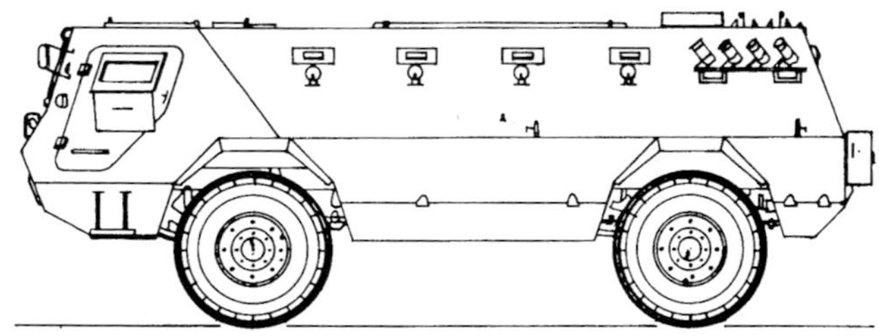

Kader Walid APC (Egypt)

Above: Walid APC

SPECIFICATIONS

Crew:	2 + 8/10
Configuration:	4 x 4
Armament:	1 x 7.62mm MG
Ammunition:	1,000 x 7.62mm
Length:	6.12m
Width:	2.57m
Height:	2.3m
Ground clearance:	0.4m
Wheelbase:	Not available
Weight, combat:	12,000kg (estimate)
Weight, empty:	9,200kg (estimate)
Power-to-weight ratio:	14hp/tonne (estimate)
Engine:	168hp diesel
Maximum road speed:	86km/hr
Maximum range:	800km
Fuel capacity:	Not available
Fording:	0.8m (estimate)
Vertical obstacle:	0.5m (estimate)
Trench:	Not applicable
Gradient:	60%
Side slope:	30%
Armour:	8mm (maximum) (estimate)
Armour type:	Steel
NBC system:	None
Night vision equipment:	None

DEVELOPMENT

Walid (4 x 4) was developed in the 1960s and used for the first time in the 1967 Middle East campaign. Consists of a German Magirus Deutz chassis made in Egypt and fitted with open-topped armoured body. Walid 2 was introduced in 1981 and is based on Mercedes-Benz automotive components. It has now been succeeded in production by Fahd (4 x 4) APC (qv).

Commander and gunner sit to rear of engine, troop compartment at rear, 7.62mm MG normally mounted on forward part of hull roof firing forwards. Additional weapons can be mounted round top of hull. Walid has no amphibious capability and no central tyre pressure regulation system.

VARIANTS

Only known variants are minelayer with ramp at rear for laying mines on surface, and multiple rocket launcher with 12 rockets in ready-to-launch position. The latter has 12 80mm D-3000 rockets with a maximum range of 2,500m. There is also a six round version with six 122mm

D-6000 smoke rockets with a maximum range of 6000m.

STATUS
Production complete. In service with Burundi, Sudan and Yemen.

MANUFACTURER
Kader Factory, Cairo, Egypt.

KEY RECOGNITION FEATURES

- Fully enclosed engine compartment front with horizontal armoured grille to protect radiator, troop compartment rear with vertical sides and rear with sides sloping slightly inwards, three circular firing ports each side
- Commander's and driver's doors open forwards, rear door with spare wheel and tyre open to left, firing port each side
- Similar in appearance to the Russian BTR-40 (4 x 4) APC but Walid is larger with rear wheel arches straight rather than curved, as in BTR-40

Above: Walid with launcher for smoke rockets (Egyptian Army)

Right: Walid in mine-laying role with doors open (Christopher F Foss)

ACMAT APC (TPK 420 BL) (France)

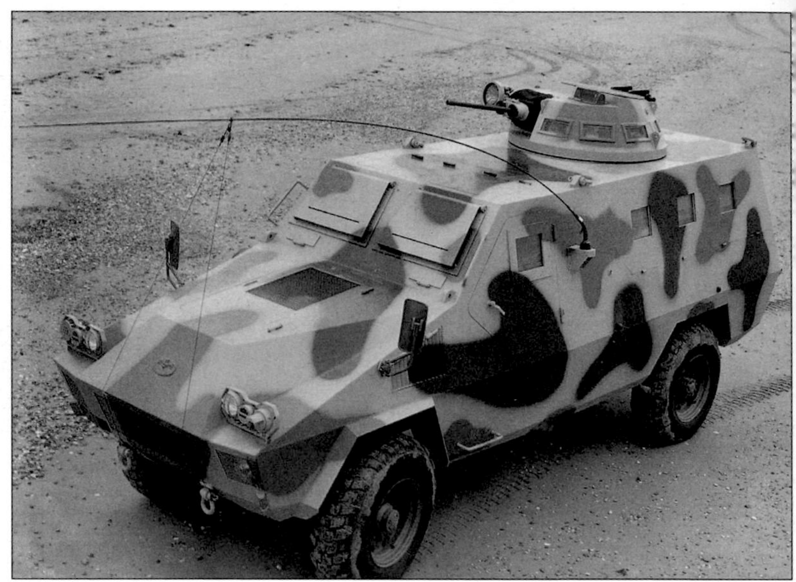

Above: ACMAT BL light armoured car with one-man turret armed with 12.7mm M2 HB and 7.62mm MGs

SPECIFICATIONS

Crew:	2 + 8/10
Configuration:	4 x 4
Armament:	See text
Length:	5.98m
Width:	2.1m
Height hull top:	2.205m
Ground clearance (axle):	0.273m
Ground clearance (hull):	0.5m
Wheelbase:	3.6m
Weight, combat:	7,800kg
Weight, empty:	6,000kg
Power-to-weight ratio:	18.49hp/tonne
Engine:	Perkins Model 6.354.4 6-cylinder diesel developing 138hp at 2,800rpm
Maximum road speed:	95km/hr
Maximum range:	1,600km
Fuel capacity:	310 lit
Fording:	0.8m
Trench:	Not applicable
Gradient:	65%
Side slope:	40%
Armour:	5.8mm (maximum)
Armour type:	Steel
NBC system:	None
Night vision equipment:	None

DEVELOPMENT

TPK 420 BL was designed as a private venture by ACMAT and is a VLRA (4 x 4) 2,500kg long-range reconnaissance vehicle with an armoured body. First prototype completed in 1980 and production commenced same year. Engine is at far front with driver and commander to its immediate rear and troop compartment extending right to rear of vehicle. Troops sit at rear on bench seats down each side. One version has fully enclosed roof with three sliding bullet-proof windows each side allowing some occupants to use small arms from inside. Other model has open roof and sides hinged outwards and downwards at mid-point for rapid exit or return fire.

Optional equipment on open-topped version includes 81mm TDA mortar firing to rear, 7.62mm or 12.7mm pintle-mounted MGs or Euromissile MILAN ATGW. Fully enclosed version can have air-

conditioning system and be used as command or radio vehicle.

VARIANTS

VBL light armoured car is essentially the fully enclosed APC with one-man turret on roof armed with 7.62mm or 12.7mm MG. The VBL can be fitted with different radios and an air conditioning system and be modified for more specific roles such as an ambulance or command post vehicle.
6 x 6 version still at prototype stage, designated TPK 650 CTL.
There are also a number of specialised reconnaissance vehicles and an ambulance.

STATUS

In production. In service with a number of countries including Botswana, Central African Republic, Cote d'Ivoire, Gabon, Saudi Arabia, Senegal and Zimbabwe.

MANUFACTURER

ACMAT, Ateliers de Construction Mécanique de l'Atlantique, Saint-Nazaire, France.

KEY RECOGNITION FEATURES

- Engine front with radiator grilles under nose, sloped windscreen with two windows covered by armoured shutters hinged at top, side door to immediate rear of windscreen which opens forwards

- Horizontal roof line that extends to rear, two doors in hull rear, troop compartment at rear has three square bullet-proof windows each side

- Two road wheels each side with hull sides sloping inwards from just above road wheels

Below: ACMAT armoured ambulance with higher roof line

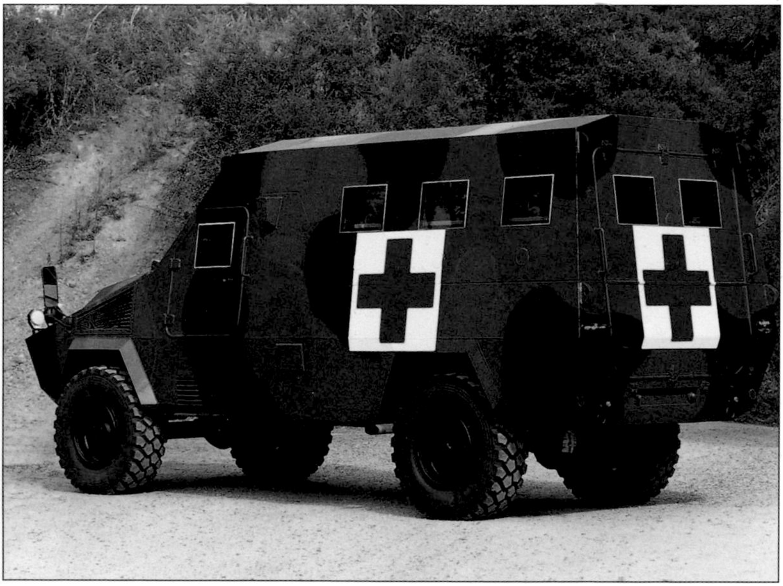

Panhard VBL Scout Car (France)

SPECIFICATIONS

Crew:	3
Configuration:	4 x 4
Armament:	1 x 7.62mm MG, 1 x MILAN ATGW launcher
Ammunition:	3000 x 7.62mm, 6 x MILAN ATGW
Length:	3.87m
Width:	2.02m
Height:	1.7m (hull top), 2.14m (with 7.62mm MG)
Ground clearance:	0.37m
Wheelbase:	2.45m
Weight, combat:	3,590kg
Weight, empty:	2,890kg
Power-to-weight ratio:	29.57hp/tonne
Engine:	Peugeot XD3T, 4-cylinder turbocharged diesel developing 105hp at 4150rpm
Maximum road speed:	95km/hr
Maximum water speed:	4.5km/hr
Maximum road range:	600km, 800km with onboard fuel cans
Fording:	0.9m (see text)
Trench:	0.50m
Gradient:	50%
Side slope:	30%
Armour:	11.5mm (maximum)
Armour type:	Steel
NBC system:	Yes
Night vision equipment:	Yes (passive for driver)

(Above relates to French Army VBL in combat/anti-tank role)

DEVELOPMENT

In 1978 the French Army issued a requirement for a new light reconnaissance/anti-tank vehicle, the Véhicule Blindé Léger (VBL). Panhard and Renault each built prototypes for competitive evaluation and in February 1985 the Panhard VBL was selected, although at this time the vehicle was already in production for Mexico. The French Army has two basic versions of the VBL, combat/anti-tank with a three-man crew armed with a MILAN ATGW launcher and 7.62mm MG, and intelligence/scout with a two-man crew and armed with one 7.62mm and one 12.7mm MG.

All versions have engine front and crew compartment rear with three roof hatches and three doors. It is fully amphibious, with propeller at hull rear, and standard equipment includes central tyre pressure system. Options include heater, powered steering and air-conditioning system.

By late 2004 the total VBL order book stood at 2,272 for home and export.

VARIANTS

Panhard has proposed over 20 models of the VBL for the export market including radar (battlefield and air defence), anti-aircraft (Mistral SAMs), anti-tank (MILAN, HOT or TOW ATGWs) and internal security to name but a few. There is also a long wheelbase version of the VBL.

STATUS

In production. In service with Cameroon, Djibouti, France, Gabon, Greece, Indonesia, Kuwait, Oman, Mexico, Niger, Nigeria, Portugal, Qatar, Rwanda and Togo.

MANUFACTURER

Société de Constructions Mécaniques Panhard et Levassor, Paris, France.

KEY RECOGNITION FEATURES

- Almost vertical hull front, sloping glacis plate with large access panel in upper part, forward part of rear crew compartment slopes to rear, horizontal roof with three hatches, single door in hull rear

- Two large road wheels, hull above wheel arches slope inwards, single forward-opening door in each side with bullet-proof window in upper part

- Heavy armament, eg 12.7mm M2 HB MG or MILAN, is mounted on circular hatch at rear

Left: Panhard VBL LWB with TOW ATGW

Right: Panhard VBL LWB in command role

Below: Panhard VBL with MILAN ATGW (Christian Dumont)

Panhard M3 APC (France)

Above: Panhard M3 internal security vehicle

SPECIFICATIONS

Crew:	2 + 10
Armament:	See text
Length:	4.45m
Width:	2.4m
Height:	2.48m (with twin 7.62mm MG turret)
Height to hull top:	2m
Ground clearance:	0.35m
Wheelbase:	2.7m
Weight, combat:	6,100kg
Weight, unloaded:	5,300kg
Power-to-weight ratio:	14.75hp/tonne
Engine:	Panhard Model 4 HD 4-cylinder air-cooled petrol developing 90hp at 4,700rpm
Maximum road speed:	90km/hr
Maximum water speed:	4km/hr
Maximum road range:	600km
Fuel capacity:	165 lit
Fording:	Amphibious
Vertical obstacle:	0.3m
Trench (1 channel):	0.8m
Trench (5 channels):	3.1m
Gradient:	60%
Side slope:	30%
Armour:	12mm (maximum)
Armour type:	Steel
NBC system:	Optional
Night vision equipment:	Optional

DEVELOPMENT

M3 (4 x 4) was developed by Panhard as a private venture, first prototype completed in 1969 and first production vehicles in 1971. Well over 1,200 have been built for export with sales made to some 35 countries. Ninety-five per cent of automotive components are identical to those of the Panhard AML range 4 x 4 armoured cars. Panhard M3 is used for a wide range of roles including internal security, ambulance and command post.

Driver sits front, engine to his rear, troop compartment occupies remainder of vehicle. Troops enter and leave via single door in sides and twin doors in rear. Eight firing ports. Wide range of turrets, mounts and cupolas can be mounted on roof armed with cannon, machine guns and ATGWs such as MILAN.

Vehicle is fully amphibious, propelled by its wheels. Wide range of optional equipment including front-mounted winch, air-conditioning system and two electrically operated smoke grenade dischargers.

VARIANTS

M3/VDA anti-aircraft vehicle with one-man power-operated turret armed with twin 20mm cannon. Before firing, four outriggers are lowered to ground for a more stable firing platform. This version known to be in service with Ivory Coast, Niger and United Arab Emirates (Abu Dhabi).
M3/VAT repair vehicle with lifting gear at rear.
M3/VPC command vehicle with extensive communications equipment.
M3/VLA engineer vehicle with front-mounted obstacle-clearing blade.
M3/VTS ambulance which carries four stretcher patients or six walking wounded, or a mixture, plus its crew.
M3 radar can be fitted with wide range of radars including RASIT battlefield surveillance radar or RA 20S surveillance radar.
Buffalo APC which in 1986 replaced Panhard M3 in production. Essentially a Panhard M3 with additional external stowage spaces and original petrol engine replaced by 146hp V-6 petrol or 95hp diesel. This model now in service with Benin, Colombia and Rwanda. The 95hp diesel is the same Peugeot XD3T that is fitted to the Panhard VBL (4 x 4) light armoured vehicle and can be backfitted to the Panhard AML.

STATUS

Production complete, replaced in production by Buffalo. M3 known to be in service with Algeria, Bahrain, Burkina Faso, Bosnia-Herzegovina, Burundi, Chad, Democratic Republic of Congo, Gabon, Ireland, Ivory Coast, Kenya, Lebanon, Malaysia, Morocco, Niger, Nigeria, Saudi Arabia, Senegal, Togo, United Arab Emirates.

MANUFACTURER

Société de Constructions Mécaniques Panhard et Levassor, Paris, France.

KEY RECOGNITION FEATURES

- Pointed front with well-sloped glacis plate, driver's position in upper part, horizontal roof with main armament normally centre, secondary armament rear

- Vertical hull sides with upper part sloping inwards, three observation/firing hatches each side, vertical hull rear with two outward-opening doors each with firing port

- Two large road wheels each side with forward-opening door between, wheels outside hull envelope with mudguards which blow off if vehicle runs over mine

Below: Panhard M3 (4 x 4) with twin 7.62mm MG turret

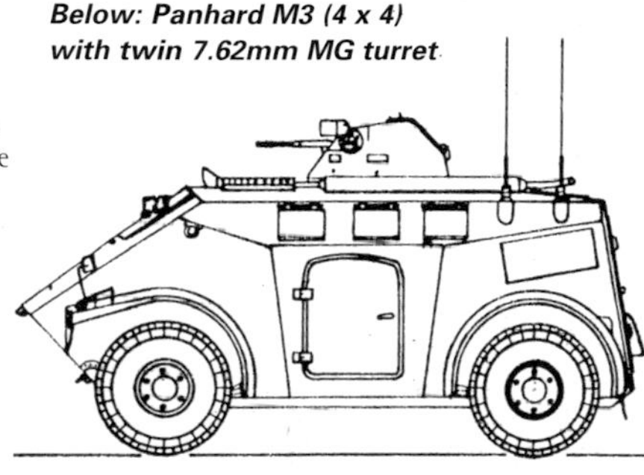

Right: Panhard M3 VDA with twin 20mm SPAAG

Panhard AML Light Armoured Car (France)

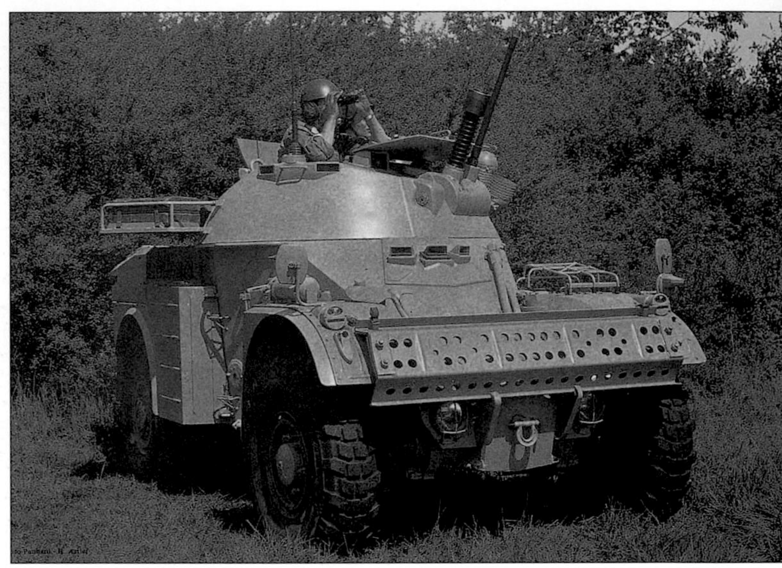

Above: Panhard AML with HE60-12 turret

SPECIFICATIONS (H 90 VERSION)

Crew:	3
Configuration:	4 x 4
Armament:	1 x 90mm, 1 x 7.62mm MG coaxial, 2 x 2 smoke grenade dischargers
Ammunition:	20 x 90mm, 2,000 x 7.62mm
Length gun forwards:	5.11m
Length hull:	3.79m
Width:	1.97m
Height overall:	2.07m
Ground clearance:	0.33m
Wheelbase:	2.5m
Weight, combat:	5,500kg
Power-to-weight ratio:	16.36hp/tonne
Engine:	Panhard Model 4 HD 4-cylinder air-cooled petrol developing 90hp at 4,700rpm. Late production models have Peugeot XD 3T diesel developing 98hp and a range of 700 to 800km
Maximum road speed:	90km/hr
Maximum road range:	600km
Fuel capacity:	156 lit
Fording:	1.1m
Vertical obstacle:	0.3m
Trench with one channel:	0.8m
Trench with three channels:	3.1m
Gradient:	60%
Side slope:	30%
Armour:	8-12mm (hull)
Armour type:	Steel
NBC system:	None
Night vision equipment:	Optional

DEVELOPMENT

Panhard AML (Automitrailleusse Legere) was developed for the French Army with first prototypes completed in 1959 and first production vehicles in 1961. By 2004 over 4,800 vehicles had been built for home and export (including those built under licence in South Africa by Sandock-Austral). Panhard M3 (4 x 4)

armoured personnel carrier (qv) shares 95 per cent automotive components of AML and also has been built in large numbers.

All AMLs have similar layout with driver front, turret centre and engine rear. The Hispano-Suiza two-man H 90 turret traverses through 360° and the 90mm gun elevates from -8° to +15°. Main armament comprises 90mm gun which fires HE, HEAT, canister and smoke projectiles. 7.62mm machine gun is mounted coaxial with left of main armament and 7.62mm or 12.7mm machine gun can be mounted on turret roof.

VARIANTS

AML with Lynx 90 turret, replaced H 90 turret, similar armament but can have powered traverse, laser rangefinder and night vision equipment, commander's cupola raised on left side.
AML with HE-60-7 turret, 60mm mortar and twin 7.62mm MGs.
AML with HE60-12 turret, 60mm mortar and 12.7mm MG.
AML with HE60-20 turret, 60mm mortar and 20mm cannon.
AML with HE60-20 Serval turret, replaced above in production.
AML with S 530 turret, twin 20mm anti-aircraft cannon, used only by Venezuela.
AML with diesel engine, late production AMLs have Panhard diesel replaced by more fuel efficient Peugeot diesel which is also installed in the Panhard VBL (4 x 4) (qv) light armoured vehicle. Panhard also now offer an upgrade package that can include the new diesel engine, improved automotives, new exhaust and upgraded weapons. For the H 90 turret, for example, the 90mm gun can be modified to fire APFSDS ammunition, a laser rangefinder added for improved first round hit probability and passive night vision equipment installed.
South African-built vehicle is known as Eland and ran through to Mk 7 in two basic versions: **Eland 60** with 60mm mortar and 7.62mm MG and **Eland 90** with 90mm gun and 7.62mm coaxial MG. Both have roof-mounted 7.62mm MG, different engine and detailed differences to French-built vehicles.

KEY RECOGNITION FEATURES

- Well-sloped inverted-V glacis plate with driver's hatch in upper part, horizontal hull top with engine rear, stowage boxes project forward of rear wheels. Diesel engine version has different hull rear

- Turret has bustle that extends over hull rear, vertical sides slope slightly inwards. 90mm gun has prominent double-baffle muzzle brake, no fume extractor or thermal sleeve. Two smoke grenade dischargers each side at turret rear

- Two large road wheels each side with large rearward-opening door to rear of first road wheel. Left door has spare wheel and tyre. Sand channels normally carried across lower hull front

STATUS

Production as required. In service with Algeria, Argentina, Bahrain, Benin, Bosnia-Herzegovina, Burkina Faso, Burundi, Chad, Democratic Republic of Congo, Djibouti, Ecuador, El Salvador, Gabon, Guinea, Ireland, Ivory Coast, Kenya, Lebanon, Lesotho, Malawai, Malaysia, Mauritania, Morocco, Niger, Nigeria, Portugal, Rwanda, Saudi Arabia, Senegal, Somalia, South Africa, Sudan, Togo, Tunisia, Uganda, United Arab Emirates, Venezuela, Yemen and Zimbabwe.

MANUFACTURERS

Société de Constructions Mécaniques Panhard et Levassor, Paris, France; Sandock Austral (today called BAE Systems Land Systems), South Africa.

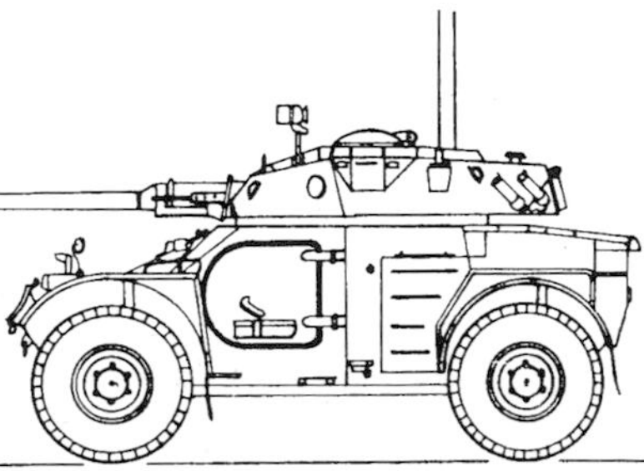

Right: Panhard AML with H 90 90mm turret

Berliet VXB-170 APC (France)

Above: VXB-170 (4 x 4) without armament (Pierre Touzin)

SPECIFICATIONS

Crew:	1 + 11
Configuration:	4 x 4
Armament:	1 x 7.62mm MG, 2 x 2 smoke grenade dischargers (optional)
Ammunition:	1,000 x 7.62mm
Length:	5.99m
Width:	2.5m
Height:	2.05m (without armament)
Ground clearance:	0.45m
Wheelbase:	3m
Weight, combat:	12,700kg
Weight, empty:	9,800kg
Power-to-weight ratio:	13.38hp/tonne
Engine:	Berliet model V800 M V-8 diesel developing 170hp at 3,000rpm
Maximum road speed:	85km/hr
Maximum water speed:	4km/hr
Road range:	750km
Fuel capacity:	220 lit
Fording:	Amphibious
Vertical obstacle:	0.3m
Trench:	Not applicable
Gradient:	60%
Side slope:	30%
Armour:	7mm
Armour type:	Steel
NBC system:	None
Night vision equipment:	Optional

DEVELOPMENT

VXB-170 was developed as a private venture by Société des Automobiles Berliet under the designation BL-12; first prototype completed in 1968. With a number of improvements it was adopted by the French Gendarmerie for internal security, the first of 155 vehicles delivered in 1973. In 1975 Berliet became part of the Renault Group which also included Saviem, so production of VXB-170 was phased out after completion of existing orders; the French Army adopted the VAB (4 x 4) to meet its future requirements.

VXB-170 has an all-welded steel hull, driver front and troop compartment extending right to rear of vehicle, except for engine compartment on left side at rear. In addition to the three doors there are five hatches in roof, one for driver with larger circular hatch to rear on which main armament is normally mounted.

French Gendarmerie vehicles are blue and normally have hydraulically operated obstacle clearing blade at hull front and are fitted with roof-mounted BTM 103 light turret armed with 7.62mm MG and 40mm grenade launcher. Turret traverse is 360° and weapon elevation from -15° to +60°.

VXB-170 is fully amphibious, propelled by its wheels, and optional equipment includes heater, night vision equipment, NBC system, front-mounted winch and bullet-proof tyres.

VARIANTS
Wide range of variants were projected and prototypes of some were built, for example with a two-man turret from the AML armed with 60mm mortar and 7.62mm MGs. None entered production.

STATUS
Production complete. In service with France (Gendarmerie), Gabon and Senegal.

MANUFACTURER
Société des Automobiles Berliet, Bourge, France. This company no longer exists.

KEY RECOGNITION FEATURES

- Four large road wheels, hull has pointed nose with driver far front, large windscreen to front and sides
- Lower half of hull vertical, top half sloping slightly inwards, single door in each hull side which opens forwards
- Engine compartment left rear with grilles in roof, entry door in right hull rear

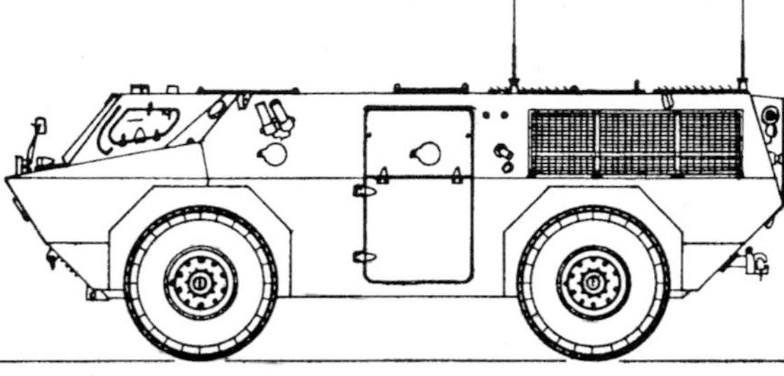

Right: VXB-170 (4 x 4) without armament

Left: VXB-170 (4 x 4) showing amphibious capabilities

Left: VXB-170 (4 x 4) with cupola-mounted MG (Pierre Touzin)

Krauss-Maffei Wegmann Dingo All Protected Vehicle (Germany)

Above: Dingo APV armed with 7.62mm MG (Krauss-Maffei Wegmann)

SPECIFICATIONS

Crew:	5
Configuration:	4 x 4
Armament:	1 x 7.62mm MG
Ammunition:	500 x 7.62mm
Length:	5.40m
Width:	2.30m
Height:	2.30m
Ground clearance:	0.42m
Wheelbase:	3.25m
Weight, combat:	8,800kg
Weight, unloaded:	7,400kg
Power-to-weight ratio:	27.27hp/tonne
Engine:	Mercedes-Benz diesel developing 240hp
Maximum road speed:	90km/h
Maximum road range:	700km
Fuel capacity:	Not available
Fording:	1.20m
Vertical obstacle:	Not available
Trench:	Not available
Gradient:	60%
Side slope:	30%
Armour:	Classified
Armout type:	Steel/Laminate
NBC system:	Optional
Night vision equipment:	Optional

DEVELOPMENT

The All Protected Vehicle (APV) was originally developed as a private venture by Krauss-Maffei Wegmann with the first of a number of prototypes being completed in 1995.

This was followed by a pre-production model in 1996 with a third vehicle to production standard following in 1997. Late in 1999 the German Army awarded Krauss-Maffei Wegmann a contract for 56 vehicles and the first of these was handed over in August 2000. Since then additional orders have been placed with a total of 137 units now delivered.

The vehicle essentially consists of a Mercedes-Benz UNIMOG U-1550L (4 x 4) cross-country chassis fitted with a heavily armoured crew compartment in the centre that provides the crew with protection from small arms fire, shell splinters and anti-tank and anti-personnel mines. The engine compartment is the front and the unarmoured cargo area at the rear.

The commander and driver are seated at the front with another three crew seats to the rear with all crew seats being provided with a full safety harness. Standard equipment on German

Army vehicles includes an air conditioning system, heater, anti-skid braking system, GPS navigation system, run flat tyres, communications and a reversing camera system. It can also be fitted with a central tyre pressure regulation system that allows the driver to adjust the tyre pressure to suit the terrain being crossed. Different wheelbase lengths are available as are different engine/transmission configurations.

Various weapon stations can be mounted on the roof of the vehicle with German Army vehicles normally being fitted with a 7.62mm MG3 machine gun that can be aimed and fired from within the vehicle in complete safety.

VARIANTS

According to Krauss-Maffei Wegmann the Dingo APV can be adopted for a wide range of battlefield roles such as armoured personnel carrier, light reconnaissance vehicle, command and control vehicle, material transport vehicle, weapon carrier, ambulance, light air defence vehicle, missile launching vehicle and forward observer vehicle. Tha latest model is the Dingo 2 based on a Mercedes-Benz U5000 (4 x 4) chassis with the first German Army order being for 52 units with deliveries starting in 2005.

KEY RECOGNITION FEATURES

- Vertical hull front in three parts with left and right parts having horizontal louvres. Bonnet slopes slightly upwards to large one-piece bullet proof windscreen that slopes slightly to the rear. Horizontal roof with 7.62mm machine gun mount on forward part

- Vertical hull sides with upper part sloping slightly inwards with two forward opening doors in either side of the hull which have a large bullet proof window in their upper part

- Two large road wheels with lower part of hull sloping inwards so that it forms a V shape for enhaced protection against mines

STATUS

Production. In service with Germany Army.

MANUFACTURER

Krauss-Maffei Wegmann, Munich, Germany.

Below: Dingo 2 APV armed with 7.62mm MG

Rheinmetall Landsysteme TM 170 APC (Germany)

SPECIFICATIONS

Crew:	2 + 10
Configuration:	4 x 4
Armament:	Optional
Length:	6.14m
Width:	2.47m
Height:	2.32m (hull top)
Ground clearance:	0.48m
Wheelbase:	3.25m
Weight, combat:	11,650kg
Weight, unloaded:	8800kg
Power-to-weight ratio:	18hp/tonne
Engine:	Daimler-Benz OM366 supercharged diesel developing 240hp at 1400rpm
Maximum road speed:	100km/hr
Maximum water speed:	9km/hr
Maximum road range:	870km
Fuel capacity:	200 lit
Fording:	Amphibious
Vertical obstacle:	0.6m
Trench:	Not applicable
Gradient:	80%
Side slope:	40%
Armour:	8mm (estimate)
Armour type:	Steel
NBC system:	Optional
Night vision equipment:	Optional

DEVELOPMENT

TM 170 (4 x 4) was developed as a private venture by Thyssen Henschel (today called Rheinmetall Landsysteme) and entered production in 1979. It consists of a UNIMOG (4 x 4) cross-country truck chassis with an all-welded steel body for protection from small arms fire and shell splinters.

Engine compartment is front with commander and driver to its immediate rear and troop compartment extending right to rear of vehicle. Wide range of weapon stations can be mounted on top of hull to rear of commander's and driver's position, such as turret with twin 7.62mm MGs or one-man turret with 20mm cannon.

Basic vehicle is fully amphibious, propelled by its wheels or two waterjets which give maximum speed of 9km/hr. Before entering the water a trim vane is erected at the front and bilge pumps switched on. Wide range of optional equipment available including NBC system, night vision equipment, obstacle clearing blade, smoke grenade dischargers, winch, flashing lights, fire extinguishing system, heater, spherical firing ports and loudspeaker.

VARIANTS

TM 170 can be adapted for a wide range of roles including communications and workshop vehicles. More recent version is TM 170 Hardliner with a number of detailed improvements.

Rheinmetall Landsysteme also built prototypes of TM 125 and TM 90 (4 x 4) armoured personnel carriers, but they did not enter production and are no longer being offered.

STATUS

Production as required. In service with Germany, Kuwait and Macedonia.

MANUFACTURER

Rheinmetall Landsysteme GmbH, Kassel, Germany.

KEY RECOGNITION FEATURES

- Box-type engine compartment front, radiator grille under nose with slightly sloping glacis plate, almost vertical windscreen which can be covered by two armoured shutters hinged at bottom, horizontal roof with hull rear sloping inwards

- Two road wheels each side, bullet-proof window in upper part of hull front which can be covered by hinged shutter, single door in each side of hull and hatch in hull rear

- Troop compartment has firing ports in sides and rear, hull sides are welded midway up then slope inwards at top and bottom

Left: TM 170 (4 x 4)

Right: TM 170 (4 x 4) from the rear (Christopher F Foss)

Right: TM 170 (4 x 4) with obstacle clearing blade

Rheinmetall Landsysteme UR-416 APC (Germany)

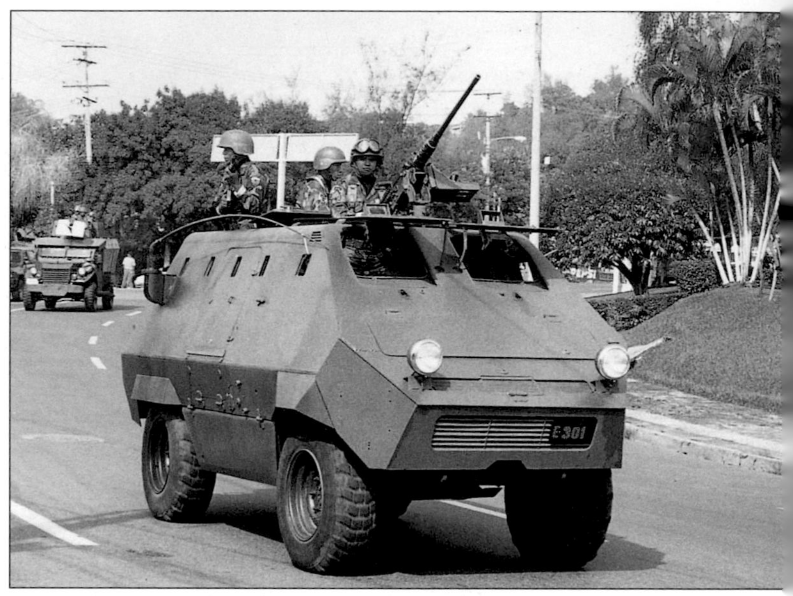

Above: UR-416 with 12.7mm MG (Julio Montes)

SPECIFICATIONS

Crew:	2 + 8
Configuration:	4 x 4
Armament:	1 x 7.62mm MG
Ammunition:	1,000 x 7.62mm
Length:	5.1m
Width:	2.25m
Height:	2.52m (with turret), 2.25m (hull top)
Ground clearance:	0.44m
Wheelbase:	2.9m
Weight, combat:	7,600kg
Weight, empty:	5,400kg
Power-to-weight ratio:	16.5hp/tonne
Engine:	Daimler-Benz OM 352 6-cylinder water-cooled diesel developing 120hp at 2,800rpm
Maximum road speed:	81km/hr
Maximum road range:	600 to 700km
Fuel capacity:	150 lit
Fording:	1.3m
Vertical obstacle:	0.55m
Trench:	Not applicable
Gradient:	70%
Side slope:	35%
Armour:	9mm
Armour type:	Steel
NBC system:	None
Night vision equipment:	Optional

DEVELOPMENT

UR-416 was developed by Rheinstahl Maschinenbau (which is today known as Rheinmetall Landsysteme) as a private venture, first prototype completed in 1965. Production commenced in 1969, and since then over 1,000 have been built, mostly for export where it is normally used in internal security by police or other paramilitary units.

UR-416 is a Mercedes-Benz (4 x 4) UNIMOG cross-country truck chassis with an all-welded body that provides protection from small arms fire and shell splinters.

Commander and driver sit front with engine forward and below, leaving the whole of the rear

ear for troops. Basic model has three doors, one ıch side and one in rear, and is fitted with ırious weapons on the roof ranging from simple ntle-mounted 7.62mm MG to turret armed with)mm cannon.

Optional equipment includes spherical firing ɔrts with vision devices, fire detection and ‹tinguishing system, air-conditioning system, ɜater, run-flat tyres, smoke grenade dischargers ıd 5,000kg-capacity winch.

'ARIANTS

R-416 can be adopted for wide range of roles ıcluding ambulance, anti-tank (recoilless rifle or ıissile), internal security (with wide range of ɜquipment including obstacle-clearing blade ·ont), reconnaissance and workshop. Latest ɜrsion is UR-416 M which has ·any detailed improvements ıcluding better visibility and ·rmoured flaps.

'TATUS

roduction complete. Known users ıclude Argentina, Ecuador, l Salvador, Germany, Greece, :enya, Morocco, Netherlands, 'akistan, Peru, Qatar, Saudi Arabia, ·pain, Togo, Turkey, Venezuela and :imbabwe.

MANUFACTURER

ʀheinmetall Landsysteme GmbH, :assel, Germany.

KEY RECOGNITION FEATURES

- Box-shaped hull with front sloping to rear, horizontal roof, sloping rear which sometimes has spare wheel, hull sides slope inwards from above wheel arches

- Radiator grilles on lower hull front with observation flaps at top which hinge upwards for normal use, firing ports in sides and rear of hull

- Armament normally mounted on forward part of roof, two road wheels each side with single door in each side and one rear

Above: UR-416 with 12.7mm MG (Julio Montes)

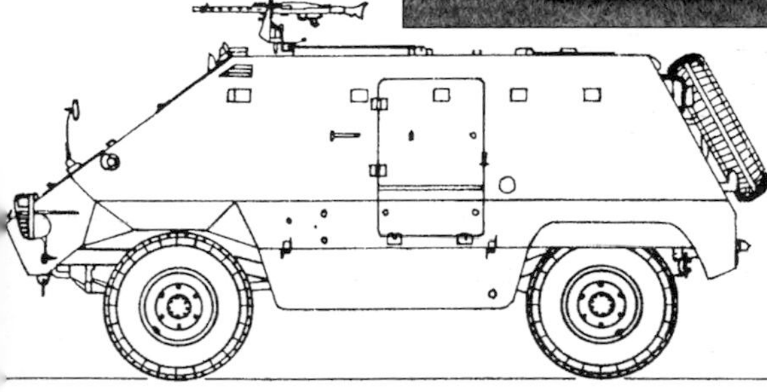

Left: UR-416 (4 x 4) with 7.62mm MG

Rheinmetall Landsysteme Condor APC (Germany)

Above: Condor (4 x 4) in command post role (Richard Stickland)

SPECIFICATIONS

Crew:	2 + 12
Configuration:	4 x 4
Armament:	1 x 20mm, 1 x 7.62mm MG (coaxial), 2 x 3 smoke grenade dischargers
Ammunition:	220 x 20mm, 500 x 7.62mm
Length:	6.13m
Width:	2.47m
Height:	2.79m (turret top), 2.18m (hull top)
Ground clearance:	0.475m
Wheelbase:	3.275m
Weight, combat:	12,400kg
Weight, empty:	9,200kg
Power-to-weight ratio:	13.54hp/tonne
Engine:	Daimler-Benz OM 352A 6-cylinder supercharged water-cooled diesel developing 168hp
Maximum road speed:	100km/hr
Maximum water speed:	10km/hr
Maximum road range:	900km
Fuel capacity:	280 lit
Fording:	Amphibious
Vertical obstacle:	0.55m
Trench:	Not applicable
Gradient:	60%
Side slope:	30%
Armour:	Classified
Armour type:	Steel
NBC system:	Optional
Night vision equipment:	Optional

DEVELOPMENT

Condor was developed by the now Rheinmetall Landsysteme (previously Henschel Wehrtechnik) as a private venture, first prototype completed in 1978. Wherever possible standard commercial components were used in the design to keep procurement and life-cycle costs to a minimum.

Largest order for Condor was placed by Malaysia in 1981 and consisted of 459 vehicles including ambulance, APC with twin 7.62mm MG, fitter's vehicle with crane, command post vehicle and APC with FVT900 one-man turret with 20mm cannon, 7.62mm MG coaxial with main armament and smoke grenade dischargers each side.

Driver sits front left, engine compartment to is right and troop compartment extending right o rear. Condor is fully amphibious, propelled by a ropeller mounted under hull rear. Before ntering the water a trim vane is erected at front f hull. Optional equipment includes heater and vinch. The latter has 50m of cable and can be sed to the front or rear of the vehicle.

KEY RECOGNITION FEATURES

- Box-type hull with driver's position far front left side, distinctive windows to front and sides, nose slopes back under hull and glacis slopes up to horizontal hull roof that extends right to rear, all four corners of hull angled
- Two large road wheels each side with forward-opening door in each side and another door in rear
- Hull sides slope inwards top and bottom with external wheel arches

VARIANTS

he company offers wide range of armament ncluding turret with twin 7.62mm MGs, pintle-nounted 7.62mm and 12.7mm MGs and ATGWs uch as HOT, MILAN and TOW. There are also ommand post and recovery versions of the Condor.

STATUS

Production as required. In service with Argentina, Malaysia, Portugal, Thailand, Turkey, Jruguay and other countries.

MANUFACTURER

Rheinmetall Landsysteme GmbH, Kassel, Germany.

Right: Condor (4 x 4) with 20mm turret

Below: Condor (4 x 4) with MG turret (Richard Stickland)

FUG Amphibious Scout Car (Hungary)

Above: FUG (4 x 4)

SPECIFICATIONS

Crew:	2 + 4
Configuration:	4 x 4
Armament:	1 x 7.62mm MG
Ammunition:	1250 x 7.62mm
Length:	5.79m
Width:	2.5m
Height:	1.91m (hull top), 2.25m (OT-65A turret top)
Ground clearance:	0.34m
Wheelbase:	3.3m
Power-to-weight ratio:	15.87hp/tonne
Engine:	Csepel D.414.44 4-cylinder in-line water-cooled diesel developing 100hp at 2,300rpm
Maximum road speed:	87km/hr
Maximum water speed:	9km/hr
Road range:	600km
Fuel capacity:	200 lit
Fording:	Amphibious
Vertical obstacle:	0.4m
Trench:	1.2m
Gradient:	60%
Side slope:	30%
Armour:	13mm (maximum)
Armour type:	Steel
Night vision equipment:	Yes (driver only, infra-red)

DEVELOPMENT

FUG (Felderito Uszo Gepkosci) entered service with the Hungarian Army in 1964 and fulfils a similar role to the Russian BRDM-1 (4 x 4) amphibious scout car. Major differences are that FUG has engine rear and is propelled by two water jets at rear (BRDM-1 has one). Before entering water, bilge pumps are switched on and trim vane, stowed under nose when not required, is erected. A 7.62mm SGMG MG is pintle-mounted on forward part of roof.

When travelling across rough country, two powered belly wheels are lowered each side to improve mobility. All FUGs have central tyre pressure regulation system.

VARIANTS

Ambulance, but probably limited to walking wounded only as sole means of entry and exit is via roof hatches.

Radiological-chemical reconnaissance vehicle, mounted on each side of hull rear is a rack that dispenses lane marking poles.

OT-65A is a former Czechoslovak modification, a basic FUG fitted with OT-62B turret (full tracked APC armed with 7.62mm M59T machine gun). 82mm T-21 Tarasnice recoilless rifle on right side of turret. There are a number of other specialised

ormer Czechoslovakian versions including recce, IBC and fitted with radar.
PSZH-IV APC, there is a separate entry overleaf or the PSZH-IV (4 x 4) vehicle.

STATUS

Production complete. In service with Czech Republic, Hungary (basic FUG is OT-65) and lovakia.

MANUFACTURER

Hungarian state arsenals.

KEY RECOGNITION FEATURES

- Glacis plate slopes up to crew compartment which has sloping front and sides, roof hatches are only means of entry
- Engine compartment rear, roof almost parallel to crew compartment, exhaust pipe on right side
- Twin belly wheels each side which are raised when travelling on roads

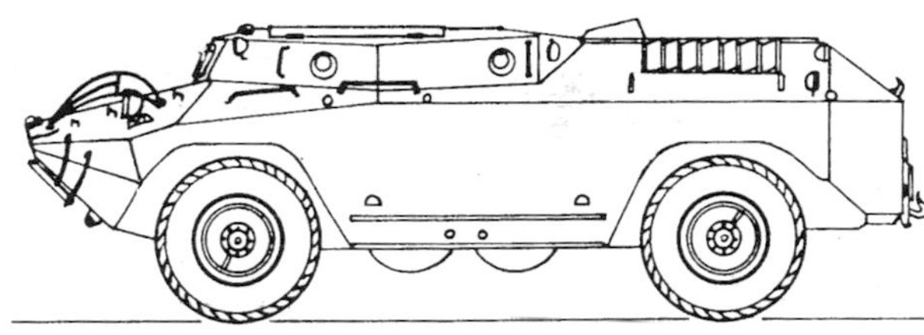

***Right:** FUG (4 x 4) without armament*

***Right:** FUG (4 x 4) radiological-chemical reconnaissance vehicle with trim vane erected*

***Right:** FUG (4 x 4) without armament*

PSZH-IV APC (Hungary)

Above: PSZH-IV

SPECIFICATIONS

Crew:	3 + 6
Configuration:	4 x 4
Armament:	1 x 14.5mm MG (main), 1 x 7.62mm MG (coaxial)
Ammunition:	500 x 14.5mm, 2,000 7.62mm
Length:	5.695m
Width:	2.5m
Height:	2.308m
Ground clearance:	0.42m
Wheelbase:	3.3m
Weight, combat:	7,600kg
Power-to-weight ratio:	13.15hp/tonne
Engine:	Csepel D.414.44 4-cylinder in-line water-cooled diesel developing 100hp at 2,300rpm
Maximum road speed:	80km/hr
Maximum water speed:	9km/hr
Road range:	500km
Fuel capacity:	200 lit
Fording:	Amphibious
Vertical obstacle:	0.4m
Trench:	0.6m (with channels)
Gradient:	60%
Side slope:	30%
Armour:	14mm (maximum)
Armour type:	Steel
NBC system:	Yes
Night vision equipment:	Yes (infra-red for gunner and driver)

DEVELOPMENT

PSZH-IV APC was developed in former Czechoslovakia after FUG (4 x 4) armoured amphibious scout car. PSZH-IV used to be called FUG-66 or FUG-70 as it was originally thought to be a reconnaissance vehicle, not an APC.

Commander and driver sit front with one-man manually operated turret to rear. The 14.5mm KPVT and 7.62mm PKT MGs have manual elevation from -5° to +30°, turret traverse is manual through 360°. Commander and driver can leave via their roof hatches but the only means of entry and exit for troops and gunner is the small two-part door in each side of hull.

Unlike the former Soviet BRDM-2 (4 x 4) amphibious reconnaissance vehicle, PSZH-IV does not have belly wheels to improve cross-country mobility. It is, however, fully amphibious, propelled by two waterjets mounted to rear of hull. Standard equipment includes central tyre pressure regulation system and NBC system.

ARIANTS

here are at least two command post versions of SZH-IV, one with turret and one without turret. here is also an ambulance and radiological-hemical reconnaissance vehicle.

The latter is very similar to the former Soviet RDM-2 vehicle designated the BRDM-2RKhb and s distinguishable by the two rectangular racks ositioned one either side of the hull rear that ispense lane marking pennants into the ground. his is designated the PSZH-CH/D-944VS.

TATUS

roduction complete. In service with Czech epublic (OT-66), Hungary and Slovakia.

MANUFACTURER

ungarian state arsenals.

KEY RECOGNITION FEATURES

- Turret with no roof hatches over forward part of hull, 14.5mm MG right and 7.62mm MG left
- Forward-opening door in each side of hull to rear of first road wheel station. Upper part of hull either side slopes inwards
- Trim vane for amphibious operations stowed on glacis plate

Below and bottom: PSZH-IV

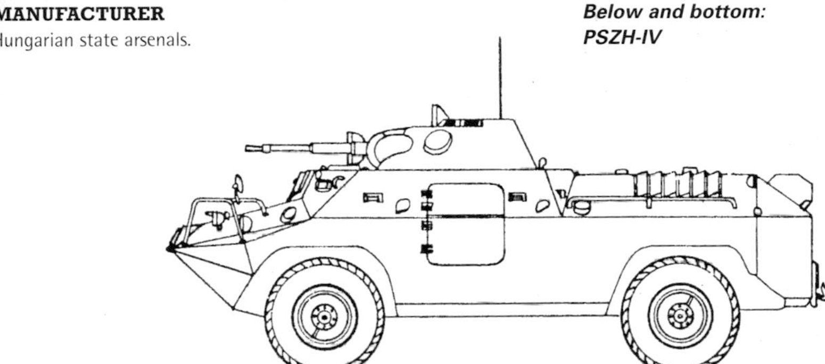

RAM Family of Light AFVs (Israel)

Above: RAM TCM-20 AA (anti-aircraft)

SPECIFICATIONS (RAM V-1)

Crew:	2 + 7
Configuration:	4 x 4
Armament:	Depends on role
Ammunition:	Depends on role
Length:	5.52m
Width:	2.03m
Height overall:	1.72m
Ground clearance (hull):	0.575m
Ground clearance (axles):	0.31m
Wheelbase:	3.9m
Weight, combat:	5,750kg
Weight, unloaded:	4,300kg
Power-to-weight ratio:	22.05hp/tonne
Engine:	Deutz air-cooled 6-cylinder diesel developing 132bhp
Maximum road speed:	96km/hr
Maximum road range:	800km
Fuel capacity:	160 lit
Fording:	1.00m
Vertical obstacle:	0.8m
Trench:	Not applicable
Gradient:	64%
Side slope:	35%
Armour:	8mm
Armour type:	Steel
NBC system:	None
Night vision equipment:	Optional

DEVELOPMENT

In the early 1970s RAMTA Structures and Systems, a subsidiary of Israel Aircraft Industries, designed and built as a private venture the RBY Mk1 light armoured reconnaissance vehicle which was subsequently built for home and export markets. It could be used for a wide range of roles and with various weapon systems including pintle-mounted 7.62mm MGs up to a 106mm recoilless rifle. In 1979 the RAM family of light AFVs was announced by the same company and this has now replaced the RBY in production. The RAM family has been expanded into two basic groups: RAM V-1 open top and RAM V-2 closed top. Main improvements on the original RBY Mk1 are increased ground clearance owing to larger tyres, increased range of action (original petrol engine replaced by diesel) and automatic transmission.

VARIANTS

Infantry fighting vehicle has three pintle-mounted 7.62mm MGs, one anti-tank rocket launcher.

Infantry combat vehicle as above but also carries 52mm mortar and night vision equipment.

TCM-20 AA fitted with one-man power-operated turret, armed with twin 20mm cannon, to provide more stable firing platform. Stabilisers lowered to ground before firing.

Close-range anti-tank has 106mm M40 recoilless rifle.

Long-range anti-tank has Raytheon Systems Company TOW ATGW launcher and two 7.62mm MGs.

RAM V-2 AFV has fully enclosed troop compartment for crew of eight or ten, and can be fitted with wide range of weapon stations including 7.62mm and 12.7mm MGs and 40mm grenade launcher.

KEY RECOGNITION FEATURES

- Spare tyre in horizontal position at front, open-topped crew compartment centre with four upward-opening hatches in forward part (two front, one each side), engine compartment rear. No side doors

- Two large wheels each side at extreme ends of vehicle, high ground clearance, extensive external stowage

STATUS

Production as required. RAM and RBY series vehicles are in service with Botswana, Cameroon, Democratic Republic of Congo, Gabon, Guatemala, Israel, Lesotho and Morocco.

MANUFACTURER

RAMTA Structures and Systems, Israel Aircraft Industries, Beer Sheba, Israel.

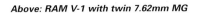

Above: RAM V-1 with twin 7.62mm MG

Below: RAM V-1 with Raytheon TOW ATGW launcher

Fiat/Oto Melara Type 6616 Armoured Car (Italy)

SPECIFICATIONS

Crew:	3
Configuration:	4 x 4
Armament:	1 x 20mm, 1 x 7.62mm MG (coaxial), 2 x 3 smoke grenade dischargers
Ammunition:	400 x 20mm, 1,000 x 7.62mm
Length gun forwards:	5.37m
Length hull:	5.37m
Width:	2.5m
Height:	2.035m (turret roof)
Ground clearance:	0.44m (hull centre), 0.37m (axles)
Wheelbase:	2.75m
Weight, combat:	8,000kg
Power-to-weight ratio:	20.20hp/tonne
Engine:	Model 8062.24 supercharged liquid-cooled in-line diesel developing 160hp at 3,200rpm
Maximum road speed:	100km/hr
Maximum water speed:	5km/hr
Maximum road range:	700km
Fuel capacity:	150 lit
Fording:	Amphibious
Vertical obstacle:	0.45m
Trench:	Not applicable
Gradient:	60%
Side slope:	30%
NBC system:	Optional
Night vision equipment:	Optional

DEVELOPMENT

Type 6616 (4 x 4) was originally a joint development by FIAT and Oto Melara and shares many components with Type 6614 (4 x 4) armoured personnel carrier. FIAT was responsible for the hull, automotive components and final assembly; Oto Melara for the complete two-man turret.

First prototype was completed in 1972 and first order placed by the Italian Carabinieri. Production was completed after about 300 vehicles had been built for the home and export markets.

The turret has full power traverse through 360° and the 20mm Rheinmetall MK 20 Rh 202 cannon elevates from -5° to +35°. The 7.62mm MG is mounted coaxial above the 20mm cannon. Type 6616 is fully amphibious, propelled by its wheels. Optional equipment includes 4,500kg capacity

winch, NBC system, air-conditioning system and fire extinguishing system. A 106mm M40 recoilless rifle can be mounted on turret roof.

VARIANTS

For trials purposes, the FIAT-Oto Melara Type 6616 armoured car has been fitted with a number of different weapon systems as listed below, but so far none of these has entered production for the Type 6616:

Oto Melara OTO T 90 CKL turret armed with 90mm gun.

Oto Melara turret armed with Oto Melara 60mm High Velocity Gun System.

Oto Melara turret armed with 25mm cannon and 7.62mm coaxial machine gun.

STATUS

Production complete. In service with Italian Carabinieri, Peru, Somalia (current status uncertain) and other undisclosed countries. This vehicle is no longer marketed.

MANUFACTURER

IVECO-FIAT, Bolzano, Italy.

KEY RECOGNITION FEATURES

- Nose slopes back under hull, well-sloped glacis plate with driver's half-circular position on right side, turret centre

- Square turret with sides sloping slightly inwards, commander's cupola on left extends slightly over turret side, chamfer between turret front and sides

- Two large road wheels each side, horizontal louvres above both rear wheel stations, spare wheel often on hull rear, small hatch in lower part of hull side between wheels

***Above left:* Type 6616 (4 x 4)**

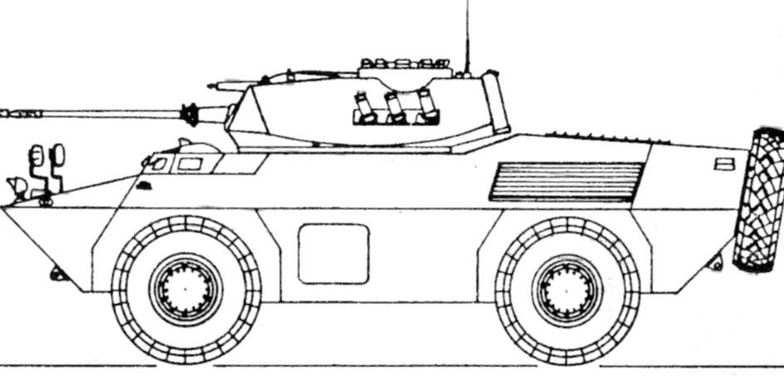

***Right:* Type 6616 (4 x 4)**

***Below:* Type 6616 (4 x 4)**

IVECO/Oto Melara Puma APC (Italy)

Above: Puma (6 x 6) APC

SPECIFICATIONS

Crew:	1 + 6
Configuration:	4 x 4
Armament:	1 x 7.62mm or 12.7mm MG, 2 x 3 smoke grenade dischargers
Length:	5.085m
Width:	2.10m
Height hull top:	1.678m
Ground clearance:	0.385m
Weight, combat:	7,000kg
Power-to-weight ratio:	25.7hp/tonne
Engine:	IVECO Type 8042 TCA 4-cylinder diesel developing 180hp at 3,000rpm
Maximum road speed:	115km/hr
Range:	700km
Fuel capacity:	150 lit
Fording:	1m
Vertical obstacle:	Not available
Trench:	Not available
Gradient:	60%
Side slope:	30%
Armour:	Classified
Armour type:	Steel
NBC system:	Yes
Night vision equipment:	Yes (passive)

DEVELOPMENT

IVECO/Oto Melara has considerable experience in the design, development and production of wheeled armoured vehicles and the Puma family has been developed to meet the requirements of the Italian Army for a vehicle to operate with the IVECO/ Oto Melara Centauro (8 x 8) tank destroyer/armoured car (qv).

The first prototype of the Puma was completed in 1988 and by 1990 a total of five vehicles had been built. The Italian Army subsequently awarded the company a contract to build six specialised versions of the Puma, one each for the MILAN and TOW ATGW systems, one for the Mistral SAM system, one 81mm mortar carrier, one ambulance and one command post vehicle. In 1999 the Italian Army placed a contract for the supply of 240 Puma (6 x 6) and 300 Puma (4 x 4).

The engine is at the front of the vehicle with the driver being seated towards the front on the left side and the troop compartment at the rear. Doors are provided in the sides and rear and on the roof is the commander's cupola that can be fitted with a 12.7mm or 7.62mm machine gun.

Standard equipment includes an integrated air conditioning system, fire detection and suppression system, power-operated winch, powered steering and run flat tyres.

VARIANTS

The 4 x 4 version of the Puma can be adopted for a wide range of roles in addition to those ordered by the Italian Army, for example NBC reconnaissance and internal security. More recently a 6 x 6 version of the Puma has been developed; this has the same automotive components as the Puma 4 x 4 including engine, automatic transmission and suspension and has a combat weight of 8,400kg. This version can carry eight men plus the driver and can be fitted with a wider range of armament stations. Its fuel capacity has been increased to 270 litres.

STATUS

In production. In service with Italian Army.

MANUFACTURER

IVECO/Oto Melara, Bolzano, Italy.

KEY RECOGNITION FEATURES

- Lower part of hull is vertical, well-sloped glacis plate that leads up to horizontal roof, vertical hull rear with lower part sloping inwards. Upper sides of hull slope inwards. Headlamps are recessed into front of hull

- Driver's hatch front left of roof with commander's cupola in centre and small rectangular roof hatch at rear. Large door in hull rear

- Two large road wheels either side with large door in centre that opens forwards, all doors have firing port and associated vision block above

Right: Puma (4 x 4) APC

Below: Puma (4 x 4) without armament installed

Fiat/Oto Melara Type 6614 APC (Italy)

Above: Type 6614 armed with 12.7mm MG

SPECIFICATIONS

Crew:	1 + 10
Configuration:	4 x 4
Armament:	1 x 12.7mm MG
Ammunition:	1,000 x 12.7mm
Length:	5.86m
Width:	2.5m
Height:	1.78m (hull top), 2.18m (MG mount)
Ground clearance:	0.37m (axles)
Wheelbase:	2.9m
Weight, combat:	8,500kg
Power-to-weight ratio:	18.82hp/tonne
Engine:	IVECO Model 8062.24 supercharged liquid-cooled in-line diesel developing 160hp at 3,200rpm
Maximum road speed:	100km/hr
Maximum water speed:	4.5km/hr
Maximum road range:	700km
Fuel capacity:	142 lit
Fording:	Amphibious
Vertical obstacle:	0.4m
Trench:	Not applicable
Gradient:	60%
Side slope:	30%
Armour:	6 to 8mm
Armour type:	Steel
NBC system:	None
Night vision equipment:	Optional

DEVELOPMENT

Type 6614 was a joint development between FIAT and Oto Melara, former responsible for hull and automotive components, latter for weapons installation. The vehicle shares many components with the FIAT/Oto Melara Type 6616 armoured car, for which there is a separate entry.

Driver sits front left, engine compartment to his right, whole remaining area to rear for 10 fully equipped troops, each with individual seats, and one manning the externally mounted 12.7mm HB MG. Gun is mounted on an M113 type cupola with no provision for aiming the weapon from inside the vehicle. Ten circular firing ports, each with vision block above, in troop compartment, four in each side of hull and one each side of rear ramp.

Type 6614 is fully amphibious, propelled by its wheels. Standard equipment includes ventilation

system and electrically operated bilge pumps. Optional equipment includes front-mounted winch, night vision equipment, air conditioning system, fire extinguishing system for wheel arches, smoke grenade dischargers and different armament installations such as turret with twin 7.62mm MG.

VARIANTS

Type 6614 can be used for a wide range of roles such as internal security and reconnaissance. Projected variants included ambulance, cargo carrier, command post and mortar carrier. For operations in the Balkans Italian Army vehicles have been fitted with additional passive armour.

STATUS

Production as required. In service with Argentina, Italy (police and air force), South Korea (licensed production), Peru, Somalia, Tunisia and Venezuela.

MANUFACTURERS

FIAT/Oto Melara, Bolzano, Italy; Asia Motors Company, Seoul, South Korea.

KEY RECOGNITION FEATURES

- Two large road wheels each side with entry door between, large ramp at rear opens downwards
- Pointed hull front, driver's position front left, hull roof to rear in line with driver's roof
- Hull sides above wheel arches slope inwards, large rectangular horizontal louvres above first wheel station on each side

Below: Type 6614 with 12.7mm MG

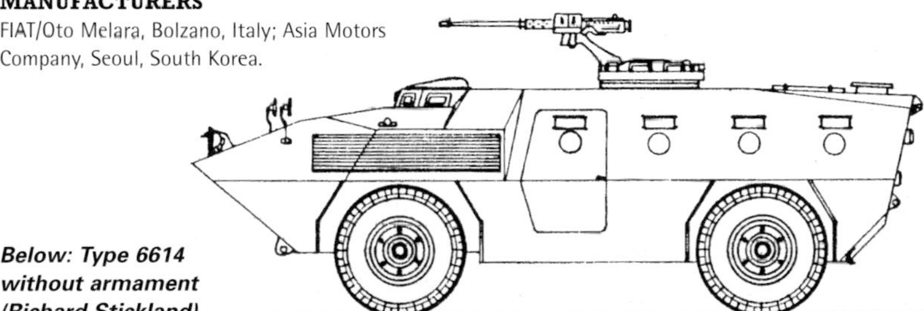

Below: Type 6614 without armament (Richard Stickland)

Boneschi MAV 5 APC (Italy)

Above: MAV 5 APC (Richard Stickland)

SPECIFICATIONS

Crew:	2 + 4
Armament:	1 x 7.62mm MG (typical)
Ammunition:	1000 x 7.62mm (typical)
Length:	4.66m
Width:	2.00m
Height:	2.15m
Ground clearance:	Not available
Weight, combat:	4,450kg
Weight, empty:	3,850kg
Power-to-weight ratio:	23.1hp/tonne
Ground pressure:	Not available
Engine:	IVECO turbo charged 4-cylinder diesel developing 103hp
Maximum road speed:	100km/h
Maximum road range:	600km
Fuel capacity:	75 lit
Fording:	0.70m
Vertical obstacle:	Not available
Trench:	Not available
Gradient:	60%
Side slope:	30%
Armour:	6mm
Armour type:	Steel
NBC system:	No
Night vision equipment:	No

DEVELOPMENT

The MAV 5 (4 x 4) light armoured vehicle was developed by Carrozzeria Boneschi and IVECO and is essentially an IVECO 40.10 (4 x 4) truck chassis fitted with a fully armoured body that provides the occupants with protection from small arms fire and shell splinters.

The Italian Army has taken delivery of over 200 vehicles and these have been deployed overseas to such places as Albania, Bosnia, Kosovo and Somalia. The Italian Carabinieri has also taken delivery of a small quantity of vehicles.

The driver and commander are seated at the front of the vehicle with the powerpack forward and below their position thus leaving the area to the rear clear for the troop compartment. This has four individual seats that face the front, although other seating arrangements are possible.

In either side is a door than opens to the front while at the rear is a door that opens to the right. The standard production vehicle has a single roof

hatch over which is mounted a 7.62mm machine gun although other armament options are possible.

Standard equipment includes internal lighting and rifle racks while special equipment includes an air conditioning system, anti-tear gas filtering system and a fire detection and suppression system for the engine compartment.

It can also be fitted with a more powerful diesel engine as well as different types of tyres, including run-flat, exhaust brake and an air/ electrical connection system for a trailer.

VARIANTS

The MAV 5 can be fitted with additional armour to provide a higher level of protection against mines, this being called the MAV (MP). The basic vehicle can also be adopted for a number of specialist roles such as command post vehicle.

KEY RECOGNITION FEATURES

- Box-shaped hull with vertical hull front containing radiator and sloping bonnet which leads up to one-piece windsceen which slopes slightly to rear

- Horizontal roof on which can be mounted a 7.62mm machine gun, vertical hull rear, upper part of latter slopes slighly inwards with single piece door with firing port and window in upper part

- Upper part of hull sides slope slightly inwards with single door in each side between front and rear wheels with window in upper part. Two additional small windows in rear troop compartment either side with firing port below

STATUS

Production complete. In service with Italy (army and Carabinieri). The Terrier Light Armoured Unit (LAU) is almost identical and is used by United Arab Emirates in IS role.

MANUFACTURER

Carrozzeria Boneschi Srl, Milan, Italy.

Right: MAV 5 APC

Right: MAV 5 APC (Richard Stickland)

IVECO Light Multirole Vehicle (Italy)

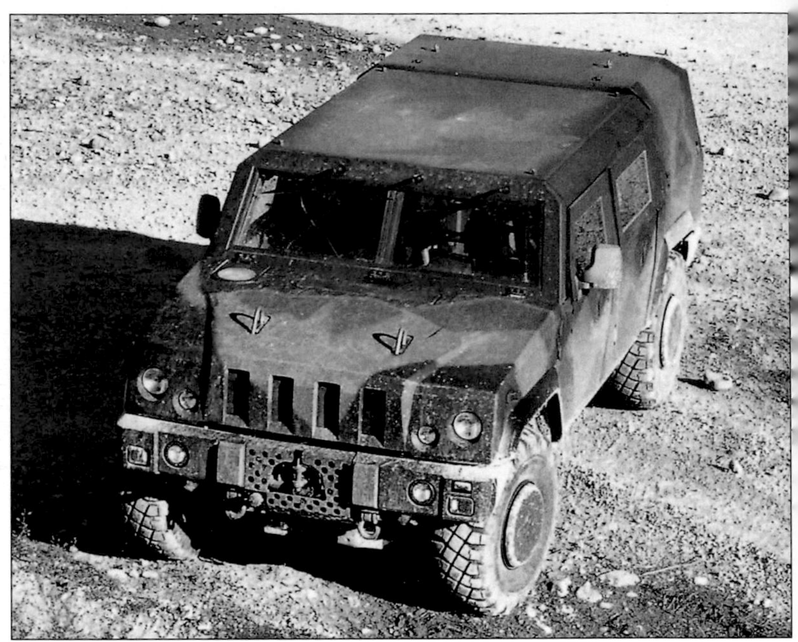

Above: IVECO Light Multirole Vehicle

SPECIFICATIONS

Crew:	1 + 4
Configuration:	4 x 4
Armament:	1 x 12.7mm MG
Ammunition:	1,000 x 12.7mm
Length:	4.812m
Width:	2.42m
Height:	2.05m (without armament)
Ground clearance:	0.473m
Weight, combat:	7,000kg
Weight, empty:	4,300kg
Power-to-weight ratio:	26.4hp/tonne
Engine:	IVECO turbocharged 4-cylinder diesel developing 185hp
Maximum road speed:	130km/h
Maximum road range:	500km
Fuel capacity:	Not available
Fording:	1.5m (with preparation)
Vertical obstacle:	0.5m
Trench:	Not available
Gradient:	60%
Side slope:	30%
Armour:	Floor armour fitted as standard, rest is optional
Armour type:	Laminate
NBC system:	Optional
Night vision equipment:	Optional

DEVELOPMENT

The Light Multirole Vehicle (LMV) was developed by IVECO Defence Vehicles Division under the company designation M 65E19 WM-4 x 4 to meet emerging requirements for a 4 x 4 vehicle with increased payload and therefore able to undertake a wide range of roles on the battlefield.

First prototypes were completed in 2001 with the first customer being the British Army which has ordered 401 units with an option on another 400 vehicles to meet its requirement for a Future Command and Liaison Vehicle (FCLV). These will

be integrated in the UK and fitted with an AEI overhead weapon station armed with a 7.62mm machine gun, a BAE day/night sighting system and the Bowman communications system. Prime UK contractor is BAE Systems Land Systems (previously Alvis Vickers). The UK calls the vehicles the Multirole Light Vehicle.

The second customer is the Italian Army which has ordered an initial batch of 60 vehicles for further trials with the eventual requirement expected to be for up to 1,150 over a five-year period.

To reduce costs, the LMV uses standard commercial parts wherever possible and has the engine at the front, crew compartment in the middle and the small load area at the rear. All production vehicles will have an armoured floor that provides a high level of protection against mines with an applique amour package being an option. A variety of weapon stations armed with 7.62mm and 12.7mm machine guns can be installed on the roof of the MLV.

Standard equipment includes powered steering, auxiliary heater, air conditioning system, front mounted winch and heated front windscreen. It is currently offered in two wheelbase versions, of 3.2m and 3.5m, with payloads of 2,300kg and 2,500kg.

VARIANTS

These are expected to include anti-tank with TOW missiles, special forces, ambulance, cargo, command and control and air defence but it is envisioned that a wide range of other variants will eventually be developed.

KEY RECOGNITION FEATURES

- Almost vertical hull front with four large vertical louvres with two headlamps either side, slightly sloping bonnet leads up to two-piece windscreen that slopes slightly to the rear. Horizontal roof extends to the hull rear which is vertical
- Hull sides are vertical with two forward opening doors in either side with oblong window in upper part. Chamfer to upper part of hull
- Wheels are at extreme ends of the chassis with wheel arches extending outwards. Weapon station would normally be mounted on forward part of roof

STATUS

In production. Entering service with Italy and the UK.

MANUFACTURER

IVECO Defence Vehicles Division, Bolzano, Italy.

Below: IVECO Light Mutirole Vehicle

Multipurpose carrier/LBV (Fennek) (Netherlands)

Above: Fennek of the German Army

SPECIFICATIONS

Crew:	3
Configuration:	4 x 4
Armament:	1 x 12.7mm MG
Ammunition:	500 x 12.7mm
Length:	5.58m
Width:	2.55m
Height:	2.2m
Weight, combat:	10,400kg
Weight, empty:	8,700kg
Power-to-weight ratio:	23.07hp/tonne
Engine:	Deutz 6-cylinder turbocharged intercooled diesel developing 240hp
Maximum road speed:	112km/hr
Maximum range:	1,000km
Fuel capacity:	Not available
Fording:	1.0m
Vertical obstacle:	Not available
Trench:	Not available
Gradient:	60%
Side slope:	35%
Armour:	Classified
Armour type:	Aluminium
NBC system:	Optional
Night vision equipment:	Optional

DEVELOPMENT

The Multipurpose carrier (MPC) was developed as a private venture by SP aerospace and vehicle systems with the first prototype being completed in 1992. It was designed to undertake a wide range of military and paramilitary roles, with the former including command and control and battlefield surveillance.

The driver is seated at the front with bulletproof windows to his front and rear, providing the same level of protection as the hull. The other crew members, typically the commander and radio operator, are seated in the centre. The powerpack is at the rear. A variety of weapons can be mounted on the roof, including machine guns, grenade launchers and ATGWs. Optional equipment includes an NBC system and an amphibious kit.

VARIANTS

The LBV, another version of the MPC has been developed as a new reconnaissance vehicle for the Royal Netherlands Army and the German Army. Four prototypes have been built, two for each army. Late in 2001, the Netherlands Ministry of

Defence (MoD) awarded the ARGE Fennek consortium a contract worth about €500 million for the supply of 612 Fennek (4 x 4) reconnaissance vehicles for the German and Netherlands armies.

The ARGE Fennek consortium originally comprised SP aerospace and vehicle systems of Netherlands (owned by RDM) and Krauss-Maffei Wegmann (KMW) of Germany.

The German Army will take delivery of 202 vehicles of which 178 will be in the reconnaissance version and 24 in the combat engineer version. These will be armed with a 40mm automatic grenade launcher.

The Royal Netherlands Army will take delivery of a total of 410 vehicles of which 202 will be in the reconnaissance version, 130 in Medium Range Anti-Tank (MRAT) (with the RAFAEL Armament and Development Authority Gill missile system) and 78 general purpose vehicles. The Netherlands vehicles will be armed with a 12.7mm machine gun.

The German Army has also ordered an artillery observation vehicle.

KEY RECOGNITION FEATURES

- Nose slopes back under vehicle with front of vehicle angled back at 45°, horizontal roof extends to rear, vertical hull rear. Upper hull sides slope inwards

- Large driver's windscreen at front with another window either side sloping to rear. Roof hatches in forward part of roof with engine louvres in roof at rear

- Two large road wheels either side with large forward opening door in either side

STATUS

In production. In service with Germany and Netherlands.

MANUFACTURER

The original developer, SP aerospace and vehicle systems, no longer exists. Krauss-Maffei Wegmann GmbH, Kassel, Germany, is the German part of the original consortium.

Top right: Fennek (German Army)

Right: Fennek (Netherlands Army)

BRAVIA Chaimite APC (Portugal)

Above: Chaimite V-200 with 12.7mm M2 MG (Richard Stickland)

SPECIFICATIONS

Crew:	11
Configuration:	4 x 4
Armament:	See text
Ammunition:	See text
Length:	5.606m
Width:	2.26m
Height:	2.26m (turret top), 1.84m (hull top)
Ground clearance:	0.61m (hull)
Wheelbase:	2.667m
Weight, combat:	7,300kg
Power-to-weight ratio:	32hp/tonne
Engine:	Model M75 V-8 water-cooled petrol developing 210hp at 4,000rpm (or V-6 diesel)
Maximum road speed:	110km/hr
Maximum water speed:	9km/hr
Maximum road range:	1050km
Fuel capacity:	300 lit
Fording:	Amphibious
Vertical obstacle:	0.9m
Trench:	Not applicable
Gradient:	65%
Side slope:	40%
Armour:	7.94mm (maximum)
Armour type:	Steel
NBC system:	None
Night vision equipment:	Optional

DEVELOPMENT

Chaimite range of 4 x 4s was designed by BRAVIA to meet requirements of the Portuguese armed forces, first prototype completed in 1966 and production commencing soon afterwards. In appearance Chaimite is very similar to the Cadillac Gage (now Textron Marine & Land Systems) LAV-150 and AV Technology Corporation Dragoon families of 4 x 4 vehicles. Both of these have their own entry in this section.

Crew number depends on mission but typically could be 11: commander, driver, gunner and eight fully equipped infantry. Chaimite is fully amphibious, propelled by its wheels. Standard equipment includes a front-mounted winch with capacity of 4,530kg, optional equipment includes night vision equipment.

VARIANTS

V-200 is basic vehicle normally fitted with a one-man MG turret, twin 7.62mm MG with 500 rounds of ready-use ammunition (250 per gun), 9,000 carried in reserve in hull, or turret with one 12.7mm and one 7.62mm MG.
V-300 can be fitted with variety of 20mm turrets.
V-400 can be fitted with 90mm turrets.
V-500, command and communications vehicle.
V-600, 81mm or 120mm mortar carrier.
V-700, ATGW vehicle.
V-800, unarmed ambulance.
V-900, crash rescue vehicle.
V-1000, riot control/internal security vehicle.

A 6 x 6 version, **BRAVIA Mk II,** was projected but as far as is known this never entered production or service.

BRAVIA has also stated that there is an 8 x 8 **BRAVIA Mk III APC** but this has never entered production or service. BRAVIA has also designed and built the Tigre Mk II (6 x 6) APC which is essentially a truck with an armoured body.

STATUS

Production complete. Known to be in service with Lebanon, Libya (status uncertain), Peru, Philippines and Portugal.

MANUFACTURER

BRAVIA SARL, Lisbon, Portugal.

KEY RECOGNITION FEATURES

• Similar in appearance to the now Textron Marine and Land Systems V-100/V-150 and V-200 (4 x 4) range with four large road wheels, single two-part hatch in each side of hull between wheels, nose angled inwards, glacis well-sloped then almost vertical to horizontal hull top that extends to rear

• Hull rear angled inwards at an angle of about 45°, engine in left hull rear with additional entry hatch to right

• Top half of hull above wheel hatches slopes slightly inwards, rectangular vision blocks with firing ports beneath

Above: Chaimite V-200 with twin 7.62mm MG turret

Left: Chaimite V-200 without armament installed (Richard Stickland)

TABC-79 APC (Romania)

Above: TABC-79 (4 x 4) APC

SPECIFICATIONS

Crew:	3 + 4
Configuration:	4 x 4
Armament:	1 x 14.5mm MG, 1 x 7.62mm MG
Ammunition:	500 x 14.5mm, 2,000 x 7.62mm
Length:	5.65m
Width:	2.805m
Height:	2.335m (with turret)
Ground clearance:	0.485m
Wheelbase:	2.9m
Weight, combat:	9275kg
Weight, empty:	8575kg
Power-to-weight ratio:	16.66hp/tonne
Engine:	798.05N2 turbo charged diesel developing 154hp
Maximum road speed:	80km/hr
Maximum road range:	700km
Fuel capacity:	Not available
Fording:	Amphibious
Vertical obstacle:	0.3m
Trench:	0.70m
Gradient:	60%
Side slope:	30%
Armour:	8mm (maximum)
Armour type:	Steel
NBC system:	Yes
Night vision equipment:	Yes

DEVELOPMENT

The TABC-79 (4 x 4) APC was developed specifically to meet the requirements of the Romanian Army and uses some automotive components of the TAB-77 (8 x 8) APC.

The driver is seated at the front of the vehicle on the left with the vehicle commander to his right. Mounted on the roof to the rear of the commander's and driver's position is the one-man manually operated turret which is the same as that fitted to the TAB-71M (8 x 8), TAB-77 (8 x 8) and the Mountaineers Combat Vehicle. This is armed with one 14.5mm and one 7.62mm machine gun.

The engine compartment is at the rear of the vehicle on the left side and in addition to the entry doors in either side there is also a door in the hull rear on the right side as well as a single roof hatch.

Standard equipment includes infra-red night vision equipment and an NBC system. The

TABC-79 (4 x 4) APC is fully amphibious being propelled in the water by a single waterjet mounted at the rear of the hull. Before entering the water the bilge pumps are switched on and the trim vane erected at the front of the hull. When not required this lays back on the glacis plate.

VARIANTS

TAB-79A PCOMA, armoured artillery observation post vehicle, armed with 7.62mm machine gun.
TAB-79AR, self-propelled 82mm mortar system which can also be deployed away from the vehicle if required.
TAB RCH-84, armoured chemical and radiological reconnaissance vehicle, no turret, fitted with racks of pennants to mark contaminated areas. Armed with 7.62mm pintle-mounted machine gun.
TCG-80, this is an unidentified variant, may be a recovery vehicle.
AM 425, latest version of TAB-79 APC; the chassis is used as basis for Romanian equivalent of the Russian SA-9 SAM, the A95.
TABC-79M, as TAB-79 but no turret.
TAB-C, similar to TABC-79.

KEY RECOGNITION FEATURES

- Box-type hull with nose sloping back under hull front, trim vane folds back onto glacis plate, two windows in hull front with shutters above, horizontal hull top, vertical hull rear

- Upper part of hull slopes slightly inwards as does lower half, two large wheels either side with door in lower half of hull

- Turret mounted towards front of vehicle has flat top and well-sloped sides

STATUS

Production complete. In service with Romania.

MANUFACTURER

ROMARM SA, Bucharest, Romania.

Below: TABC-79 (4 x 4) APC

ABI armoured car (Romania)

SPECIFICATIONS

Crew:	2 + 4
Configuration:	4 x 4
Armament:	1 x 12.7mm and 1 x 7.62mm MG (see text)
Ammunition:	Not available
Length:	4.22m
Width:	2.225m
Height:	1.65 m (hull top) 2.12 m (turret top)
Ground clearance:	0.195m
Wheelbase:	2.35m
Weight,combat:	4,000kg
Weight, unloaded:	3,500 kg (estimate)
Power-to-weight ratio:	17hp/tonne
Engine:	Model D-127 4-stroke diesel developing 68hp at 3,200rpm
Maximum road speed:	90 km/h
Maximum road range:	600 km
Fuel capacity:	Not available
Fording:	0.30m
Vertical obstacle:	Not available
Trench:	Not available
Gradient:	40%
Side slope:	20%
Armour:	4–10mm
Armour type:	Steel
NBC system:	Yes
Night vision equipment:	Yes

DEVELOPMENT

The ABI (4 x 4) armoured car is essentially an armoured body mounted on the chassis of the ARO-240 (4 x 4) light vehicle. The vehicle has been designed mainly for the light scout role and internal security roles.

The diesel powerpack is at the front with the commander and driver seated to the immediate rear and they enter the vehicle via a forward opening side door in either side which has a firing port in the upper part. The four troops are carried in the rear and enter and leave via two doors in the hull rear. Firing ports allow the troops to fire their weapons from within the vehicle with some degree of safety.

Various types of turrets and weapons can be mounted on the roof. One version of the ABI, called the AM 100 ALG is fitted with one person turret which can be armed with a 7.62mm PKMS machine gun. Another version is fitted with a fully enclosed one person turret armed with a 12.7mm and 7.62mm machine

gun. Turret traverse is a full 360° with elevation from -5° to +25° under manual control.

Mounted at the front of the hull is a light obstacle clearing device and various types of optional equipment can be provided such as different communications equipment and day and night observation devices.

VARIANTS

None apart from different armament installations.

STATUS

Production as required. In service with Algeria, Romania and possibly some other countries.

MANUFACTURER

ROMARM SA, Bucharest, Romania.

Left: Romanian AM 100 ALG armoured car without machine gun installed in turret (ROMARM)

Below: ABI armoured car with turret armed with external 12.7mm MG

KEY RECOGNITION FEATURES

- Lower part of hull front vertical with upper part slightly sloping to rear. Middle part has horizontal lourves for the radiator with bonnet almost horizontal. Front of crew compartment slopes to rear with bullet proof window in left side which is covered by an armoured shutter hinged at the top with firing port to right. Single door in either side with firing port in upper part

- Hull roof horizontal with observation slits just below roof line and covering frontal arc. Various types of turret and weapon station can be mounted on turret roof

- Lower part of hull slopes inwards with upper part of rear wheeled covered by armour. Upper part of hull slopes inwards with firing ports in sides. Twin doors in hull rear

BRDM-1 Amphibious Scout Car (Russia)

SPECIFICATIONS

Crew:	5
Configuration:	4 x 4
Armament:	1 x 7.62mm MG
Ammunition:	1,250 x 7.62mm
Length:	5.7m
Width:	2.25m
Height:	1.9m (without MG)
Ground clearance:	0.315m
Wheelbase:	2.8m
Weight, combat:	5,600kg
Power-to-weight ratio:	16.7hp/tonne
Engine:	GAZ-40P 6-cylinder water-cooled in-line petrol developing 90hp at 3,400rpm
Maximum road speed:	80km/hr
Maximum water speed:	9km/hr
Road range:	500km
Fuel capacity:	150 lit
Fording:	Amphibious
Vertical obstacle:	0.4m
Trench:	1.22m
Gradient:	60%
Side slope:	30%
Armour:	10mm (maximum)
Armour type:	Steel
NBC system:	None
Night vision equipment:	Yes (infra-red for driver only)

DEVELOPMENT

BRDM-1 (4 x 4) was developed in the mid-1950s and entered service with the Russian Army in 1957, but it has been replaced in all front-line Russian units by the later BRDM-2 (4 x 4) amphibious reconnaissance vehicle.

BRDM-1 is fully amphibious, propelled by a single waterjet mounted at hull rear. Before entering a trim vane is erected at hull front and bilge pumps switched on. On each side of hull, between road wheels, is a set of powered belly wheels that are lowered to the ground to improve cross-country mobility. Tyre pressure regulation system is fitted as standard.

Typical armament comprises 12.7mm DShKM MG at front and 7.62mm SGMB MG at rear of crew compartment.

VARIANTS

BRDM-1 Model 1957 had open roof, but only a few were built.

BRDM-1 Model 1958 is the most common, with enclosed roof and hatches.

BRDM-U is command model with four radio antennas compared with one in standard vehicle.

BRDM-RKhb radiological-chemical reconnaissance vehicle has two rectangular packs at rear for dispensing poles with pennants.

BRDM-1 with three Snapper ATGWs (raised from inside for launching); rarely seen today.

3RDM-1 with four Swatter ATGWs (raised from nside for launching); rarely seen today.

3RDM-1 with six Sagger ATGWs (raised from nside) complete with overhead armour protection; rarely seen today.

STATUS

Production complete. In service with Albania, Bulgaria, Congo, Cuba, Guinea, Kazakhstan, Mozambique, Sudan, Vietnam and Zambia. In most of these countries the vehicle is now found n reserve units.

MANUFACTURER

Molotov GAZ plant, Gorkiy, Russia.

Left: BRDM-1 (4 x 4) amphibious scout car with 7.62mm and 12.7mm MGs installed

KEY RECOGNITION FEATURES

- Pointed nose containing engine slopes upwards towards crew compartment that extends almost to rear of vehicle. Only means of entry and exit via roof hatches

- Hull sides and rear vertical, but front, sides and rear of crew compartment slope inwards with two armoured covers on front and two firing ports in sides

- On each side of hull between roadwheels are two belly wheels that are raised when travelling on roads. Trim vane under nose when not in use

- Mounted low down at the hull rear is a single water jet that is covered up while the vehicle is in land mode

Above: BRDM-1 (4 x 4) amphibious scout car with belly wheels lowered

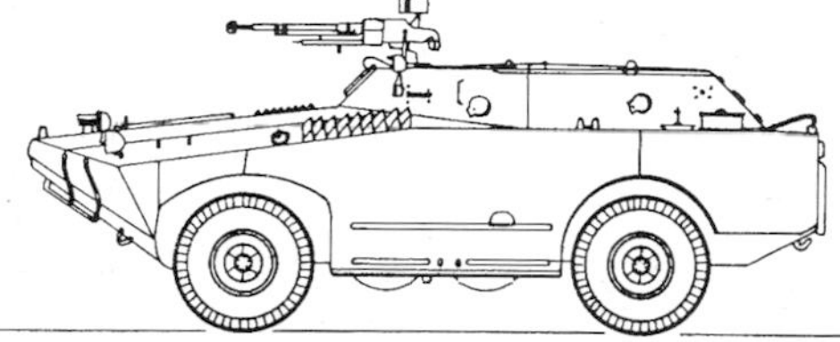

Right: BRDM-1 (4 x 4)

BRDM-2 Amphibious Scout Car (Russia)

Above: BRDM-2 amphibious scout car (Michael Jerchel)

SPECIFICATIONS

Crew:	4
Configuration:	4 x 4
Armament:	1 x 14.5mm MG (main), 1 x 7.62mm MG (coaxial)
Ammunition:	500 x 14.5mm, 2,000 7.62mm
Length:	5.75m
Width:	2.35m
Height:	2.31m
Ground clearance:	0.43m
Wheelbase:	3.1m
Weight, combat:	7,000kg
Power-to-weight ratio:	20hp/tonne
Engine:	GAZ-41 V-8 water-cooled petrol developing 140hp at 3,400rpm
Maximum road speed:	100km/hr
Maximum water speed:	10km/hr
Road range:	750km
Fuel capacity:	290 lit
Fording:	Amphibious
Vertical obstacle:	0.4m
Trench:	1.25m
Gradient:	60%
Side slope:	30%
Armour:	3-7mm
Armour type:	Steel
NBC system:	Yes
Night vision equipment:	Yes (driver and commander, infra-red)

DEVELOPMENT

BRDM-2 was developed as the replacement for the BRDM-1 (4 x 4) and was first seen in public during 1966. Main improvements are better road and cross-country performance, heavier armament in fully enclosed turret, more powerful rear-mounted engine, improved amphibious capabilities, NBC system and night vision equipment.

Commander and driver sit side-by-side at front with roof hatch behind. Turret is the same as on the OT-64 Model 2A (8 x 8), BTR-70 and BTR-60PB (8 x 8) armoured personnel carriers and has no roof hatch. The 14.5mm KPVT MG is mounted on left with 7.62mm PKT MG right; both have manual elevation from -5° to +30° and manual traverse through 360°.

Standard equipment on all BRDM-2s includes central tyre pressure system, decontamination kit, winch and land navigation system. Two powered belly wheels can be lowered to the ground each side to improve cross-country mobility.

VARIANTS

BRDM-2-RKhb radiological-chemical reconnaissance vehicle has two rectangular racks, one each side at rear, which dispense lane marking poles with pennants.
BRDM-2U command vehicle retains turret of BRDM-2 but has additional communications equipment.
BRDM-2U command vehicle normally has turret replaced by small roof-mounted generator and two roof-mounted antennae.
SA-9 Gaskin SAM system is based on BRDM-2 chassis.
BRDM-2 with Sagger ATGWs.
BRDM-2 with Spandrel ATGWs.
BRDM-2 with Swatter ATGWs.
Upgraded BRDM-2: Various countries are now upgrading their BRDM-2 vehicles with new engines and removing the belly wheels.

STATUS

Production complete. In service with Algeria, Angola, Benin, Bulgaria, Burundi, Cape Verde Islands, Congo, Croatia, Cuba, Czech Republic, Egypt, Equatorial Guinea, Eritrea, Estonia, Ethiopia, Gaza, Guinea, Guinea-Bissau, Hungary, India, Indonesia, Kazakhstan, Kyrgyzstan, Latvia, Libya, Lithuania, Macedonia, Madagascar, Mali, Mauritania, Mongolia, Mozambique, Namibia, Nicaragua, Peru, Poland, Romania, Russia, Serbia and Montenegro, Seychelles, Slovakia, Slovenia, Somalia, Sudan, Syria, Tanzania, Turkmenistan, Ukraine, Uzbekistan, Vietnam, Yemen and Zambia.

KEY RECOGNITION FEATURES

- Lower part of hull has vertical sides and rear, upper part slopes inwards, engine compartment roof slopes down to rear
- Belly wheels raised when travelling on roads, trim vane under nose when not required
- Turret on centre of hull roof with flat top. Only means of entry and exit via two circular hatches forward of turret

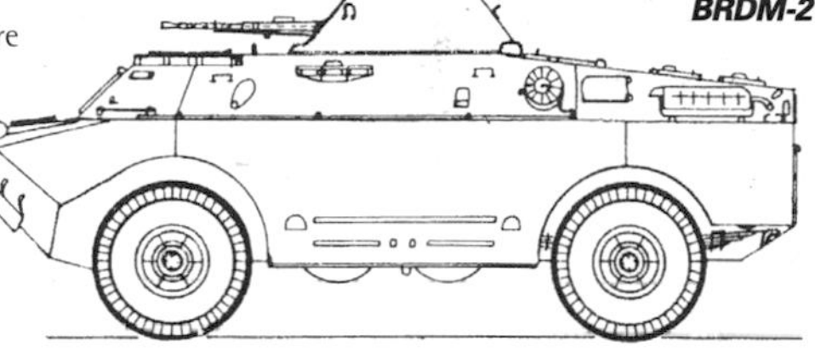

BRDM-2

MANUFACTURER

Molotov GAZ Plant, Gorkiy, Russia.

Below: BRDM-2 amphibious scout car (Michael Jerchel)

BRDM-2 ATGW versions (Russia)

Above: BRDM-2

SPECIFICATIONS (BRDM-2 SAGGER)

Crew:	2-3
Configuration:	4 x 4
Armament:	Launcher with 6 Sagger ATGW
Ammunition:	14 x Sagger ATGW (total)
Length:	5.75m
Width:	2.35m
Height:	2.01m (launcher retracted)
Ground clearance:	0.43m
Wheelbase:	3.1m
Weight, combat:	7,000kg
Power-to-weight ratio:	20hp/tonne
Engine:	GAZ-41 V-8 water-cooled petrol developing 140hp at 3,400rpm
Maximum road speed:	100km/hr
Maximum water speed:	10km/hr
Maximum road range:	750km
Fuel capacity:	290 lit
Fording:	Amphibious
Vertical obstacle:	0.4m
Trench:	1.25m
Gradient:	60%
Side slope:	30%
Armour:	14mm (maximum)
Armour type:	Steel
NBC system:	Yes
Night vision equipment:	Infra-red (driver)

DEVELOPMENT

BRDM-2 Sagger was developed in the late 1960s to replace versions of the earlier BRDM-1 with Snapper, Swatter or Sagger ATGWs (none of which remain in service). First used operationally by Egyptian and Syrian armies in 1973 Middle East conflict. Automotively, BRDM-2 (Sagger) is identical to standard BRDM-2 amphibious scout vehicle. Fully amphibious, propelled by single waterjet mounted in hull rear, central tyre pressure regulation system, and between road wheels each side are two powered belly wheels lowered to ground when vehicle is crossing rough ground.

When in firing position the six-round Sagger launcher, complete with overhead armour protection, is raised above roof of vehicle and missiles can be launched from inside vehicle or up to 80m away with the aid of a separation sight

nd cable. Further eight missiles carried internally or manual reloading. Sagger has maximum range f 3,000rpm. In 1977 Sagger was being converted om its normal wire command guidance system o a semi-automatic infra-red system.

'ARIANTS

RDM-2 with Spandrel ATGWs, first seen in 977, has five AT-5 Spandrel ATGWs in ready-to-unch position on roof, a further 10 being arried internally. AT-5 Spandrel has range of ,000m; gunner keeps cross-hair of sight on arget to ensure a hit. Some BRDM-2s (Spandrel) ave been seen with two AT-4 Spigot (right) and hree AT-5 Spandrel (left) ATGW in the ready-to-unch position.

RDM-2 with Swatter-C ATGW, first seen in 1973, as quadruple launcher for AT-2 Swatter converted om original radio-to-line-of-sight to semi-active nfra-red command guidance.

TATUS

roduction complete. Known users of BRDM-2 agger include Algeria, Czech Republic, Egypt, lungary, Libya, Morocco, Nicaragua, Poland, Romania, Russia, Serbia and Montenegro, Slovakia and Syria.

KEY RECOGNITION FEATURES

- Hull identical to BRDM-2 (4 x 4) amphibious scout car except turret replaced by retractable launcher for six Sagger ATGWs
- When in action six-round Sagger launcher complete with overhead armour protection is raised above hull roof
- Gunner's sight protrudes from hull roof to right of driver

MANUFACTURER

Molotov GAZ plant, Gorkiy, Russia.

Below: BRDM-2 (Spandrel)

BTR-40 APC (Russia)

Above: BTR-40 (Michael Jerchel)

SPECIFICATIONS

Crew:	2 + 8
Configuration:	4 x 4
Armament:	1 x 7.62mm MG
Ammunition:	1,250 x 7.62mm
Length:	5m
Width:	1.9m
Height:	1.75m (without armament)
Ground clearance:	0.275m
Wheelbase:	2.7m
Weight, combat:	5,300kg
Power-to-weight ratio:	15hp/tonne
Engine:	GAZ-40 6-cylinder water-cooled in-line petrol developing 80hp at 3,400rpm
Maximum road speed:	80km/hr
Range:	285km
Fuel capacity:	120 lit
Fording:	0.8m
Vertical obstacle:	0.47m
Trench:	0.7m (with channels)
Gradient:	60%
Side slope:	30%
Armour:	8mm (maximum)
Armour type:	Steel
NBC system:	None
Night vision equipment:	Yes (driver only, infra-red)

DEVELOPMENT

BTR-40 was developed from 1944, essentially a lengthened and modified GAZ-63 (4 x 4) truck chassis with fully armoured body. Entered service with the former Soviet Army in 1950 and used both as APC and command and reconnaissance vehicle; in the latter role it was replaced in the late 1950s by BRDM-1 (4 x 4) which had better cross-country mobility and was fully amphibious. Three pintle mounts for MGs round hull top.

In the former Soviet Army the BTR-40 was often referred to as the Sorokovke. As far as it is known, none remain in front line service with the Russian Army.

VARIANTS

Original version did not have firing ports. Models built from the 1950s were designated BTR-40V and have central tyre pressure regulation system. Some BTR-40s have 4,500kg winch mounted at front of vehicle.

BTR-40A anti-aircraft vehicle has same turret as BTR-152A armed with twin 14.5mm MGs; no longer in front line Russian service.

BTR-40B APC has overhead armour protection for troop compartment, carries six troops plus two-man crew.

BTR-40Kh is chemical reconnaissance vehicle with equipment at rear to dispense marking pennants.

BTR-40 zhd has steel wheels for running on railway lines.

STATUS

Production complete. In service with Burundi, Cuba, Guinea, Guinea-Bissau, Indonesia, North Korea, Laos, Mali, Mozambique, Syria, Tanzania, Vietnam and Yemen. In many of these countries the vehicle is in second-line use, often with militia units.

MANUFACTURER

Russian state arsenals.

KEY RECOGNITION FEATURES

- Engine front with open-topped troop compartment rear, firing ports each side and entry door at rear which normally has spare wheel and tyre

- Armoured air intake grille under nose, engine compartment roof sloping up towards commander's and driver's flap that can be locked in horizontal open position

Below: BTR-40 (4 x 4) APC

Aligator light reconnaissance vehicle (Slovakia)

Above: Aligator (4 x 4) (Stefan Marx)

SPECIFICATIONS

Crew:	1 + 5
Configuration:	4 x 4
Armament:	1 x 7.62mm or 1 x 12.7mm MG
Ammunition:	1,000 rounds approx
Length:	4.365m
Width:	2.20m
Height:	1.95m
Ground clearance:	0.385m
Wheelbase:	2.82m
Weight, combat:	6,700kg
Weight, empty:	6,000kg
Power-to-weight ratio:	28.20hp/tonne
Engine:	Deutz BF6 1013 water-cooled turbocharged and intercooled diesel developing 189hp at 2,300rpm
Maximum road speed:	120km/h
Maximum water speed:	See text
Road range:	600km
Fuel capacity:	160 lit
Fording:	See text
Vertical obstacle:	0.4m
Trench:	0.8m
Gradient:	60%
Side slope:	40%
Armour:	Classified
Armour type:	Steel
NBC system:	Optional
Night vision equipment:	Optional

DEVELOPMENT

In many respects the Aligator (4 x 4) light armoured reconnaissance vehicle is very similar to the French Panhard VBL (4 x 4) scout car of which well over 2,200 units have been built or ordered for the home and export markets.

The prototypes of the Aligator were built by the Transmisie company with the Kerametal company providing funding. First prototypes of the Aligator were completed in 1996 with the first eight production vehicles for the Slovakian Army being completed in 2001–2002.

The hull of the Aligator is of all welded steel rmour construction that provides the occupants vith protection from 7.62mm armour piercing ttack. If required an applique armour kit can be itted which provides a higher level of ballistic rotection.

The commander and driver are seated at the ront of the Aligator with the remaining three rew members being seated on individual seats in he rear of the vehicle.

Standard equipment on the Aligator includes ommunications system, run flat tyres, powered teering, fire detection and suppression system nd hull mounted searchlights. A wide range of ptional equipment can be fitted including arious weapon systems, NBC system, air onditioning systen, passive night vision quipment, winch, auxiliary power unit, central yre pressure regulation system and an mphibious kit. The latter includes a propeller nounted under the rear of the hull.

KEY RECOGNITION FEATURES

- Almost vertical hull front with glacis plate sloping slightly upwards. Upper part of hull front slopes slightly to rear with two large bullet proof windows. Hull roof is horizontal and extends to rear with three roof hatches, one either side at the front and a larger one at the rear

- Two large road wheels, one at either end of hull and in either side is a large door that opens forwards with a bullet proof window in the upper part. Large door in hull rear that opens to left with small window in upper part

- Various armament installations can be fitted on the turret roof and electrically operated smoke grenade launchers can be installed on either side of the hull

VARIANTS

Observation and reconnaissance post (ORP).
Police Modification (PCM).
Mobile Command Post (MCP).
Police Support Operations (PSO).
Armoured personnel carrier (6 x 6) has been proposed.
Mine detection vehicle (two examples built).

STATUS

Production as required. In service with Slovakia.

MANUFACTURER

Kerametal Company Ltd, Bratislava, Slovakia.

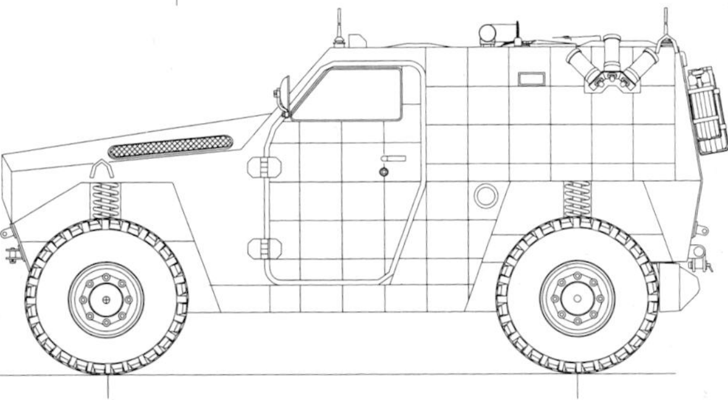

Aligator (4 x 4) (Karametal)

BOV-VP APC (Slovenia)

SPECIFICATIONS

Crew:	2 + 8
Configuration:	4 x 4
Armament:	1 x 7.62mm MG, 2 x 3 smoke grenade dischargers
Length:	5.7m
Width:	2.534m
Height:	2.335m (hull roof) 1.99m (hull top)
Ground clearance:	0.325m
Wheelbase:	2.75m
Weight, combat:	9,400kg
Power-to-weight ratio:	15.94hp/t
Engine:	Deutz type F 6L 413 F 6-cylinder diesel developing 150hp at 2,650rpm
Maximum road speed:	95km/hr
Range:	500km
Fuel capacity:	220 lit
Fording:	1.1m
Vertical obstacle:	0.54m
Trench:	0.64m
Gradient:	55%
Side slope:	30%
Armour:	8mm (Maximum) (estimate)
NBC system:	No
Night vision equipment:	Yes (infra-red for driver)

DEVELOPMENT

In the early 1980s the then Yugoslavia introduced the first of what was to become a family of 4 x 4 armoured vehicles using many commercial automotive components such as engine, transmission and suspension. In many respects this series, known as BOV, is similar to the American LAV-150 series multi-mission vehicle developed in the 1960s and has since been built in large numbers, mainly for export.

BOV-VP APC has commander and driver front, each provided with a roof hatch, raised troop compartment centre, engine and transmission rear. Troops normally enter and leave via door in side of hull between road wheels. Armament comprises 7.62mm or 12.7mm pintle-mounted MG with bank of three electrically operated smoke grenade dischargers mounted on hull side firing forwards.

Standard equipment includes day/night vision

quipment, heater and communications quipment. Some BOV-VP vehicles have been itted with wire mesh screens along side of the ıull that folds forwards through 90° when equired.

VARIANTS

3OV-1 is anti-tank version. Mounted on hull roof are two pods, each containing three ATGWs based on Russian AT-3 Sagger but fitted with semi-automatic guidance system.
3OV-3 triple 20mm SPAAG system.
3OV-30 twin 30mm SPAAG system.
3OV-SAN is ambulance model and has similar hull to the APC.

STATUS

Production complete. In service with Croatia, Serbia and Montenegro and Slovenia.

MANUFACTURER

MPP Vozila doo, Ptujska, Slovenia.

KEY RECOGNITION FEATURES

- Nose angled at 45° with slightly sloped glacis plate leading up to almost vertical windscreen for commander and driver, horizontal roof for crew compartment drops down to rear in line with back wheels

- Cupola in middle of roof with externally mounted 12.7mm MG, upper part of troop compartment sides has rectangular windows with circular firing ports between

- Two large road wheels each side with hull sides sloping inwards from just above wheel arches

Left: BOV-1 anti-tank vehicle

Below: BOV-3 triple 20mm SPAAG

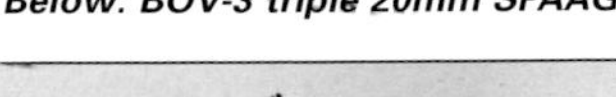

OMC RG-31 Nyala APC (South Africa)

Above: OMC RG-31 Nyala APC

SPECIFICATIONS

Crew:	2 + 10
Configuration:	4 x 4
Armament:	1 x 7.62mm MG (optional)
Ammunition:	Depends on role
Length:	6.40m
Width:	2.47m
Height:	2.72m
Ground clearance:	0.40m
Wheelbase:	3.40m
Weight, combat:	8,400kg
Weight unloaded:	7,368kg
Power-to-weight ratio:	20hp/tonne
Engine:	Mercedes-Benz OM 366A liquid cooled 6-cylinder direct injection diesel developing 167 hp at 2,800 rpm
Maximum road speed:	105km/h
Maximum road range:	900km (estimated)
Fuel capacity:	200 lit
Fording:	1m
Vertical obstacle:	Not available
Trench:	Not available
Gradient:	60%
Side slope:	40%
Armour:	Classified
Armour type:	Steel
NBC system:	No
Night vision equipment:	No

DEVELOPMENT

The RG-31 Nyala mine protected 4 x 4 armoured personnel carrier was developed by OMC to provide the occupants with a high level of protection against anti-tank mines, small arms fire and splinters. The lower part of the hull is V-shaped to help deflect mine blast upwards. To reduce procurement and support costs the RG-31 Nyala is based on proven Mercedes-Benz UNIMOG components. The vehicle has also been referred to as the Charger and is very similar to the Mamba, covered in a separate entry, which is no longer in production.

The engine compartment is at the front with the commander and driver to the rear and with the troops being seated four down either side on individual seats with seat belts facing inwards with an additional single seat to the rear of the front seats.

Standard equipment on current production vehicles includes powered steering, air

conditioning system and a five-tonne electrically operated winch that is mounted at the front of the vehicle.

The RG-31 Nyala is available in left and right hand configurations and a wide range of optional equipment is available including run flat insert, a higher level of armour protection, communications equipment, weapons mounts and a customised internal layout.

As a result of mergers and acquisitions in late 2004 Alvis OMC became BAE Systems Land Systems OMC.

VARIANTS

Quick interventional vehicle with larger cab and flatbet rear area with fold down sides and rear.
Weapons carrier armed with various 7.62mm and 12.7mm machine gun and 20mm cannon
81mm mortar carrier.
Anti-tank with 106mm recoiless rifle or guided missiles.
Bomb disposal.
Internal security.
Command post.

STATUS

In production. In service with many countries including Colombia, Cote d'Ivoire, Rwanda, South Africa, the United Nations and the US.

KEY RECOGNITION FEATURES

- Vertical hull front with horizontal radiator grille in centre, long horizontal bonnet which slopes slightly upwards then almost vertical two part bullet proof windscreen, horizontal roof with roof hatches

- On lower part of hull sides are vertical stowage boxes with slight step to the upper part of the hull sides which are also vertical with integral bullet proof windows. Vertical hull rear with large door with bullet proof window in upper part

- Two large road wheels either side with spare road wheel on lower part of either hull side. It should be noted that the design of the vehicle is modular so appearance can change. Some recent models, for example, have been fitted with side doors

MANUFACTURER

BAE Systems Land Systems OMC, Benoni, South Africa.

Below: OMC RG-31 Nyala APCs

OMC RG-32M APC APC (South Africa)

Above: OMC RG-32M armed with remote-controlled 7.62mm MG

SPECIFICATIONS

Crew:	1 + 4
Configuration:	4 x 4
Armament:	1 x 7.62mm MG (typical)
Ammunition:	1,000 x 7.62mm (typical)
Length:	4.6m
Width:	1.8m
Height:	1.95m
Ground clearance:	0.247m
Weight, combat:	5,100kg
Weight, empty:	4,000kg
Power-to-weight ratio:	32.8hp/tonne
Engine:	VM Motori HR694HT2 turbocharged 6-cylinder in-line diesel developing 148hp
Maximum road speed:	120km/h
Maximum road range:	750km
Fuel capacity:	100 lit
Fording:	0.60m
Vertical obstacle:	Not available
Trench:	0.60 m
Gradient:	60%
Side slope:	36%
Armour:	Classified
Armour type:	Steel
NBC system:	Optional
Night vision equipment:	Optional

DEVELOPMENT

The RG-32 series of armoured personnel carriers/ armoured patrol vehicles was originally developed in South Africa for the police market and was produced in 4 x 4 and 4 x 2 configurations.

Further development resulted in the RG-32M which has a host of improvements including all-wheel drive, larger wheels and tyres, more robust axles, differential locks on both axles and more powerful diesel coupled to automatic transmission.

It has an adaptable military type rear body with canopy or fully enclosed module, roof mounted hatch with 7.62mm or 12.7mm machine gun and is suitable for adaptation for a wide range of roles and missions.

To meet different market requirements the RG-32M is available in left and right hand drive configurations and also has a higher level of mine

protection including capping on the weld seams and special door locks.

The RG-32M has been entered in a number of international competitions and in 2004 was selected by the Swedish Army. A typical military role is command and control.

To reduce overall life cycle costs the RG-32M (with the M in the designation standing for military) uses proven commercial sub-systems wherever possible such as engine, transmission and axles.

The engine is at the front with the armour-protected crew capsule in the middle. The driver is seated on the left with another seated on the right. An additional three people are seated to the rear. If extensive communications equipment is installed then the crew is reduced to four people.

Normal means of entry and exit are via two doors in either side that open to the front. The front and side windows are of bullet proof construction and circular firing ports can be provided in the side doors.

The vehicle is normally provided with a circular roof hatch that opens to the rear and this can be locked in the vertical position if required. A 7.62mm or 12.7mm machine gun can be mounted at this position and for some trials a 7.62mm remote control machine gun has been fitted. This is provided with a day/night sighting system with the weapon being aimed and fired by the gunner under complete armour protection.

KEY RECOGNITION FEATURES

- Vertical hull front with horizontal radiator grille in centre and headlamps either side, horizontal bonnet which slopes slightly upwards then almost vertical one-part windscreen, horizontal roof hatch which usually has one-piece circular hatch cover on which can be mounted a 7.62mm machine gun

- Vertical hull sides with two forward opening doors with a bullet proof window in the upper part. Vertical hull rear with integral stowage area. The latter can have large door that opens to the left and side access flaps that open upwards

- Two road wheels each side which are positioned well to the front and rear. Can be fitted with front mounted winch

VARIANTS

The RG-32M can be adapted for a wide range of specialised roles with alternative body styles being offered for different user requirements.

STATUS

Development complete. Entering production.

MANUFACTURER

BAE Systems Land Systems OMC, Benoni, South Africa.

Right: OMC RG-32M with all doors and hatches open

OMC Mamba Mk II APC (South Africa)

SPECIFICATIONS

Crew:	2 + 9
Configuration:	4 x 4
Armament:	1 x 12.7mm MG (optional)
Length:	5.46m
Width:	2.205m
Height:	2.495m
Ground clearance:	0.39m
Wheelbase:	2.90m
Weight, combat:	6800kg
Weight, empty:	5710kg
Power-to-weight ratio:	18.47hp/t
Engine:	Daimler-Benz OM 352 6-cylinder water-cooled diesel developing 123hp at 2800rpm
Maximum road speed:	102km/h
Maximum road range:	900km
Fuel capacity:	200 lit
Fording:	1m
Vertical obstacle:	0.4m
Trench:	0.9m
Gradient:	60%
Side slope:	40%
Armour:	Classified
Armour type:	Steel
NBC:	No
Night vision equipment:	No

Above: Mamba II (4 x 4) APC (Richard Stickland)

DEVELOPMENT

The first Mamba was a 4 x 2 vehicle and was produced in significant numbers for a variety of missions. Further development resulted in the Mamba Mk II which has a number of improvements including 4 x 4 drive and a higher ground clearance. The hull of the Mamba Mk II is V-shaped to provide a high level of protection against anti-tank mines. Wherever possible standard UNIMOG components are used in the design of the vehicle.

The engine compartment is at the front with the commander and driver in the centre and the troop compartment extending right to the rear. Only means of entry is via the large door in the rear of the hull and the roof hatches. Bullet proof windows are fitted all round and these provide the same level of protection as the armoured hull.

The basic model is unarmed although various weapon systems can be fitted.

As a result of mergers and acquisitions late in

2004 Alvis OMC became BAE Systems Land Systems OMC.

VARIANTS
Projected roles include ambulance, command post vehicle, utility vehicle, recovery, VIP transport and logistics support. Can be fitted with various weapons including machine guns.

STATUS
Production complete. In service with Congo, South Africa and Sweden.

MANUFACTURER
BAE Systems Land Systems OMC, Benoni, South Africa.

KEY RECOGNITION FEATURES

- Vertical hull front with grill in centre, long horizontal bonnet which slopes slightly upwards, then almost vertical bullet proof windscreen, horizontal roof with eight hatches

- Hull sides vertical with large bullet proof windows in sides and rear, large door in rear. Side and rear windows have firing ports

- Two large road wheels either side with spare wheel carried on left side of hull

Above: Mamba II (4 x 4) APC (Christopher F Foss)

Right: Mamba II (4 x 4) APC (Christopher F Foss)

OMC Casspir Mk III APC (South Africa)

SPECIFICATIONS

Crew:	2 + 10
Configuration:	4 x 4
Armament:	1 to 3 7.62mm MGs
Length:	6.9m
Width:	2.45m
Height:	3.125m
Ground clearance:	0.41m (axles)
Weight, combat:	12,580kg
Weight, empty:	11,040kg
Power-to-weight ratio:	13.51hp/tonne
Engine:	ADE-352T, 6-cylinder diesel developing 170hp at 2,800rpm
Maximum road speed:	90km/hr
Maximum road range:	850km
Fuel capacity:	220 lit
Fording:	1.0m
Vertical obstacle:	0.5m
Trench:	1.06m
Gradient:	65%
Side slope:	40%
Armour:	Classified
Armour type:	Steel
NBC system:	None
Night vision equipment:	None

DEVELOPMENT

The original Casspir family of vehicles was developed in the late 1970s but from 1981 production was undertaken by TFM which has since developed the Casspir Mk II and Mk III vehicles of which well over 2,000 have been built.

Above: Casspir Mk III APC (Christopher F Foss)

Although designed mainly for internal security operations, it has been used for offensive operations in South Africa. A unique feature of the Casspir is that it has been designed to give its crew a high degree of protection against anti-tank mines and for this reason the vehicle has a very high ground clearance with the hull having a V-shape to help deflect the blast from any mines. The large cross-country wheels are outside of the main armour envelope.

There have been three main models of the Casspir, the Mk I, Mk II and Mk III, all of which have incorporated improvements as a result of operational experience. Wherever possible standard commercial components are used in the construction of the Casspir family of vehicles.

The engine compartment is at the front, commander and driver to the immediate rear with the troop compartment extending right to the rear. The troops are seated five either side facing each other. There are minor differences between production runs and there are a number of local modifications.

Standard equipment includes long range fuel tank, drinking water tank, two spare wheels and tyres and fire extinguishers.

Optional equipment includes floodlights, searchlights and obstacle clearing equipment. As well as the 7.62mm MGs, a rubber bullet launcher can be fitted.

The original manufacturer was TFM but this company was subsequently taken over by Reumech OMC which in turn was taken over by Vickers Defence Systems of the UK. The company then became Vickers OMC, which was taken over by Alvis and became Alvis OMC. Late in 2004 BAE took over Alvis and the company became BAE Systems Land Systems OMC.

KEY RECOGNITION FEATURES

- Lower part of hull is V-shaped with upper part of hull sides and rear vertical, single wheel at each end of the vehicle outside of the armour envelope
- Bonnet-type engine compartment at the front with horizontal engine louvres with chamfer between sides and top, large bullet-proof windows at front and along sides of hull. The bullet-proof windows along sides towards rear have firing ports below
- Horizontal hull top with forward part armoured and often mounting a 7.62mm machine gun, early models had open roof but late production models had fully enclosed rear troop compartment, twin doors in rear

VARIANTS

Blesbok, this is a cargo carrier and retains the fully armoured cab.
Duiker, this is a 5,000 litre fuel tanker and retains the fully armoured cab.
Gemsbok, recovery vehicle with recovery equipment at very rear of hull and fitted with extended armoured cab.
Ambulance, similar to Casspir Mk III APC but modified for ambulance role.
Police, increased visibility.
Artillery fire control.
Mine clearing, two versions.
Mine sensor vehicle.
81mm mortar.
106mm recoilless rifle.

STATUS

Production as required. In service with Angola, India, Mozambique, Namibia, Nigeria, Peru, South Africa and Uganda.

MANUFACTURER

BAE Systems Land Systems OMC, Benoni, South Africa.

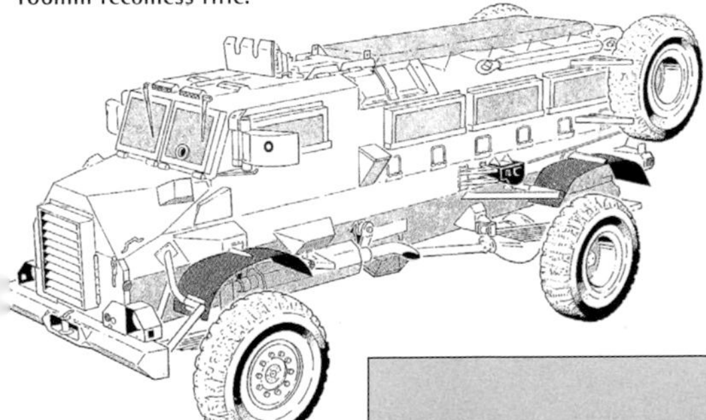

Above: Casspir Mk III APC

Right: Casspir with 106mm recoilless rifle

OMC RG-12 Patrol APC (South Africa)

Above: RG-12 APC

SPECIFICATIONS

Crew:	2 + 6
Configuration:	4 x 4
Length:	5.2m
Width:	2.45m
Height:	2.64m
Ground clearance:	0.322m
Weight, combat:	9,200kg
Weight, empty:	7,420kg
Power-to-weight ratio:	18.4hp/tonne
Engine:	ADE 366T diesel developing 170hp
Maximum road speed:	100km/hr
Range:	1,000km
Fuel capacity:	250 lit
Fording:	Not available
Vertical obstacle:	Not available
Trench:	Not available
Gradient:	50%
Side slope:	40%
Armour:	Classified
Armour type:	Steel
NBC system:	None
Night vision equipment:	None

DEVELOPMENT

The RG-12 patrol armoured personnel carrier was developed as a private venture by the TFM company (which is today BAE Systems Land Systems OMC) which also manufactures the Casspir (4 x 4) range of armoured personnel carriers (qv). The first prototypes were completed early in 1990 with first production vehicles being completed later the same year.

The RG-12 is designed mainly for internal security operations and wherever possible standard commercial components are used in the construction of the vehicle. Both 4 x 4 and 4 x 2 versions of the RG-12 were manufactured.

The complete powerpack is mounted at the front of the vehicle with the commander being seated on the left and the driver on the right, each being provided with a forward opening door. The three troops are seated either side facing outwards and enter and leave the vehicle via door in the side that can be rapidly opened. In addition

there is a door in the rear that gives access to the spare wheel and storage. A tropical roof is fitted and a roof hatch is provided above the commander's seat.

Standard equipment includes an air conditioning system, powered steering, protection against 7.62mm ball attack, floodlights, flashing beacons, hand held spotlight, siren, public address system, fire extinguishers and drinking water tank. All windows are covered by wire mesh screens and a barricade removal device is provided at the front of the hull. Can also be fitted with the Mobile Adjustable Ramp System for use in hijack suituations.

VARIANTS

There are no variants of the RG-12. The company also manufactured a similar vehicle called the RCV 9. This carries nine men, including the driver and has a combat weight of 6,900kg. This has been built in production quantities and sold to Colombia as well as within South Africa. It is no longer being marketed.

STATUS

Production. In service in Canada, Colombia, Italy (ordered 2004), Ivory Coast, Malawi, Mozambique, South Africa and United Arab Emirates, plus other countries mainly in police service.

KEY RECOGNITION FEATURES

- Box-type hull with sloping windscreen at front, vertical hull sides and rear, horizontal radiator grille in centre of hull front

- Large square windows in front, sides and rear of vehicle that are usually covered by wire mesh screens, two doors in each side of vehicle, one over first road wheel and one between road wheels

- Total of four road wheels which are at extreme ends of vehicle, horizontal roof raised for air conditioning system

MANUFACTURER

BAE Systems Land Systems OMC, Benoni, South Africa.

Below: RG-12 with Mobile Adjustable Ramp System

SANTA BARBARA BLR APC (Spain)

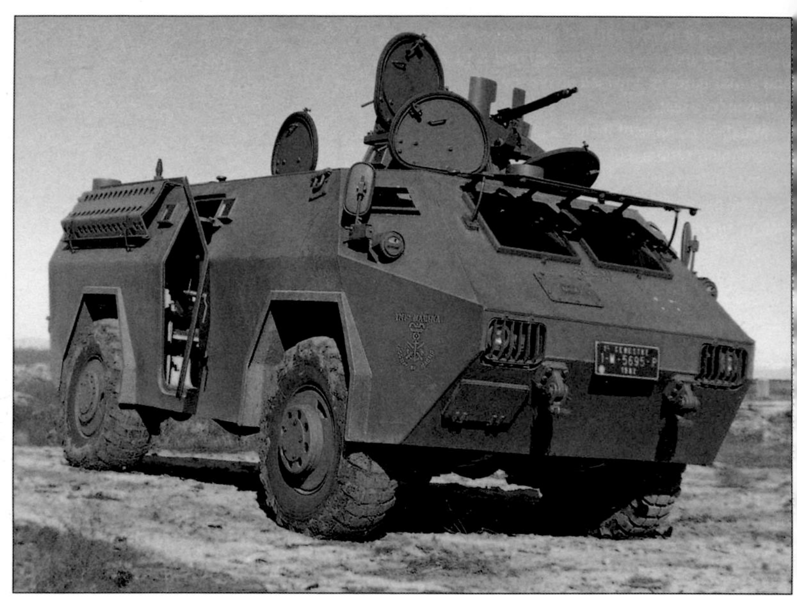

Above: BLR with 7.62mm MG

SPECIFICATIONS

Crew:	1 + 12
Configuration:	4 x 4
Armament:	1 x 7.62mm MG
Ammunition:	1,000 x 7.62mm
Length:	5.65m
Width:	2.5m
Height:	2m (hull top)
Ground clearance:	0.32m
Wheelbase:	3.15m
Weight, combat:	12,000kg
Weight, unloaded:	9,600kg
Power-to-weight ratio:	17.5hp/tonne
Engine:	Pegaso 6-cylinder turbo-charged in-line diesel developing 210hp at 2,100rpm
Maximum road speed:	93km/hr
Maximum range:	570km
Fuel capacity:	200 lit
Fording:	1.1m
Vertical obstacle:	Not available
Trench:	Not applicable
Gradient:	60%
Side slope:	30%
Armour:	8mm (maximum) (estimate)
Armour type:	Steel
NBC system:	None
Night vision equipment:	None

DEVELOPMENT

BLR (Blindado Ligero de Ruedas), also known previously as Pegaso BLR 3545, has been designed mainly for use in internal security. Its hull gives the crew complete protection from small arms fire and shell splinters, commander and driver sit front and whole of rear is occupied by troop compartment with exception of engine compartment which is centre of hull at rear. To reduce procurement and life cycle costs, standard commercial components are used in the vehicle wherever possible.

Armament depends on role, but typically is one-man cupola with externally mounted 7.62mm MG. Standard equipment includes ventilation system, choice of manual or automatic transmission, fire suppression system for both

engine compartment and wheels, bullet-proof tyres and 4,500kg capacity winch.

Wide range of optional equipment includes smoke/CS gas dischargers, PTO, specialised riot control equipment and various communications systems.

VARIANTS

Manufacturer suggested alternative weapon systems including 12.7mm MG, 20mm or 25mm cannon and turret-mounted 90mm gun. More specialised versions could include ambulance and command.

STATUS

Production as required. In service with Ecuador, Spanish Marines and Guardia Civil.

MANUFACTURER

Santa Barbara Sistemas, Madrid, Spain. (Now owned by General Dynamics of the United States.)

KEY RECOGNITION FEATURES

- Box-type hull with sloping nose, flat roof, vertical hull rear, vertical hull sides with top sloping slightly inwards

- Two large road wheels each side with forward-opening door between, two doors rear, one each side of central engine compartment which has louvres in roof and hull rear

- Depending on model, has various types of observation/firing device in hull sides, normally has cupola or turret on forward part of hull top to rear of commander's and driver's position

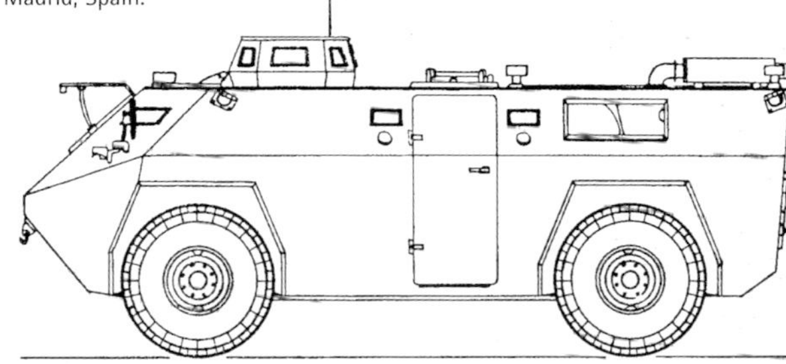

Right: BLR without armament

Right: BLR from rear with doors open

MOWAG Eagle Armoured Recon Vehicle (Switzerland)

Above: Eagle Mk I

SPECIFICATIONS

Crew:	4
Configuration:	4 x 4
Armament:	1 x 7.62mm MG, 1 x 6 smoke grenade launchers
Ammunition:	400 x 7.62mm
Length:	4.90m
Width:	2.28m
Height:	1.75m (hull top)
Ground clearance:	0.4m
Wheelbase:	3.30m
Weight, combat:	5,100kg
Weight, empty:	3,900kg
Power-to-weight ratio:	31.3hp/tonne
Engine:	General Motors Type 6.5 1 NA V-8 diesel developing 160hp at 1700rpm
Maximum road speed:	125km/h
Maximum road range:	450km
Fuel capacity:	95 lit
Fording:	0.76m
Vertical obstacle:	Not available
Trench:	Not applicable
Gradient:	60%
Side slope:	40%
Armour:	Classified
Armour type:	Steel
NBC:	Yes
Night vision equipment:	None (optional)

DEVELOPMENT

The Eagle Armoured Reconnaissance Vehicle was developed by MOWAG to meet the requirements of the Swiss Army and following trials with three prototype vehicles a production order was placed for 156 units with the first of these being delivered early in 1995.

The Eagle essentially consists of the chassis of the US Army General High Mobility Multipurpose Wheeled Vehicle (HMMWV), of which over 170,000 have been built for the US Army and for export, fitted with a armoured body that provides the occupants with protection from small arms fire and shell splinters.

The engine is at the front, driver and commander in the centre and another two people to the rear. Mounted on the hull top is a one man turret with a 7.62mm machine gun mounted on the right side. Turret traverse is through 360° with weapon elevation from -10° to +20°. A day/night thermal imaging device is fitted on the forward part of the turret. The bullet proof windows provide the same level of protection as the hull.

Standard equipment includes an NBC system, power steering and run flat tyres. A wide range of optional equipment can be fitted including central tyre pressure system, heater and a winch.

VARIANTS
First production vehicles are now known as Eagle Mk I. This was followed by the Eagle Mk II and finally the Eagle Mk III which is a forward observation vehicle for the Swiss Army. The new Mk IV is based on a new DURO (4 x 4) chassis.

STATUS
Production of Mks I, II and III complete; Mk IV ready for production. In service with Denmark and Switzerland.

MANUFACTURER
MOWAG Motorwagenfabrik AG, Kreuzlingen, Switzerland.

KEY RECOGNITION FEATURES

- Vertical hull front with radiator grille in centre, horizontal bonnet leading up to windscreen with two large windows that slope slightly to the rear. Horizontal roof with turret in centre, hull slopes sharply down with lower part vertical
- Lower part of hull sides vertical with upper part sloping slightly inwards. Two doors in each side with windows in upper part
- Two large road wheels either side

Right: MOWAG Eagle Mk II

Below: Eagle artillery observation vehicle

MOWAG Piranha APC (Switzerland)

Above: Piranha (6 x 6) with 12.7mm MG

SPECIFICATIONS

Model:	6 x 6	8 x 8
Crew: (max)	14	16
Length:	6.25m	6.96m
Width:	2.66m	2.66m
Height (hull top):	1.985m	1.985m
Weight, combat:	12,500kg	18,500kg
Weight, empty:	9,500kg	12,500kg
Power-to-weight ratio:	28hp/t	21.6hp/t
Engine type:	(all diesel)	
hp:	350	400
Maximum road speed:	100km/hr	100km/hr
Maximum water speed:	10km/hr	10km/hr
Maximum road range:	600km	600km
Fuel capacity: (lit)	200 (lit)	300 (lit)
Fording:	All fully amphibious	
Vertical obstacle:	0.6m	0.6m
Gradient:	60%	60%
Side slope:	30%	30%
Armour (maximum):	10mm	10mm
NBC system:	Standard on all vehicles	
Night vision equipment:	Optional on all vehicles	

DEVELOPMENT

In the early 1970s MOWAG started development of a range of 4 x 4, 6 x 6 and 8 x 8 armoured vehicles which have many common components and a wide range of roles. The family was subsequently called Piranha, first prototype completed in 1972 and first production vehicles in 1976.

In addition to being manufactured by MOWAG in Switzerland the Piranha family is also made in Canada (by the now General Dynamics Land Systems – Canada which has now taken over MOWAG of Switzerland), Chile (FAMAE) and the UK (the then Alvis Vehicles). In the last case they are all for export (Kuwait, Oman and Saudi Arabia).

There are separate entries for the Canadian (6 x 6), Canadian (8 x 8) LAV-25 and Bison (8 x 8) APCs.

All Piranhas have similar layout with driver front left, engine right, rear taken by troop compartment which has roof hatches and twin doors in rear. Troop compartment can have firing ports and vision devices and a wide range of weapon systems can be installed on roof.

Piranha is fully amphibious, propelled by two propellers under hull at rear. Before entering water a trim vane is erected at front and bilge pumps switched on.

Vehicle can be used for wide range of roles

including ambulance, anti-tank armed with ATGWs, cargo, command, internal security, mortar carrier, recovery, reconnaissance and radar carrier.

Standard equipment includes NBC and air conditioning system; optional equipment includes winch and night vision equipment.

KEY RECOGNITION FEATURES

- Pointed hull front with lower part sloping back to first road wheel station and upper part sloping up to horizontal hull top that extends to rear. Trim vane normally folded up under nose.

- Driver sits front left with engine compartment to right, troop compartment extends right to rear with troops entering via two doors in rear. Hull sides slope inward top and bottom just above road wheels

- MOWAG Piranha produced in 4 x 4, 6 x 6 and 8 x 8 versions but all have similar layout. In 6 x 6 rear two road wheels are close together, in 8 x 8 road wheels are equally spaced

VARIANTS

4 x 4 can have various weapon stations up to turret-mounted 20mm cannon.
6 x 6 can have various turrets up to two-man turret armed with 90mm gun. Swiss Army has 310 in anti-tank role with Norwegian Kvaerner-Eureka turret and twin TOW ATGW in ready-to-launch position.
8 x 8 version can have wide range of turrets and weapon systems including Euromissile Mephisto launcher with four HOT ATGWs, 90mm turret, 105mm turret with low recoil force gun and multiple rocket launchers.

In 1994 the prototype of a MOWAG 10 x 10 Piranha was built and fitted with a 105mm gun. In 1996 the MOWAG Piranha Generation III of 6 x 6, 8 x 8 and 10 x 10 vehicles was launched with increased armour and mobility.

Latest version is Piranha IV which is currently undergoing trials.

Above: Piranha (8 x 8) with 12.7mm MG

STATUS

Production. In service or on order for (all 8 x 8 unless otherwise stated) Australia, Botswana, Canada (6 x 6 and 8 x 8), Chile (8 x 8 and 6 x 6), Denmark, Ghana (4 x 4, 6 x 6 and 8 x 8), Ireland, Liberia (4 x 4), New Zealand, Nigeria, Oman, Qatar, Saudi Arabia, Sierra Leone (6 x 6), Spain, Sweden (10 x 10), Switzerland (8 x 8 and 6 x 6) and US (Army and Marines).

MANUFACTURER

MOWAG Motorwagenfabrik AG, Kreuzlingen, Switzerland (but see text).

Above: Piranha (8 x 8) with 90mm turret

MOWAG Roland APC (Switzerland)

Above: MOWAG Roland with remote-controlled 7.62mm machine gun

SPECIFICATIONS

Crew:	3 + 3
Configuration:	4 x 4
Armament:	1 x 7.62mm MG
Ammunition:	1,000 x 7.62mm
Length:	4.44m
Width:	2.01m
Height turret top:	2.03m
Ground clearance:	0.4m
Wheelbase:	2.5m
Weight, combat:	4,700kg
Weight, empty:	3,900kg
Power-to-weight ratio:	42.9hp/tonne
Engine:	V-8 4-stroke water-cooled petrol developing 202hp at 3,900rpm
Maximum road speed:	110km/hr
Maximum road range:	550km
Fuel capacity:	154 lit
Fording:	1m
Vertical obstacle:	0.4m
Trench:	Not applicable
Gradient:	60%
Side slope:	30%
Armour:	8mm (maximum) (estimate)
Armour type:	Steel
NBC system:	None
Night vision equipment:	Optional

DEVELOPMENT

Roland was designed by MOWAG in the early 1960s as a private venture for a wide range of roles including internal security, armoured personnel carrier and reconnaissance vehicle. First prototypes completed in 1963, first production vehicles in 1964. Driver sits front left with crew compartment to rear. Each side of hull has entry hatch with firing port and observation hatch. Additional door in right rear side, engine compartment left rear.

Roland normally has three-man crew consisting of commander, machine gunner and driver and carries three fully equipped troops. A

7.62mm or 12.7mm MG can be mounted on top of hull on simple pintle mount, or turret armed with similar weapon can be installed.

Standard model has manual transmission with one reverse and four forward gears, but was also available with fully automatic transmission with one reverse and three forward gears.

Wide range of optional equipment was available including smoke grenade dischargers, night vision equipment, MOWAG-designed firing ports allowing some occupants to aim and fire from inside, obstacle clearing blade at full front, searchlights and MOWAG bullet-proof cross-country wheels consisting of metal discs each side of tyre to support tyre when punctured and give additional traction when moving across country.

Late production vehicles had a fully automatic transmission in place of the manual transmission and a slightly longer wheelbase. This model has a combat weight of 4,900kg and power-to-weight ratio of 41hp/tonne.

KEY RECOGNITION FEATURES

- Nose slopes back under vehicle, well-sloped glacis plate with driver's hatch in upper part, flat roof with engine compartment in left side, vertical rear with louvres in left side and door in right side

- Hull side welded in middle with upper and lower parts sloping inwards. Some vehicles have air louvres over left rear wheel

- Two wheels each side, sides of wheel arches outside armour envelope, door mid-way between wheel arches is hinged at top

Below: MOWAG Roland

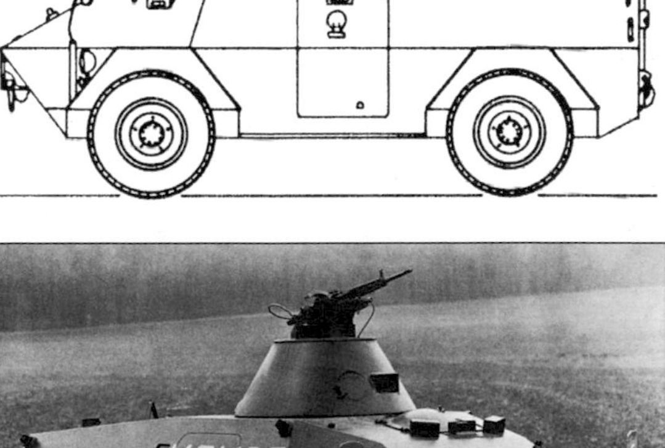

VARIANTS

No variants except for different armament installations.

STATUS

Production complete. In service with many countries including Argentina, Bolivia, Chile, Ghana, Greece, Liberia, Mexico and Sierra Leone.

MANUFACTURER

MOWAG Motor-wagenfabrik AG, Kreuzlingen, Switzerland.

Right: MOWAG Roland with remote-controlled 7.62mm machine gun and cross-country wheels

Otokar Cobra APC (Turkey)

Above: Otokar Cobra APC with cupola-mounted 12.7mm MG

SPECIFICATIONS

Crew:	2 + 11
Armament:	1 x 12.7mm MG (typical)
Ammunition:	1,000 x 12.7mm
Length:	5.229m
Width:	2.2m
Height:	2.1m (without armament)
Ground clearance:	0.365 m
Weight, combat:	6,300kg
Weight, empty:	4800kg
Power-to-weight ratio:	31 hp/t
Ground pressure:	Not available
Engine:	General Motors V8 turbocharged diesel developing 190hp at 3,400rpm
Maximum road speed:	115km/h
Maximum road range:	500km
Fuel capacity:	120 lit
Fording:	1m
Vertical obstacle:	0.32m
Trench:	Not available
Gradient:	70%
Side slope:	40%
Armour:	Classified
Armour type:	Steel
NBC system:	Optional
Night vision equipment:	Optional

DEVELOPMENT

The Cobra (4 x 4) armoured personnel carrier was developed by Otokar based on their extensive experience in the design, development and production of other 4 x 4 armoured cars and armoured personnel carriers which are based on a Land Rover (4 x 4) chassis.

The Cobra has an integral all welded steel armoured hull and automotive components from the American General High Mobility Multipurpose Wheeled Vehicle (4 x 4) which is used in large numbers by the US Army and many other countries.

The powerpack is at the front of the Cobra with the commander and driver being seated in the centre and the troop compartment extending to the rear; entry to this is normally via a large

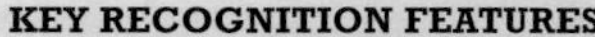

door in the rear although there is a door in either side.

A wide range of weapon stations can be mounted on the roof such as remote controlled 7.62mm and 12.7mm machine guns or a one person turret armed with similar weapons with electrically operated smoke grenade launchers either side.

Optional equipment on the Cobra includes a central tyre pressure inflation system, electric winch, NBC system, various day and night periscopes and specialised communications equipment.

An amphibious version of the Cobra has been developed this being propelled in the water by two waterjets mounted one either side at the hull rear.

VARIANTS

In addition to the basic APC other variants have been projected including reconnaissance vehicle, command and control vehicle, ambulance and TOW missile carrier.

STATUS

Production. In service with Maldives and Turkey.

MANUFACTURER

Otokar Otobus Karoseri Sanayi AS, Adapazari, Turkey.

KEY RECOGNITION FEATURES

- Vertical hull front which slopes back under nose of vehicle, bonnet slopes up to two part windscreen which is angled to the rear, horizontal roof in the centre on which is mounted the weapon station, to the rear of this are two roof hatches

- Pointed hull rear with large door that opens to left with integral vision block and firing port below

- Upper part of hull slopes inwards with wheels almost at extreme ends of vehicle. In each side of the hull is a side windscreen behind which is a forward opening door and to the rear of this are vision blocks with firing ports below

Right: Otokar Cobra

Above: Otokar Cobra APC without armament

Above: Otokar Cobra APC with turret mounted MG

Otokar Akrep (Scorpion) light reconnaissance vehicle (Turkey)

Above: Otokar Akrep in IS role (Otokar)

SPECIFICATIONS

Crew:	3
Configuration:	4 x 4
Armament:	2 x 7.62mm MG
Ammunition:	230 + 3,000 x 7.62mm
Length:	4.19m (with winch)
Width:	1.91m
Height:	2.563m (with weapons), 2.01m (without weapons)
Ground clearance:	0.23m
Wheelbase:	2.694m
Weight, loaded:	3,700kg
Weight, empty:	3,200kg
Power-to-weight ratio:	36hp/tonne
Ground pressure:	Not available
Engine:	Land Rover V-8 3.5 litre water-cooled petrol devloping 134hp at 5,000 rpm or Rover 300 TDI 4-cylinder turbocharged diesel developing 111hp at 4,000rpm
Max road speed:	125km/h
Max road range:	650km (petrol engine) 1,000km (diesel engine)
Fuel capacity:	110 lit
Fording:	0.65m
Vertical obstacle:	0.315m
Trench:	Not available
Gradient:	70%
Side slope:	40%
Armour:	Classified
Armour type:	Steel
NBC system:	No
Night vision equipment:	Yes

DEVELOPMENT:

The Akrep (Scorpion) was developed as a private venture by Otokar Otobus Karoseri Sanayi AS and is essentially a locally produced Land Rover (4 x 4) chassis fitted with a hull armoured body that provides the occupants with protection from small arms fire. First prototypes were completed in 1993 with first production vehicles following in 1994. It shares many components with the Otokar APC (4 x 4) covered in the following entry.

The layout of the Akrep is conventional with the engine at the front and commander and driver to the immediate rear. These two crew

members enter and leave via a door in either side. The gunner is seated in the rear and aims and fires the twin 7.62mm machine guns by remote control using a day/night sighting system.

Standard equipment includes powered steering, air conditioning system, heater, smoke extraction system and run flat tyres. A wide range of optional equipment is also available including a power-operated front-mounted winch, electrically-operated smoke grenade launchers, communications system and a 24 V electrical system. It is offered powered by a petrol engine or a more fuel efficient diesel engine which can be coupled to a manual or fully automatic transmission.

VARIANTS

As an alternative to the remote controlled 7.62mm machine guns various other types of turrets can be fitted armed with 7.62mm or 12.7mm machine guns.

Internal security – fitted additional sensors, wire mesh protection and siren.

Radar – can be fitted with various types of battlefield surveillance radar.

Missile carrier – armed with various surface-to-air missile systems or anti-tank guided missiles.

STATUS

Production as required. In service with Turkish Land Forces Command and other users.

MANUFACTURER

Otokar Otobus Karoseri Sanayi AS, Istanbul, Turkey.

KEY RECOGNITION FEATURES

- Vertical hull front with horizontal radiator grill and headlamps either side. Bonnet slopes upwards with louvres in its lower part. Two part windscreen slopes to the rear. Roof is almost horizontal with forward part sloping downwards

- Upper and lower part of hull sides slope inwards with forward opening door in either side with bullet proof window in the upper part. Large door in hull rear that opens to the left with small bullet proof window in its upper part

- Two road wheels at extreme ends of vehicle with replacement wheel and tyre sometimes carried on right side of hull. Armament is normally mounted on centre of roof

Right: Otokar Akrep with battlefield surveillance radar (Otokar)

Otokar APC (Turkey)

Above: Otokar APC with 7.62mm MG

SPECIFICATIONS

Crew:	2 + 6
Configuration:	4 x 4
Armament:	1 x 7.62mm MG, 1 x 6 smoke grenade launchers
Ammunition:	1000 x 7.62mm
Length:	4.155m
Width:	1.81m
Height:	2.26m (hull top) 2.75m with MG
Weight, combat:	3600kg
Weight, empty:	3000kg
Power-to-weight ratio:	37hp/t
Engine:	Land Rover V-8 3.5 litre petrol developing 134hp at 5000rpm or Rover 300 Tdi 4-cylinder turbocharged diesel developing 111hp at 4000rpm
Maximum road speed:	125km/hr
Maximum range:	500km
Fuel capacity:	85 lit
Fording:	0.6m
Vertical obstacle:	0.315m
Trench:	Not applicable
Gradient:	70%
Side slope:	40%
Armour:	Classified
Armour type:	Steel
NBC system:	No
Night vision equipment:	No

DEVELOPMENT

The Otokar APC was developed for the Turkish army with first prototypes completed in 1993 and production vehicles in 1994. In many respects it is similar to the Shorland S 55 (qv). It consists of a modified Land Rover Defender 4 x 4 chassis, fitted with a fully-armoured body that provides protection from small arms fire. The engine is at the front as in a normal Land Rover, with the

ommander and driver behind it, each provided vith a forward-opening side door with window. 'he six troops are seated three to either side, acing each other. They enter and exit via door loors in the hull rear. Firing ports and vision levices are provided in the sides and rear of the roop compartment, and a 7.62mm machine gun nount is fitted on the forward part of the roof. 'he mount can be traversed through 360° and levated from -12° to +65°.

/ARIANTS

Vone, although the vehicle can be adapted for a variety of roles. The similar Otokar Akrep Scorpion) light reconnaissance vehicle, also based on the Land Rover Defender, has a crew of three and has a remotely-controlled 7.62mm machine gun on the roof.

STATUS

n production. In service with Turkey and other undisclosed countries.

MANUFACTURER

Otokar Otobus Karoseri Sanayi AS, Istanbul, Turkey.

KEY RECOGNITION FEATURES

- Conventional layout, with armour-plated engine compartment front with horizontal louvres in centre, bonnet slopes slightly upwards to windscreen which slopes to rear

- Front of roof has sloping front with searchlight on top, hull top horizontal and rear hull vertical. Machinegun mount on roof with spare wheel to rear. Forward-opening door in each side has bullet-proof window in upper part. Three small firing ports with window above in either side of troop compartment

- Two wheels each side with extended wheel arches above. Lower hull sides are vertical, upper part slopes slightly inwards

Below: Otokar APCs on the production line

Shorland Armoured Patrol Car (UK/Australia)

Above: Shorland S52

SPECIFICATIONS

Crew:	3
Configuration:	4 x 4
Armament:	1 x 7.62mm MG
Ammunition:	1600 x 7.62mm
Length:	4.49m
Width:	1.8m
Height:	1.8m (roof)
Ground clearance:	0.324m
Wheelbase:	2.79m
Weight, combat:	3,600kg
Power-to-weight ratio:	37.8bhp/tonne
Engine:	Rover 4-stroke V-8 petrol developing 134bhp at 5000rpm (or diesel engine)
Maximum road speed:	120km/hr
Maximum road range:	630km
Fuel capacity:	136 lit
Fording:	0.5m
Vertical obstacle:	0.23m
Trench:	Not applicable
Gradient:	60%
Side slope:	30%
Armour:	8mm
Armour type:	Steel
NBC system:	None
Night vision equipment:	None

(Above relates to late production S52 vehicle)

DEVELOPMENT

Shorland was originally developed in 1965 to meet the requirements of Royal Ulster Constabulary for Northern Ireland. First production vehicles were completed in 1965 since when well over 1,000 have been built, mostly for export. No longer used by the British Army. Shorland is a modified long wheelbase Land Rover (4 x 4) chassis with a fully armoured body for protection from small arms fire and shell splinters.

First production vehicles were Mk 1s, followed by the Mk 2, 3, 4 and 5, the main difference being the Land Rover chassis used. Mk 5 has improved coil suspension and wider wheel track. Late production models are known as the Series 5 with the Armoured Patrol Car being designated the S52.

The 7.62mm MG mounted in turret has manual traverse and elevation and four electrically-operated smoke grenade dischargers can be mounted each side, firing forwards. Optional equipment includes various radios, air conditioning system and loud hailer. Different vision arrangements are also available as is a version powered by a 107bhp diesel engine. Latest production vehicles have a redesigned rear, angled 45° and a slightly different hull front.

The Shorland was originally manufactured by

norts in Northern Ireland but all future roduction will be undertaken by Tenix Defence ystems in Australia

ARIANTS

52 is the basic Shorland armoured patrol car.
53 is mobile air defence vehicle. Mounted on the urret roof is a lightweight mounting with three avelin SAMs in the ready-to-launch position.
54 is an anti-hijack vehicle with a special turret itted with a mounting for a sniper's rifle.
55 is the APC and covered in the APC section.

TATUS

roduction as required. In service with 40 countries ncluding Argentina, Bahrain, Botswana, Burundi, yprus, Guyana, Kenya, Lesotho, Libya, Malaysia, Mali, Portugal, Syria, Thailand and United Arab mirates.

MANUFACTURER

enix Defence Systems, Bandiana, Victoria, ustralia. (So far no Australian production has een undertaken.)

KEY RECOGNITION FEATURES

- Land Rover chassis with armoured engine compartment front, crew compartment centre, commander and driver each have forward-opening side door with drop-down vision port in upper part and windscreen to front, which can be covered by two armoured shutters hinged at top

- One-man six-sided turret on hull roof, turret rear in line with rear of crew compartment which then drops down to back of vehicle which is almost in line with engine compartment

- Two large road wheels each side that extend from hull side, extended wheel arches above

Shorland

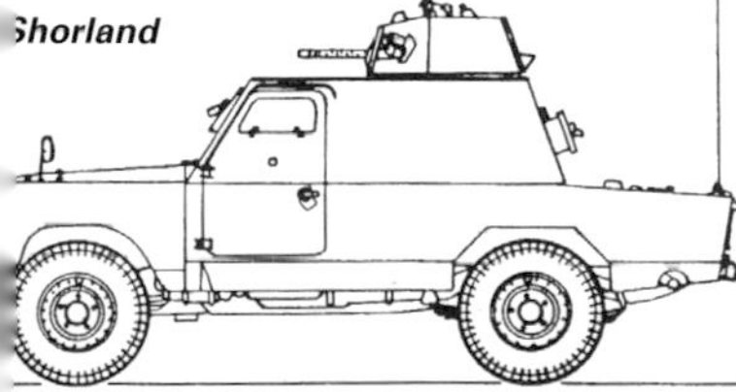

Above: Shorland S52

Left: Shorland S54

Daimler Ferret Scout Cars (UK)

SPECIFICATIONS Mk 2/3

Crew:	2
Armament:	1 x 7.62mm MG, 2 x 3 smoke grenade dischargers
Ammunition:	1,000 x 7.62mm
Length:	3.835m
Width:	1.905m
Height:	1.879m
Ground clearance:	0.33m
Wheelbase:	2.286m
Weight, combat:	4,400kg
Weight, empty:	3,640kg
Power-to-weight ratio:	29.35bhp/tonne
Engine:	Rolls-Royce B60 Mk 6A 6-cylinder in-line water-cooled petrol developing 129bhp at 3,750rpm
Maximum road speed:	93km/hr
Maximum road range:	306km
Fuel capacity:	96 lit
Fording:	0.914m
Fording with preparation:	1.524m
Vertical obstacle:	0.406m
Trench with channels:	1.22m
Gradient:	46%
Side slope:	30%
Armour:	8-16mm

Above: Daimler Ferret Mk 2/3

Armour type:	Steel
NBC system:	None
Night vision equipment:	None

DEVELOPMENT

Ferret series 4 x 4 scout car was developed by the Daimler company shortly after the Second World War for the British Army. First prototypes were completed in 1949 with production running from 1952 to 1971. Total production amounted to 4,409 vehicles for home and export. It is no longer used by the British Army.

Ferret Mk 2/3 has driver at front, commander centre and engine rear. Turret has manual traverse through 360°, 7.62mm machine gun with manual elevation from -15° to +45°. Turret is identical to that on many Alvis Saracen (6 x 6) APCs. Spare wheel carried on left side of hull, emergency hatch on opposite side. Channels were often carried across front of hull for crossing ditches or sandy terrain.

VARIANTS

Ferret Mk 1 has no turret and open top, normally has pintle-mounted 7.62mm MG.

Mk 1/2 has crew of three and low profile turret with 7.62mm machine gun.

Mk 2 is similar to Mk 2/3, with turret.
Mk 2/2 was for Far East, no longer in service.
Mk 2/4 has additional armour.
Mk 2/5 is Mk 2 brought up to Mk 2/4 standard.
Mk 2/6 is Mk 2/3 with Vigilant ATGW mounted each side of turret. No longer operational with any country.
Mk 2/7 is Mk 2/6 with missiles removed and equals Mk 2/3.
Mk 3 is Mk 1 with same modifications as Mk 4.
Mk 4 is Mk 2/3 rebuilt with many improvements including larger wheels and flotation screen.
Mk 5 had Swingfire ATGWs. No longer in service.

Further development of Mk 4 (or 'big wheeled Ferret') resulted in Fox (qv). A number of companies offer upgrade packages for the Ferret including a more fuel-efficient diesel engine.

KEY RECOGNITION FEATURES

- Driver front, turret centre, engine compartment rear with roof that slopes down slightly each side with louvres at far rear top. Top half of hull rear vertical, lower half slopes back under hull rear

- Well-sloped glacis plate, driver has hatch hinged at top that opens downwards and similar smaller hatch each side. Upper part of hull front, sides and rear slope inwards

- Two large road wheels each side with spare wheel and tyre on left side of hull

STATUS

Production complete. In service with Bahrain, Burkina Faso, Cameroon, Central African Republic, India, Indonesia, Kenya, Madagascar, Malawi, Malaysia, Mauritius, Myanmar, Nepal, Qatar, South Africa, Sri Lanka, Sudan and Zimbabwe.

MANUFACTURER

Daimler Limited, Coventry, UK.

Below: Ferret Mk 1

Below: Daimler Ferret Mk 1

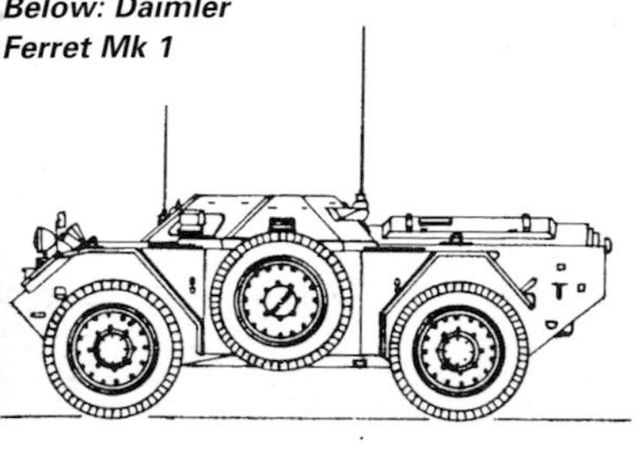

Below: Daimler Ferret Mk 4

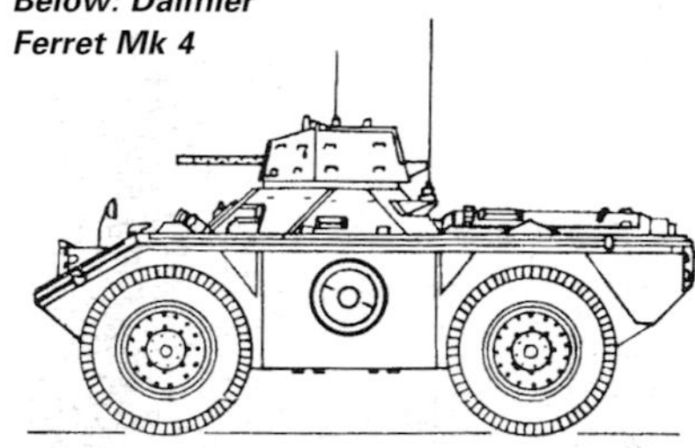

Fox Light Armoured Car (UK)

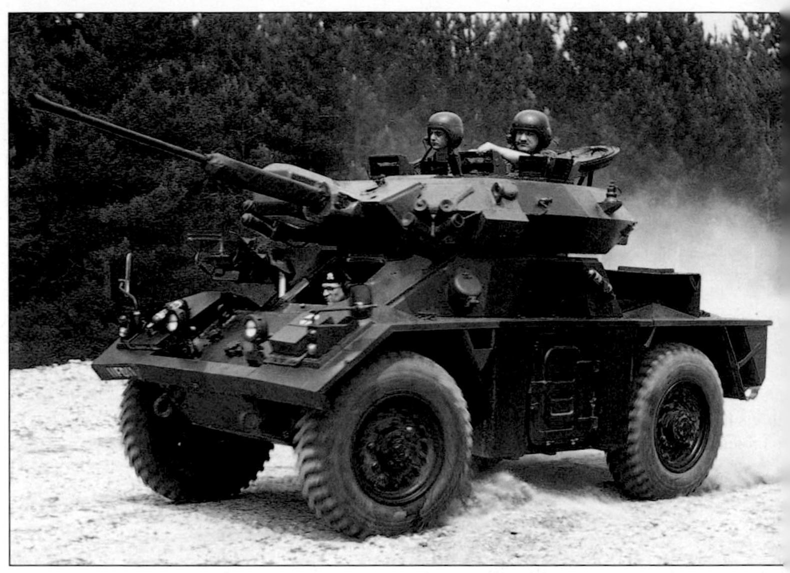

Above: Fox (4 x 4)

SPECIFICATIONS

Crew:	3
Configuration:	4 x 4
Armament:	1 x 30mm cannon, 1 x 7.62mm MG (coaxial), 2 x 4 smoke grenade dischargers
Ammunition:	99 x 30mm, 2,600 x 7.62mm
Length gun forwards:	5.08m
Length hull:	4.166m
Width:	2.134m
Height overall:	2.2m
Height to turret top:	1.981m
Ground clearance:	0.3m
Wheelbase:	2.464m
Weight, combat:	6120kg
Weight, empty:	5733kg
Power-to-weight ratio:	30.04bhp/tonne
Engine:	Jaguar XK 4.2 litre 6-cylinder petrol developing 190bhp at 4,500rpm
Maximum road speed:	104km/hr
Maximum water speed:	5.23km/hr
Maximum road range:	434km
Fuel capacity:	145 lit
Fording:	1m, amphibious with preparation
Vertical obstacle:	0.5m
Trench with channels:	1.22m
Gradient:	46%
Side slope:	30%
Armour:	Classified
Armour type:	Aluminium
NBC system:	None
Night vision equipment:	Yes (passive for driver and gunner)

DEVELOPMENT

Combat Vehicle Reconnaissance (Wheeled) was developed in the 1960s by the then Fighting Vehicles Research and Development Establishment (FVRDE) at the same time as the Combat Vehicle Reconnaissance (Tracked) Scorpion. The prototypes were built by Daimler, Coventry, the first completed in 1967. Production was undertaken by the then Royal Ordnance Factory, Leeds, first production vehicles completed in 1973. In 1986 Royal Ordnance Leeds was taken over by Vickers

)efence Systems. The production line for Fox was ıowever closed some time ago.

Driver sits front, two-man turret centre, engine ınd transmission rear. Turret has manual traverse hrough 360° and 30mm RARDEN cannon levates from -14° to +40°. Ammunition consists f APDS-T, APSE-T, HEI-T and training.

The Fox light armoured car is fitted with a lotation screen and when this is erected the vehicle s propelled and steered in the water by its wheels. 'hese were removed from British Army vehicles.

/ARIANTS

Vlany variants of the Fox were projected but none of these entered service. The Fox has been phased ıut of service with the British Army and their urrets have been fitted onto the Scorpion chassis :o produce the Sabre reconnaissance vehicle. Some 30mm Fox Turrets were fitted onto British Army FV432 series APCs.

KEY RECOGNITION FEATURES

- Two large road wheels each side with stowage box between, flotation screen carried on hull top (sometimes removed)
- Well-sloped glacis plate with large driver's hatch opening to right in upper part
- Turret in hull centre with two hatch covers opening to rear, long 30mm RARDEN cannon with day/night sight on right, turret welded in middle and upper and lower parts sloping inwards

STATUS

Production complete. In service with Malawi and Nigeria.

MANUFACTURER

Vickers Defence Systems, Leeds, UK (facility no longer exists).

Above: Fox (4 x 4) without flotation screen

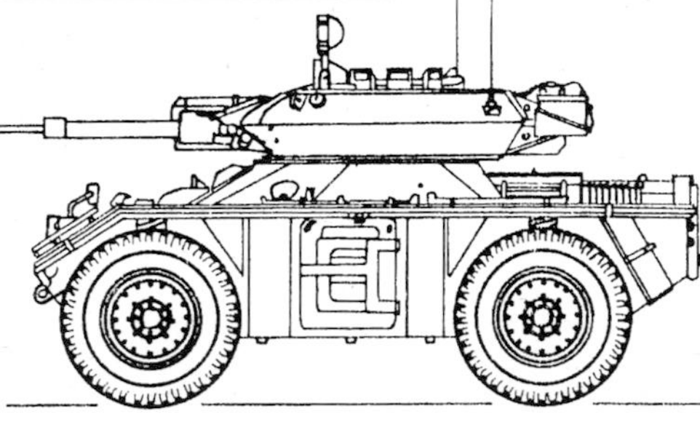

Right: Fox (4 x 4)

Saxon APC (UK)

Above: Saxon command post (Richard Stickland)

SPECIFICATIONS

Crew:	2 + 8 (or 10)
Configuration:	4 x 4
Armament:	1 x 7.62mm MG
Ammunition:	1,000 x 7.62mm
Length:	5.169m
Width:	2.489m
Height:	2.628m (commander's cupola)
Ground clearance:	0.41m (hull), 0.29m (axles)
Wheelbase:	3.073m
Weight, combat:	11,660kg
Weight, empty:	9,940kg
Power-to-weight ratio:	14.06bhp/tonne
Engine:	Bedford 500 6-cylinder diesel developing 164bhp at 2,800rpm
Maximum road speed:	96km/hr
Maximum road range:	480km
Fuel capacity:	153 lit
Fording:	1.12m
Vertical obstacle:	0.41m
Trench:	Not applicable
Gradient:	60%
Side slope:	30%
Armour:	Classified
Armour type:	Steel
NBC system:	None
Night vision equipment:	None

DEVELOPMENT

Saxon (4 x 4) was developed as a private venture by GKN Defence, first prototype completed in 1976 and first production vehicles in 1976. In 1983 it was adopted by the British Army for infantry battalions based in UK but deployed to Germany in wartime.

Driver sits front left or front right, engine in lower part of hull and troop compartment extending right to rear. Troops on bench seats down both sides and enter via side doors or two doors at rear. Commander has fixed cupola or turret with single or 7.62mm twin MGs.

Optional equipment includes air-conditioning system, front-mounted winch, heater, grenade launchers, barricade remover, searchlights, front-mounted winch and replacement of Bedford engine by Perkins T6.3544 diesel developing 195hp at 2,500rpm.

Final production vehicles for the British Army re powered by a Cummins 6BT 5.91 litre turbo-harged 6-cylinder diesel engine developing 60hp coupled to a fully automatic transmission. ate production models for British Army are called axon Patrol and were for Northern Ireland.

It was originally designed and built by GKN)efence which merged with Alvis to form Alvis 'ehicles. This in turn merged with Vickers Defence ystems to form Alvis Vickers. In late 2004 this ompany was taken over and is today BAE ystems Land Systems.

VARIANTS

:ommand vehicle - fitted with additional :ommunications equipment.
Ambulance - in service with British Army.
Recovery - in service with British Army, has winch vith capacity of 16 tonnes.
ncident control vehicle - prototype only for IS applications.
Water cannon - prototype only.

STATUS

Production complete. In service with Bahrain, Hong Kong, Malaysia, Nigeria, Oman, United Arab Emirates and UK.

MANUFACTURER

BAE Systems Land Systems, UK.

KEY RECOGNITION FEATURES

- Box-shaped hull with front sloping to rear and driver's position offset to right, horizontal louvres on front and left side of hull, single door in right side of hull and twin doors rear

- Flat roof with commander's fixed cupola on forward part with rear-opening hatch, vision block in each side and 7.62mm MG on external DISA mount

- Two large road wheels each side with stowage bins on left side of hull and wire stowage box on roof

(Note: left-hand drive model available; export vehicles have door in left side of hull)

Below: Saxon (4 x 4) with MG turret

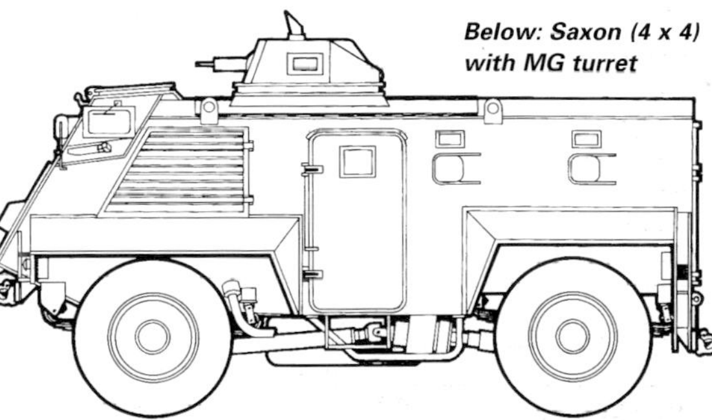

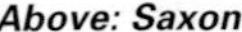

Above: Saxon

Above: Saxon Patrol (Richard Stickland)

Tenix Defence Systems Shorland S 55 APC (UK/Australia

Above: Shorland S 55 (4 x 4)

SPECIFICATIONS

Crew:	2 + 6
Configuration:	4 x 4
Armament:	2 x 4 smoke grenade dischargers
Length:	4.25m
Width:	1.8m
Height:	2.28m
Ground clearance:	0.324m
Wheelbase:	2.795m
Weight, combat:	3,600kg
Power-to-weight ratio:	37.2hp/tonne
Engine:	Rover V-8 water-cooled petrol developing 134bhp at 5,000rpm
Maximum road speed:	120km/hr
Maximum range:	630km
Fuel capacity:	136 lit
Fording:	0.50m
Vertical obstacle:	0.23m
Trench:	Not applicable
Gradient:	60% (estimate)
Side slope:	30% (estimate)
Armour:	8mm (estimate)
Armour type:	Steel
NBC system:	None
Night vision equipment:	None

DEVELOPMENT

In the early 1970s Short Brothers developed an APC based on a Land Rover (4 x 4) chassis to work with its Shorland Armoured Patrol Vehicle on a similar chassis. First prototype completed in 1973 under the designation SB 301.

This was followed in production by SB 401 with improved armour protection and more powerful engine, and in 1980 SB 501 was introduced, based on new Land Rover One-Ten chassis with wider wheelbase and improved coil spring suspension. Depending on year of manufacture there are minor exterior differences between vehicles, especially hull front; for example, on early vehicles radiator grille was short distance back from front mudguards whereas on SB 501 it is slightly forward of radiator.

Layout of all versions virtually identical with engine front, commander and driver to its rear (left-hand and right-hand drive models available) and troop compartment rear, three men each side facing.

Wide range of optional equipment including long-range fuel tank, smoke grenade dischargers, flashing lamps, air-conditioning system and roof-mounted 7.62mm MG.

To date all production of the vehicle has been undertaken in Northern Ireland but sales and marketing is carried out by Tenix Defence Systems of Australia who own the rights of all the Shorland vehicles. As of late 2004 there had been no production of the vehicle in Australia.

VARIANTS

No variants but see also Shorland Armoured Patrol Vehicle (ACRVs). Late production vehicles had different hull front, three small vision blocks with associated firing ports in either side of hull and integral bullet-proof windows for commander and driver.

STATUS

Production as required. In service with more than 20 countries including Malaysia, Pakistan, Papua New Guinea Defence Force and Turkey.

MANUFACTURER

Tenix Defence Systems, Bandiana, Victoria, Australia.

KEY RECOGNITION FEATURES

- Conventional layout with armour plated engine compartment front, angled windscreen with armoured louvres hinged at top, hull top above commander. Driver has integral spotlight, horizontal roof over rear troop compartment, vertical hull rear

- Single forward-opening door each side with outward-opening observation panel in upper part, two rectangular firing ports in hull sides that slope slightly inwards, two doors rear each with firing port

- Two road wheels each side with rounded front and square cut rear wheel arches (see variants)

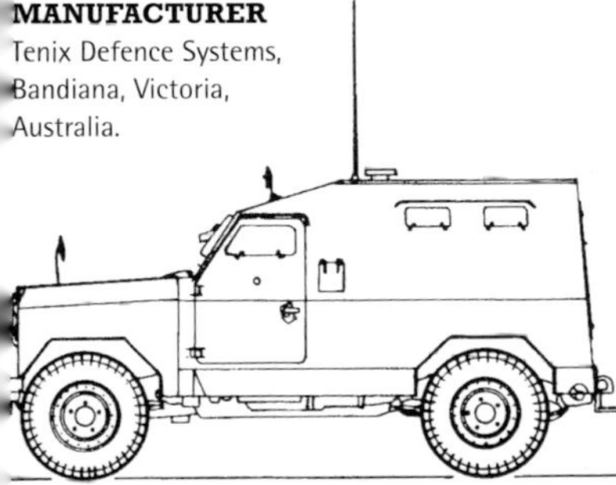

Above: Shorland (4 x 4) APC

Above left: Shorland SB 501 (4 x 4) APC

Left: Shorland S 55 (4 x 4) APC on One-Ten chassis

Glover Webb Armoured Patrol Vehicle (UK)

Above: Glover Webb Armoured Patrol Vehicle

SPECIFICATIONS

Crew:	2 + 6
Configuration:	4 x 4
Armament:	nil
Ammunition:	nil
Length:	4.55m
Width:	1.79m
Height:	2.08m
Ground clearance:	0.32m
Wheelbase:	2.794m
Weight, combat:	Not available
Weight, empty:	Not available
Power-to-weight ratio:	Not available
Engine:	Rover V-8 petrol developing 114 hp
Maximum road speed:	120km/h
Maximum road range:	Not available
Fuel capacity:	Not available
Fording:	Not available
Vertical obstacle:	0.23m
Trench:	Not applicable
Gradient:	60%
Side slope:	30%
Armour:	Classified
Armour type:	Steel
NBC:	No
Night vision equipment:	No

DEVELOPMENT

The Glover Webb Armoured Patrol Vehicle (APV) was originally developed to meet the requirements of the British Army for use in Northern Ireland with the first of about 100 vehicles being completed in 1986. These were built by Glover Webb which no longer exists.

The vehicle is essentially a Land Rover chassis fitted with an armoured body that provides the occupants with protection from small arms fire and shell splinters. The engine is at the front, commander and driver in the centre and the troop compartment at the rear. The troops are seated three down each side facing each other.

VARIANTS

Can be provided with firing ports in rear troop compartment and roof mounted 7.62mm machine gun. Glover Webb have also built quantities of Hornet (4 x 4) armoured car based on a modified Land Rover chassis. This is fitted with a roof mounted turret armed with a 7.62mm machine gun.

Many other companies build light armoured vehicles based on the Land Rover (4 x 4) Defender chassis including NP Aerospace of the UK who has built over 1000 of the CAV 100 vehicles, many for the British Army. These are also referred to as 'Snatch' vehicles.

STATUS

Production complete. No longer marketed. In service with British Army, Police and other undisclosed users.

MANUFACTURER

Glover Webb, Hamble, Hampshire, UK.

KEY RECOGNITION FEATURES

- Conventional layout with armour plated engine compartment front with wire mesh screen across front, bonnet horizontal to windscreen which can be provided with wire mesh screen that hinges forward onto bonnet when not required

- Front part of roof has slightly sloping front with searchlight above, hull top horizontal and hull rear vertical. Hatch in roof of British Army vehicles. Forward opening door in each side has bullet proof window in upper part. Troops enter and leave via twin doors in rear each of which has vision block

- Two wheels each side with arches above, lower part of hull sides are vertical with upper part sloping slightly inwards

Right: CAV 100 APC of the British Army (Richard Stickland)

Right: Glover Webb Hornet

Tactica APC (UK)

Above: Tactica water cannon background with bonneted Tactica in front

SPECIFICATIONS

Crew:	2 + 12
Configuration:	4 x 4
Armament:	Nil (see text)
Ammunition:	Nil (see text)
Length:	5.6m
Width:	2.2m
Height:	2.35m
Ground clearance:	0.3 m
Wheelbase:	Depends on model
Weight, combat:	10,000kg
Weight, empty:	6,500kg
Power-to-weight ratio:	See text
Engine:	Mercedes, Perkins or Renault turbocharged diesel engine
Maximum road speed:	120km/h
Maximum road range:	650km
Fuel capacity:	167 lit
Fording:	Not available
Vertical obstacle:	Not available
Trench:	Not applicable
Gradient:	60%
Side slope:	30%
Armour:	Classified
Armour type:	Steel
NBC:	No
Night vision equipment:	No

DEVELOPMENT

The Tactica APC (4 x 4) was developed as a private venture by Glover Webb who were taken over by GKN Defence. As a result of mergers the Telford facility is now part of BAE Systems Land Systems. First prototype of the Tactica was completed in 1988 with first production vehicles being completed the following year.

Two versions of the Tactica are currently offered, one with a forward control type hull which can carry up to 14 men and the other with a conventional bonnet type hull which can carry up to 10 men. Different wheelbase models are available as are different diesel engines.

The conventional bonnet type has the engine at the front, commander and driver in the centre and the troop compartment at the rear. The troops normally enter and leave via two doors in the hull rear. The basic model is unarmed but can be fitted with a variety of roof mounted weapon stations including a pintle mounted 7.62mm or 12.7mm machine gun or one man turret armed with similar weapons.

Standard equipment includes power steering

and a wide range of optional equipment is available according to mission requirements.

VARIANTS

The vehicle can be adopted for a wide range of roles, for example fitted with a water cannon and for use in command post role. The UK uses the vehicles to transport EOD teams.

STATUS

Production as required. In service with Argentina (UN role), Ghana, Indonesia, Kuwait, Mauritius, Norway (EOD), Saudi Arabia, Singapore, UK and other countries.

MANUFACTURER

BAE Systems Land Systems, Telford, Shropshire, UK.

KEY RECOGNITION FEATURES

- Conventional layout with armour-plated engine compartment front with horizontal louvres in the centre, bonnet slopes slightly upwards to windscreen which slopes to rear

- Front part of roof has slightly sloping front with hull top horizontal and hull rear vertical, lower part of hull rear slopes inwards. Forward opening door in each side has bullet proof window in upper part. Three firing ports with bullet proof window above in either side of rear troop compartment

- Two wheels each side, lower part of hull sides slope slightly inwards, upper part of hull are vertical, twin door in hull rear with two firing ports with vision blocks above

Right: Tactica APC

Right: Tactica in forward control configuration

Simba APC (UK)

Above: Simba with 25mm turret

SPECIFICATIONS

Crew:	3 + 8/10
Configuration:	4 x 4
Armament:	1 x 7.62mm MG
Ammunition:	1000 x 7.62mm
Length:	5.35m
Width:	2.50m
Height:	2.19m (low profile cupola)
Ground clearance:	0.45m (hull), 0.33m (axles)
Wheelbase:	2.972m
Weight, combat:	11,200kg
Weight, empty:	9,500kg
Power-to-weight ratio:	18.75 bhp/tonne
Engine:	Perkins 210Ti turbocharged intercooled diesel developing 210bhp at 2500rpm
Maximum road speed:	100km/h
Maximum road range:	660km
Fuel capacity:	296 lit
Fording:	1m
Vertical obstacle:	0.45m
Trench:	Not applicable
Gradient:	60%
Side slope:	40%
Armour:	8mm (maximum) (estimate)
Armour type:	Steel
NBC:	No (optional)
Night vision equipment:	No (optional)

DEVELOPMENT

The Simba light combat vehicle was designed as a private venture by GKN Defence (which is today BAE Systems Land Systems) specifically for the export market and following trials was selected by the Philippines Armed Forces who placed an order for 150 vehicles.

Of these 150 vehicles, eight vehicles were delivered complete, two in knocked down kit form and the remaining 148 were assembled in the Philippines at a facility owned by the joint venture company Asian Armoured Vehicle Technologies Corporation.

The driver is seated front left with the powerpack to his right and the troop compartment extending to the rear. The troops sit on seats down either side and can leave the vehicle via the door in the rear or the door in left side of the hull. Most vehicles used by the Philippines have a one man turret armed with a

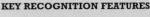

12.7mm M2 machine gun. Some vehicles were fitted with a one person turret armed with a 25mm cannon and 7.62mm MG.

A wide range of optional equipment can be fitted including front mounted winch, heater and/or air conditioning system and various weapon systems.

VARIANTS

AIFV, two man 20mm or 25mm turret.
Fire support vehicle, two man 90mm turret.
Internal security, wide range of equipment.
Anti-tank, HOT or TOW ATGW.
Mortar, 81mm on turntable.

STATUS

Production complete. In service with Philippines Armed Forces.

MANUFACTURER

BAE Systems Land Systems, Telford, Shropshire, UK.

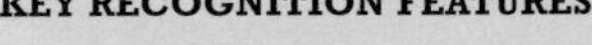

KEY RECOGNITION FEATURES

- Box-shaped hull sloping up to raised drivers position on left side, engine compartment on right side with louvres on lower part of glacis plate. Horizotal roof extends to rear, vehicle hull rear with large door

- Upper part of hull slopes inwards with two part door in left side of hull and single hatch in right side of hull. Various armament options can be mounted on roof

- Two large road wheels each side, lower part of hull slopes inwards

Right: Simba fitted with 12.7mm MG turret

Above: Simba

Above: Simba

Cadillac Gage Ranger APC (USA)

Above: Ranger as used by US Air Force (Michael Jerchel)

SPECIFICATIONS

Crew:	2 + 6
Configuration:	4 x 4
Armament:	1 x 7.62mm MG
Ammunition:	1,000 x 7.62mm
Length:	4.699m
Width:	2.019m
Height:	1.981m
Ground clearance:	0.203m
Wheelbase:	2.641m
Weight, combat:	4,536kg
Power-to-weight ratio:	40hp/tonne
Engine:	Dodge 360 CID V-8 liquid-cooled petrol developing 180hp at 3,600rpm
Maximum road speed:	112.65km/hr
Maximum road range:	482km
Fuel capacity:	121 lit
Fording:	0.60m
Vertical obstacle:	0.254m
Trench:	Not applicable
Gradient:	60%
Side slope:	30%
Armour:	7mm (maximum) (estimate)
Armour type:	Steel
NBC system:	None
Night vision equipment:	None

DEVELOPMENT

Ranger was developed as a private venture in the late 1970s by the now Textron Marine & Land Systems and following completion was selected by the US Air Force for a Security Police Armored Response/Convoy Truck to patrol air bases and other high value targets. First production vehicles completed in 1980 and by 1995 over 700 were built.

It is essentially a Chrysler truck chassis with a shorter wheelbase fitted with armoured body for protection from small arms fire and shell splinters. Engine is front, commander and driver to rear and crew compartment far rear.

Basic vehicle is fitted with roof-mounted 7.62mm MG which normally has a shield, but a wide range of other weapon systems can be installed including turret with twin 7.62mm MG or turret with one 7.62mm and 12.7mm MG. The turret has manual traverse through a full 360° with weapon elevation being from -14° to +55°. Luxembourg has five vehicles with this turret armed with twin 7.62mm MGs.

Standard equipment includes air conditioning system and heater, optional equipment includes grenade launchers, flashing lights, spotlight and front-mounted winch.

VARIANTS

In addition to different weapon stations, Ranger can be used as command post vehicle, ambulance and light reconnaissance vehicle.

STATUS

Production complete. No longer marketed. In service with Indonesia and Luxembourg. In US Air Force and Navy it has now been replaced by the M1116 (4 x 4) armoured personnel carrier based on an AM General HMMWV (4 x 4) chassis with additional armour.

MANUFACTURER

Textron Marine & Land Systems, New Orleans, Louisiana, US.

KEY RECOGNITION FEATURES

- Vertical hull front with horizontal armoured radiator louvres, horizontal bonnet top which then slopes upwards to crew compartment, horizontal roof and almost vertical hull rear

- Single door in each hull side which opens to the front, with firing port and vision block, twin doors in rear each with firing port, left door also has vision block and ventilator

- Two road wheels each side with hull sides above road wheels sloping slightly inwards

Below: Ranger in police role

Cadillac Gage ASV 150 (USA)

Above: ASV 150

SPECIFICATIONS

Crew:	1 + 3
Armament:	1 x 40mm grenade launcher, 1 x 12.7mm MG (coaxial), 2 x 4 smoke grenade launchers
Ammunition:	600 x 40mm, 800 x 12.7mm
Length hull:	6.07m
Width:	2.56m
Height overall:	2.59m
Height hull roof:	2.05m
Ground clearance:	0.46m
Weight, combat:	13,408kg
Weight, empty:	11,884kg
Power-to-weight ratio:	19.39hp/tonne
Ground pressure:	Not available
Engine:	Cummins 6CTA 8.3 turbocharged diesel developing 260hp at 2200rpm
Maximum road speed:	100km/h
Maximum road range:	708km
Fuel capacity:	264 lit
Fording:	1.50m
Vertical obstacle:	0.60m
Trench:	Not applicable
Gradient:	60%
Side slope:	30%
Armour:	Classified
Armour type:	Steel plus composite
NBC system:	Yes
Night vision equipment:	Yes

DEVELOPMENT

The Cadillac Gage ASV 150 was developed by Textron Marine & Land Systems to meet the requirements of the US Army Military Police for an Armored Security Vehicle (ASV). Following trials with prototype vehicles the first production order was placed in early 1999 for 94 vehicles under the US Army designation of the M1117. First production vehicles were delivered in the second quarter of the year 2000. By late 2004 the order book stood at 132 for the US Army and 43 for Iraq.

The ASV 150 is a further development of the Cadillac Gage Textron LAV-150 ST and in future the ASV 150 will be the only vehicle offered by the company.

The ASV 150 has many improvements over the LAV-150 ST including the replacement of older suspension by a new fully independent suspension which gives an improved ride over rough terain. The steel hull is fitted with applique passive armour developed by the German company of IBD.

The commander and driver are seated at the front with the turret in the centre, powerpack at the left rear and narrow aisle at the right rear.

The one person power-operated turret is armed with a 40mm Mk 19 grenade launcher and a 12.7mm M2 machine gun. Turret traverse is a full 360° with elevation from -8° to +48°.

Standard equipment includes a fire detection and suppression system and a front mounted power operated winch. A central tyre pressure regulation system is fitted as standard which allows the driver to adjust the tyre pressure to suit the type of terrain being crossed.

VARIANTS

The are no variants of the ASV 150 so far but in the future it is expected that the vehicle will be capable of being fitted with a wide range of armament systems up to and including a two person turret armed with a 90mm gun. An NBC reconnaissance version is also projected. Iraq has two versions: APC with pintle mounted machine gun and command post vehicle.

STATUS

Production. In service with Iraq and US.

MANUFACTURER

Textron Marine & Land Systems, New Orleans, Louisiana, US.

KEY RECOGNITION FEATURES

- Very similar in appearance to LAV-150 (4 x 4) and Dragoon (4 x 4) covered in following entries but has different hull shape with engine left rear and applique armour

- Pointed hull front with horizontal roof, hull sides above rear wheel arches slope inwards, hull rear slopes inwards with horizontal louvres on left side and two part hatch on right side

- Two large road wheels each side with two-part hatch between which has firing port and window in upper part, turret in centre of hull roof

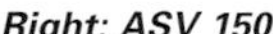

Right: ASV 150

Right: ASV 150

Cadillac Gage LAV-150 AFV Range (USA)

Above: Cadillac Gage LAV-200 Commando mortar carrier

SPECIFICATIONS

Crew:	3 + 2
Configuration:	4 x 4
Armament:	1 x 20mm, 1 x 7.62mm MG (coaxial), 1 x 7.62mm MG (anti-aircraft), 2 x 6 smoke grenade dischargers
Ammunition:	400 x 20mm, 3,200 x 7.62mm
Length:	5.689m
Width:	2.26m
Height:	2.54m (turret roof), 1.981m (hull roof)
Ground clearance:	0.381m (axles), 0.648m (hull)
Wheelbase:	2.667m
Weight, combat:	9,888kg
Power-to-weight ratio:	20.42bhp/tonne
Engine:	V-504 V-8 diesel developing 202bhp at 3,300rpm
Maximum road speed:	88.54km/hr
Maximum water speed:	5km/hr
Maximum range:	643km
Fuel capacity:	303 lit
Fording:	Amphibious
Vertical obstacle:	0.609m
Trench:	Not applicable
Gradient:	60%
Side slope:	30%
Armour:	Classified
Armour type:	Steel
NBC system:	None
Night vision equipment:	Optional

DEVELOPMENT

In 1962 Cadillac Gage (now Textron Marine & Land Systems) started private venture development work on a 4 x 4 light armoured vehicle which became known as LAV-100, first prototype completed in 1963 and first production vehicle in 1964. It was powered by a Chrysler petrol engine and used on a large scale in South Vietnam. A scaled-up version, LAV-200, was also built but was sold only to Singapore.

In 1971 LAV-100 and LAV-200 were replaced in production by LAV-150 with a number of improvements including replacement of petrol engine by diesel. In 1985 LAV-150 was replaced in production by LAV-150S which has longer

wheelbase and therefore greater weight. So far over 3,200 vehicles have been built.

In all versions commander and driver are at front with troop compartment extending to rear except for engine compartment left rear. All versions are fully amphibious, propelled by their wheels, have a front-mounted winch and run flat tyres. A wide range of armament can be fitted as well as other specialised equipment.

VARIANTS

These are many and include: turret with twin 7.62mm or one 7.62mm and one 12.7mm MG; turret with 20mm cannon and 7.62mm MG (one- or two-man versions); two-man turret with 25mm cannon and 7.62mm MG; one-man turret with 40mm grenade launcher and 12.7mm MG; anti-aircraft with 20mm Vulcan cannon; two-man turret with 90mm gun and 7.62mm coaxial and 7.62mm AA MG; 81mm mortar carrier; TOW ATGW; command or APC with pod; recovery; base security; ambulance; and emergency rescue vehicle.

US Army designation is **M706** and some are used as surrogate Russian systems such as **SA-9**.

There is also a 6 x 6 version, Commando LAV-300 (qv).

Singapore has a number of variants of LAV-200 including recovery and air defence with RBS-70 SAM.

Armoured Security Vehicle, this is a further development of the LAV-150 and is covered in a seperate entry.

KEY RECOGNITION FEATURES

- Very similar in appearance to Dragoon (qv) except engine is left side at rear, not right
- Pointed hull front with horizontal roof, hull sides above curved wheel arches slope inwards, hull back cut off top and bottom and points rear
- Two large road wheels each side with two-part hatch between, similar hatch right rear, armament mounted on hull roof centre of vehicle

STATUS

Production complete. In service with Bolivia (LAV-100), Botswana (LAV-150), Cameroon (LAV-150), Chad (LAV-150S), Dominican Republic (LAV-150), Gabon (LAV-150), Guatemala (LAV-150), Indonesia (LAV-150), Jamaica (LAV-150), Malaysia (LAV-100 and LAV-150), Mexico (LAV-150 ST), Philippines (LAV-150), Saudi Arabia (LAV-150), Singapore (LAV-150 and LAV-200), Somalia, Sudan (LAV-150 and LAV-150 S), Taiwan (LAV-150), Thailand (LAV-150), Turkey (LAV-150), US (LAV-100), Venezuela (LAV-150).

MANUFACTURER

Textron Marine & Land Systems, New Orleans, Louisiana, US.

Right: Cadillac Gage LAV-150 Commando with turret mounted 90mm gun

AV Technology Dragoon armoured vehicle (USA)

Above: Dragoon APC with 12.7mm MG

SPECIFICATIONS

Crew:	3 + 6
Configuration:	4 x 4
Armament:	1 x 20mm cannon, 1 x 7.62mm MG (coaxial)
Length:	5.89m
Width:	2.49m
Height:	2.819m (overall), 2.082m (hull top)
Ground clearance:	0.685m (hull centre), 0.381m (axles)
Wheelbase:	3.10m
Weight, combat:	12,700kg
Weight, empty:	11,204kg
Power-to-weight ratio:	23.62bhp/tonne
Engine:	Detroit Diesel 6V-53T 6-cylinder liquid-cooled turbocharged diesel developing 300bhp at 2,800rpm
Maximum road speed:	115.9km/hr
Maximum water speed:	5.5km/hr
Maximum road range:	869km
Fuel capacity:	350 lit
Fording:	Amphibious
Vertical obstacle:	0.609m
Trench:	Not applicable
Gradient:	60%
Side slope:	30%
Armour:	Classified
Armour type:	Steel
NBC system:	Optional
Night vision equipment:	Optional

DEVELOPMENT

Dragoon AFV family was originally developed by the Verne Corporation to meet requirements of the US Army Military Police. The requirement subsequently lapsed and the company built two prototypes first shown in 1978. A small quantity of vehicles was built for the US Army and Navy in 1982. The US Army vehicles were supplied to the 9th Infantry Division High Technology Test Bed in two versions: electronic warfare and optical surveillance. The US Navy used them for patrolling nuclear weapon storage sites. AV Technology is now owned by General Dynamics Land Systems.

To reduce life-cycle and procurement costs Dragoon uses components of M113A2 full-tracked APC and M809 five-tonne (6 x 6) truck.

Commander and driver sit front with troops carried to rear, wide range of weapon stations mounted on hull top, up to two-person 90mm

Kenerga gun with 7.62mm coaxial MG in power-operated turret.

Dragoon is fully amphibious, propelled by its wheels, standard equipment includes front-mounted winch and wide range of optional equipment.

In 1984 the Verne Corporation and the Arrowpointe Corporation merged to form AV Technology Corporation and since then the vehicle has been further developed into the following basic versions: APC, Patroller armoured security vehicle, armoured command vehicle, 81mm armour mortar carrier, 90mm turret, 40mm/12.7mm turret, armoured maintenance vehicle, electronic warfare, armoured logistic support vehicle and TOW ATGW carrier.

Latest production model is the Dragoon 2 which has many improvements.

KEY RECOGNITION FEATURES

- Similar in appearance to Cadillac Gage (now Textron Marine & Land Systems) LAV-100/LAV-150 (4 x 4) vehicles except that powerpack is on right side rear, not left

- Pointed front with almost horizontal roof, hull sides above curved wheel arches slope inwards, hull back slopes to rear at about 60°

- Two large road wheels each side with two-part hatch between similar hatch left rear, armament mounted on hull roof centre of vehicle

VARIANTS

Dragoon can be used for wide range of roles including APC, reconnaissance, recovery, command/communications, riot control, engineer, security/escort, 81mm mortar carrier, anti-tank with TOW, ambulance and logistics.

STATUS

Production as required. In service with American forces, Thailand, Turkey, Venezuela and a number of civil authorities. It is envisioned that future production of the Dragoon will be in Spain by General Dynamics Santa Barbara Sistemas.

MANUFACTURER

AV Technology, Detroit, Michigan, US.

Above right: Dragoon with two-man 90mm turret

Right: Dragoon Patroller armoured security vehicle

Cadillac Gage Scout (USA)

SPECIFICATIONS

Crew:	1 + 1 or 1 + 2
Configuration:	4 x 4
Armament:	2 x 7.62mm MG
Ammunition:	2,600 x 7.62mm
Length:	5.003m
Width:	2.057m
Height:	2.159m
Wheelbase:	2.743m
Track:	1.660m
Weight, combat:	7240kg
Power-to-weight ratio:	20.58hp/tonne
Engine:	Cummins V-6 diesel developing 155hp at 3,300rpm
Maximum road speed:	88km/hr
Maximum road range:	846km
Fuel capacity:	378 lit
Fording:	1.168m
Vertical obstacle:	0.609m
Trench:	1.14m
Gradient:	60%
Side slope:	30%
Armour:	8mm (maximum) (estimate)
Armour type:	Steel
NBC system:	None
Night vision equipment:	Optional

Above: Commando Scout with 1m pod and armed with two 7.62mm machine guns

DEVELOPMENT

Commando Scout (4 x 4) was developed as a private venture by Cadillac Gage (now part of Textron Marine & Land Systems), the first prototype shown in 1977. Although its main role is reconnaissance it is suitable for a wide range of roles with little modification, such as anti-tank and command post. In 1983 Indonesia ordered 28 Commando Scouts and in 1986 Egypt ordered 112, all of which were delivered by mid-1987. Since then there has been no production of this vehicle.

The fuel tank is at the front, driver to immediate rear on left side, engine to his right. The turret is mounted rear, gunner enters via turret hatch cover or via two-part hatch in hull rear, upper part opens upwards and lower part downwards.

Standard equipment includes run flat tyres, power steering and air compressor with 15.24m hose. Optional equipment includes siren/public address system, various radio installations, slave cable, auxiliary cable, smoke grenade system and fragmentation grenade system as well as a wide range of one person turrets.

VARIANTS

40mm/12.7mm turret, armed with 40mm grenade launcher and 12.7mm MG as fitted to US Marine Corps AAV7A1 vehicles.
Twin/combination MG (1m) Cadillac Gage turret, with twin 7.62mm or twin 12.7mm MG or combination of both. Turret traverses 360°, weapon elevates from -10° to +55°.
Command pod, with three-man crew (driver, commander and radio operator) and raised pod on which a 7.62mm or 12.7mm MG is mounted.
Anti-tank, with Raytheon Systems Company TOW ATGW launcher with one missile in ready-to-launch position and six missiles in reserve.

KEY RECOGNITION FEATURES

- Nose slopes back at 45° to first road wheel station, well-sloped glacis plate which extends half way along to horizontal roof at rear on which turret is mounted
- Driver's hatch upper left side of glacis plate with air louvres to right, exhaust pipe right side of hull, two-part hatch in hull rear
- Two large road wheels each side with hull sides sloping inwards top and bottom

STATUS

Production complete. Can be placed back into production. In service with Egypt and Indonesia.

MANUFACTURER

Textron Marine & Land Systems, New Orleans, Louisiana, USA.

Right: Commando Scout with 1m turret and twin 7.62mm MG

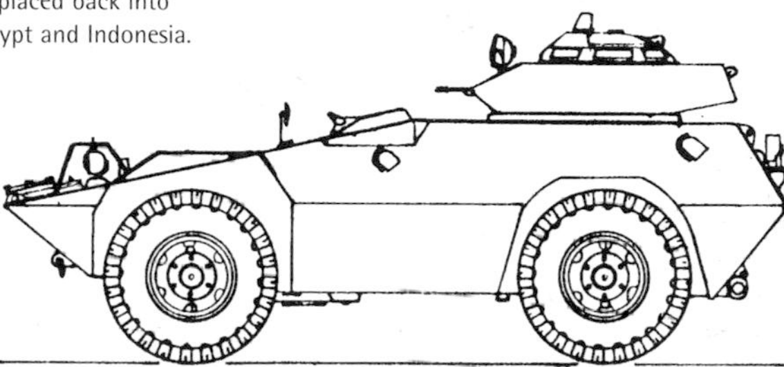

Above: Commando Scout with Command Pod and 12.7mm MG

O'Gara-Hess M1114 armoured vehicle (USA)

Above: M1114 armoured HMMWV with roof mounted 7.62mm machine gun (Richard Stickland)

SPECIFICATIONS

Crew:	1 + 3
Armament:	1 x 12.7mm MG typical)
Ammunition:	1,000 x 12.7mm typical)
Length hull:	4.99m
Width:	2.3m
Height:	1.9m
Ground clearance:	0.30m
Weight, combat:	5,489kg
Weight, empty:	4,445kg
Power-to-weight ratio:	34.61hp/tonne
Engine:	V-8 turbocharged diesel developing 190 hp at 3,400rpm
Maximum road speed:	125km/h
Maximum road range:	443km
Fuel capacity:	94 lit
Fording:	0.762m
Vertical obstacle:	Not available
Trench:	Not available
Gradient:	60%
Side slope:	40%
Armour:	Classified
Armour type:	Classified
NBC system:	No
Night vision equipment:	No

DEVELOPMENT

The M1114 is essentially an Enhanced Capacity Vehicle model of the AM General High Mobility Multipurpose Wheeled Vehicle HMMWV (4 x 4) up-armoured by the O'Gara-Hess & Eisenhardt Armoring Company to provide the occupants with protection from 7.62mm armour-piercing attack through a full 360°, shell splinters and mines.

The first examples were completed in 1994 and by late 2004 well over 3,000 had been built with deliveries to continue for some years.

The layout of the M1114 is similar to the HMMWV with the engine at front, crew compartment in centre and load area at rear. Access to the latter is via an upward opening hatch. The vehicle is normally left hand drive with the vehicle commander to the right and another

two people seated to the rear.

Mounted on the roof of the vehicle is a hatch on which various types of weapon can be installed such as 7.62mm or 12.7mm machine gun or a 40mm automatic grenade launcher. Standard equipment includes an air conditioning system, powered steering and an automatic transmission. Options include passive night vision equipment.

VARIANTS

The US Air Force has a further development of the M1114 called the M1116 which is used for a number of missions including Security Police, Civil Engineer and Explosive Ordnance Disposal Base Recovery After Attack.

STATUS

Production. In service with Egypt, Israel, Luxembourg, Qatar, Slovenia, United Arab Emirates and US.

MANUFACTURER

O'Gara-Hess & Eisenhardt Armoring Company, Fairfield, Ohio, US.

KEY RECOGNITION FEATURES

- Vertical hull front with vertical louvres with headlamp either side, slightly sloping bonnet leads up to vertical armoured windsceen. Horizontal roof with rear sloping downwards to vertical hull rear

- Sides are vertical with two forward opening doors in each side with a square window in the upper part. Wheels are at extreme ends of vehicle. There is a vertical air inlet pipe (retractable) to the front of the right windscreen

- Armament is mounted in centre of roof and on some models will be seen fitted with a shield

Below: US Air Force M1116 with 40mm automatic grenade launcher

6 x 6 VEHICLES

Steyr-Daimler-Puch Pandur APC (Austria)

Above: Pandur with 12.7mm for Austrian Army

SPECIFICATIONS

Crew:	2 + 8
Configuration:	6 x 6
Armament:	1 x 12.7mm MG, 2 x 3 smoke grenade launchers
Ammunition:	1000 x 12.7mm
Length:	5.697m
Width:	2.5m
Height:	1.82m
Ground clearance:	0.43m
Wheelbase:	1.53m + 1.53m
Weight, combat:	13,500kg
Weight, empty:	10,300kg
Power-to-weight ratio:	19.25 hp/tonne
Engine:	Steyr WD 612.95 6-cylinder turbocharged diesel, developing 260 hp at 2400rpm
Maximum road speed:	100km/h
Maximum road range:	700km
Fuel capacity:	275 lit
Fording:	1.5m
Vertical obstacle:	0.5m
Trench:	1.1m
Gradient:	70%
Side slope:	40%
Armour:	8mm (estimate)
Armour type:	Steel
NBC system:	Yes
Night vision equipment:	Yes

DEVELOPMENT

The Pandur 6 x 6 armoured personnel carrier was developed as a private venture by Steyr-Daimler-Puch. The first prototypes were shown in 1985 and in 1994 the Austrian army ordered 68 Pandurs for use by Austrian forces serving with the UN. Deliveries began in 1995.

The driver is seated front left, with the commander to his rear and the engine compartment to the right. The troop compartment extends to the rear and has roof hatches and firing ports/vision devices. The version for the Austrian army has a raised rear troop compartment with spall liners, mine protection mats and a heater. The commander/gunner has a 12.7mm machine gun in a protected position.

Standard equipment includes power steering, fire detection and suppression systems and a central tyre pressure regulation system. An amphibious version has been developed.

VARIANTS

Ambulance.
Anti-aircraft.
Anti-tank (HOT or TOW).
Armoured reconnaissance scout vehicle (30mm).
Armoured reconnaissance fire support vehicle (90mm).
Command and control vehicle.
Mechanised Infantry Combat Vehicle.
Reconaissance vehicle.
Amphibious model has longer hull and more powerful engine.
Recovery and repair.
Mortar carrier (81mm).
LWB, the standard Pandur has a wheel base of 1.53m + 1.53m but a version is also available with a wheel base of 1.53m + 1.83m which gives the vehicle greater internal volume.
Pandur II, this is the latest model with a more powerful engine and many other improvements and there is also a Pandur II 8 x 8 which ran for the first time late in 2001.

KEY RECOGNITION FEATURES

- Box-like hull with nose sloping back under front of vehicle, well-sloped glacis plate with driver to left rear and engine compartment to the right. Horizontal hull top extends to rear

- Upper part of hull sides above road wheels slope inwards with optional firing ports/vision devices in either side

- Three road wheels either side with equal space between them

Above: Pandur ambulance as supplied to Kuwait

STATUS

Production as required. In service or on order for Austria, Belgium, Kuwait, Slovenia and the US.

MANUFACTURER

Steyr-Daimler-Puch AG, Vienna, Austria.

Above: Pandur for US Army with 12.7mm MG

Above: Pandur with two person 90mm turret

SIBMAS APC (Belgium)

Above: SIBMAS (6 x 6) with 90mm CM 90 turret

SPECIFICATIONS

Crew:	3 + 11
Configuration:	6 x 6
Armament:	Depends on role
Ammunition:	Depends on role
Length, hull:	7.32m
Width:	2.5m
Height, turret top:	2.77m
Height, hull top:	2.24m
Ground clearance:	0.4m
Wheelbase:	2.8m + 1.4m
Weight, combat:	14,500 to 18,500kg (depends on role)
Weight, unloaded:	13,200kg (eg without turret)
Power-to-weight ratio (at 16,000kg):	20hp/tonne
Engine:	MAN D 2566 MK 6-cylinder in-line water-cooled turbocharged diesel developing 320hp at 1,900rpm
Maximum road speed:	100km/hr
Maximum water speed (wheels):	4km/hr
Maximum water speed (propellers):	11km/hr
Maximum road range:	1,000km
Fuel capacity:	400 lit
Fording:	Amphibious
Vertical obstacle:	0.7m
Trench:	1.5m
Gradient:	70%
Side slope:	40%
Armour:	Classified
Armour type:	Steel
NBC system:	Optional
Night vision equipment:	Optional

DEVELOPMENT

SIBMAS (6 x 6) wheeled armoured vehicle range was designed as a private venture from 1975 by BN Constructions Ferroviaires et Métalliques, first prototype completed in 1976. In appearance SIBMAS is similar to the South African Ratel (6 x 6) infantry fighting vehicle (qv).

In 1981 Malaysia ordered 196 SIBMAS vehicles, delivered between 1983 and 1985 in two versions: 162 Armoured Fire Support Vehicle 90s (AFSV-90) with CM 90 turret, and 24 ARVs. In mid-1985 the SIBMAS Division of BN was transferred to Belgian Mechanical Fabrication. The SIBMAS production line was closed some time ago and the vehicle is no longer being marketed.

Drivers sits front with weapon station on roof to his rear, troop compartment extends to rear of hull, engine compartment is left rear of vehicle. Three entry doors, one in each side and one at

ear, and three roof hatches. Troop compartment as firing ports and vision devices.

Standard equipment includes run flat tyres and ptional equipment includes night vision quipment, propellers, winch, heater, air onditioning system and NBC pack. Wide range of urrets including twin 7.62mm MG, 20mm annon, twin 20mm anti-aircraft, up to two-man urret with 90mm gun.

ARIANTS

IBMAS can be adapted for a wide range of roles ncluding mortar carrier, cargo vehicle, command ost, ambulance and recovery (used by Malaysia, vith 20,000kg winch, 10,500kg crane and front nd rear stabilising blades).

AFSV-90 has two-man CM 90 turret armed with 0mm Cockerill gun with 7.62mm coaxial and .62mm anti-aircraft MG and eight smoke/ ragmentation grenade launchers each side of urret.

TATUS

Production complete. No longer marketed. n service with Malaysia only.

MANUFACTURER

Cockerill Mechanical ndustries.

KEY RECOGNITION FEATURES

- Long box-shaped hull, driver front, large windows to front and sides, horizontal roof, hull rear slopes inwards with engine compartment left and entry door right rear
- Hatch over driver's position, turret to immediate rear of driver's position, three rectangular roof hatches to turret rear, one left and two right. Externally mounted 7.62mm anti-aircraft MG on roof at right rear
- Three large road wheels, forward-opening door each side of hull to rear of first road wheel station, two rear road wheels close together

Right: SIBMAS (6 x 6) with 90mm CM 90 turret

Right: SIBMAS (6 x 6) ARV

ENGESA EE-11 Urutu APC (Brazil)

Above: ENGESA EE-11 Urutu (6 x 6) with one-man machine gun turret

SPECIFICATIONS (Mk VII)

Crew:	1 + 12
Configuration:	6 x 6
Armament:	1 x 12.7mm MG, 2 x 2 smoke grenade dischargers
Ammunition:	1,000 x 12.7mm
Length:	6.1m
Width:	2.65m
Height top of MG mount:	2.9m
Height hull top:	2.125m
Ground clearance:	0.38m
Wheelbase:	3.05m
Weight, combat:	14,000kg
Weight, unloaded:	11,000kg
Power-to-weight ratio:	18.6hp/tonne
Engine:	Detroit Diesel 6V-53T 6-cylinder water-cooled diesel developing 260hp at 2,800rpm
Maximum road speed:	105km/hr
Maximum water speed:	8km/hr
Maximum road range:	850km
Fuel capacity:	380 lit
Fording:	Amphibious
Vertical obstacle:	0.6m
Trench:	Not applicable
Gradient:	60%
Side slope:	30%
Armour:	Classified
Armour type:	Steel (2 layers)
NBC system:	Optional
Night vision equipment:	Optional

DEVELOPMENT

EE-11 Urutu (6 x 6) was developed to meet the requirements of Brazilian Army with first prototype completed in 1970 and first production vehicles in 1974. It shares many automotive components with ENGESA EE-9 Cascavel (6 x 6) armoured car developed at the same time. ENGESA is no longer trading.

All vehicles have same basic layout with driver front left, powerpack to right and troop compartment extending back to rear. Troops enter and leave via door in each side and one in rear (except on Mk V which has no door in right side owing to larger engine compartment). Armament is usually mounted to rear of driver and ranges from pintle-mounted 7.62mm or 12.7mm MG to turret with 60mm breech-loaded mortar or 25mm cannon. Over top of troop compartment are four roof hatches.

EE-11 Urutu has had seven marks, I, II, III, IV, V, VI and VII, main difference being the engine (Mercedes-Benz or Detroit Diesel) and

transmission (manual or automatic). Late production vehicles have run flat tyres and central tyre pressure regulation system. The Mk VII has the turbocharged diesel in place of the standard 6V-53 developing 212hp installed in the Mk III. Vehicle is fully amphibious, propelled by its wheels. Before entering the water a trim vane is erected at front of hull. Wide range of optional equipment was available including firing ports, vision blocks, 5,000kg capacity winch, NBC system and night vision devices.

VARIANTS

In addition to armament options, the following versions were available: 81mm mortar carrier, ambulance with higher roof, cargo carrier, armoured fire support vehicle with 90mm turret as fitted to EE-9 Cascavel armoured car, command post vehicle, recovery vehicle, anti-aircraft vehicle with twin 20mm cannon, and internal security vehicle with obstacle-clearing blade at front of hull.

STATUS

Production complete. Known users include Angola, Bolivia, Brazil (Army and Marines), Chile, Colombia, Cyprus, Ecuador, Gabon, Guyana, Jordan, Libya, Morocco, Nigeria, Paraguay, Surinam, Tunisia, United Arab Emirates, Uruguay and Venezuela.

KEY RECOGNITION FEATURES

- Nose slopes back to just forward of front road wheels at 60°, recessed headlamps, glacis plate has driver's position left and engine compartment right, horizontal roof and vertical hull rear, large door in rear opening to left

- Hull sides vertical half-way up then slope slightly inwards to hull roof, single door on left side of hull to rear of first road wheel station, earlier Mks have door in each side, four outward-opening roof hatches over rear troop compartment

- Three road wheels each side with rear wheels close together, ENGESA boomerang suspension which keeps both wheels in contact with ground

MANUFACTURER

ENGESA, São José dos Campos, Brazil. This company is no longer trading.

Below: ENGESA EE-11 Urutu (6 x 6) with 90mm turret

ENGESA EE-9 Cascavel Armoured Car (Brazil)

Above: ENGESA EE-9 Cascavel

SPECIFICATIONS (Mk IV)

Crew:	3
Configuration:	6 x 6
Armament:	1 x 90mm, 1 x 7.62mm MG (coaxial), 1 x 7.62mm or 12.7mm MG (anti-aircraft), 2 x 3 smoke grenade dischargers
Ammunition:	44 x 90mm, 2,200 x 7.62mm
Length gun forwards:	6.2m
Length hull:	5.2m
Width:	2.64m
Height to top of commander's cupola:	2.68m
Height to turret roof:	2.28m
Ground clearance:	0.34m (front axle)
Ground clearance:	0.5m (hull centre)
Wheelbase:	2.343m + 1.414m
Weight, combat:	13,400kg
Weight, empty:	10,900kg
Power-to-weight ratio:	15.82hp/tonne
Engine:	Detroit Diesel model 6V-53N 6-cylinder water-cooled diesel developing 212hp at 2,800rpm
Maximum road speed:	100km/hr
Maximum range:	880km
Fuel capacity:	390 lit
Fording:	1m
Vertical obstacle:	0.6m
Trench:	Not applicable
Gradient:	60%
Side slope:	30%
Armour:	Classified
Armour type:	Steel (2 layers)
NBC system:	None
Night vision equipment:	Optional (passive for commander, gunner and driver)

DEVELOPMENT

EE-9 Cascavel (6 x 6) was developed by ENGESA to meet the requirements of the Brazilian Army and shares many common components with EE-11 Urutu (6 x 6) APC, developed about the same time. First prototypes of EE-9 were completed in

November 1970, pre-production vehicles following in 1972–73 and first production vehicles in 1974.

First production vehicles for the Brazilian Army had 37mm guns, while those for export had a French 90mm turret as installed on the AML 90 (4 x 4) armoured car. For some years all production EE-9s have had an ENGESA ET-90 turret armed with an ENGESA EC-90 gun.

Marks I, II, III, IV and V of EE-9 Cascavel have been built so far by ENGESA. Layout of all vehicles is similar with driver front left, two-man turret centre, engine and transmission rear. Turret has a 90mm gun which elevates from -8° to +15° under manual control, turret traverses manually through 360°. A 7.62mm MG is mounted coaxial to left of main armament, plus a cupola with externally mounted 12.7mm M2 HB MG which can be aimed and fired from inside the vehicle.

Standard equipment includes central tyre pressure regulation system and run flat tyres. A wide range of optional equipment includes different sights, laser rangefinder, fire detection and suppression system, fire-control system, power traverse and different engines, 190hp Mercedes-Benz diesel or 212hp Detroit diesel.

KEY RECOGNITION FEATURES

- Nose slopes back under hull with recesses in upper part for headlamps, well-sloped glacis plate leads up to horizontal hull top which extends to rear, driver's position front left, turret centre, engine rear. Vertical hull rear with horizontal air louvres

- Turret has flat sides and rear which slope slightly inwards, smoke grenade dischargers mounted each side at rear, 90mm barrel has muzzle brake with three vertical slots, commander's cupola on left side of turret roof

- Three road wheels each side (rear two mounted close together on boomerang suspension to maintain contact with ground)

VARIANTS

No variants except for models mentioned above.

STATUS

Production complete. In service with Bolivia, Brazil (Army and Marines), Burkina Faso, Chad, Chile, Colombia, Cyprus, Ecuador, Gabon, Ghana, Iran, Libya, Nigeria, Paraguay, Surinam, Togo, Tunisia, Uruguay, Zimbabwe and other countries.

MANUFACTURER

ENGESA, São José dos Campos, Brazil. This company is no longer trading.

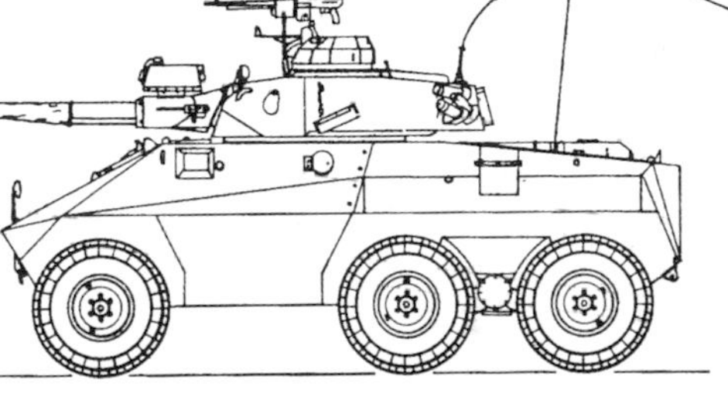

Above: ENGESA EE-9 Cascavel

Right: ENGESA EE-9 Cascavel with 7.62mm AA MG

General Dynamics Land Systems – Canada Armoured Vehicle General Purpose (Canada)

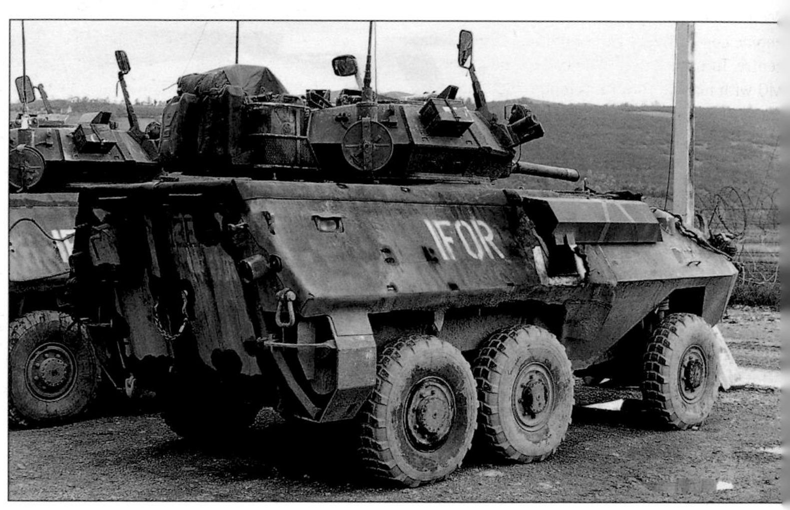

Above: Cougar 76mm Wheeled Fire Support Vehicle (Richard Stickland)

SPECIFICATIONS

Crew:	3 + 6
Configuration:	6 x 6
Armament:	1 x 12.7mm MG, 1 x 7.62mm MG (coaxial), 2 x 4 smoke grenade dischargers
Ammunition:	1,000 x 12.7mm, 4,400 x 7.62mm
Length:	5.968m
Width:	2.53m
Height overall:	2.53m
Height hull top:	1.85m
Ground clearance:	0.392m
Wheelbase:	2.04m + 1.04m
Weight, combat:	10,500kg
Power-to-weight ratio:	20.46hp/tonne
Engine:	Detroit Diesel 6V-53T, 6-cylinder diesel developing 215hp
Maximum road speed:	101.5km/hr
Maximum water speed:	7km/hr
Maximum road range:	603km
Fuel capacity:	204 lit
Fording:	Amphibious
Vertical obstacle:	0.381m to 0.508m
Trench:	Not applicable
Gradient:	60%
Side slope:	30%
Armour:	10mm (maximum)
Armour type:	Steel
NBC system:	None
Night vision equipment:	Yes (passive for driver)

Note: Above relates to Wheeled Armoured Personnel Carrier Grizzly

DEVELOPMENT

In 1974 the Canadian Armed Forces issued a requirement for an Armoured Vehicle General Purpose and after evaluating three prototype vehicles selected the Swiss MOWAG Piranha 6 x 6. Production was undertaken in Canada by the now General Dynamics Land Systems – Canada, first production vehicles completed in 1979. By the time production was completed in 1982, 491 had been built in three versions. More recently the company has built the Light Armored Vehicle (LAV) family of vehicles for Australia, Canada, New Zealand, the US Marine Corps and Saudi Arabia and the Bison (8 x 8) for the Canadian Armed Forces (qv).

Grizzly Wheeled Armoured Personnel Carrier (WAPC) has driver front left, commander to rear, engine compartment front right and turret in centre. Turret has one 12.7mm and one 7.62mm MG with manual traverse through 360° and elevation from -8° to +55°. Six infantrymen sit rear and enter and leave via two doors in hull rear. All three versions fully amphibious with two propellers, one each side at rear. Before entering the water a trim vane is erected at front and bilge pumps switched on.

VARIANTS

Cougar 76mm Gun Wheeled Fire Support Vehicle (WFSV) is fitted with complete Scorpion turret with 76mm gun and 7.62mm coaxial MG. A total of 195 was built.

Husky Wheeled Maintenance and Recovery Vehicle, of which 27 were built, has roof-mounted hydraulic crane and crew of three.

All Canadian Armed Forces 6 x 6 vehicles are now fitted with the upgraded suspension fitted to the 8 x 8 vehicles which gives improved cross-country mobility.

Note: The 76mm model is being phased out of service and the complete family is being re-roled including ambulance, SAM carrier, radio rebroadcast, mobile repair team vehicle, armoured personnel carrier and fitted with surface plough mine disruption device.

KEY RECOGNITION FEATURES

- Pointed hull front with nose sloping under hull to front wheel station, well-sloped glacis plate leads up to horizontal hull top which extends to vertical hull rear with two doors. Turret mounted centre of hull roof

- Hull side welded mid-way up then slopes inwards at top and bottom, two firing ports with vision block above each over second and third road wheel station

- Three road wheels each side with distinct gap between first and second, propeller to immediate rear of third road wheel

STATUS

Production complete. In service with Canada.

MANUFACTURER

General Dynamics Land Systems – Canada, London, Ontario, Canada.

Below: Grizzly Wheeled Armoured Personnel Carrier (Michael Jerchel)

NORINCO WZ 523 APC (China)

SPECIFICATIONS

Crew:	2 + 10
Configuration:	6 x 6
Armament:	1 x 12.7mm MG
Ammunition:	600 x 12.7mm
Length:	6.02m
Width:	2.55m
Height with MG:	2.73m
Weight, combat:	11,200kg
Power-to-weight ratio:	14.73hp/tonne
Engine:	EQ 6105 water-cooled petrol developing 165hp
Maximum road speed:	80km/hr
Maximum water speed:	7km/hr
Maximum range:	600km
Fuel capacity:	255 lit
Fording:	Amphibious
Gradient:	60%
Side slope:	30%

DEVELOPMENT

During a parade in Beijing in October 1984 a new Chinese 6 x 6 APC was seen in public for the first time. It is very similar to the Belgian SIBMAS and South African Ratel (6 x 6) and is believed to have the Chinese designation WZ 523; US Army refers to it as M1984. It is fully amphibious, propelled by two waterjets mounted one each side of hull at rear. Main armament comprises roof-mounted 12.7mm Type 54 MG with lateral protection for gunner.

Above: Type WZ 523 (6 x 6) (via G Jacobs)

KEY RECOGNITION FEATURES

- Long box-shaped hull similar to Belgian SIBMAS (6 x 6) APC, trim vane mounted on glacis plate, windscreen above covered by shutters hinged at top, horizontal hull top, vertical hull rear with single door opening to right

- Hull sides almost vertical, door in each side to rear of first road wheel, 12.7mm roof-mounted MG, roof hatches above rear troop compartment

- Three road wheels each side, second and third road wheels close together

VARIANTS

No known variants, but other models could include command post vehicle, ambulance, mortar carrier and anti-tank vehicle with missiles.

STATUS

Production complete.

MANUFACTURER

Chinese state arsenals.

NORINCO WZ 551 APC (China)

Above: WZ 551 with 25mm turret

SPECIFICATIONS

Crew:	2 + 11
Configuration:	6 x 6
Armament:	1 x 25mm cannon, 1 x 7.62mm MG, 2 x 4 smoke grenade dischargers
Ammunition:	400 x 25mm, 1000 x 7.62mm
Length:	6.73m
Width:	2.86m
Height:	2.10m (hull top), 2.89m (turret top)
Ground clearance:	0.41m
Wheelbase:	1.9m + 1.9m
Weight, combat:	15,000kg
Weight, empty:	13,000kg
Power-to-weight ratio:	21.33hp/tonne
Engine:	Deutz BF8L 413FC V8 diesel developing 320 hp at 2500rpm
Maximum road speed:	90km/h
Maximum road range:	800km
Fuel capacity:	400 lit (estimate)
Fording:	Amphibious
Vertical obstacle:	0.5m
Trench:	1.2m
Gradient:	60%
Side slope:	30%
Armour:	8mm (maximum) (estimate)
Armour type:	Steel
NBC system:	Yes
Night vision equipment:	Yes

DEVELOPMENT

The NORINCO (Chinese North Industries Corporation) WZ 551 (6 x 6) APC is very similar in appearance to the French VAB (4 x 4 and 6 x 6) series which are covered in a seperate entry and was first observed in the mid-1980s. Although the 6 x 6 version is the most common, a quantity of 4 x 4 models have been built and there is also an 8 x 8 version.

The layout is similar to the VAB with the commander and driver at the front, engine compartment to rear of the driver and troop compartment extending to the rear. The latter has roof hatches, firing ports and a large door that opens to the right.

The specification relates to the model armed with a one-man turret armed with a 25mm externally mounted cannon and a 7.62mm coaxial

machine gun. Turret traverse is 360° with weapon elevation from -8° to +55°.

The WZ 551 is fully amphibious being propelled in the water by two shrouded propellers which are mounted one either side at the rear of the hull and standard equipment includes run flat tyres and a fire detection and suppression system.

Specifications relate to latest production model which has more powerful engine; earlier models had 256hp diesel.

VARIANTS

Ambulance, raised roof.
Anti-tank (4 x 4) with Red Arrow 8 ATGW
APC, armed with 12.7mm MG.
IFV, turret armed with 25mm cannon and 7.62mm MG.
IFV, turret of WZ 501 IFV (similar to Russian BMP-1).
NGV-1 IFV, fitted with Giat Industries Dragar turret.
Anti-tank (4 x 4) with Red Arrow 9 ATGW.
105mm (6 x 6) armoured car (prototype).
Other variants include ARC, 120mm turret-mounted mortar and forward observation vehicle.

KEY RECOGNITION FEATURES

- Box-type hull with nose sloping back under hull front, almost horizontal glacis plate leading to well-sloped hull front with two large windows with flaps above. Horizontal hull roof and almost vertical hull rear with one large door

- Upper part of hull slopes inwards with firing ports in either side towards rear, exhaust pipe runs alongside upper part of left hull side. When armed, turret is normally on centre of hull roof

- Three large rubber-tyred road wheels each side with shrouded propeller at rear each side

STATUS

In production. In service with Bosnia-Herzegovina (4 x 4 anti-tank), China, Oman and Sri Lanka.

MANUFACTURER

Chinese state factories.

Right: WZ 551 with 25mm turret

Right: WZ 551 without armament installed

Patria Vehicles XA-200 APC (Finland)

Above: XA-180 of Finnish Army in ambulance role (Richard Stickland)

SPECIFICATIONS

Crew:	3 + 8
Configuration:	6 x 6
Armament:	1 x 12.7mm MG, 1 x 4 smoke grenade dischargers
Ammunition:	1,000 x 12.7mm (estimate)
Length:	7.45m
Width:	2.95m
Height:	2.60m
Ground clearance:	0.4m
Weight, combat:	22,000kg
Weight, empty:	16,000kg
Power-to-weight ratio:	13.4hp/tonne
Engine:	Valmet 6-cylinder, water-cooled, turbocharged diesel developing 295hp
Maximum road speed:	90km/hr
Fuel capacity:	290 lit
Vertical obstacle:	0.6m
Trench:	1m
Gradient:	70%
Side slope:	60%
Armour:	10mm (maximum) (estimate)
Armour type:	Steel
NBC system:	Optional
Night vision equipment:	Optional

DEVELOPMENT

To replace Russian-supplied BTR-60PB (8 x 8) APCs in service with Finnish Army, SISU (today Patria Vehicles) and Valmet each built prototypes of a new 6 x 6 APC in 1982. Following extensive trials with both vehicles SISU XA-180 was selected in 1983 and is now in production and service with Finnish Army.

Hull is all-welded armour with commander and driver front, engine compartment to rear of driver on left side and troop compartment rear. Troops sit five each side at rear on bench seats, and enter and leave via twin doors in hull rear, one of which has firing port and vision block. Two roof hatches over troop compartment and three vision blocks in each side with firing port beneath. Early production vehicles were fully amphibious but later vehicles are heavier and are not amphibious. Before entering water a trim vane is erected at front of hull. Standard equipment includes front-mounted winch with 50m of 16mm cable and capacity of 10 tonnes, engine compartment fire suppression system. Armament normally comprises a roof-mounted 7.62mm or 12.7mm MG, the latter can be ring or turret mounted.

The XA-180 has now been followed in

production by the improved XA-185 which has a more powerful engine.

Latest production model is the XA-200 series which will be baseline for all future vehicles. The XA-203 is the APC model with the XA-202 being the systems platform. This has a higher roof line and greater internal volume.

VARIANTS

Air defence, armed with now Thales Air Defence Crotale New Generation SAM system, used by Finland only.

Radar, Finland has a number of vehicles with the Giraffe air surveillance radar.

AMOS 120mm mortar (prototype)

Other versions are believed to include command post with projected versions including anti-tank, mortar carrier, ambulance and repair and recovery.

The latest Patria Vehicles project is the Armoured Modular Vehicle (8 x 8) (qv) now in production for Finland and Poland.

STATUS

Production. In service with Finland, Ireland (UN), Netherlands, Norway and Sweden.

MANUFACTURER

Patria Vehicles, Hameenlinna, Finland.

KEY RECOGNITION FEATURES

- Hull sides and rear almost vertical with flat roof and pointed nose, trim vane on nose top
- Commander and driver at far front, each with side door, large windscreen covered by shutter hinged at top
- Three equally spaced road wheels each side, two doors in hull rear, shrouded propeller under each hull side at rear

Above right: Patria Vehicles XA-203 series APC

Right: XA-181 chassis with Crotale SAM

Panhard ERC 90 F4 Sagaie Armoured Car (France)

Above: Panhard ERC 90 F1 Lynx

SPECIFICATIONS

Crew:	3
Configuration:	6 x 6
Armament:	1 x 90mm, 1 x 7.62mm MG (coaxial), 1 x 7.62mm MG AA (optional), 2 x 2 smoke grenade dischargers
Ammunition:	20 x 90mm, 2,000 x 7.62mm
Length gun forwards:	7.693m
Length hull:	5.098m
Width:	2.495m
Height:	2.254m (overall), 1.502m (hull top)
Ground clearance:	0.294m (road), 0.344m (cross-country)
Wheelbase:	1.63m + 1.22m
Weight, combat:	8,300kg
Power-to-weight ratio:	17.5hp/tonne
Engine:	Peugeot V-6 petrol developing 155hp at 5,250rpm
Maximum road speed:	95km/hr
Maximum water speed (wheels):	4.5km/hr
Maximum water speed (hydrojets):	7.2km/hr
Maximum road range:	700km
Fuel capacity:	242 lit
Fording:	Amphibious
Vertical obstacle:	0.8m
Trench:	1.1m
Gradient:	60%
Side slope:	30%
Armour:	10mm (maximum hull) (estimate)
Armour type:	Steel
NBC system:	Optional
Night vision equipment:	Optional (passive)

DEVELOPMENT

ERC (Engin de Reconnaissance Cannon) 6 x 6 armoured cars were developed as a private venture by Panhard from 1975, first production vehicles completed at its new Marolles factory in 1979. ERC shares many common components with the Panhard VCR 6 x 6 armoured personnel carriers developed at the same time. Although the ERC range was developed specifically for export it was adopted by the French Army, first vehicles delivered in 1984.

Driver sits front, two-man turret centre, engine and transmission rear. GIAT TS 90 turret is armed

with 90mm gun that fires canister, HE, HE long-range, HEAT, smoke and APFSDS ammunition. Turret has manual traverse through 360°, manual elevation from -8° to +15°. This is usually referred to as the ERC-1 Sagaie.

Basic vehicle is fully amphibious, propelled by its wheels, although waterjets can be fitted if required. Steering is power-assisted on front two wheels. Centre road wheel each side is normally raised when travelling. A wide range of optional equipment is available including NBC system, night vision, land navigation, air conditioning system and heater.

French Army vehicles are being upgraded with new engine. These will no longer be amphibious and middle road wheel will be in lowered position.

KEY RECOGNITION FEATURES

- Well-sloped glacis plate with driver's hatch in upper part which cannot be seen from side owing to large sheet metal covering, rear-opening side door between first and second wheel stations

- Turret centre of hull, long-barrelled 90mm gun with thermal sleeve and single baffle muzzle brake, two smoke grenade dischargers each side of turret towards rear

- Three road wheels each side with largest gap between first and second road wheel, sheet metal sides above rear road wheels ribbed horizontally

VARIANTS

ERC 90 F4 Sagaie TTB 190 has SAMM 90mm TTB 190 turret.

ERC 90 F4 Sagaie 2 is slightly larger with two engines.

ERC 90 F1 Lynx has Hispano-Suiza Lynx 90mm turret as on AML armoured car. This is usually referred to as the ERC-1 Lynx.

ERC anti-aircraft, Gabon has model with turret armed with twin 20mm cannon.

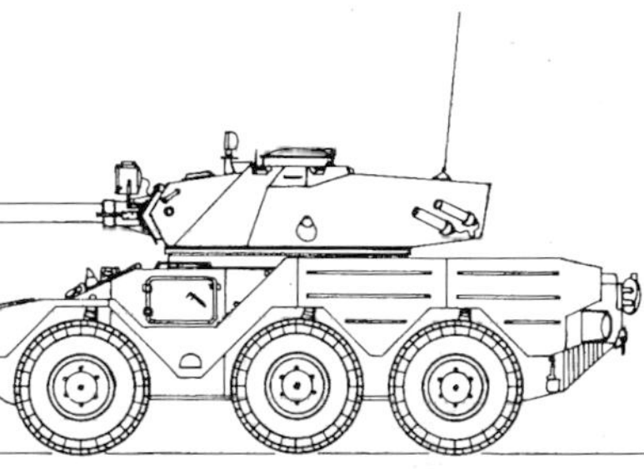

Above: Panhard ERC 90 F4 Sagaie

STATUS

Production complete but can be resumed if further orders are placed. In service with Argentina (Lynx 90), Chad (Lynx 90), France (ERC 90 F4 Sagaie), Gabon (Sagaie 2 TTB 190 and twin 20mm TAB 220 turret), Ivory Coast (ERC 90 F4 Sagaie), Mexico (Lynx) and Nigeria.

MANUFACTURER

Société de Constructions Mécaniques Panhard et Levassor, Paris, France.

Right: Panhard ERC 90 F4 Sagaie

GIAT AMX-10RC Reconnaissance Vehicle (France)

Above: AMX-10RC (6 x 6)

SPECIFICATIONS

Crew:	4
Configuration:	6 x 6
Armament:	1 x 105mm, 1 x 7.62mm MG (coaxial), 2 x 2 smoke grenade dischargers
Ammunition:	38 x 105mm, 4,000 x 7.62mm
Length gun forwards:	9.15m
Length hull:	6.357m
Width:	2.95m
Height:	2.66m (overall), 2.29m (turret top)
Ground clearance:	0.35m (normal)
Wheelbase:	1.55m + 1.55m
Weight, combat:	15,880kg
Weight, empty:	14,900kg
Power-to-weight ratio:	16.45hp/tonne
Engine:	Baudouin Model 6F 11 SRX diesel developing 280hp at 3000rpm
Maximum road speed:	85km/hr
Maximum water speed:	7.2km/hr
Maximum road range:	1,000km
Fuel capacity:	Not available
Fording:	Amphibious
Vertical obstacle:	0.8m
Trench:	1.65m
Gradient:	50%
Side slope:	30%
Armour:	Classified
Armour type:	Aluminium
NBC system:	Yes
Night vision equipment:	Yes (passive for commander, gunner and driver)

DEVELOPMENT

AMX-10RC was developed by the AMX to meet a French Army requirement to replace the Panhard EBR (8 x 8) armoured car. First prototype was completed in 1971, first production vehicles completed in 1978 and final deliveries made to French Army in 1987. The Moroccan vehicles are not fitted with a waterjet propulsion system.

Layout is conventional with driver front left, three-man turret centre, loader left, commander and gunner right, engine and transmission rear. The 105mm gun is mounted in a turret which traverses 360˚, gun elevates from -8˚ to +20˚. Computerised fire-control system includes laser rangefinder and LLLTV system for both

commander and gunner. The 105mm gun fires HEAT, HE and practice rounds with an APFSDS round introduced in 1987.

AMX-10RC is fully amphibious, propelled by two waterjets. The driver can adjust suspension to suit terrain.

VARIANTS

AMX-10RC driver training vehicle.

French Army AMX-10RC vehicles are now being upgraded in a number of key areas including installation of a thermal camera, decoy system, additional armour, central tyre pressure regulation system, electronic control system for the transmission and a Land Battlefield Management System. When upgraded, the amphibious capability will be removed.

STATUS

Production complete. In service with France, Morocco and Qatar.

MANUFACTURER

GIAT Industries, Roanne, France.

KEY RECOGNITION FEATURES

- Pointed nose with trim vane folded back onto glacis plate, driver has half-circular cupola on left side of glacis, hull top to his rear horizontal, vertical hull rear

- Turret centre of hull, commander's cupola right and large periscopic sight to his front, 105mm gun with double baffle muzzle brake overhangs front of vehicle

- Three equally spaced road wheels each side which can be raised or lowered by driver. French Army vehicles have waterjet inlets to rear of last road wheels with outlet on hull rear

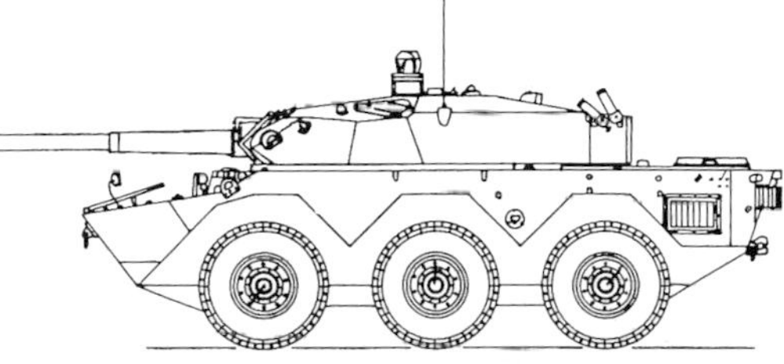

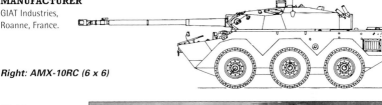

Right: AMX-10RC (6 x 6)

Right: AMX-10RC (6 x 6) with applique armour

Panhard VCR APC (France)

Above: Panhard VCR (6 x 6) APC with 12.7mm MG

SPECIFICATIONS

Crew:	3 + 9
Configuration:	6 x 6
Armament:	Depends on role
Ammunition:	Depends on role
Length:	4.875m
Width:	2.5m
Height with 7.62mm MG:	2.56m
Height hull top:	2.13m
Ground clearance:	0.315m (4 wheels), 0.37m (6 wheels)
Wheelbase:	1.66m + 1.425m
Power-to-weight ratio:	18.35hp/tonne
Engine:	Peugeot PRV V-6 petrol developing 145hp at 5,500rpm
Maximum road speed:	90km/hr
Maximum water speed:	4km/hr
Maximum road range:	700km
Fuel capacity:	242 lit
Fording:	Amphibious
Vertical obstacle:	0.8m
Trench:	1.1m
Gradient:	60%
Side slope:	30%
Armour:	12mm (maximum)
Armour type:	Steel
NBC system:	Optional
Night vision equipment:	Optional (passive)

DEVELOPMENT

VCR (Véhicule de Combat à Roues) was developed as a private venture by Panhard and shares many automotive components with Panhard ERC range of 6 x 6 armoured cars. VCR was first shown in 1977 and entered production in 1979. Largest order to date is 100 VCT/TH anti-tank vehicles for Iraq. These are no longer operational.

VCR is fully amphibious, propelled by its wheels. Standard equipment includes run flat tyres, optional equipment includes front-mounted winch, air conditioning system, NBC system and passive night vision equipment. Wide range of weapon stations including turret-mounted 12.7mm MG at front and ring-mounted 7.62mm MG at rear. Other options include turret with 60mm breech-loaded mortar, turret- or ring-mounted 20mm cannon, turret with MILAN ATGWs in ready-to-launch position.

VARIANTS

VCR/AT repair vehicle has block and tackle at rear, tools and spare parts.
VCR/AA anti-aircraft vehicle has Saab Bofors Dynamics RBS-70 SAM, prototype only.
VCR/TH anti-tank vehicle has Euromissile UTM-800 turret with four HOT ATGW in ready-to-launch position, GIAT Mascot 7.62mm remote-controlled MG rear.
VCR/IS ambulance has higher roof and medical equipment.
VCR/PC command post vehicle has extensive communications equipment. Also variant in electronic warfare role.
VCR/TT (4 x 4) is essentially 6 x 6 with centre wheel removed each side and replaced by waterjet. Used only by Argentina.

STATUS

Production as required. In service with Argentina (4 x 4), Gabon, Mexico and United Arab Emirates.

MANUFACTURER

Société de Constructions Mécaniques Panhard and Levassor, Paris, France.

KEY RECOGNITION FEATURES

- Glacis plate at about 45° with driver's hatch in upper part, step up to hull roof which extends to vertical hull rear with large door

- Commander's cupola rear of driver on left side, engine compartment right, main armament on forward part of roof and secondary armament on rear. Rear troop compartment has two upward-opening flaps in each side

- Three road wheels each side, second wheel normally raised while travelling on roads. Hull sides vertical except for rear troop compartment which slopes inwards mid-way up

***Below:** Panhard VCR/IS ambulance (background) and electronic warfare model (foreground)*

Renault Trucks Defense VAB APC (France)

Above: VAB (4 x 4) command post (Pierre Touzin)

SPECIFICATIONS (4 x 4)

Crew:	2 + 10
Configuration:	4 x 4
Armament:	1 x 12.7mm MG (typical)
Length:	5.98m
Width:	2.49m
Height (hull top):	2.06m
Ground clearance:	(axles) 0.4m, (hull) 0.5m
Wheelbase:	3m
Weight, combat:	13,000kg
Weight, empty:	10,200kg
Power-to-weight ratio:	16.92hp/tonne
Engine:	Renault MIDS 06.20.45 six-cylinder in-line water-cooled turbocharged diesel developing 220hp at 2,200rpm
Maximum road speed:	92km/hr
Maximum water speed:	8km/hr
Maximum road range:	1,000km
Fuel capacity:	300 lit
Fording:	Amphibious
Vertical obstacle:	0.6m
Trench:	Not applicable
Gradient:	60%
Side slope:	35%
Armour:	Classified
Armour type:	Steel
NBC system:	Yes
Night vision equipment:	Yes (passive for driver)

DEVELOPMENT

Prototypes of both 4 x 4 and 6 x 6 versions were built by Renault and Panhard to meet requirements of French Army for a Forward Area Armoured Vehicle (Véhicule de l'Avant Blindé). The 4 x 4 configuration was selected with first production vehicles completed at Saint Chamond in 1976. By 2004 about 5,000 VABs had been built with production being undertaken as required.

All versions have a similar layout with driver front left, commander/machine gunner right, engine compartment rear of driver, small passageway on right and troop compartment rear with seats down each side, roof hatches, two doors at rear and three hatches in each side. Fully amphibious, propelled by its wheels or by waterjets mounted at rear of hull. Before entering water a trim vane is erected at front.

VARIANTS

Variants are numerous and include: infantry combat vehicle (with various turrets mounting 25mm or 20mm cannon); VAB Echelon (repair vehicle); VCAC HOT anti-tank vehicle with Mephisto system with four HOT missiles; VCAC HOT anti-tank vehicle with UTM 800 turret with four HOT missiles; VAB PC (command vehicle); VAB Transmission (communications vehicle); VAB engineer vehicle; electronic warfare carrier (Bromure); VAB Sanitaire (ambulance); VMO (internal security vehicle); VTM 120 (mortar towing vehicle with 120mm mortar); VPM 81 (81mm mortar in rear); anti-aircraft (2 x 20mm cannon, used by Oman); NBC reconnaissance; recovery; TOW ATGW; and anti-aircraft with MBDA Mistral SAMs. VAB components also used in VBC-90 (6 x 6) armoured car.

Most French Army VABs are now being upgraded.

STATUS

Production as required. In service with Brunei, Central African Republic, Cyprus, France, Indonesia, Italy (NBC only), Ivory Coast, Lebanon, Mauritius, Morocco, Oman, Qatar, United Arab Emirates and other undisclosed countries.

MANUFACTURER

Renault Trucks Defense, Limoges, France.

KEY RECOGNITION FEATURES

- Box-type hull with nose sloping back under hull front, almost horizontal glacis plate leading to well-sloped hull front with two windows, horizontal roof and almost vertical hull rear with two large opening rear doors

- Upper part of hull sides slope inwards, single door with window in each side of forward part of hull, three upward-opening shutters in each side at rear, exhaust pipe on right side of hull

- Two large rubber-tyred road wheels each side in 4 x 4 model, also 6 x 6 version with three equally spaced road wheels each side, waterjets sometimes mounted under hull at rear. Light armament normally mounted over front right of vehicle.

Below: VAB (6 x 6) with turret armed with 20mm cannon and 7.62mm MG (Michael Jerchel)

Rheinmetall Landsysteme Transportpanzer 1 (Fuchs) APC (Germany)

Above: Transportpanzer 1 of the German Army with applique armour (Michael Jerchel)

SPECIFICATIONS

Crew:	2 + 10
Configuration:	6 x 6
Armament:	1 x 7.62mm MG, 1 x 6 smoke grenade dischargers
Ammunition:	1,000 x 7.62mm (estimate)
Length:	6.83m
Width:	2.98m
Height:	2.30m (hull top)
Ground clearance:	0.506m (hull), 0.406m (axle)
Wheelbase:	1.75m + 2.05m
Weight, combat:	19,000kg
Weight, empty:	14,400kg
Power-to-weight ratio:	16.84hp/tonne
Engine:	Mercedes-Benz Model OM 402A V-8 liquid-cooled diesel developing 320hp at 2,500rpm
Maximum road speed:	105km/hr
Maximum water speed:	10.5km/hr
Maximum road range:	800km
Fuel capacity:	390 lit
Fording:	Amphibious
Vertical obstacle:	0.6m
Trench:	1.1m
Gradient:	70%
Side slope:	35%
Armour:	Classified
Armour type:	Steel
NBC system:	Yes
Night vision equipment:	Yes (driver has passive periscope)

DEVELOPMENT

After building numerous prototypes of 4 x 4 and 6 x 6 amphibious armoured load carriers, the 6 x 6 was placed in production as Transportpanzer 1 (Fuchs) with 996 delivered to the German Army between 1979 and 1986.

Since then production has been resumed for the NBC reconnaissance vehicle which has been adopted by the US Army as the M93. During the Middle East conflict of 1991, Germany supplied these vehicles to Israel, the United Kingdom and the United States.

Commander and driver sit at far front, engine

compartment to their immediate rear on left side, small passageway on right side. Troop compartment extends right to rear, troops enter and leave via twin doors in rear. Transportpanzer 1 is fully amphibious, two propellers mounted on each side under hull rear. Standard equipment includes NBC system, power-assisted steering on front two axles and engine compartment fire extinguishing system. Normal armament for German Army vehicles is 7.62mm MG above hull front on right side.

VARIANTS

Models in service with Germany Army:
RASIT radar carrier with radar retracted into hull for travelling.
Command and communications vehicle with extensive communications equipment.
NBC reconnaissance vehicle.
Engineer vehicle carrying demolitions.
Electronic warfare, TPz 1 Eloka.
Supply carrier.
Many German vehicles have been upgraded with additional armour and protection for roof mounted 7.62mm MG.
Transportpanzer 1 could be adopted for a wide range of roles including ambulance, mortar vehicle (81mm or 120mm), ATGW carrier, ambulance, cargo carrier, recovery or maintenance vehicle and infantry fighting vehicle with various types of weapon stations and firing ports/vision blocks.
Venezuela has taken delivery of 10 Transportpanzer 1s with 1 x 12.7mm MG and 1 x 7.62mm MG on roof.

KEY RECOGNITION FEATURES

- Long box-shaped hull with pointed front, trim vane retracted onto glacis plate above which is large one-piece window covered by armoured shutter hinged at top, forward-opening door each side at hull front

- Flat horizontal roof with two circular hatches over front of vehicle, three hatches over rear troop compartment, twin doors at rear

- Three large road wheels each side with hull above sloping inwards. Six forward-firing smoke grenade dischargers and exhaust pipe on left side of hull

STATUS

Production complete. In service with Germany, Netherlands (electronic warfare), Saudi Arabia, UK (NBC and electronic warfare), US (NBC) and Venezuela.

MANUFACTURER

Rheinmetall Landsysteme GmbH, Kassel, Germany.

Below: Transportpanzer 1 NBC of the British Army (Richard Stickland)

Komatsu Type 87 Reconnaissance and Patrol Vehicle (Japan)

Above: Type 87 Reconnaissance and Patrol Vehicle (Paul Beaver)

SPECIFICATIONS

Crew:	5
Configuration:	6 x 6
Armament:	1 x 25mm cannon, 1 x 7.62mm MG (coaxial), 2 x 3 smoke grenade dischargers
Length:	5.99m
Width:	2.48m
Height:	2.8m
Ground clearance:	0.45m
Wheelbase:	1.5m + 1.5m
Weight, combat:	15,000kg
Power-to-weight ratio:	20.33hp/tonne
Engine:	Isuzu 10PBI 10-cylinder water-cooled diesel developing 305hp at 2,700rpm
Maximum road speed:	100km/hr
Maximum road range:	500km
Fuel capacity:	Not available
Fording:	1m
Vertical obstacle:	0.6m
Trench:	1.5m
Gradient:	60%
Side slope:	30%
Armour:	Classified
Armour type:	Aluminium
NBC system:	None
Night vision equipment:	Yes

DEVELOPMENT

Type 87 Reconnaissance and Patrol Vehicle has been developed to meet the requirements of the Japanese Ground Self Defence Force by Komatsu and shares many automotive components with the Type 82 Command and Communications Vehicle developed by Mitsubishi Heavy Industries. It is believed that the total requirement is for 250 vehicles.

Driver sits front right with radio operator to his left, two-man turret centre, engine rear on right side, observer facing rear on left side.

Two-man power-operated turret sits commander on right and gunner on left and has Oerlikon Contraves 25mm KBA cannon with 7.62mm Type 74 MG mounted coaxial to left. Type 87 has no amphibious capability.

VARIANTS

No variants.

STATUS

Production. In service with Japanese Ground Self Defence Force.

MANUFACTURER

Komatsu Limited, Minato-Ku, Japan.

KEY RECOGNITION FEATURES

- Box-shaped hull with flat nose, well-sloped glacis plate with driver's position on right side, horizontal hull top, vertical rear with engine on right side
- Turret in centre of hull has eight sides, all of which are vertical, 25mm cannon in forward part with 7.62mm coaxial MG to right
- Three large equally spaced road wheels each side with forward-opening door in left side between second and third road wheels

***Right:* Type 87 Reconnaissance and Patrol Vehicle (Kensuke Ebata)**

***Below:* Type 87 Reconnaissance and Patrol Vehicle (Kensuke Ebata)**

Mitsubishi Type 82 Command and Communications Vehicle (Japan)

Above: Type 82 with roof mounted cupola with 12.7mm MG (Kensuke Ebata)

SPECIFICATIONS

Crew:	3
Configuration:	6 x 6
Armament:	1 x 12.7mm MG, 1 x 7.62mm MG
Length:	5.72m
Width:	2.48m
Height without armament:	2.37m
Ground clearance:	0.45m
Wheelbase:	1.5m + 1.5m
Weight, combat:	13,500kg
Weight, empty:	12,000kg
Power-to-weight ratio:	22.4hp/tonne
Engine:	Isuzu 10PBI water-cooled diesel developing 305hp at 2,700rpm
Maximum road speed:	100km/hr
Maximum range:	500km
Fuel capacity:	Not available
Fording:	1m
Vertical obstacle:	0.6m
Trench:	1.5m
Gradient:	60%
Side slope:	30%
Armour:	Classified
Armour type:	Steel (not confirmed)
NBC system:	None
Night vision equipment:	Yes (driver)

DEVELOPMENT

In the early 1970s the Japanese Ground Self Defence Force issued a requirement for a new wheeled reconnaissance vehicle and, following trials with both 4 x 4s and 6 x 6s, the latter was selected for further development. This was subsequently standardised as Type 82 command and communications vehicle, the first ten approved in the 1982 defence budget. Under current plans it is expected that 250 vehicles will be supplied to the Japanese Ground Self Defence Force.

Driver sits front right, another crew member on left (who also mans pintle-mounted 7.62m MG

above his position). Engine compartment is towards hull front on left side with passageway to rear crew compartment on right.

Remainder of crew sit on individual seats at rear and enter via a large door in hull rear; there is also a door between the second and third road wheels on the left side and between the first and second road wheels on the right side. All doors have vision port which can also be used as firing port. There are extra two vision ports on the right side and one on the left. The 12.7mm M2 HB MG has a shield and is mounted on the forward right part of the rear crew compartment roof, commander's cupola on the left.

More recently some vehicles have been fitted with a new roof-mounted cupola armed with 12.7mm MG that can be aimed and fired from within the vehicle.

KEY RECOGNITION FEATURES

- Three closely spaced large road wheels each side with hull line above road wheels

- Snub nose with glacis plate sloping up towards windscreen that extends across front of vehicle with smaller windows to sides, all of which can be covered by hatch covers hinged top; 7.62mm MG above forward hull

- Front two-thirds of hull roof horizontal, then slopes upwards at an angle for remaining third on which 12.7mm MG is mounted, large door in hull rear opens to right

VARIANTS

NBC reconaissance vehicle. Automotive components of Type 82 are also used in the Type 87 reconnaissance and patrol vehicles (qv).

STATUS

In production. In service with the Japanese Ground Self Defence Force.

MANUFACTURER

Mitsubishi Heavy Industries, Tokyo, Japan.

Below: Type 82 command and communications vehicle (Kensuke Ebata)

BTR-152 APC (Russia)

Above: *BTR-152V1 (6 x 6) APC (Michael Jerchel)*

SPECIFICATIONS (BTR-152V1)

Crew:	2 + 17
Configuration:	6 x 6
Armament:	1 x 7.62mm MG
Ammunition:	1,250 x 7.62mm
Length:	6.55m
Width:	2.32m
Height:	2.36m (without armament)
Ground clearance:	0.295m
Wheelbase:	3.3m + 1.13m
Weight, combat:	8,950kg
Power-to-weight ratio:	12.29hp/tonne
Engine:	ZIL-123 6-cylinder in-line water-cooled petrol developing 110hp at 3,000rpm
Maximum road speed:	75km/hr
Road range:	600km
Fuel capacity:	300 lit
Fording:	0.8m
Vertical obstacle:	0.6m
Trench:	0.69m
Gradient:	55%
Side slope:	30%
Armour:	4mm to 13.5mm
Armour type:	Steel
NBC system:	None
Night vision equipment:	Yes (driver only, infra-red, on BTR-152V3)

DEVELOPMENT

BTR-152 was developed after the Second World War, basically a much modified truck chassis with armoured body. First production vehicles were completed in 1950 but it was replaced many years ago in the Russian Army by BTR-60P series 8 x 8 APCs.

Commander and driver sit to rear of fully enclosed engine compartment at front, open-topped troop compartment to rear. Around top of troop compartment are three sockets for mounting 7.62mm or 12.7mm MGs. Some vehicles have front-mounted winch with capacity of 5,000kg.

Late production vehicles have the central tyre pressure regulation system that allows the driver to adjust tyre pressure to suit terrain being crossed.

VARIANTS

BTR-152, first model, no winch or tyre pressure system.

BTR-152V has external central tyre pressure regulation system, command version is BTR-1521.

BTR-152V1 has front-mounted winch and central tyre pressure regulation system with external air lines.

BTR-152V2 has central tyre pressure regulation

system with external air lines, no winch.
BTR-152V3 has front-mounted winch, infra-red driving lights, central tyre pressure regulation system with internal air lines.
BTR-152K, same as BTR-152V3 but with full overhead armour protection for troop compartment.
BTR-152U command vehicle with much higher roof for command staff to stand upright, often tows trailer with generator.
BTR-152A anti-aircraft vehicle with turret armed with twin 14.5mm MGs, also fitted in BTR-40P.
BTR-152 with 23mm ZU-23 LAAG, some of which were captured by Israel in Lebanon, summer 1982.
BTR-152 with 12.7mm MGs. Egypt used BTR-152s with former Czechoslovak Quad 12.7mm M53 turret in rear.

STATUS

Production complete. In service with Angola, Cambodia, Central African Republic, Congo, Cuba, Ethiopia, Guinea, Guinea-Bissau, North Korea, Laos, Mali, Mozambique, Nicaragua, Sudan, Syria, Tanzania, Vietnam and Yemen.

MANUFACTURER

State production facilities.

KEY RECOGNITION FEATURES

- 6 x 6 chassis with rear wheels mounted close together, sides and rear of troop compartment vertical, with corners sloping inwards
- Engine front with open-topped troop compartment rear, firing ports each side, single door each side to rear of engine compartment, twin doors rear with spare wheel and tyre
- Nose of BTR-152 has armoured louvres for engine cooling

Below: BTR-152K (6 x 6)

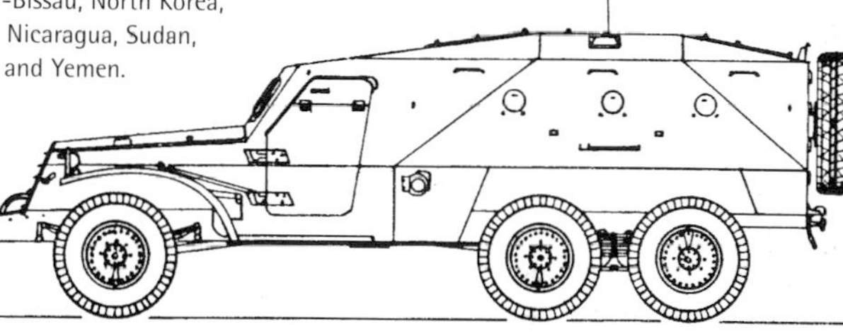

Right: BTR-152K (6 x 6) APC

OMC Ratel 20 Infantry Fighting Vehicle

(South Africa)

Above: Ratel (6 x 6) fitted with turret for launching Swift ATGWs (Christopher F Foss)

SPECIFICATIONS

Crew:	4 + 7
Configuration:	6 x 6
Armament:	1 x 20mm cannon, 1 x 7.62mm MG (coaxial), 1 x 7.62mm MG (anti-aircraft), 1 x 7.62mm MG (anti-aircraft, rear), 2 x 2 smoke grenade dischargers
Ammunition:	1,200 x 20mm, 6,000 x 7.62mm
Length of hull:	7.212m
Width:	2.516m
Height overall:	2.915m
Height hull top:	2.105m
Ground clearance:	0.34m
Wheelbase:	2.809m + 1.4m
Weight, combat:	18,500kg
Weight, empty:	16,500kg
Power-to-weight ratio:	15.24hp/tonne
Engine:	Bussing D 3256 BTXF 6-cylinder in-line turbocharged diesel developing 282hp at 2,200rpm
Maximum road speed:	105km/hr
Maximum road range:	860km
Fuel capacity:	430 lit
Fording:	1.2m
Vertical obstacle:	0.6m
Trench:	1.15m
Gradient:	60%
Side slope:	30%
Armour:	20mm (maximum)
Armour type:	Steel
Night vision equipment:	Optional

DEVELOPMENT

Ratel range of 6 x 6s was developed to meet the requirements of South African Army, first prototype completed in 1974 and first production vehicles in 1979. Production continued until early 1987 with about 1,200 built in three marks (I, II and III) for both home and export.

Driver sits front with three large bullet-proof windows for observation to front and sides; windows can be covered by armoured shutters hinged at bottom.

Mounted on roof to rear of driver is manual turret with commander left and gunner right, turret traverse 360°, 20mm cannon and 7.62mm coaxial MG elevating from -8° to +38°, second 7.62mm MG on turret roof for air defence.

Seven infantrymen sit centre of vehicle with firing ports, vision blocks and roof hatches. Engine compartment is left rear with passageway, 7.62mm anti-aircraft MG mounted above on the right side.

VARIANTS

Ratel 60 IFV has crew of 11 and two-man turret armed with 60mm mortar, 7.62mm coaxial and 7.62mm anti-aircraft MG, second 7.62mm anti-aircraft MG at right rear.
Ratel 90 FSV (fire support vehicle) has 10-man crew and similar turret to Eland 90 (4 x 4) armoured car's with 90mm gun, 7.62mm coaxial and 7.62mm anti-aircraft MG right rear.
Ratel 12.7mm command has nine-man crew and two-man turret with 12.7mm MG, 7.62mm anti-aircraft MG and second 7.62mm anti-aircraft MG right rear.
Ratel repair, basic Ratel fitted with a front mounted jib for carrying out repairs in the field.
Ratel 81mm mortar has no turret and 81mm turntable mounted mortar firing through roof hatches.
Ratel anti-tank, fitted with new turret armed with three Swift laser guided ATGWs in ready-to-launch position and 7.62mm MG. In service with South African Armoured Corps.
Artillery observation vehicle with mast mounted sensor pod.

KEY RECOGNITION FEATURES

- Long box-shaped hull, driver front, large windows to his front and sides, horizontal roof and vertical rear with engine on left rear side, entry door on right rear side

- Circular turret with raised cupola for commander on left side of roof to rear of driver, externally mounted 7.62mm anti-aircraft MG on roof at right rear

- Three large road wheels, forward-opening door to rear of first road wheel, four firing ports and vision blocks in each side, two rear wheels close together

STATUS

Production complete. In service with Jordan, Morocco and South Africa.

MANUFACTURER

BAE Systems Land Systems OMC, Benoni, South Africa.

Above right: Ratel 90 (6 x 6) FSV

Right: Ratel 20 (6 x 6) IFV (Christopher F Foss)

Santa Barbara Sistemas BMR-600 IFV (Spain)

Above: BMR-600 with 12.7mm MG as used by Spanish Army

SPECIFICATIONS

Crew:	2 + 10
Configuration:	6 x 6
Armament:	1 x 12.7mm MG
Ammunition:	2,500 x 12.7mm
Length:	6.15m
Width:	2.5m
Height:	2.36m (including armament), 2m (hull top)
Ground clearance:	0.4m
Wheelbase:	1.65m + 1.65m
Weight, combat:	14,000kg
Power-to-weight ratio:	22hp/tonne
Engine:	Pegaso 9157/8 6-cylinder in-line diesel developing 310hp at 2,200rpm
Maximum road speed:	103km/hr
Maximum water speed:	9km/hr
Maximum range:	1,000km
Fuel capacity:	400 lit
Fording:	Amphibious
Vertical obstacle:	0.6m
Trench:	1.35m
Gradient:	60%
Side slope:	30%
Armour:	38mm (maximum) (estimate)
Armour type:	Aluminium
NBC system:	Optional
Night vision equipment:	Optional

DEVELOPMENT

BMR-600 (Blindado Medio de Ruedas) was designed by the Spanish Army and Pegaso, first prototype completed in 1975 and first production vehicles delivered in 1979. It shares many components with the VEC (see following entry). Company designation for BMR-600 was BMR 3560.50.

Driver sits front left, MG cupola to his immediate rear, engine compartment to right, troop compartment extends to rear and has roof hatches and ramp at rear.

BMR-600 is fully amphibious, propelled by waterjets one each side at rear of hull. Standard equipment includes power steering, engine compartment fire extinguishing system, run flat tyres and winch. Optional equipment includes different tyres, communications equipment, firing

orts/vision blocks, night driving equipment and ir conditioning system.

Spanish Army BMR-600s have cupola with xternally mounted 12.7mm M2 HB MG which an be aimed and fired from inside. Wide range of veapon stations available including turret-nounted 20mm cannon.

Spanish Army BMR-600 vehicles are being itted with a Scania DS9 diesel developing 310hp t 2,200rpm. These have a number of other nprovements including additional passive rmour.

KEY RECOGNITION FEATURES

- Long box-shaped hull with pointed front and driver's compartment offset to left side
- Three large road wheels each side with equal gap between, hull line above wheel arches slopes slightly inwards, exhaust pipe right side of hull, power operated ramp at rear
- Basic Spanish Army BMR-600 has cupola with externally mounted 12.7mm MG on hull top to rear of driver's position

VARIANTS

ommand vehicle (3560.51).
adio communications vehicle (3560.56).
lissile launcher (eg HOT) (3560.57).
1mm mortar carrier (3560.53E).
ombat vehicle with heavier armament such as 0mm gun (3564, for export only).
mbulance (3560.54).
ecovery and maintenance ehicle (3560.55).
owing 120mm mortar.

There is also a ersion with the 20mm mortar nounted in the rear of ne vehicle; this is esignated the 3560.59E.

Below: BMR-600 with 7.62mm MG

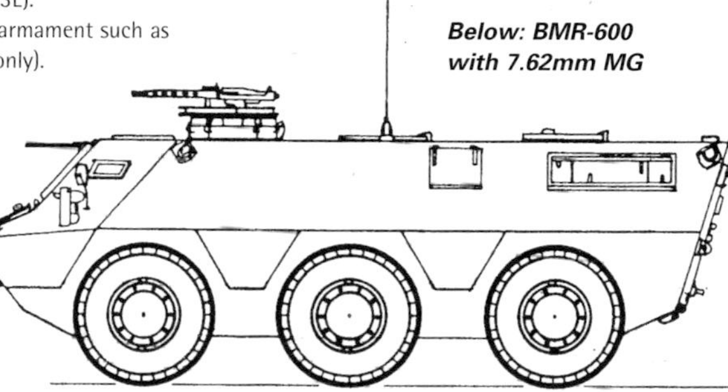

STATUS

roduction as required. n service with Egypt, eru, Saudi Arabia and pain.

MANUFACTURER

anta Barbara Sistemas, Madrid, Spain.

Right: BMR-600 ecovery and naintenance vehicle (Richard Stickland)

Santa Barbara Sistemas VEC Cavalry Scout Vehicle (Spain)

Above: VEC (6 x 6) fitted with 25mm TC2
turret and upgraded to VEC 2 standard
(Richard Stickland)

SPECIFICATIONS

Crew:	5
Configuration:	6 x 6
Armament:	1 x 25mm, 1 x 7.62mm MG (coaxial), 2 x 3 smoke grenade dischargers
Ammunition:	170 x 25mm (turret), 250 x 7.62mm (turret)
Length:	6.1m
Width:	2.5m
Height:	2.51m (turret roof), 2.00m (hull top)
Ground clearance:	0.4m
Wheelbase:	1.65m + 1.65m
Weight, combat:	13,750kg
Power-to-weight ratio:	22.25hp/tonne
Engine:	Scania DS9 diesel developing 310hp at 2,20rpm
Maximum road speed:	103km/hr
Maximum water speed	
(wheels):	3km/hr
(waterjets):	9km/hr
Maximum road range:	800km
Fuel capacity:	400 lit
Fording:	Amphibious
Vertical obstacle:	0.6m
Trench:	1.5m
Gradient:	60%
Side slope:	30%
Armour:	Classified
Armour type:	Aluminium
NBC system:	Optional
Night vision equipment:	Optional

DEVELOPMENT

VEC (Vehiculo de Exploracion de Caballeria) was developed by Pegaso to meet the requirements of the Spanish Army and uses many common components of the BMR-600 (6 x 6) infantry fighting vehicle. First five prototypes were completed in 1977–78, with a total Spanish Army

requirement for 235 vehicles. (VEC is also known as Pegaso VEC 3562.) Driver sits front centre, two-man turret centre (Italian Oto Melara T25 made under licence in Spain), engine to turret rear on left side. Fourth crew man sits turret rear on right side, fifth crew man to his front.

The T25 turret has full powered traverse through 360°, elevation powered from -10° to +50°, and 7.62mm MG mounted above.

The Spanish designation for the T25 turret is the CETME TC-15/M242. The 25mm cannon is the American M242 Bushmaster from ATK Gun Systems Company which is also installed in the Bradley M2/M3 used by the US Army.

VEC is fully amphibious, propelled by its wheels; waterjets are an optional extra. Steering is power-assisted on front and rear axles, suspension is adjustable.

Optional equipment includes NBC system, night vision equipment, winch with capacity of 4,500kg, fire-extinguishing system, larger tyres and land navigation system.

VARIANTS

VEC for the export market has a wide range of other turrets to meet different mission requirements, such as anti-tank missile, air-defence (gun or missile), or French Hispano-Suiza 90mm turret as fitted to Panhard AML armoured car. Spanish Army has some vehicles fitted with 20mm turret and 90mm turret (from AML). the VEC has been upgraded to the enhanced VEC 2 standard with new diesel engine and additional passive armour.

KEY RECOGNITION FEATURES

- High hull with well-sloped glacis plate with central driver's position, horizontal hull top with sloping back
- Turret centre of hull with slightly sloping front and sides, distinct chamfer between turret front and sides
- Three equally spaced road wheels each side with hull above road wheels sloping inwards

STATUS

Production complete. In service with the Spanish Army.

MANUFACTURER

Santa Barbara Sistemas, Madrid, Spain.

Below: Upgraded VEC with applique armour and T25 turret

Alvis Saracen APC (UK)

Above: Saracen (6 x 6) APC

SPECIFICATIONS

Crew:	2 + 10
Configuration:	6 x 6
Armament:	1 x 7.62mm MG (turret), 1 x 7.62mm MG ring), 2 x 3 smoke grenade dischargers
Ammunition:	3,000 x 7.62mm
Length:	5.233m
Width:	2.539m
Height:	2.463m (turret top), 2m (hull top)
Ground clearance:	0.432m
Wheelbase:	1.524m + 1.524m
Weight, combat:	10,170kg
Weight, empty:	8,640kg
Power-to-weight ratio:	15.73hp/tonne
Engine:	Rolls-Royce B80 Mk 6A 8-cylinder petrol developing 160hp at 3,750rpm
Maximum road speed:	72km/hr
Maximum range:	400km
Fuel capacity:	200 lit
Fording:	1.07m, 1.98m with preparation
Vertical obstacle:	0.46m
Trench:	1.52m
Gradient:	42%
Side slope:	30%
Armour:	16mm (maximum)
Armour type:	Steel
NBC system:	None
Night vision equipment:	None

DEVELOPMENT

Alvis Saracen APC (FV603) was developed shortly after the Second World War and shares many components with Alvis Saladin (6 x 6) armoured car. First prototype completed in 1952; 1,838 vehicles were built by the time production was completed in 1972. The Saracen APC was finally phased out of service with the British Army in 1993 and these have all now been disposed of.

Driver sits front of crew compartment, section commander to his left rear, radio operator right

ear, four troops on each side facing. Turret has nanual traverse through 360° and 7.62mm MG elevates from -12° to +45°. A 7.62mm Bren LMG s normally mounted to rear of turret for anti-aircraft role.

VARIANTS

Saracen with reverse-flow cooling has different front and top engine covers.
FV604 Saracen command vehicle is similar to FV603 but can have tent erected to rear of hull.
FV610 command vehicle has much higher roof and no MG turret.
FV611 is ambulance with same hull as above.
The company now offers an upgrade for the FV600 series, including the Saracen which ncludes the installation of a Perkins Phaser 180 MTi 180hp diesel engine. This is known to have been adopted by Indonesia.

STATUS

Production complete. In service with Indonesia, Jordan, Lebanon, Mauritania, Nigeria, South Africa (for sale) and Sri Lanka.

KEY RECOGNITION FEATURES

- Engine compartment far front, horizontal radiator louvres which extend to rear of first road wheel station, raised troop compartment to rear, hull sides sloping slightly inwards

- Troop compartment has three rectangular firing ports in each side, two outward-opening doors in hull rear which each have rectangular firing port

- Three large equally spaced road wheels each side, MG turret on hull roof centre and 7.62mm MG on ring mount to immediate rear

MANUFACTURER

Alvis, Coventry, UK. (This site has now closed and the design authority is now BAE Systems Land Systems.)

Below: Saracen (6 x 6) APC

Alvis Saladin Armoured Car (UK)

Above: Saladin

SPECIFICATIONS

Crew:	3
Configuration:	6 x 6
Armament:	1 x 76mm gun, 1 x 7.62mm MG (coaxial), 1 x 7.62mm MG (anti-aircraft), 2 x 6 smoke grenade dischargers
Ammunition:	42 x 76mm, 2,750 x 7.62mm
Length gun forward:	5.284m
Length hull:	4.93m
Width:	2.54m
Height to top of gunner's periscope:	2.39m
Height to turret top:	2.19m
Ground clearance:	0.426m
Wheelbase:	1.524m + 1.524m
Weight, combat:	11,590kg
Weight, empty:	10,500kg
Power-to-weight ratio:	14.66hp/tonne
Engine:	Rolls-Royce B80 Mk 6A 8-cylinder petrol developing 170bhp at 3,750rpm
Maximum road speed:	72km/hr
Range:	400km
Fuel capacity:	241 lit
Fording:	1.07m
Vertical obstacle:	0.46m
Trench:	1.52m
Gradient:	46%
Side slope:	30%
Armour:	8-32mm
Armour type:	Steel
NBC system:	None
Night vision equipment:	None

DEVELOPMENT

Saladin (FV601) (6 x 6) armoured car was developed by the then Alvis of Coventry for the British Army and shares many components with Alvis Saracen (6 x 6) armoured personnel carrier. Almost 1,200 vehicles were produced between 1959 and 1972. Has been replaced in British Army by Alvis Scorpion CVR(T).

Main armament comprises 76mm gun with 7.62mm machine gun mounted coaxial to right and similar weapon on right side of turret roof.

Turret traverse is powered through 360° with weapon elevation from -10° to +20°. Gun fires same ammunition as 76mm gun on Alvis Scorpion, although actual gun is different.

VARIANTS

No variants. Saladin turret has been fitted to some Australian M113A1 series APCs for fire support role but these now in reserve.

Alvis have developed an upgrade kit for the Saladin which includes the replacement of the petrol engine by a more fuel-efficient Perkins diesel. This has been sold to Indonesia.

STATUS

Production complete. In service with Bahrain, Honduras, Indonesia, Jordan, Lebanon, Mauritania, Portugal, Sri Lanka, Sudan, Tunisia and United Arab Emirates.

MANUFACTURER

Alvis, Coventry, UK. (This site has now closed and the design authority is now BAE Systems Land Systems.)

KEY RECOGNITION FEATURES

- Driver front, well-sloped glacis plate, turret centre, engine rear. Engine has six rectangular covers on top, upper part of hull rear vertical, lower part sloping back under hull, cylindrical silencer on right side at rear

- Three equally spaced road wheels identical to those of Alvis Saracen APC

- Turret has flat sides and vertical rear with short-barrelled 76mm gun in external mantlet, 7.62mm MG on right side of roof, cable drum on turret rear

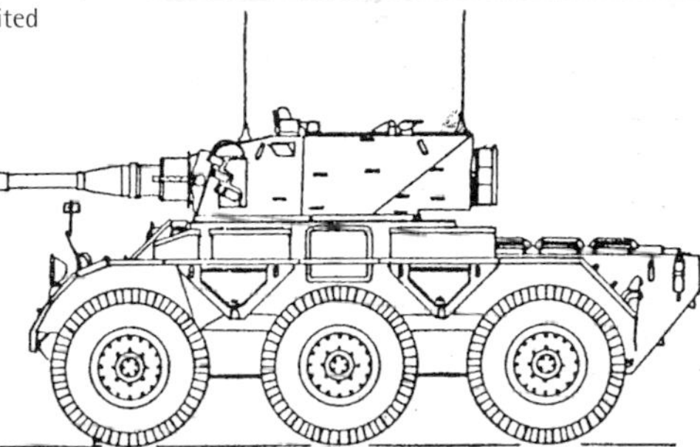

***Right:* Saladin**

***Below:* Saladin (Christopher F Foss)**

Cadillac Gage LAV-300 AFV Range (USA)

SPECIFICATIONS

Crew:	3 + 9
Configuration:	6 x 6
Armament:	1 x 90mm, 1 x 7.62mm MG (coaxial), 1 x 7.62mm MG (anti-aircraft), 2 x 6 smoke grenade dischargers
Length:	6.4m
Width:	2.54m
Height:	2.7m (turret roof), 1.98m (hull top)
Ground clearance:	0.533m (hull), 0.381m (axle)
Wheelbase:	2.209m + 1.524m
Weight, combat:	14,696kg
Power-to-weight ratio:	17.36bhp/tonne
Engine:	Cummins 6 CTA 8.3 turbocharged, 6-cylinder in-line diesel developing 260hp at 1,900rpm
Maximum road speed:	105km/hr
Maximum water speed:	3km/hr
Maximum range:	925km
Fuel capacity:	435 lit
Fording:	Amphibious
Vertical obstacle:	0.609m
Trench:	Not applicable
Gradient:	60%
Side slope:	30%
Armour:	Classified
Armour type:	Steel
NBC system:	Optional
Night vision equipment:	Optional

DEVELOPMENT

LAV-300 range of 6 x 6s was developed by Cadillac Gage as a private venture to complement its 4 x 4s. First prototypes completed in 1979, first production vehicles in 1982.

Driver sits front left, engine compartment to his right, troop compartment extending right to rear. Troops enter and leave via twin dors in hull rear, roof hatches also provided. LAV-300 is fully amphibious, propelled by its wheels. Standard equipment includes front-mounted winch with capacity of 9,072kg. Wide range of optional equipment includes air conditioning system and heater.

Cadillac Gage vehicles are manufactured by Textron Marine & Land Systems.

VARIANTS

LAV-300 can be fitted with wide range of turrets

including one-man turret with twin 7.62mm or one 7.62mm and one 12.7mm MGs, ring mount with 7.62mm or 12.7mm MG, one- or two-man turret with 20mm cannon and 7.62mm MG, two-man turret with 25mm cannon and 7.62mm coaxial MG, two-man turret with 76mm or 90mm gun, 7.62mm coaxial and 7.62mm AA MG. **More specialised versions** include TOW anti-tank, ambulance, 81mm mortar, recovery, cargo carrier, command post vehicle and air defence vehicle (gun or missile), some of which have raised roof to rear of driver's position. The 81mm mortar carrier, for example, has the standard hull with hatches that open either side to enable mortar to be used.

All future LAV-300 production will be to the latest enhanced Mk II standard.

KEY RECOGNITION FEATURES

- Long box-type hull with pointed front, horizontal hull top and vertical rear. Weapon station normally on hull top in line with second road wheel
- Three large road wheels each side with distinctive gap between first and second, hull sides above road wheels slope inwards
- Twin doors at rear each with firing port and vision block above, small door in left side of hull to rear of first wheel station, firing ports with vision block above in hull sides

STATUS

Production as required. Sales have been made to Kuwait, Panama and the Philippines. Of these three countries only the Philippines' vehicles are operational.

MANUFACTURER

Textron Marine & Land Systems, New Orleans, Louisiana, US.

Above left : LAV-300 with two person turret with 90mm gun, 7.62mm coaxial and 7.62mm anti-aircraft MGs

Below: LAV-300 with one person turret armed with twin machine guns

8 x 8 VEHICLES

General Dynamics Land Systems – Canada Bison APC (Canada)

SPECIFICATIONS

Crew:	2 + 8
Configuration:	8 x 8
Armament:	1 x 7.62mm MG, 2 x 4 smoke grenade dischargers
Ammunition:	2,000 x 7.62mm (estimate)
Length:	6.452m
Width:	2.5m
Height:	2.21m
Weight, combat:	12,936kg
Weight, empty:	11,072kg
Power-to-weight ratio:	21.25hp/tonne
Engine:	Detroit Diesel Model 6V-53T 6-cylinder diesel developing 275hp at 2,800rpm
Maximum road speed:	100km/hr
Maximum water speed:	9.7km/hr
Maximum range:	665km
Fuel capacity:	Not available
Fording:	Amphibious
Vertical obstacle:	0.381 to 0.508m
Trench:	2.06m
Gradient:	60%
Side slope:	30%
Armour:	Classified
Armour type:	Steel
NBC system:	Yes
Night vision equipment:	Yes (commander and driver)

DEVELOPMENT

In 1988, the Diesel Division of General Motors of Canada (today General Dynamics Land Systems – Canada) designed and built the prototype of an 8 x 8 APC as a private venture. This was based on the chassis and automotive components of the Light Armoured Vehicle (LAV) that it has built for the United States Marine Corps (qv). The Canadian Army subsequently placed an order for 199 of a modified version, for the Militia, called the Bison and first production vehicles were completed in late 1990.

The driver is seated at the front of the vehicle on the left with the commander being seated to his rear with a raised cupola, the powerpack is to

the right of the driver with the remainder of the hull being occupied by the troop compartment. The infantry are seated on seats on either side of the troop compartment and enter via a large hydraulic operated ramp in the rear. Over the top of the troop compartment are hatches that open either side of the roof. There is no provision for the troops to fire their weapons from within the vehicle.

The Bison is fully amphibious being propelled in the water by two propellers mounted at the rear of the hull and before entering the water a trim vane is erected at the front of the vehicle which, when not required, folds back under the nose. Steering is power assisted on the front four road wheels and standard equipment includes a winch and fire detection and suppression system.

Canada's Bison vehicles are being re-roled.

KEY RECOGNITION FEATURES

- Long hull with nose sloping back under front to first road wheel station, well-sloped glacis plate leading to horizontal roof, above second/third road wheel roof is raised and extends to rear of vehicle. Hull rear is vertical with ramp that contains a door

- Four road wheels either side with slightly larger gap between second and third road wheels, upper part of hull slopes inwards on front half of vehicle, rear half almost vertical with extensive external stowage

- Raised commander's cupola in line with second road wheel on left side of hull, 7.62mm MG on ring type mount

VARIANTS

The Canadian Armed Forces order comprises 149 APCs, 18 command post vehicles, 16 81mm mortar carriers and 16 maintenance and repair vehicles that are fitted with a hydraulic crane.

Coyote, 8 x 8 vehicle with LAV-25 turret plus mast sensors for recce role.

LAV-III, 8 x 8 vehicle with LAV-25 turret, troop carrier.

STATUS

Production complete. In service with Australia, Canada and the National Guard in the US.

MANUFACTURER

General Motors Defense, London, Ontario, Canada.

Above left: Bison (8 x 8) APC

Right: Bison APC from the rear with ramp lowered

General Dynamics Land Systems – Canada Light Armored Vehicle 25 (LAV-25) (Canada)

Above: LAV-25 (8 x 8) with 25mm turret for Canada

SPECIFICATIONS (LAV-25)

Crew:	3 + 8
Configuration:	8 x 8
Armament:	1 x 25mm, 1 x 7.62mm MG (coaxial), 1 x 7.62mm MG (anti-aircraft, optional), 2 x 4 smoke grenade dischargers
Ammunition:	420 x 25mm, 1,740 x 7.62mm
Length:	6.393m
Width:	2.667m
Height overall:	2.692m
Ground clearance:	0.595m
Wheelbase:	1.1m + 1.135m + 1.04m
Weight, combat:	16,329kg
Weight, empty:	14,243kg
Power-to-weight ratio:	21.43hp/tonne
Engine:	Caterpillar 3126B diesel developing 350hp
Maximum road speed:	99km/hr
Maximum range:	500km
Fuel capacity:	300 lit
Fording:	1.5m
Vertical obstacle:	0.6m
Trench:	1.981m
Gradient:	60%
Side slope:	30%
Armour:	10mm (estimate)
NBC system:	None
Night vision equipment:	Yes (passive, commander, gunner and driver)

Note: Specifications relate to latest Canadian vehicle, not original LAV.

DEVELOPMENT

To meet a US Marine Corps requirement for a Light Armored Vehicle (LAV) prototypes were built by Diesel Division, General Motors of Canada, Alvis and Cadillac Gage. In 1982 Diesel Division, General Motors of Canada (which is today called General Dynamics Land Systems – Canada and also owns MOWAG of Switzerland) 8 x 8 (based

on Swiss MOWAG Piranha series) was selected and 758 ordered over a five-year period from FY82 to FY85 in six basic versions. US Army was also involved in the programme but subsequently withdrew. First production vehicles were delivered in October 1983 with final deliveries in 1987.

LAV has driver front left, engine compartment to right, two-man power-operated turret to rear, troop compartment at far rear. Six troops sit three each side back to back, six firing ports and vision blocks. Vehicle is fully amphibious with two propellers mounted at rear. Before entering the water a trim vane is erected at front of vehicle and bilge pumps switched on. Turret is armed with 25mm M242 Chain Gun, with 7.62mm M240 MG mounted coaxial and optional 7.62mm or 12.7mm MG on turret roof for anti-aircraft defence. Turret traverse is 360°, weapon elevation from -10° to +60°.

VARIANTS

LAV logistics has two-man crew, higher roof and crane. In service.
LAV mortar has 81mm mortar in rear. In service.
LAV maintenance/recovery has five-man crew, crane. In service.
LAV anti-tank has three-man crew, same turret as M901s. **Improved TOW vehicle** has two TOW in ready-to-launch position. In service.
LAV command and control is similar to logistics with higher hull. In service.
LAV Mobile Electronic Warfare Support System (MEWS), raised roof. In service.
Anti-aircraft (Marine Corps), fitted with turret armed with 25mm cannon and Stinger SAMs.
Saudi Arabia has many variants including 120mm Armoured Mortar System, 90mm assault gun and anti-tank with HOT ATGW.
LAV can be fitted with many other weapon systems.
Bison (8 x 8) APC (qv).
Coyote, recce vehicle for Canada (25mm turret).
LAV-III – (8 x 8) with latest 25mm turret, for Canadian Army.
Stryker – is US Army model with eight variants in service.

KEY RECOGNITION FEATURES

- Long hull with nose sloping back under front to first road wheel station, well-sloped glacis plate leading to horizontal roof, vertical hull rear with two doors
- Four road wheels each side, upper part of hull sloping inwards, equal gap between first and second and third and fourth road wheels
- Turret to rear of vehicle and offset to left, flat front, sides and rear that slope inwards, basket rear

STATUS

Production. The Piranha series is in service or in order for Australia (8 x 8), Botswana (8 x 8), Canada (6 x 6 and 8 x 8), Chile (6 x 6 and 8 x 8), Denmark (8 x 8), Ghana (4 x 4, 6 x 6 and 8 x 8), Ireland (8 x 8), Liberia (4 x 4), New Zealand (8 x 8), Nigeria (8 x 8), Oman (8 x 8), Qatar (8 x 8), Saudi Arabia (8 x 8), Sierra Leone (6 x 6), Sweden (10 x 10), Switzerland (8 x 8 and 6 x 6), Spain (8 x 8) and US (Army and Marines).

MANUFACTURER

General Dynamics Land Systems – Canada, London, Ontario, Canada.

Below: LAV-III (8 x 8) with 25mm turret for Canada

OT-64C(1) (SKOT-2A) APC (Former Czechoslovakia)

Above: OT-64C(1) SKOT-2A)
(Richard Stickland)

SPECIFICATIONS

Crew:	2 + 10
Configuration:	8 x 8
Armament:	1 x 14.5mm MG (main), 1 x 7.62mm MG (coaxial)
Ammunition:	500 x 14.5mm, 2,000 x 7.62mm
Length:	7.44m
Width:	2.55m
Height:	2.71m (turret top), 2.06m (hull top)
Ground clearance:	0.46m
Wheelbase:	1.3m + 2.15m + 1.3m
Weight, combat:	14,500kg
Weight, unloaded:	12,800kg
Power-to-weight ratio:	12.41hp/tonne
Engine:	Tatra 928 18 V-8 air-cooled diesel developing 180hp at 2,000rpm
Maximum road speed:	94.4km/hr
Maximum water speed:	9km/hr
Maximum road range:	710km
Fuel capacity:	330 lit
Fording:	Amphibious
Vertical obstacle:	0.5m
Trench:	2m
Gradient:	60%
Side slope:	30%
Armour:	14mm (max turret), 10mm (max hull
Armour type:	Steel
NBC system:	Yes
Night vision equipment:	Yes (infra-red for driver)

DEVELOPMENT

OT-64 (Obrneny Transporter) series 8 x 8 was developed by the former Czechoslovakia and Poland from 1959, first production vehicles completed in 1964. In these countries it was originally used in place of the similar Soviet-designed and built BTR-60 (8 x 8). Tatra of Czechoslovakia built the chassis and FSC/Lubin of Poland the armoured body.

OT-64 (designated SKOT by Poland) is fully amphibious with two propellers at the rear. Before entering the water a trim vane is erected at the front and bilge pumps switched on. All vehicles have powered steering on front four wheels and central tyre pressure regulation system.

VARIANTS

OT-62A (SKOT), original model armed with pintle-mounted 7.62mm MG (Poland) or unarmed (Czechoslovakia). Some fitted with two Sagger ATGWs over rear troop compartment.
OT-64B (SKOT-2), used only by Poland. Square plinth with pintle-mounted 7.62mm or 12.7mm MG with shield.
OT-64C(1) (SKOT-2A) has same turret as fitted to Soviet BRDM-2, BTR-60PB and BTR-70 vehicles

and armed with one 14.5mm KPVT and one 7.62mm PKT coaxial MG with elevation from -4° to +29°. Turret traverse is 360°. Both elevation and traverse are manual.
OT-64C(2) (SKOT-2AP), used only by Poland. Same as SKOT-2A but has new turret with same armament, curved top for higher elevation of +89.5°. Turret also fitted to OT-62C.
OT-64C(1) with **OT-62B turret**. Morocco has a few of these local conversions.
DPT-64, is OT-64 modified for repair role.
OT-64 R-2M and **R-2AM** are command versions.
OT-64 R-3MT and **OT-64 R-4MT** are radio versions.
OT-93 is SKOT with new turret armed with single 7.62mm MG
WPT, armoured repair and maintenance vehicle.
Other versions include artillery resupply, minelayer, repair and maintenance, OT-64 R-3Z, OT-64 R4 and OT-64 R6, all of which are Polish. Upgraded versions have recently been developed in Poland including command post and 98mm mortar.

STATUS

Production complete. In service with Algeria, Angola, Cambodia, Czech Republic, India, Libya, Morocco (status uncertain), Poland, Sierra Leone, Slovakia, Sudan, Syria, Uganda (status uncertain) and Uruguay.

KEY RECOGNITION FEATURES

- 8 x 8 chassis with equal spaces between first/second and third/fourth wheels, larger gap between second/third

- Blunt nose with vertical hull sides sloping slightly inwards at top, rear slopes outwards, exhaust pipes on both sides of hull, trim vane front

- OT-64C(1) has flat topped turret on plinth just forward of third wheel station

MANUFACTURER

Polish and former Czechoslovakian state factories.

Below: OT-62C(1) (SKOT-2A) (8 x 8)

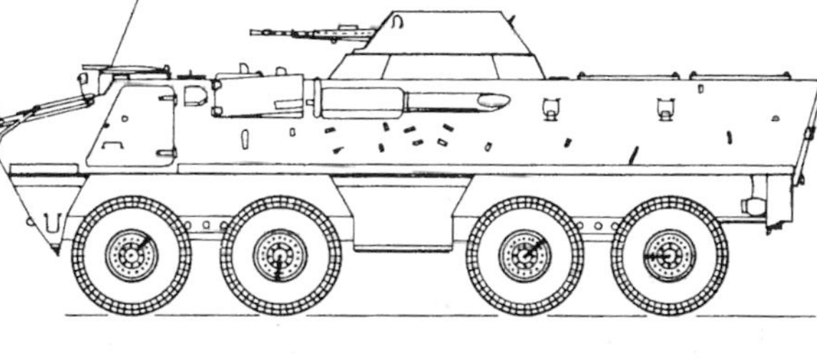

Right: OT-64 series APC from the rear (Richard Stickland)

Patria Vehicles Armoured Modular Vehicle

(Finland)

Above: Patria Vehicles AMV armed with 12.7mm MG

SPECIFICATIONS

Crew:	3 + 8 (but depends on role)
Configuration:	8 x 8
Armament:	1 x 12.7mm MG
Ammunition:	1,000 x 12.7mm
Length:	7.7m
Width:	2.8 m
Height:	2.3 m (hull top)
Ground clearance:	0.45 m
Weight, combat:	28,000kg
Weight, empty:	16,000kg
Power-to-weight ratio:	19.14hp/tonne
Engine:	Scania DC12 6-cylinder turbo charged diesel with an output of between 335 and 536hp
Maximum road speed:	100km/h
Maximum road range:	800km/h
Fuel capacity:	Not available
Fording:	1.5m
Vertical obstacle:	0.7m
Trench:	2m
Gradient:	60%
Side slope:	30%
Armour:	Classified
Armour type:	Steel
NBC system:	Yes
Night vision equipment:	Yes
Note:	Weight and height depend on weapon fit

DEVELOPMENT

Based on their experience in the design, development and production of the XA-180 series of 6 x 6 APC and variants, Patria Vehicles developed the Armoured Modular Vehicle (AMV) in close co-operation with the Finnish Defence Force (FDF). The first prototype of the AMV was completed in 2001 and was followed by additional trials vehicles.

The Finnish Defence Force placed an order for two vehicles in 2002, one fitted with a 12.7mm remote controlled machine gun and one with a two person turret armed with a 30mm cannon. Late in 2002 Poland selected the AMV and placed an order for 690 units of which 658 will be in 8 x 8 configuration and 32 the 6 x 6 reconnaissance model. The first 40 are coming from Finland with the remainder being manufactured in Poland.

Poland has ordered seven versions of the AMV including 313 fitted with a new Oto Melara HITFIST 30P turret armed with a 30/40mm MK44 cannon and 7.62mm coaxial machine gun.

The Finnish Defence Force has ordered 24 AMV

(4 + 20) fitted with the twin 120mm AMOS (Advanced Mortar System) with an option of an additional 100 units in the infantry fighting vehicle configuration.

The driver is seated at the front left with another crew position to his rear and the power pack to the right. Remainder of area to the rear is occupied by the troop compartment and is provided with roof hatches. Normal means of entry and exit is via a large power-operated door in the hull rear.

Three models of the AMV are being marketed: basic; system platform; and modular carrier. Basic models include infantry fighting vehicle, armoured personnel carrier kit, command kit and ambulance kit. System platform models include command kit, communication kit, mast version, large ambulance kit and workshop version. The modular carrier includes a container carrier version and missile modular carrier.

As well as an NBC system and night vision equipment, standard equipment on the AMV includes winch, power steering on the front four road wheels and a central tyre pressure regulation system that allows the driver to adjust the tyre pressure to the terrain being crossed. When fitted with a lighter weapon fit the vehicle can be amphibious.

KEY RECOGNITION FEATURES

- Nose of vehicle slopes slightly back underneath hull front to first road wheel station. Well-sloped hull front up to above rear of first road wheel station then horizontal roof to hull rear. Hull rear slopes slightly inwards with large door in rear

- Four large road wheels either side with slightly wider gap between second and third road wheels. Hull sides above road wheels hull sides slope slightly inwards

- Driver's station in forward part of hull roof on left side with weapons station normally installed on centre of hull roof in line with second and third road wheels

VARIANTS

The AMV can be adapted for a wide range of roles and missions and be fitted with a wide range of weapon stations up to 105mm in calibre.

STATUS

In production. Entering service with Poland and on order for Finland.

MANUFACTURER

Patria Vehicles, Hameenlinna, Finland.

Above right: Patria Vehicles AMV armed with 12.7mm MG

Right: Patria Vehicles AMV with turret mounted 30mm cannon

GIAT Industries VBCI infantry combat vehicle

(France)

Above: GIAT Industries VCI with Dragar 25mm turret

SPECIFICATIONS

Crew:	2 + 9
Configuration:	8 x 8
Armament:	1 x 25mm cannon, 1 x 7.62mm MG (co-axial)
Ammunition:	Not available
Length:	7.80m
Width:	2.98m
Height:	2.26m
Ground clearance:	0.50m
Weight, combat:	28,000kg
Weight, empty:	18,000kg
Power-to-weight ratio:	19.64hp/tonne
Engine:	Renault diesel developing 550hp
Maximum road speed:	100km/h
Maximum road range:	750km
Fuel capacity:	Not available
Fording:	1.2m (1.5m with preparation)
Vertical obstacle:	0.7m
Trench:	2m
Gradient:	60%
Side slope:	30%
Armour:	Classified
Armour type:	Aluminium plus add-on titanium
NBC system:	Yes
Night vision equipment:	Yes

DEVELOPMENT

To replace the current full tracked AMX-10P infantry combat vehicle used by the French Army, GIAT Industries is developing the VBCI (Vehicule Blindé de Combat d'Infanterie) 8 x 8 armoured vehicle.

The total French Army requirement is for 550 VCI (Vehicule Blindé de Combat d'Infanterie) and 150 of the Vehicule Poste de Commandement (VCP) command post vehicle model. This is fitted with a 12.7mm machine gun cupola and has extensive communications for its specialist role.

Five prototypes have been built, four in the VCI and one in the VCP configuration, with the first contract being for 54 VCI and 11 VPC which should be delivered in 2008/2009. Production is to be built up to 100 units a year.

The hull of the VCI is of welded aluminium to which an additional layer of titanium armour has been added for a higher level of protection. Internal spall liners are fitted and the floor has been designed to provide a high level of

protection against anti-tank mines.

The VCI has the driver front left with the power pack to the right. The commander is seated to the rear of the driver and would normally dismount with the infantry. The commander can also take over control of the latest generation Dragar turret and aim and fire the weapons.

The new generation Dragar turret is armed with a 25mm M811 dual feed stabilised cannon, a 7.62mm machine gun mounted coaxial to the right and is provided with grenade launchers and day/night sights.

The infantry are seated four down either side of the hull on individual seats and enter and leave the vehicle via a large power operated ramp in the hull rear.

Standard equipment includes powered steering on the front four wheels, a central tyre pressure regulation system, fire/explosion detection and suppression system, battle information system and a defensive aids suit.

KEY RECOGNITION FEATURES

- Pointed nose with well-sloped glacis plate with driver's hatch in left side and horizontal roof that extends to rear. Hull rear is vertical but slopes slightly inwards with large power operated ramp in rear

- Commander's position to rear of driver and turret in forward part of hull roof and offset slightly to right. Turret has pointed front with 7.62mm machine gun mounted coaxial on right side of turret

- Four large road wheels either side with upper part of hull sides sloping slightly inwards

VARIANTS

The only variant announced so far is the command post model but a number of other variants are under consideration including an engineering vehicle, mortar carrier, anti-tank missile carrier and a version armed with a 120mm smooth bore gun fed by an automatic loader.

STATUS

Development. Not yet in production or service.

MANUFACTURER

GIAT Industries, Roanne, France.

Above right: GIAT Industries VCI fitted with Dragar 25mm turret (Christopher F Foss)

Right: GIAT Industries VCI with Dragar 25mm turret (Christopher F Foss)

Rheinmetall Landsysteme Spähpanzer Luchs Reconnaissance Vehicle (Germany)

Above: Luchs (8 x 8) (Michael Jerchel)

SPECIFICATIONS

Crew:	4
Configuration:	8 x 8
Armament:	1 x 20mm, 1 x 7.62mm MG (anti-aircraft), 2 x 4 smoke grenade dischargers
Ammunition:	375 x 20mm (turret), 100 x 7.62mm (turret)
Length:	7.743m
Width:	2.98m
Height:	2.905m (MG rail), 2.125m (hull top)
Ground clearance:	0.44m (hull), 0.58m (axles)
Wheelbase:	1.4m + 2.356m + 1.4m
Weight, combat:	20,000kg
Power-to-weight ratio:	20hp/tonne
Engine:	Daimler-Benz OM 403 A 10-cylinder 90° V-4 stroke multifuel developing 390hp at 2,500rpm (diesel fuel)
Maximum road speed:	90km/hr
Maximum water speed:	10km/hr
Maximum range:	730km
Fuel capacity:	500 lit
Fording:	Amphibious
Vertical obstacle:	0.6m
Trench:	1.9m
Gradient:	60%
Side slope:	30%
Armour:	Classified
Armour type:	Steel
NBC system:	Yes
Night vision equipment:	Yes (passive for commander, gunner and driver)

DEVELOPMENT

In the mid-1960s the then West German Army issued a requirement for a new 8 x 8 armoured amphibious reconnaissance vehicle and after trials with two competing designs the Daimler-Benz model was selected. In December 1973 Rheinstahl Wehrtechnik (now Rheinmetall Landsysteme) was awarded a contract for 408 vehicles. First production vehicles, known officially as the Spähpanzer Luchs, were delivered in 1975 and production continued until early 1978.

Driver sits front left, to his rear is the two-man turret, engine is rear on right side, second driver/

radio operator is left side facing rear. Turret has full power traverse through 360°, weapon elevation from -15° to +69°. Manual controls provided for emergency use. The 7.62mm MG is mounted on a ring mount above commander's hatch on left side.

Luchs is fully amphibious, propelled by two propellers mounted rear. Steering is power-assisted and all eight wheels can be steered. When originally introduced into service Luchs had infra-red night vision equipment for all crew members, but this has now been replaced by thermal night vision equipment. Luchs has the same speed forwards and backwards.

KEY RECOGNITION FEATURES

- High hull with well-sloped glacis plate on forward part of which is trim vane, horizontal hull top, turret slightly forward of vehicle centre, sloping hull rear

- Vertical hull sides sloping inward above wheels, access door in left hull side between second and third road wheels

- Four large road wheels each side with equal space between first/second and third/fourth road wheels, two propellers under hull rear

VARIANTS

The Luchs A1 has new radios and the Luchs A2 has the thermal vision equipment.

STATUS

Production complete. In service with Germany Army only. Now being replaced by the Fennek (4 x 4) reconnaissance vehicle.

MANUFACTURER

Rheinmetall Landsysteme GmbH, Kassel, Germany.

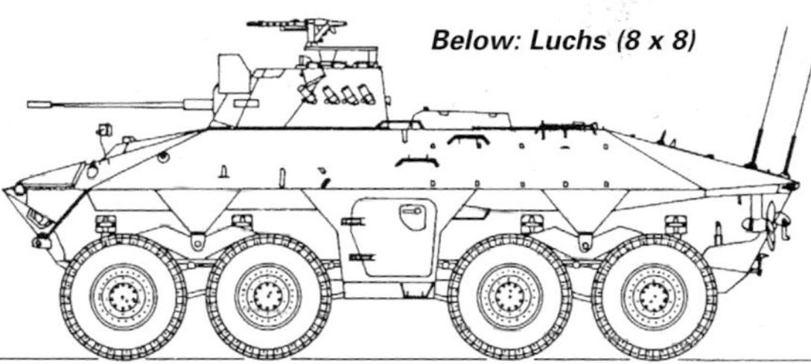

Below: Luchs (8 x 8)

Below: Luchs (8 x 8) (BP)

ARTEC Boxer Multi-Role Armoured Vehicle (MRAV) (International)

Above: Boxer (8 x 8) MRAV without armament installed (ARTEC GmbH)

SPECIFICATIONS

Crew:	3 + 8 (but depends on role)
Configuration:	8 x 8
Armament:	1 x 12.7mm MG (typical)
Ammunition:	1,000 x 12.7mm
Length:	7.927m
Width:	2.99m
Height:	2.376m (roof)
Ground clearance:	0.504m
Weight, combat:	33,000kg
Weight, empty:	25,000kg
Power-to-weight ratio:	21.51hp/tonne
Engine:	MTU diesel developing 710hp
Maximum road speed:	103km/h
Maximum road range:	1,050km
Fuel capacity:	Not available
Fording:	1.5m
Vertical obstacle:	0.8m
Trench:	2m
Gradient:	60%
Side slope:	30%
Armour:	Classified
Armour type:	Steel plus applique
NBC system:	Yes
Night vision equipment:	Yes

DEVELOPMENT

The Boxer Multi Role Armoured Vehicle (MRAV) was originally developed by the ARTEC consortium to meet the operational requirements of Germany, Netherlands and the United Kingdom with the original initial production order expected to be for a total of 600 vehicles, 200 for each country.

ARTEC includes Krauss-Maffei Wegmann and Rheinmetall Landsysteme of Germany, Stork of the Netherlands and the now BAE Systems Land Systems (previously Alvis Vickers). The UK has now pulled out of the programme and as of September 2004 no firm production orders had been placed for Boxer.

Boxer consists of two key parts, the chassis and the removable mission module mounted at the rear. The chassis includes the complete drive line, engine compartment front left and driver to the front right.

The basic mission module is for eight troops who are seated four down either side facing each other. The troops can rapidly enter and leave Boxer via the large power operated ramp in the rear that is also fitted with an emergency escape

door. There are no firing ports in the hull as this was not a requirement.

Each country has selected a different weapon station/armament for Boxer which can be a 7.62mm or 12.7mm machine gun or a 40mm automatic grenade launcher which can be aimed and fired under armour protection.

When compared to other wheeled vehicles, Boxer has a high level of protection against not only small arms fire and shell splinters but also anti-tank mines and top attack weapons. In addition to the basic all welded steel armour Boxer also has an applique layer of passive armour.

More specialised versions of the Boxer, for example ambulance (or medical treatment vehicle as it is referred to), have a higher roof line to the rear of the driver's station for greater internal volume.

As well as an NBC system and night vision equipment, standard equipment on all Boxer vehicles includes power steering on the front four road wheels and a central tyre pressure regulation system that allows the driver to adjust the tyre pressure to the terrain being crossed.

VARIANTS

These include command vehicle, communications, mortar carrier, carrying anti-tank guided missile teams, medical treatment and evacuation vehicle, cargo carrier, battle damage repair vehicle and pioneer vehicle.

KEY RECOGNITION FEATURES

- Nose of vehicle slopes well back underneath hull front to first road wheel station. Well-sloped hull front up to above second wheel station then horizontal roof to hull rear. Hull rear slopes slightly inwards with large ramp in rear

- Four large road wheels either side with slightly wider gap between second and third road wheels. Hull sides vertical but just above road wheels hull sides slope slightly inwards

- Driver's station in forward part of hull roof on right side with commander's cupola in middle of roof and armed with externally mounted weapon

STATUS

Prototypes. Not yet in production or service.

MANUFACTURER

See text.

Below: Boxer (8 x 8) MRAV armed with 7.62mm machine gun (ARTEC GmbH)

Consortium IVECO-Oto Melara Centauro Tank Destroyer (Italy)

SPECIFICATIONS

Crew:	4
Configuration:	8 x 8
Armament:	1 x 105mm, 1 x 7.62mm MG (coaxial), 1 x 7.62mm MG (anti-aircrft), 2 x 4 smoke grenade dischargers
Ammunition:	40 x 105mm, 4,000 x 7.62mm
Length with gun:	8.555m
Length hull:	7.85m
Width:	3.05m
Height:	2.735m
Ground clearance:	0.417m
Wheelbase:	1.6m + 1.45m + 1.45m
Weight, combat:	25,000kg
Power-to-weight ratio:	20.8hp/tonne
Engine:	IVECO FIAT VTCA V-6 turbocharged diesel developing 520hp at 2,300rpm
Maximum road speed:	105 + km/hr
Range:	800km
Fuel capacity:	540 lit
Fording:	1.5m
Vertical obstacle:	0.55m
Trench:	1.2m
Gradient:	60%
Side slope:	30%

Above: IVECO FIAT Centauro

Armour:	Classified
Armour type:	Steel
NBC system:	Yes
Night vision equipment:	Yes (passive)

DEVELOPMENT

The Centauro (8 x 8) tank destroyer is the first of a complete new family of armoured vehicles developed for the Italian Army to enter production. The others are the Ariete MBT (qv), Dardo IFV (qv) and the Puma range of 4 x 4 and 6 x 6 vehicles (qv). Oto Melara has responsibility for the tracked vehicles and armament aspects of all vehicles. IVECO is responsible for the wheeled vehicles and automotive aspects of all tracked vehicles.

Following trials with a number of prototypes the Italian Army placed an order for the vehicle and the first production vehicles were completed in 1991. IVECO at Bolzano built the chassis of the Centauro and integrate this with the complete turret which is supplied by Oto Melara at La Spezia.

The driver is seated on the left side of the vehicle at the front with the powerpack to his right and the power-operted turret at the rear. The commander and gunner are seated on the right with the loader being seated on the left. In addition to the two roof hatches there is also a

hatch in the rear for crew escape and ammunition resupply. Turret traverse is a full 360° with weapon elevation from -6° to +15°, turret traverse and weapon elevation is powered with manual controls being provided for emergency use. The computerised fire control system is similar to that used in the Ariete MBT and includes a commander's stabilised sight and day/night sight for the gunner. Suspension system is of the hydropneumatic type with steering being power assisted on the front four wheels and standard equipment includes a central tyre pressure regulation system that allows the ground pressure to be adjusted to suit the type of terrain being crossed, winch located in the front of the hull and a fire detection and suppression system. For operations in the Balkans the Centauro has been fitted with additional armour and two roof-mounted 7.62mm MG each provided with a shield.

Italy has taken delivery of 40 vehicles while Spain has received 22 and ordered another 62.

KEY RECOGNITION FEATURES

- High hull with well-sloped glacis plate, nose slopes back under hull. Horizontal hull roof with hull rear containing a door that opens to the right, hull rear slopes inwards

- Turret mounted towards rear of vehicle with distinctive external mantlet, turret sides slope slightly inwards with bank of four smoke grenade dischargers either side, 105mm gun extends over front of vehicle and has muzzle brake, thermal sleeve and fume extractor

- Four large road wheels either side with slightly larger gap between first and second road wheels. Upper part of hull slopes inwards with louvres in right side of hull above first and second road wheels

VARIANTS

VBC, APC version of Centauro with various turrets including 25mm, 60mm and 12.7mm (prototypes).
120mm, mortar (under development).
Command post (prototype).
Recovery vehicle (design stage).
Ambulance (prototype).

STATUS

In production. In service with Italy and Spain.

MANUFACTURER

IVECO FIAT, Bolzano, Italy.

Below: IVECO FIAT Centauro

TAB-77 APC (Romania)

SPECIFICATIONS

Crew:	2 + 9
Configuration:	8 x 8
Armament:	1 x 14.5mm MG (main), 1 x 7.62mm MG (coaxial)
Ammunition:	600 x 14.5mm, 2,500 x 7.62mm
Length:	7.42m
Width:	2.95m
Height:	1.92m (turret top)
Ground clearance:	0.525m
Wheelbase:	4.392m
Weight, combat:	13,350kg
Power-to-weight ratio:	19.77hp/tonne
Engine:	2 x Model 797-05M1 diesels, each developing 132hp at 3,000rpm
Maximum road speed:	83km/hr
Maximum road range:	550km
Fuel capacity:	290 lit
Fording:	Amphibious
Vertical obstacle:	0.5m
Trench:	2m
Gradient:	60%
Side slope:	30%
Armour:	8mm (estimate)
NBC system:	Yes
Night vision equipment:	Yes

DEVELOPMENT

In the 1960s Romania developed the TAB-71 (see next entry), a version of the BTR-60PB. This was followed by the TAB-77, based on the BTR-70, but with minor differences. It has a new turret of local design and the original petrol engines are replaced by two locally manufactured diesel units. The commander and driver sit at the front with one man manually operating the turret to their rear. The troop compartment extends almost to the rear where the engine compartment is located.

The turret traverses through 360° and the turret armament elevates from -5° to +85°. The TAB-77 is fully amphibious, being propelled in the water by a single waterjet mounted in the rear. Before entering the water, bilge pumps are

switched on and the trim vane at the front is erected. Standard equipment includes a central tyre pressure regulation system, fire detection and suppression system and a winch.

VARIANTS

TAB-77 PCOMA, armoured artillery command post vehicle.
TAB-77A, armoured command post vehicle.
TERA-77L, maintenance and recovery vehicle.
B33, latest model of TAB-77 with one 268hp diesel engine but is based on more recent Russian BTR-80 (8 x 8) APC.
Zibru, latest model with new powerpack and raised hull line.
RN-94, is a joint development between Romania and Turkey and is a 6 x 6 vehicle which remains at the prototype stage (qv).

STATUS

Production complete. In service with Romania.

MANUFACTURERS

ROMARM SA, Bucharest, Romania.

KEY RECOGNITION FEATURES

- Looks very similar to the Russian BTR-80 but has different turret with distinctive sight on left side and no smoke grenade launchers on the turret rear

- Four large road wheels each side, with door in lower part of hull between second and third road wheels, upper part of hull slopes inwards, trim vane folds back on to glacis

- Pointed front with commander and driver seated towards front and turret on roof in line with second road wheel, long exhaust pipe on either side of hull above last road wheel

Above left: TAB-77 (8 x 8)

Below: TAB-77 (8 x 8)

TAB-71 APC (Romania)

SPECIFICATIONS

Crew:	3 + 8
Configuration:	8 x 8
Armament:	1 x 14.5mm MG (main), 1 x 7.62mm MG (coaxial)
Ammunition:	500 x 14.5mm, 2,000 x 7.62mm
Length:	7.22m
Width:	2.83m
Height:	2.7m (turret top)
Ground clearance:	0.47m
Wheelbase:	4.21m
Weight, combat:	11,000kg
Power-to-weight ratio:	25.4hp/tonne
Engine:	2 x V-6 liquid cooled petrol developing 140hp each
Maximum road speed:	95km/hr
Maximum water speed:	10km/hr
Maximum road range:	500km
Fuel capacity:	290 lit
Fording:	Amphibious
Vertical obstacle:	0.4m
Trench:	2m
Gradient:	60%
Side slope:	30%
Armour:	9mm (max turret), 7mm (max hull)
Armour type:	Steel
NBC system:	Yes
Night vision equipment:	Yes (infra-red for driver)

DEVELOPMENT

TAB-71 (8 x 8) was first seen in public during 1972 and is the Romanian equivalent of the former Soviet BTR-60PB (8 x 8) but with at least two major improvements: more powerful engines (2 x 140hp compared with 2 x 90hp of Soviet vehicle) and machine guns with higher elevation for use in the anti-aircraft role. TAB-71 is fully amphibious, propelled by a single waterjet at rear of hull. Central tyre pressure regulation system. Turret has manual traverse and MGs elevate manually from -5° to +85°.

VARIANTS

TAB-71M, virtually same as standard TAB-71.
TAB-71AR, TAB-71 with turret removed and fitted with 81mm mortar.
TERA-71L, TAB-71 modified for maintenance and recovery role.
TAB-71A R, TAB-71A R1 451, TAB-71A R1 452, TAB-71 modified for armoured command vehicle.

The TAB-71 was replaced in production by the TAB-77 for which there is a separate entry. **Note:** TAB-79 (4 x 4) APC (qv).

STATUS

Production complete. In service with Moldova, Romania and Serbia and Montenegro.

MANUFACTURER

Romanian state factories.

Left: TAB-71 (8 x 8) APC

KEY RECOGNITION FEATURES

- Four equally spaced road wheels each side
- Hull sides slope slightly inwards with square door in each side above second/third road wheel, three firing ports each side
- Mounted on roof of vehicle, above the second road wheel, is the turret which is similar to that of the former Soviet BTR-60PB (8 x 8) APC (qv) but has a distinctive sight mounted externally to the left of the weapons

Below: TAB-71M (8 x 8) APC

BTR-90 APC (Russia)

Above: BTR-90 (8 x 8) APC

SPECIFICATIONS

Crew:	3 + 7
Configuration:	8 x 8
Armament:	1 x 30mm cannon, 1 x 7.62mm machine gun,1 x AT-5 Spandrel ATGW launcher, 1 x 30mm grenade launcher
Ammunition:	500 x 30mm, 2,000 x 7.62mm, 4 x Spandrel ATGW and 400 x 30mm grenades
Length:	7.64m
Width:	3.20m
Height:	2.975m
Ground clearance:	0.510m
Weight, combat:	20,920kg
Weight. empty:	Not available
Power-to-weight ratio:	24.37hp/tonne
Engine:	Turbocharged multi-fuel developing 510hp
Maximum road speed:	100km/h
Maximum water speed:	9km/h
Road range:	800km
Fuel capacity:	Not available
Fording:	Amphibious
Vertical obstacle:	0.8m
Trench:	2m
Gradient:	60%
Side slope:	30%
Armour:	Classified
Armour type:	Steel
NBC system:	Yes
Night vision equipment:	Yes

DEVELOPMENT

The BTR-90 (8 x 8) armoured personnel carrier was developed in the early 1990s by the Arzamas Machine Construction Factory with the first prototype being completed in 1994.

In many respects the BTR-90 is a scaled up version of the earlier BTR-80 but has a higher level of protection, greater internal volume, more powerful armament and greater mobility. A small batch of BTR-90 vehicles are in service with the Russian Ministry of Interior.

Two crew members including driver are seated at front with large two person turret to the rear which is identical to that fitted to the Russian BMP-2 inafntry fighting vehicle. Turret traverse is a full 360° with 30mm cannon and 7.62mm coaxial machine gun having elevation from -5° to +75°. Mounted on roof is a launcher for the AT-5 Spandrel anti-tank guided weapon which has a

maximum range of 4,000m. Mounted on the turret rear on the left side is a 30mm automatic grenade launcher which is fired by remote control.

The infantry are provided with roof hatches and normally enter and leave via a side door between second and third road wheels. Firing ports and associated vision ports are provided to allow the troops to fire their weapons from within the hull.

Standard equipment for the BTR-90 includes night vision equipment, powered steering on the front four (two either side) road wheels and a central tyre pressure regulation system that allows the driver to adjust the tyre pressure to suit the terrain being crossed.

The BTR-90 vehicle is also fully amphibious being propelled in the water by two waterjets mounted one either side at the rear. Before entering the water the trim vane is erected at the front of the hull and the bilge pumps are switched on.

VARIANTS

For trials purposes the BTR-90 APC has been fitted with a new turret armed with a 100mm gun, 30mm cannon and 7.62mm machine gun.

STATUS

Production as required. In service with Russia.

KEY RECOGNITION FEATURES

- Very similar in appearance to BTR-80 (8 x 8) APC (qv) but much larger. The new hull has a distinctive arrow head front with the upper part sloping upwards to the horizontal hull top that extends to rear of vehicle. A trim vane is folded back onto the glacis plate. Large turret as fitted to Russian BMP-2 IFV is mounted over forward part of hull above first and second road wheel stations

- Upper part of hull sides slopes inwards with four road wheels either side. Larger gap between second and third road wheels with vertical side door between. Upper part opens upwards while lower part folds down to form a step

- On upper part of hull at rear are two horizontal exhaust outlets. Hull rear slopes slightly inwards to and bottom with two rectangular waterjet outlets below which are normally covered

MANUFACTURER

Arzamas Machinery Construction Plant, Russia.

Below: BTR-90 (8 x 8) APC

BTR-80 APC (Russia)

Above: BTR-80 (8 x 8) APC

SPECIFICATIONS

Crew:	3 + 7
Configuration:	8 x 8
Armament:	1 x 14.5mm MG, 1 x 7.62mm MG (coaxial), 6 smoke grenade dischargers
Ammunition:	500 x 14.5mm, 2,000 x 7.62mm
Length:	7.65m
Width:	2.90m
Height:	2.35m
Ground clearance:	0.475m
Weight, combat:	13,600kg
Power-to-weight ratio:	19.11hp/tonne
Engine:	KamAZ-7203 4-stroke V-8 water-cooled diesel developing 260hp
Maximum road speed:	90km/hr
Maximum water speed:	9.5km/hr
Road range:	600km
Fuel capacity:	300 lit
Fording:	Amphibious
Vertical obstacle:	0.5m
Trench:	2m
Gradient:	60%
Side slope:	30%
Armour:	7mm (max turret), 9mm (max hull)
Armour type:	Steel
NBC system:	Yes
Night vision equipment:	Yes (infra-red for commander and driver)

DEVELOPMENT

BTR-70 (8 x 8) had a number of improvements over the original BTR-60 (8 x 8) family but still has disadvantages including two petrol engines and poor means of entry and exit. In the early 1980s the former Soviet Army took delivery of a new vehicle, BTR-80, which has the same layout as BTR-70 but a single V-8 diesel developing 260hp. The one-man, manually-operated turret is similar to BTR-70's but the 14.5mm KPVT MG elevates to +60° so it can be used against slow-flying aircraft and helicopters. The 7.62mm PKT MG is retained. Mounted on turret rear is a bank of six 81mm smoke grenade dischargers firing forwards. There are three firing ports in each side of troop compartment. Between second and third axles is a new hatch arrangement: upper part opens to front and lower part folds down to form step allowing infantry to leave more safely.

BTR-80 is fully amphibious, propelled by a single waterjet at rear, has central tyre pressure regulation system, steering on front four road wheels, front-mounted winch, NBC system and

infra-red night vision equipment for driver and commander who sit at front of vehicle.

VARIANTS

BTR-80 M1989/1, this is a command vehicle with additional communications equipment.
120mm 2S23 self-propelled gun, details of this vehicle, essentially a BTR-80 with the turret of the 2S9 are given in the self-propelled guns section.
RKhM-4 chemical and reconnaissance vehicle.
BREM-K armoured recovery vehicle.
BTR-80A has new turret with externally mounted 30mm cannon and 7.62mm machine gun.
BTR-80K, command vehicle.
SPR-2, jamming vehicle.
BMM armoured medical vehicle.
BTR-80 with Kliver turret (prototype).
There are numerous other command versions.

KEY RECOGNITION FEATURES

- Similar in appearance to BTR-70 (8 x 8) APC (qv) but similar turret has a bank of six forward firing smoke grenade dischargers mounted on turret rear

- Between second and third road wheels is a new hatch/door arrangement, upper part opens to right and lower part opens downwards to form a ramp

- Hull rear is different from BTR-70/BTR-80 and has higher roof line with exhaust pipe almost horizontal

STATUS

Production. In service with Afghanistan, Algeria, Angola, Armenia, Azerbaijan, Bangladesh, Belarus, Estonia, Finland, Georgia, Hungary, Kazakhstan, North Korea, South Korea, Kyrgyzstan, Macedonia, Moldova, Russia, Sri Lanka, Sudan, Tajikstan, Turkey, Turkmenistan, Ukraine and Uzbekistan.

MANUFACTURER

Arzamas Machinery Construction Plant, Russia.

***Above right:* BTR-80 (8 x 8) APC**

***Right:* BTR-80A (8 x 8) APC (Christopher F Foss)**

BTR-70 APC (Russia)

Above: BTR-70 (8 x 8) (Michael Jerchel)

SPECIFICATIONS

Crew:	2 + 9
Configuration:	8 x 8
Armament:	1 x 14.5mm MG, 1 x 7.62mm MG (coaxial)
Ammunition:	500 x 14.5mm, 2,000 x 7.62mm
Length:	7.535m
Width:	2.8m
Height top of turret:	2.235m
Ground clearance:	0.475m
Wheelbase:	4.4m
Weight, combat:	11,500kg
Power-to-weight ratio:	20.86hp/tonne
Engines:	2 x ZMZ-4905 6-cylinder petrol developing 120hp (each)
Maximum road speed:	80km/hr
Maximum water speed:	10km/hr
Maximum road range:	600km
Fuel capacity:	350 lit (estimate)
Fording:	Amphibious
Vertical obstacle:	0.5m
Trench:	2m
Gradient:	60%
Side slope:	40%
Armour:	9mm (maximum) (estimate)
Armour type:	Steel
NBC system:	Yes
Night vision equipment:	Yes (infra-red for driver and commander)

DEVELOPMENT

BTR-70 is a further development of BTR-60 and was first shown in public during a Moscow parade in 1980. Main improvements over the BTR-60PB are slightly more powerful petrol engines which give improvement in power-to-weight ratio, improved vision for the troops with additional firing ports and improved armour protection. Commander and driver sit front with troop compartment extending towards rear, engines rear. Turret identical to BRDM-2 reconnaissance vehicle's, BTR-60PB's and armed with 14.5mm and a 7.62mm MG. Turret traverse is manual through 360°, weapons elevate from -5° to +30°. Steering is power-assisted on front four wheels, standard equipment includes front-mounted winch and central tyre pressure regulation system. BTR-70 is fully amphibious, propelled by a single waterjet mounted at rear of hull. Before entering the water a trim vane is erected at front and bilge pumps switched on.

VARIANTS
Some BTR-70s in Afghanistan were fitted with 30mm AGS-17 grenade launcher mounted on roof to rear of driver.
BTR-70MS is a turretless communications vehicle.
BTR-70KShM is a command/staff vehicle.
BREM is a turretless BTR-70 with bow-mounted jib crane and other equipment.
BTR-70Kh is chemical reconnaissance vehicle.
SPR-2 is a possible radar jamming variant.
Some BTR-70s have been fitted with complete turret of later BTR-80 (8 x 8) APC.
BTR-70 MBP, artillery command vehicle.
BTR-70MS, communications vehicle.

STATUS
Production complete. In service with Armenia, Azerbaijan, Bangladesh, Belarus, Bosnia, Estonia, Georgia, Kazakhstan, Krygyzstan, Macedonia, Moldova, Nepal, Pakistan, Romania, Russia, Sierra Leone, Tajikistan, Turkmenistan, Ukraine and Uzbekistan.

MANUFACTURER
Gorkiy Automobile Plant, Gorkiy, Russia.

KEY RECOGNITION FEATURES
- Similar in appearance to BTR-60PB but with small door in lower part of hull between second and third road wheels, trim vane folds back onto glacis plate (on BTR-60 it folds under nose), commander's hatch front right is slightly domed, waterjet opening in hull rear has two-piece cover with hinge at top. BTR-80 also has different hull rear

- Commander and driver sit front, turret on roof in line with second road wheel, horizontal hull top which slopes down at far rear, exhaust pipe each side of hull at rear

- Four large rubber-tyred road wheels each side with slightly larger gap between second and third

***Right:* BTR-70 (8 x 8) (Michael Jerchel)**

***Below:* BTR-70 (8 x 8)**

BTR-60PB APC (Russia)

Above: BTR-60PB (8 x 8) (Richard Stickland)

SPECIFICATIONS

Crew:	2 + 14
Configuration:	8 x 8
Armament:	1 x 14.5mm MG (main), 1 x 7.62mm MG (coaxial)
Ammunition:	500 x 14.5mm, 2,000 x 7.62mm
Length:	7.56m
Width:	2.835m
Height:	2.31m (turret top), 2.055m (hull top)
Ground clearance:	0.475m
Wheelbase:	1.35m + 1.525m + 1.35m
Weight, combat:	10,300kg
Power-to-weight ratio:	17.47hp/tonne
Engines:	2 x GAZ-49B 6-cylinder in-line water-cooled petrol developing 90hp at 3,400rpm each
Maximum road speed:	80km/hr
Maximum water speed:	10km/hr
Maximum road range:	500km
Fuel capacity:	290 lit
Fording:	Amphibious
Vertical obstacle:	0.4m
Trench:	2m
Gradient:	60%
Side slope:	40%
Armour:	7mm (max turret), 9mm (max hull)
Armour type:	Steel
NBC system:	Yes
Night vision equipment:	Yes (infra-red for commander and driver)

DEVELOPMENT

BTR-60P series 8 x 8s were developed in the late 1950s to replace BTR-152 (6 x 6) and were first seen in public in 1961. Throughout the 1960s it was continuously improved, final production model being BTR-60PB. It was replaced in production by the similar BTR-70 (8 x 8).

All members of BTR-60P series are fully amphibious, propelled by a single waterjet mounted at hull rear, have a 4,500kg capacity front-mounted winch, powered steering on front four wheels and central tyre pressure regulation system. BTR-60PB has fully enclosed troop compartment on top of which is a one-man turret almost identical to the BRDM-2 (4 x 4) amphibious scout car's. Turret has one 14.5mm

KPVT MG with 7.62mm PKT MG mounted coaxial to right, both have manual elevation from -5° to +30°, turret traverse through 360°.

VARIANTS

BTR-60P, first production model with open roof, has one to three 7.62mm MGs or 1 x 12.7mm and 2 x 7.62mm MGs.
BTR-60PA, second production model with fully enclosed troop compartment, first model with NBC system, roof-mounted 7.62mm MG.
BTR-60PB has 14.5mm/7.62mm turret of BRDM-2 and OT-64C(1).
BTR-60PBK, command version of BTR-60PB.
BTR-60 1V18, artillery observation post vehicle.
BTR-60 1V19, fire direction centre vehicle.
BTR-60 communications are numerous and normally have an R or E designation, eg BTR-60-R-409BM.
BTR-60AVS, command post vehicle.
BTR-60PAU, artillery communications vehicle.
BTR-60PU-12M, air defence command post vehicle.
BTR-60 VVS, command post vehicle.
BTR-60 ACVR M1979(2), used by towed artillery units.
BTR-60PU command vehicle.
BTR-60PU-12 command vehicle is BTR-60PA with large stowage box on right side of hull, generator and telescopic mast.
BTR-60 ACRV, artillery command and reconnaissance vehicle.

KEY RECOGNITION FEATURES

- Four road wheels each side with slightly larger gap between second and third
- Well-sloped flat top turret on forward part of roof above second wheel station, square side door above second and third axle
- Blunt nose with engine at far rear and exhaust pipe on each side at 45°

BTR-60MS radio vehicle has High Ball (NATO code name) telescopic antenna.
BTR-60PB forward air control vehicle.

STATUS

Production complete. In service with Algeria, Angola, Armenia, Azerbaijan, Belarus, Botswana, Bulgaria, Cambodia, Congo, Cuba, Djibouti, Eritrea, Estonia, Ethiopia, Finland, Guinea, Guinea-Bissau, India, Iran, North Korea, Laos, Libya, Lithuania, Macedonia, Mali, Moldova, Mongolia, Mozambique, Namibia, Nicaragua, Peru, Romania (qv TAB-72), Russia, Serbia and Montenegro, Somalia, Syria, Tajikistan, Turkey, Turkmenistan, Uganda, Ukraine, Vietnam, Yemen and Zambia.

MANUFACTURER

Gorkiy Automobile Plant, Gorkiy, Russia.

Right: BTR-60PU-12 command post vehicle

OMC Rooikat Armoured Car (South Africa)

Above: 76mm Rooikat armoured car

SPECIFICATIONS

Crew:	4
Configuration:	8 x 8
Armament:	1 x 76mm, 1 x 7.62mm MG (coaxial), 1 x 7.62mm MG (anti-aircraft), 2 x 4 smoke grenade dischargers
Ammunition:	48 x 76mm, 3,600 x 7.62mm
Length with gun:	8.2m
Length hull:	7.09m
Width:	2.9m
Height:	2.8m
Ground clearance:	0.4m
Wheelbase:	1.55m + 2.032m + 1.625m
Weight, combat:	28,000kg
Power-to-weight ratio:	20.11hp/tonne
Engine:	V-10 water-cooled diesel developing 563hp
Maximum road speed:	120km/hr
Range:	1,000km
Fuel capacity:	540 lit
Fording:	1.5m
Vertical obstacle:	1m
Trench:	2m (crawl speed), 1m (60km/hr)
Gradient:	70%
Side slope:	30%
Armour:	Classified
Armour type:	Steel
NBC system:	Yes (BC only)
Night vision equipment:	Yes (passive)

DEVELOPMENT

The first production vehicles were completed in 1989 and the first unit was equipped with Rooikats in 1990. The turret is made by Denel Ordnance with OMC being the overall prime contractor and responsible for the chassis and systems integration. As a result of mergers and acquisitions in late 2004 OMC became BAE Systems Land Systems OMC.

The driver is seated at the front of the hull, turret in the centre and the powerpack at the rear. The commander and gunner are seated on the right of the turret with the loader on the left. The commander is provided with a raised cupola

for improved all-round observation.

The stabilised 76mm gun fires APFSDS-T and HE-T rounds and has an elevation of +20° and a depression of -10°, with turret traverse being a full 360°. Turret traverse and weapon elevation/depression is all-electric with manual controls for emergency use. The Rooikat has a computerised fire control system fitted as standard. The gunner's day/night sight incorporates a laser rangefinder and the commander has a roof-mounted periscopic day sight.

The driver can select 8 x 8 or 8 x 4 drive with steering being power assisted on the front four wheels and if required the vehicle can lay its own smoke screen by injecting diesel fuel into the exhaust. A fire detection suppression system is fitted as standard.

For trials purposes the chassis has been fitted with various other turrets, including one with four long range anti-tank guided missiles.

KEY RECOGNITION FEATURES

- Almost horizontal glacis plate with driver's hatch in upper part in centre, horizontal hull top with raised engine compartment at the rear, hull rear vertical

- Turret is centre of vehicle with flat front and sides that slope slightly inwards. Long barrelled 76mm gun has thermal sleeve and fume extractor and overhangs front of vehicle

- Four large road wheels either side with larger gap between second and third road wheels, upper part of hull slopes slightly inwards, hull escape hatch in either side of hull side between second and third road wheels

VARIANTS

105mm, prototypes of a 105mm version firing NATO standard ammunition have been built. This can be fitted with various types of fire control system to meet the users specific operational requirements.

STATUS

Production complete. In service with the South African Army.

MANUFACTURER

BAE Systems Land Systems OMC, Boksburg, Transvaal, South Africa.

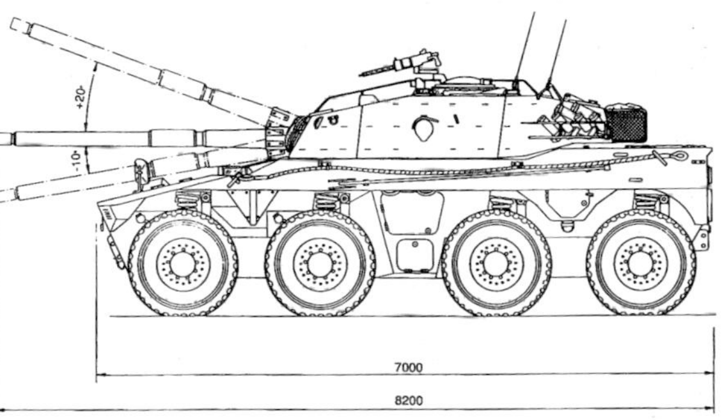

Above right: 76mm Rooikat armoured car

Right: 76mm Rooikat armoured car

Guardian Armoured Personnel Carrier (Ukraine)

Above: Guardian APC

SPECIFICATIONS

Crew:	3 + 6
Configuration:	8 x 8
Armament:	1 x 30mm cannon, 1 x 30mm grenade launcher, 1 x 7.62mm, or 12.7mm MG (co-axial), 2 x Spandrel ATGW
Ammunition:	350 x 30mm, 29 x 30mm grenade, 2,000 x 7.62mm
Length:	7.65m
Width:	2.90m
Height:	2.86m
Ground clearance:	0.47m
Weight, combat:	16,400kg
Weight, empty:	15,400kg
Power-to-weight ratio:	19.87hp/tonne
Engine:	Deutz BF6M1015 air cooled diesel developing 326hp
Maximum road speed:	100km/h
Maximum water speed:	9km/h
Maximum road range:	600–800km
Fuel capacity:	300 lit
Fording:	Amphibious
Vertical obstacle:	0.5m
Trench:	2m
Gradient:	60%
Side slope:	40%
Armour:	Classified
Armour type:	Steel
NBC system:	Yes
Night vision equipment:	Yes

DEVELOPMENT

In the mid-1990s the Ukraine developed and manufactured a copy of the Russian BTR-80 (8 x 8) amphibious APC under the designation of the BTR-94. This was fitted with a locally developed turret armed with twin 23mm cannon and a 7.62mm coaxial machine gun. As far as it is known the BTR-94 was developed for the export market with Jordan taking delivery of a total of 50 vehicles. These were transferred to Iraq in 2004.

The BTR-94 was followed by the Guardian APC which is also referred to as the BTR-3U and/or BTR-3E and was developed in conjunction with ADCOM Group International of the UAE.

Guardian is similar in layout to the BTR-80 with the commander and driver at the front, fighting compartment in the centre and the powerpack at the rear. The major difference is that the roof line to the rear of the commander's

and driver's position has been raised for greater internal volume which has increased the overall height of the vehicle and its weight.

In addition to the roof hatches, the crew can also enter the vehicle via the doors in the sides of the vehicle. The upper part contains a firing port and vision device while the lower part folds down to form a step.

A variety of weapon systems can be fitted including the locally developed one person Shakval unified battlefield module armed with a 30mm KBA-3 cannon, 7.62mm PKT or 12.7mm coaxial machine gun, 30mm AGS-17 automatic grenade launcher and two anti-tank guided weapons mounted externally on the right side. The turret is also fitted with six electrically-operated 81mm smoke grenade launchers. Turret traverse and weapon elevation is powered with the latter being from -6° to +75°.

Guardian is fully amphibious being propelled in the water by a single water jet mounted at the hull rear. Before entering the water a trim vane is erected at the front of the hull and bilge pumps are activated. Standard equipment includes a central tyre pressure regulation system and powered steering on the front four wheels.

KEY RECOGNITION FEATURES

- Similar in appearance to Russian BTR-70/ BTR-80 (8 x 8) APC with four large road wheels either side with a slightly larger gap between the second and third road wheel stations. Guardian has a distinct raised roof line to rear of driver's and commander's position at front of vehicle. Variety of weapon stations can be mounted on roof

- Blunt nose with trim vane folded on top with large windows for driver and commander which can be covered by flaps hinged at the top. Engine compartment at rear of hull with large horizontal exhaust pipes on right side of hull and stowage boxes on left

- In addition to roof hatches there is an entrance door between the second and third road wheel stations either side

VARIANTS

Guardian can be fitted with a wide range of weapon stations apart from the locally developed Shakval unified battlefield module previously mentioned. An ARV model has been developed.

STATUS

Production as required. In service with the United Arab Emirates.

MANUFACTURER

Malyshev Plant, Kiev, Ukraine.

Above right: Guardian ARV

Right: Guardian APC

SELF-PROPELLED GUNS

NORINCO 155mm PLZ45 self-propelled gun (China)

Above: NORINCO 155mm PLZ45 self-propelled gun

SPECIFICATIONS

Crew:	5
Armament:	1 x 155mm howitzer, 1 x 12.7mm anti-aircraft MG
Ammunition:	30 x 155mm, 400 x 12.7mm
Length gun forwards:	10.15m
Length hull:	6.1m
Width without skirts:	3.23m
Height with AA MG:	3.417m
Ground clearance:	0.45m
Weight, combat:	33,000kg
Weight, empty:	29,000kg (estimate)
Power-to-weight ratio:	16.40hp/tonne
Ground pressure:	Not available
Engine:	Deutz air cooled diesel developing 525hp
Maximum road speed:	56km/h
Maximum road range:	450km
Fuel capacity:	Not available
Fording:	1.2m
Vertical obstacle:	0.7m
Trench:	2.7m
Gradient:	58%
Side slope:	47%
Armour:	Classified
Armour type:	Steel
NBC system:	Yes
Night vision equipment:	Yes (driver)

DEVELOPMENT

The 155mm/45 calibre PLZ45 self-propelled howitzer was developed by NORINCO (China North

Industries Corporation) in the late 1980s and was shown for the first time in public in 1988. In many respects it is very similar to the United States M109 series of 155mm self-propelled howitzers although the PLZ45 is slightly heavier and has a longer 155mm/45 calibre ordnance.

The layout of the PLZ45 is similar to the M109 with the driver being seated at the front of the vehicle on the left side with the engine compartment to his right with the remainder of the chassis being taken up by the fighting compartment.

The fully enclosed turret is mounted at the rear of the chassis and can be traversed through a full 360°, the 155mm/45 calibre ordnance can be elevated from -3° to +72°. Firing an Extended Range Full Bore - Base Bleed (ERFB-BB) projectile a maximum range of 39km can be achieved.

A 12.7mm machine gun is mounted on the turret roof for air defence purposes and when travelling the 155mm ordnance is in a travel lock pivoted at the hull front.

Standard equipment includes an auxiliary power unit, NBC system, explosion detection and suppression system, fire detection and suppression system, muzzle velocity measuring system, inertial direction finder and a gun display unit.

KEY RECOGNITION FEATURES

- Hull has vertical sides with glacis plate sloping up to horizontal hull top which extends to hull rear which is vertical with no spades

- Large turret mounted at hull rear with vertical sides and rear, sides of turret slope towards front, no turret bustle. 155mm barrel has muzzle brake and fuze extractor

- Suspension either side has six road wheels with gap between first and second/second and third road wheels, drive sprocket at front, idler rear and three track-return rollers

VARIANTS

The only known variant is an ammunition resupply vehicle which has a similar chassis but is fitted with a raised superstructure at the rear and a hydraulic crane is mounted on the hull front.

STATUS

Production as required. In service with China and Kuwait.

MANUFACTURER

Chinese state factories (marketed by NORINCO).

Below: NORINCO 155mm PLZ45 self-propelled gun in travelling order

NORINCO 152mm Type 83 self-propelled gun (China)

Above: 152mm Type 83

SPECIFICATIONS

Crew:	5
Armament:	1 x 152mm, 1 x 12.7mm MG (AA)
Ammunition:	30 x 152mm, 650 x 12.7mm
Length gun forwards:	7.005m
Length hull:	6.405m
Width:	3.236m
Height with AA MG:	3.502m
Height turret top:	2.682m
Ground clearance:	0.45m
Weight, combat:	30,000kg
Power-to-weight ratio:	17.33hp/tonne
Ground pressure:	0.68kg/cm²
Engine:	Deutz Type 12150L diesel developing 520hp
Maximum road speed:	55km/hr
Maximum road range:	450km
Fuel capacity:	885 lit
Fording:	1.3m
Vertical obstacle:	0.7m
Trench:	2.50m
Gradient:	60%
Side slope:	40%
Armour:	10mm (maximum) (estimate)
Armour type:	Steel
NBC system:	Not known
Night vision equipment:	Yes (infra-red for driver)

DEVELOPMENT

The 152mm Type 83 was first seen in public in 1984 and Is similar to Russian 152mm self-propelled gun/howitzer M-1973 (2S3) which entered service in the early 1970s.

Driver sits front left with powerpack to his right and whole of rear occupied by large turret. Turret has hatches in roof and large forward-opening door in each side. The Type 83 ordnance is based on Type 66 152mm towed weapon and fires HE projectile to maximum range of 17,230m.

Turret traverses 360° and ordnance elevates from -5° to +63°. Semi-automatic loading device achieves rate of fire of four rounds a minute. In addition to 12.7mm MG mounted on turret roof for air defence, 7.62mm MG and Type 40 rocket launcher are carried internally.

VARIANTS

Trench digger, chassis of Type 83 is used as a basis for a trench digging machine.
425mm mine-clearing rocket launcher, based on Type 83 chassis, carries two Type 762 mine clearing rockets.
130mm self-propelled gun, for trials purposes a Type 83 has had its 155mm ordnance replaced by a 130mm gun used in the 130mm Type 59 towed artillery system.
120mm self-propelled anti-tank gun PTZ 89/ Type 89, uses hull and turret of 152mm Type 83.

STATUS

Production complete. In service with Chinese Army.

MANUFACTURER

Chinese state arsenals (marketed by NORINCO).

KEY RECOGNITION FEATURES

- Well-sloped glacis plate with driver left and louvres right, horizontal hull top with vertical hull rear and large door opening right

- Large turret mounted rear with vertical sides and rear, long 152mm ordnance with large double baffle muzzle brake and fume extractor, 12.7mm AA MG on right side of roof

- Suspension each side has six road wheels with distinct gap between first/second, third/fourth and fifth/sixth, drive sprocket front, idler rear, three track-return rollers, no skirts

Below: 152mm Type 83

NORINCO Type 85 122mm self-propelled gun (China)

SPECIFICATIONS

Crew:	6
Armament:	1 x 122mm howitzer
Ammunition:	40 x 122mm
Length gun forwards:	6.663m
Length hull:	6.125m
Width:	3.068m
Height:	2.85m (overall)
Ground clearance:	0.46m
Weight, combat:	16,500kg
Power-to-weight ratio:	19.4hp/tonne
Ground pressure:	0.67kg/cm^2
Engine:	Deutz Type BF8L413F air cooled diesel developing 320hp
Maximum road speed:	60km/h
Range:	500km
Fuel capacity:	450 lit
Fording:	Amphibious
Vertical obstacle:	0.60m
Trench:	2.2m
Gradient:	53%
Side slope:	40%
Armour:	Classified
Armour type:	Steel
NBC system:	No
Night vision equipment:	Optional

DEVELOPMENT

The NORINCO 122mm self-propelled howitzer Type 85 is essentially the chassis of the Type 85 APC (or YW 531H as it is also referred to) fitted with the complete ordnance, elevating/traverse mechanism of the Chinese equivalent of the Russian 122mm D-30 towed howitzer.

This 122mm weapon has an elevation of +70°, depression of -5° with traverse being 22.5° left and right. Firing a standard HE projectile a maximum range of 15,300m can be achieved; while firing an Extended Range Full Bore - Base Bleed projectile a maximum range of 21,000m is achieved.

The driver and commander are seated front left with the powerpack to the right with the weapon mounted at the rear. For amphibious operations an inflatable pontoon is fitted either side of the hull and held in position by hoops, the vehicle is then propelled in the water by its tracks at a maximum speed of 6km/h.

VARIANTS
None. More recently this system has been offered mounted on the chassis of the latest Type 90 full tracked APC chassis.

STATUS
Production complete. In service with China.

MANUFACTURER
Chinese state factories (marketed by NORINCO).

KEY RECOGNITION FEATURES

- Nose slopes back under hull with well-sloped glacis plate leading up to horizontal hull top which extends to the rear. Hull rear vertical with single door and stowage box either side
- 122mm howitzer mounted on top at rear with open roof, 122mm ordnance extends just over front of hull and has distinctive multi-baffle muzzle brake
- Suspension either side consists of five road wheels, drive sprocket front, idler rear and track-return rollers. Upper part of suspension covered by skirts. Upper part of hull slopes slightly inwards

***Left:* Type 85 122mm SP gun**

***Below:* Type 85 122mm SP gun**

NORINCO Type 70-1 122mm self-propelled gun
(China)

Left: 122mm Type 85 self-propelled gun (Christopher F Foss)

SPECIFICATIONS

Crew:	7 (maximum)
Armament:	1 x 122mm howitzer, 1 x 7.62mm MG
Ammunition:	40 x 122mm, 1,000 x 7.62mm
Length:	5.654m
Width:	3.07m
Height:	2.729m (top of gun), 1.91m (top of hull)
Ground clearance:	0.45m
Weight, combat:	15,400kg
Power-to-weight ratio:	16.88hp/tonne
Ground pressure:	0.6kg/cm^2
Engine:	Model 6150L 6-cylinder in-line water-cooled diesel developing 260hp at 2,000rpm
Maximum road speed:	56km/hr
Maximum road range:	500km
Fording:	1.5m
Vertical obstacle:	0.6m
Trench:	2.0m
Gradient:	60%
Side slope:	30%
Armour:	12mm (maximum)
Armour type:	Steel
NBC system:	None
Night vision equipment:	Yes (driver only, infra-red)

DEVELOPMENT

The first Chinese 122mm self-propelled gun was the Type 70 which was based on the Type 63-1 APC with four road wheels on either side. This was followed by the 122mm Type 70-1 series which have a longer chassis with five road wheel stations on either side.

The Type 70 is armed with a Chinese version of the Russian M1938 (M-30) and has short barrel with no muzzle brake and does not overhang front of vehicle. Type 70-1 retains its shield but has no protection to sides, rear or top for gun crew. 122mm howitzer has traverse of 22.5° left and right with elevation from -2.5 to +63°.

The 122mm howitzer fires separate loading ammunition including high explosive, smoke and illuminating to maximum range of 11,800m. A 7.62mm Type 67 MG, a copy of the Russian RP-46, is carried internally for both ground and anti-aircraft roles.

VARIANTS

122mm SPH Type 85 – This is based on the Type 85 APC chassis with six road wheels either side, drive sprocket at the front and idler at the rear with upper part of suspension covered by a skirt. Mounted over the rear part of the hull is the Chinese version of the Russian 122mm D-30 howitzer. This barrel has a slotted muzzle brake that overhangs the front of the vehicle.
122mm SPH Type 89 – This is similar in some

respects to the Russian 122mm 2S1 and has a new hull with six rubber tyred road wheels, drive sprocket at the front and idler at the rear. There are no return rollers. The fully enclosed turret is mounted at the rear and the barrel has a fume extractor and a muzzle brake.

Maximum range depends on ammuition/charge combination but the standard high explosive projectile has a maximum range of 15,300m while the Extended Range Full Bore – Base Bleed projectile has a maximum range of 21,000m. Mounted on the roof is a 12.7mm machine gun and there are banks of four electrically-operated smoke grenade launchers mounted on either side of the turret.

KEY RECOGNITION FEATURES

- 122mm howitzer mounted rear of hull in open mount, can be fully enclosed by tarpaulin cover

- Chassis similar to Type 531 (YW 531) APC but with additional road wheel each side

- Suspension either side has five road wheels, drive sprocket front, idler rear, three track-return rollers, upper part of track covered by skirts

STATUS

Production complete. In service with Chinese Army.

MANUFACTURER

Chinese state factories (marketed by NORINCO).

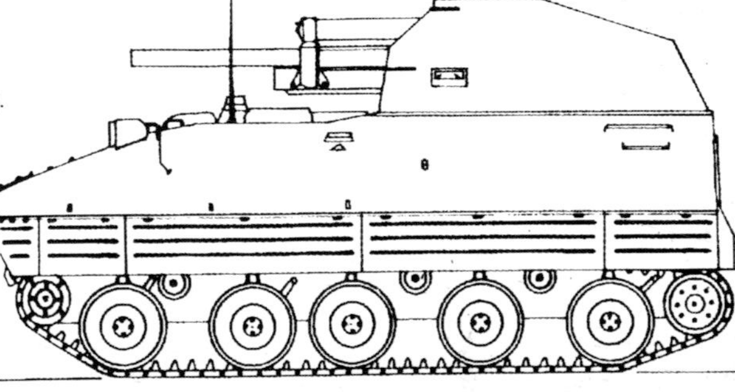

Right: 122mm Type 70-1 SPG

Below: Latest Chinese 122mm Type 89 series

ZTS Dana 152mm self-propelled gun

(Former Czechoslovakia)

Above: Zuzana 155mm

SPECIFICATIONS

Crew:	5
Configuration:	8 x 8
Armament:	1 x 152mm howitzer, 1 x 12.7mm MG
Ammunition:	60 x 152mm
Length gun forward:	11.156m
Length hull:	8.87m
Width overall:	3.00m
Height:	2.85m (turret roof)
Wheelbase:	1.65m + 3.07m + 1.45m
Weight, combat:	29,250kg
Power-to-weight ratio:	13.74hp/tonne
Engine:	Tatra 2-939-34 air-cooled diesel developing 345hp
Maximum road speed:	80km/hr
Maximum road range:	740km
Fording:	1.4m
Gradient:	60%
Side slope:	30%
Armour:	12.7mm maximum (estimated)
NBC system:	Yes
Night vision equipment:	Yes (driver only)

DEVELOPMENT

The Dana 152mm was developed for the former Czechoslovak Army in the 1970s and was first seen in public in 1980. Its correct Czechoslovak designation is Vzor 77 self-propelled howitzer Dana. The chassis is based on a Tatra 815 (8 x 8) truck with extensive modifications including fully enclosed armoured cab at front, fully enclosed armoured turret in centre and engine moved to rear. Steering is power-assisted on front four wheels with central tyre pressure regulation system fitted as standard, for driver to adjust tyre pressure while travelling.

The 152mm howitzer elevates from -4° to +70°, turret traverses 225° left and right. Turret traverse and weapon elevation hydraulic with manual controls for emergency. Three hydraulic jacks are lowered to ground before firing, one at rear and one each side between second/third road wheels. Ordnance has single baffle muzzle brake but no fume extractor, with load assist device fitted as standard. The range of the 152mm howitzer is 18,700m using standard ammunition. Rate of fire is 3 rounds per minute for a period of 30 minutes. Ammunition includes APHE, HE, illuminating and smoke.

VARIANTS

155mm Zuzana, latest model with many improvements including installation of 155mm/45 calibre ordnance which, when firing Extended Range Full Bore – Base Bleed projectiles, enables a range of 39,600m to be achieved.

A new 155mm/52 calibre system has been developed and a similar armoured 8 x 8 chassis is used for other roles.

KEY RECOGNITION FEATURES

- Cab front, turret centre, engine rear
- Eight road wheels, four front and four rear
- Turret higher than rest of vehicle with 152mm howitzer extending well over front of cab

STATUS

Production as required.
In service with Cyprus (Zuzana), Czech Republic (Dana), Libya (Dana), Poland (Dana) and Slovakia (Dana and Zuzana).

MANUFACTURER

ZTS Dubnica nad Vahom, Slovakia.

Right: Dana 152mm in firing position

Below: Zuzana 155mm

United Defense SP122 self-propelled gun (Egypt/USA)

SPECIFICATIONS

Crew:	5
Armament:	1 x 122mm howitzer, 1 x 12.7mm machine gun
Ammunition:	85 x 122mm, 500 x 12.7mm
Length gun forward:	6.957m
Width:	3.15m
Height:	2.821m without AA machine gun
Ground clearance:	0.46m
Weight, combat:	23,182kg
Power-to-weight ratio:	17.47hp/tonne
Engine:	Detroit Diesel model 8V-71T turbocharged 8-cylinder diesel developing 405 hp at 2,350 rpm
Maximum road speed:	56.3km/h
Maximum road range:	349km
Fuel capacity:	511 lit
Fording:	1.7m
Vertical obstacle:	0.61m
Trench:	1.83m
Gradient:	60%
Side slope:	40%
Armour:	Classified

KEY RECOGNITION FEATURES

- Hull has vertical sides with glacis plate sloping up to horizontal hull top that extends halfway to rear. On this has been mounted a new superstructure with vertical sides and curved front
- Mounted in front of superstructure is 122mm barrel with slotted muzzle brake, 12.7mm machine gun on turret roof
- Suspension on either side conists of seven road wheels with drive sprocket front, idler rear, no track-return rollers

Left: SP122 122mm self-propelled gun

Armour type:	Aluminium
NBC system:	No
Night vision equipment:	No

DEVELOPMENT

The SP122 was developed for the Egyptian Army by the now United Defense LP (previously BMY Combat Systems) and, following trials with two competing designs, was selected for service. Some 124 systems were delivered to Egypt in three batches with final deliveries being made in 2000.

The SP122 combines the chassis of the M109 SPG/M992 FAASV with a new, fully enclosed superstructure at the rear. In front of this is the Russian D-30 122mm gun/howitzer which has been manufactured under licence in Egypt for many years by the Abu Zaabal Engineering Industries Company.

The driver is seated front left, with the engine compartment to his right and the fighting compartment extending to the rear. The 122mm D-30 has manual traverse of up to 30° right or left and elevation from -5° to +70°. Maximum range is 15,300m firing standard HE. Longer ranges are obtainable with rocket-assisted projectiles.

VARIANTS

None.

STATUS

Production complete. In service with Eygptian Army only.

MANUFACTURER

United Defense LP, York, Pennsylvania, US.

GIAT Industries 155mm GCT self-propelled gun (France)

Above: GCT 155mm (Pierre Touzin)

SPECIFICATIONS

Crew:	4
Armament:	1 x 155mm gun, 1 x 7.62mm or 12.7mm AA MG, 2 x 2 smoke grenade dischargers
Ammunition:	42 x 155mm, 2,050 x 7.62mm or 800 x 12.7mm
Length gun forwards:	10.25m
Length hull:	6.7m
Width:	3.15m
Height:	3.25m (turret top)
Ground clearance:	0.42m
Weight, combat:	42,000kg
Weight, empty:	38,000kg
Power-to-weight ratio:	17.14hp/tonne
Engine:	Hispano-Suiza HS 110 12-cylinder water-cooled supercharged multi-fuel developing 720hp at 2,000rpm
Maximum road speed:	60km/hr
Maximum road range:	450km
Fuel capacity:	970 lit
Fording:	2.1m
Vertical obstacle:	0.93m (forwards), 0.48m (reverse)
Trench:	1.9m
Gradient:	60%
Side slope:	30%
Armour:	20mm max (estimate)
Armour type:	Steel
NBC system:	Yes
Night vision equipment:	Yes (driver only)

DEVELOPMENT

The 155mm GCT (Grande Cadence de Tir) was developed from 1969 to replace the 105mm Mk 61 and 155mm Mk F3 self-propelled guns in service with French Army. Production commenced at GIAT facility, Roanne, in 1977 and first production vehicles completed in 1978 for Saudi Arabia. A total of 241 was built with production now complete.

The 155mm gun has powered elevation from -4° to +66° with turret traverse powered through 360°. The 155mm gun is fed by a fully automatic loader that enables rate of fire of eight rounds a minute although it can also be loaded manually, in which case rate of fire is reduced to three rounds a minute. Maximum range using standard 155mm HE M107 projectile is 18,000m although other types of projectile can be fired including illuminating, smoke, extended range and anti-tank (mine).

VARIANTS

No variants although various options in fire-control system are available. For trials purposes the GCT turret has been fitted onto the chassis of the Russian T-72 MBT. A 155mm/52 calibre version has been developed to the prototype stage. The current Hispano-Suiza engine is now being replaced by a Renault E9 diesel engine.

STATUS

Production complete. In service with France, Kuwait (reserve) and Saudi Arabia.

MANUFACTURER

GIAT Industries, Roanne, France.

KEY RECOGNITION FEATURES

- Large fully enclosed flat-sided turret mounted centre of chassis, 155mm gun with double baffle muzzle brake overhanging front of vehicle

- Chassis identical to AMX-30 MBT's with five road wheels either side, idler front, drive sprocket rear, four track-return rollers. The upper part of the suspension is sometimes covered by a skirt

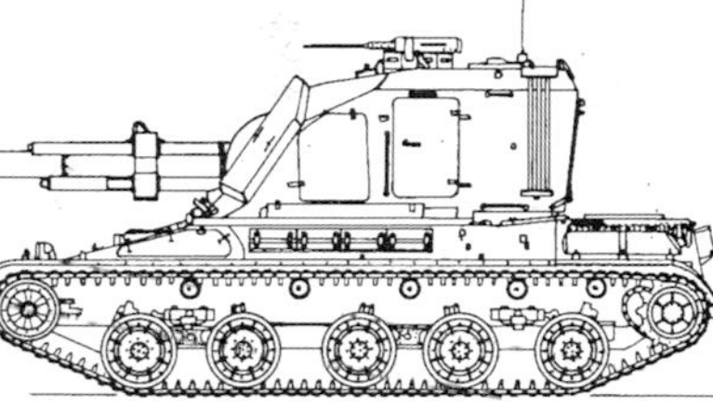

Above: GCT 155mm

Left: GCT 155mm turret on T-72 MBT chassis (Christopher F Foss)

Below: GCT 155mm (Pierre Touzin)

GIAT 155mm Mk F3 self-propelled gun (France)

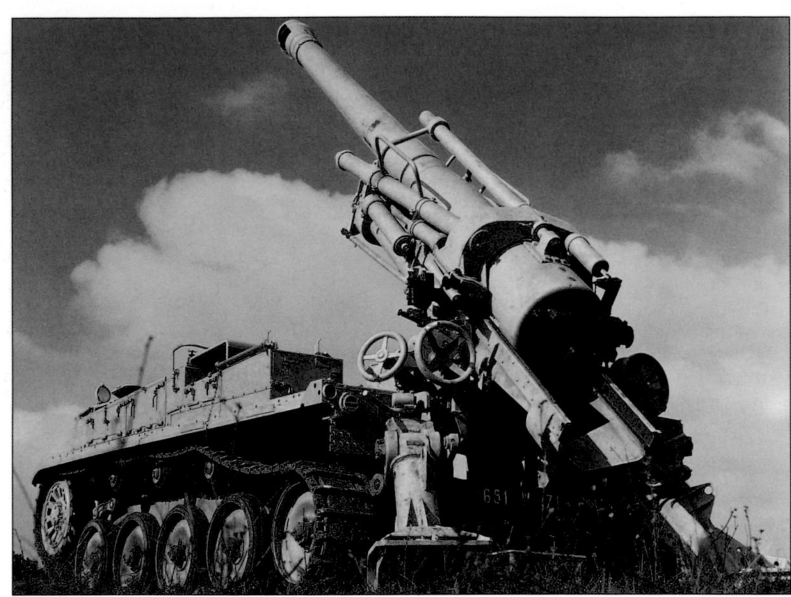

Above: 155mm Mk F3 from rear

SPECIFICATIONS

Crew:	2 (on gun)
Armament:	1 x 155mm gun
Ammunition:	None (on gun)
Length:	6.22m (excluding spades)
Width:	2.7m
Height, travelling:	2.085m
Ground clearance:	0.48m
Weight, combat:	17,400kg
Power-to-weight ratio:	14hp/tonne
Ground pressure:	0.84kg/cm^2
Engine:	SOFAM 8Gxb 8-cylinder water-cooled petrol developing 250hp at 3,200rpm (but see text)
Maximum road speed:	60km/hr
Maximum road range:	300km
Fuel capacity:	450 lit
Fording:	1m
Vertical obstacle:	0.6m (forwards), 0.4m (reverse)
Trench:	1.5m
Gradient:	40%
Side slope:	20%
Armour:	20mm (maximum)
Armour type:	Steel
NBC system:	No
Night vision equipment:	Yes (driver only)

DEVELOPMENT

The 155mm Mk F3 was developed in the 1950s based on AMX-13 light tank chassis. In French Army the system has now been replaced by 155mm GCT self-propelled gun. The 155mm gun is mounted at rear of chassis with no protection for crew from bad weather, NBC attack, small arms fire and shell splinters. Before coming into action two spades at rear of hull have to be released manually. The 155mm gun elevates to a maximum of 67°, with traverse 20° left and 30° right up to +50°, and 16° left and 30° right up to +67°. Elevation and traverse both manual. Firing a standard 155mm HE projectile maximum range is 20,047m. Other types of projectile include

illumination, smoke and rocket-assisted.

Original production models were built with SOFAM petrol engine, but can have Detroit Diesel Model 6V-53T 6-cylinder water-cooled diesel developing 280hp at 2,800rpm. This gives maximum road speed of 64km/hr with operating range increased from 300km to 400km. More recently Baudouin has offered its 6 F 11 SRY diesel developing 280hp at 3,200rpm for this and other members of AMX-13 family.

Other eight members of gun crew normally carried in 6 x 6 truck or AMX VCA tracked vehicle which carries 25 projectiles, 25 charges plus fuses.

VARIANTS

Apart from different engine options, there are no variants in service.

STATUS

Production complete. In service with Argentina, Chile, Cyprus, Ecuador, Kuwait, Morocco, Peru, Qatar, Sudan, United Arab Emirates and Venezuela.

KEY RECOGNITION FEATURES

- 155mm gun is fitted rear in unprotected mount and has barrel with double baffle muzzle brake that slightly overhangs front of vehicle. When travelling gun is locked 8° to right of centre line
- Chassis has five road wheels either side with last acting as idler, drive sprocket front and three track-return rollers
- Two large spades at rear of hull, one either side

MANUFACTURER

GIAT Industries, Roanne, France.

Below: 155mm Mk F3

GIAT Industries CAESAR 155mm self-propelled gun (France)

Above: GIAT Industries CAESAR 155mm (6 x 6) SPG in firing position (GIAT Industries)

SPECIFICATIONS

Crew:	5
Armament:	1 x 155mm gun
Ammunition:	18 x 155mm
Length:	9.95m
Width:	2.55m
Height:	3.65m
Ground clearance:	0.40m
Weight, combat:	17,400kg
Weight, empty:	15,900kg
Power-to-weight ratio:	13.63hp/tonne
Ground pressure:	Not available
Engine:	Mercedes-Benz LA 6-cylinder turbo charged diesel developing 240hp at 2,600rpm
Maximum road speed:	110km/h
Maximum road range:	600km
Fuel capacity:	200 lit
Fording:	1.20m
Vertical obstacle:	Not available
Trench:	Not available
Gradient:	60%
Side slope:	40%
Armour:	Classified
Armour type:	Steel
NBC system:	No
Night vision equipment:	No

DEVELOPMENT

The CAESAR 155mm (6 x 6) self-propelled gun was originally developed as a private venture by GIAT Industries with a technology demonstrator being shown for the first time in 1994.

This was followed by a pre-producton model and in late 2000 the French Delegation Generale pour l'Armement (DGA) awarded Giat Industries a contract for five pre-production systems for delivery to the French Army from 2002 through to 2003. These are being used for extensive trials. In mid-2004 the DGA placed a contract with GIAT Industries for 72 production systems which will be based on a new Renault Trucks Defense 6 x 6 chassis.

CAESAR essentially consists of a modified Mercedes-Benz UNIMOG U 2450 L (6 x 6) truck chassis fitted with a armoured crew cab at the

front. Mounted on the rear of the chassis is the complete upper mass of the Giat Industries 155mm/52 calibre TR towed artillery system. This can be elevated from -3° to +66° with a traverse of 17° left and 17° right under full power with manual controls being provided as a back up.

To provide a more stable firing platform a large space is hydraulically lowered to the ground before firing commences. An automatic projectile loader is fitted as standard and a computerised fire control is also installed.

Range of CAESAR depends on projectile and charge combination but is a maximum of 42,000m when firing an Extended Range Full Bore – Base Bleed projectile. Maximum rate of fire is quoted as six rounds a minute and a muzzle velocity measuring system is installed over the barrel and this feeds information to the on-board computer.

The chassis is fitted with a central tyre pressure regulation system that allows the driver to adjust the tyre pressure from within the cab when the vehicle is moving to suit the terrain being crossed. Power steering is also provided and it is fully airportable in a Lockheed Martin C-130 Hercules transport aircraft.

KEY RECOGNITION FEATURES

- Based on Mercedes-Benz 6 x 6 truck chassis with fully enclosed two door cab at the front with the front and sides sloping inwards

- Mounted at the rear is a 155mm/52 calibre ordnance that points to the front when in travelling configuration

- Either side are three rubber tyred road wheels, one under the forward control cab and two closer together at the rear. Large spade at the hull rear is retracted for travelling

VARIANTS

None.

STATUS

Five pre-production systems have been delivered to the French Army which has placed a production order for 72 units.

MANUFACTURER

GIAT Industries, Bourges, France.

Below: GIAT Industries CAESAR 155mm (6 x 6) SPG in travelling configuration (GIAT Industries)

Krauss-Maffei Wegmann 155mm PzH 2000 self-propelled gun (Germany)

Above: PzH 2000

SPECIFICATIONS

Crew:	5
Armament:	1 x 155mm, 1 x 7.62mm MG, 2 x 4 smoke grenades
Ammunition:	60 x 155mm, 1,000 x 7.62mm
Length gun forward:	11.669m
Length hull:	7.30m
Width:	3.58m
Height:	3.06m
Ground clearance:	0.44m
Weight, combat:	55,300kg
Power-to-weight ratio:	18hp/tonne
Engine:	MTU 881 diesel developing 1000hp
Maximum road speed:	60km/h
Maximum road range:	420km
Fuel capacity:	Not available
Fording:	Not available
Vertical obstacle:	1m
Trench:	3m
Gradient:	50%
Side slope:	25%
Armour:	Classified
Armour type:	Steel (see text)
NBC system:	Yes
Night vision equipment:	Yes

DEVELOPMENT

A consortium led by the then Wegmann was selected to continue development of the Panzerhaubitze 2000 155mm self-propelled artillery system for the German Army. It was accepted for service in 1995 and the initial order was for 185 vehicles. The now Krauss-Maffei Wegmann is the prime contractor, responsible for the turret and systems integration with Rheinmetall Landsysteme responsible for the complete chassis. First production systems were handed over in mid-1998.

The driver is seated at the front right with the powerpack to his left and the fighting compartment to his rear. The 155mm/52 calibre

gun elevates from -2.5° to +65° and the turret can traverse through 360°. An automatic loading system enables eight rounds to be fired in 60 seconds. The charges are loaded manually. Maximum range is 40km with assisted projectiles or 30km with conventional munitions.

The PzH 2000 can be fitted with explosive reactive armour on the upper hull and turret roof to protect it from top attack weapons.

VARIANTS

None.

STATUS

Production. In service with Germany and Greece and on order for Italy and Netherlands.

MANUFACTURER

Krauss-Maffei Wegmann GmbH, Kassel, Germany.

KEY RECOGNITION FEATURES

- Large chassis with well-sloped glacis plate, vertical sides and rear. Turret mounted at rear with long barrel mounted in turret front that overhangs vehicle. Barrel is fitted with fume extractor two-thirds back from the muzzle

- Turret overhangs rear, sides curve inwards to flat roof which is fitted with 7.62mm MG

- Suspension consists of seven road wheels with drive sprocket front and idler rear, upper part of suspension covered by wavy skirt

Below: PzH 2000

DIO Raad-2 155mm self-propelled gun (Iran)

Above: Raad-2 155mm SPG

SPECIFICATIONS

Crew:	5
Armament:	1 x 155mm, 1 x 12.7mm MG (anti-aircraft)
Ammunition:	30 x 155mm
Length, with armament:	9.14m
Length, chassis:	Not available
Width:	3.38m
Height:	2.60m (to turret roof), 3.467m (with AA MG
Ground clearance:	0.45m
Weight, combat:	36,000kg
Power-to-weight ratio:	23hp/tonne
Engine:	V-84MS diesel developing 840hp
Maximum road speed:	65km/h
Maximum road range:	450km
Fuel capacity:	Not available
Fording:	1.20m
Vertical obstacle:	0.8m
Trench:	2.4m
Gradient:	60%
Side slope:	30%
Armour:	Classified
Armour type:	Classified
NBC system:	Yes
Night vision equipment:	Optional

DEVELOPMENT

The Raad-2 155mm/39 calibre self-propelled gun has been developed by the Iranian Defence Industries Organisation, Armour Industries Group, Shahid Karimi Industrial Complex.

It was the second locally developed self-propelled artillery system to enter service with Iran with the first being the Raad-1 122mm system covered in a separate entry.

In many respects the DIO Raad-2 155mm self-propelled gun howitzer is very similar in appearance to the United Defense 155mm M109 series of self-propelled guns that are used in large numbers by Iran. The Raad-2 is however heavier and is fitted with a longer 155mm/39 calibre barrel.

Some of the automotive components of the Raad-2 are already in production in Iran for other applications. For example the road wheels and engine are from the T-72 tank and the SPAT 1200 transmission is from the upgraded T-54/T-55 tanks which have been in service with Iran for some years.

Layout is similar to the M109 with the driver's compartment front left and the powerpack front right which leaves the remainder of the chassis clear for the fighting compartment and turret which is at the rear of the vehicle.

Full enclosed turret has full 360° traverse with weapon elevation from -3° to +75° under full power control with manual back up being provided.

Maximum range depends on projectile/charge combination but firing a base bleed high explosive projectile a maximum range of 24,000m is claimed. When deployed in the firing position, two spades are lowered to the ground. These are positioned one either side of the large door in the hull rear.

VARIANTS

Raad-2M – This has a different powerpack consisting of a Ukrainian 5TDF water-cooled diesel developing 700hp. This version has a larger exhaust outlet positioned on the front right side of the hull. The exhaust outlet on the earlier Raad-2 is smaller and mounted lower.

KEY RECOGNITION FEATURES

- Chassis is very similar to US 155mm M109 with well-sloped glacis plate leading up to horizontal hull top that extends to the rear. Turret is mounted at rear with vertical front and sides. Forward parts of turret sides slope to the rear

- 155mm ordnance is mounted in forward part of the turret and appears to be similar to late production M109s with a double baffle muzzle brake and a fume extractor about two thirds of the way up the barrel. US type indirect fire sight hood in left side of the hull roof with 12.7mm AA MG on right side

- Chassis sides are vertical with suspension either side consisting of six dual rubber tyred road wheels with drive sprocket at front and idler at the rear. Upper part of suspension is covered by a skirt

STATUS

Production. In service with Iran.

MANUFACTURER

Defence Industries Organisation, Armour Industries Group, Shahid Karimi Industrial Complex, Iran.

Right: Raad-2 155mm SPG

DIO Raad-1 122mm self-propelled gun/howitzer (Iran)

SPECIFICATIONS

Crew:	4
Armament:	1 x 122mm, 1 x 12.7mm MG (anti-aircraft)
Ammunition:	35 x 122mm
Length:	6.50m
Width:	2.67m
Height:	3.00m
Ground clearance:	0.4m
Weight, combat:	17,500kg
Power-to-weight ratio:	18hp/tonne
Engine:	air cooled diesel developing 315hp
Maximum road speed:	65km/h
Maximum road range:	400km
Fuel capacity:	Not available
Fording:	Not available
Vertical obstacle:	0.8m
Trench:	2.3m
Gradient:	60%
Side slope:	30%
Armour:	Classified
Armour type:	Steel
NBC system:	Yes
Night vision equipment:	Optional

DEVELOPMENT

The Raad-1 122mm self-propelled gun/howitzer was developed by the Iranian Defence Industries Organisation, Armour Industries Group, Shahid Karimi Industrial Complex.

It was the first self-propelled artillery system to enter production in Iran and was followed by the Raad-2 155mm/39 calibre system that is covered in a separate entry. As far as it is known neither of these systems has been exported.

The chassis of the Raad-1 is a further

Below: Raad-1 122mm SPG

development of the Iranian Boraq armoured personnel carrier which is very similar to the Russian BMP-1 and its Chinese equivalent, the WZ-501.

The driver is seated front left with the powerpack to the right and the raised fighting compartment is to the immediate rear to provide greater internal volume.

Mounted on top of this is the complete turret of the Russian 122mm 2S1 self-propelled artillery system. The ordnance is fitted with a double baffle muzzle brake and and fume extractor. When travelling the ordnance is held in position by a travel lock located on the glacis plate forward of the driver's position and folded downwards when not required.

Turret traverse is a full 360° with weapon elevation from –3° to +72° with direct and indirect sights being fitted as standard. Maximum range depends on projectile/charge combination. Firing a conventional high explosive projectile maximum quoted range is stated to be 15,200m. Ammunition is identical to that used in the towed 122mm D-30 artillery system which has been manufactured in Iran for many years.

While the Boraq is fully amphibious being propelled in the water by its tracks, the overall weight of the Raad-2 may well limit its amphibious capabilities.

KEY RECOGNITION FEATURES

- Nose slopes back under hull with well-sloped ribbed glacis plate leading up to horizontal roof which extends mid-way along hull. Upper part of hull is raised with fully enclosed turret mounted above

- Turret has curved front with vertical sides that slope slightly inwards and bustle at rear. When travelling the 122mm ordnance is held in travel lock positioned on forward part of glacis plate

- Suspension either side consists of six US M113 type road wheels with drive sprocket at front and idler at the rear plus return rollers that are covered by a four part rubber skirt

VARIANTS

There are no known variants of the 122mm 2S1 although the design of the chassis allows it to be adopted for a wide range of other roles and missions.

There are a number of variants on the Boraq APC chassis including an ammunition resupply vehicle which could be used with the Raad-1 or 2 self-propelled artillery systems.

STATUS

Production. In service with Iran.

MANUFACTURER

Defence Industries Organisation, Armour Industries Group, Shahid Karimi Industrial Complex, Iran.

Soltam Systems L-33 155mm self-propelled gun (Israel)

Above: Soltam Systems L-33 155mm (IDF)

SPECIFICATIONS

Crew:	8
Armament:	1 x 155mm howitzer, 1 x 7.62mm AA MG
Ammunition:	60 x 155mm,
	1,000 x 7.62mm
Length gun forwards:	8.47m
Length hull:	6.47m
Width:	3.5m, 2.86m (over tracks)
Height:	3.45m
Ground clearance:	0.43m
Weight, combat:	41,500kg
Power-to-weight ratio:	10.08hp/tonne
Engine:	Cummins VT 8-460-Bi diesel developing 460hp at 2,600rpm
Maximum road speed:	38km/hr
Maximum road range:	260km
Fuel capacity:	820 lit
Fording:	0.9m
Vertical obstacle:	0.91m
Trench:	2.3m
Gradient:	60%
Side slope:	30%
Armour:	12–64mm
Armour type:	Steel
NBC system:	No
Night vision equipment:	Yes, driver only

DEVELOPMENT

The L-33 was developed in the 1960s by Soltam Systems to meet requirements of Israeli Army and is essentially a rebuilt Sherman tank chassis with original petrol engine replaced by a diesel and new fully enclosed superstructure. L-33 is same length as howitzer in calibres. It was first used operationally during 1973 Middle East conflict.

Soltam Systems L-33 is fitted with a modified version of the standard Soltam Systems 155mm M-68 gun/howitzer which is mounted well to rear. It has manual elevation from -4 to +52 and manual traverse of 30 left and right. When travelling, ordnance is held in travelling lock mounted on glacis plate.

The 155mm gun fires separate loading type ammunition including high explosive, smoke and illuminating, with maximum range of 20,000m with unassisted projectiles. Out of 60 rounds of ammunition carried 16 are for ready use.

OTHER ISRAELI SPGS

Romach is US 175mm M107.
Doher is US 155mm M109 series.
Slammer is local SPG on Merkava chassis (trials only).

VARIANTS

No known variants. Soltam Systems is now offering a conversion package to replace the 33 calibre barrel by a 39 calibre barrel which will fire an HE projectile to 24,000m.

STATUS

Production/conversion complete. In service with Israeli Army.

MANUFACTURER

Conversions by Soltam Systems, Haifa, Israel.

KEY RECOGNITION FEATURES

- High superstructure with vertical sides and rear. Glacis plate slopes at 45° then is vertical to roof

- 155mm howitzer has single baffle muzzle brake with fume extractor to rear, howitzer protrudes from gun compartment

- Superstructure overhangs chassis which has three bogies each with two road wheels, drive sprocket front, idler rear and three track-return rollers

Below: Soltam Systems L-33 155mm (IDF)

Oto Melara Palmaria 155mm self-propelled gun (Italy)

Above: Palmaria 155mm

SPECIFICATIONS

Crew:	5
Armament:	1 x 155mm howitzer, 1 x 7.62mm AA MG, 2 x 4 smoke grenade dischargers
Ammunition:	30 x 155mm, 1000 x 7.62mm
Length gun forward:	11.474m
Length hull:	7.265m
Width:	3.35m
Height:	2.874m (without AA MG)
Ground clearance:	0.4m
Weight, combat:	46,000kg
Weight, empty:	43,000kg
Power-to-weight ratio:	16.3hp/tonne
Engine:	MTU MB 837 Ea-500 4-stroke, turbocharged, 8-cylinder multi-fuel diesel developing 750hp
Maximum road speed:	60km/hr
Maximum road range cruising:	500km
Fuel capacity:	800 lit
Fording:	1.2m (without preparation), 4m (with preparation)
Vertical obstacle:	1m
Trench:	3m
Gradient:	60%
Side slope:	30%
Armour:	Classified
Armour type:	Hull steel, turret aluminium
NBC system:	Optional
Night vision equipment:	Optional

DEVELOPMENT

The Palmaria 155mm was developed as a private venture by Oto Melara specifically for export with first prototype completed in 1981 and first production vehicles the following year. It shares many automotive components with Oto Melara OF-40 MBT, also developed for export, and in service with United Arab Emirates.

Driver and auxiliary power unit are at front, turret centre, engine and transmission rear.

155mm howitzer has powered elevation from -5° to +70° with powered turret traverse through 360°. It fires HE projectile to maximum range of 24,700m, and other types including HE rocket-assisted, illuminating, and smoke. Palmaria fires one round per 15 seconds using automatic loader.

VARIANTS
No variants in service but its chassis has been fitted with twin 35mm ATAK turret and could be fitted with Oto Melara 76mm anti-aircraft/helicopter turret. Argentina ordered 25 turrets for installation on lengthened TAM tank chassis, with final deliveries during 1986/87.

STATUS
Production complete but can be resumed if required. In service with Libya and Nigeria, turret in service with Argentina on modified TAM chassis.

MANUFACTURER
Oto Melara, La Spezia, Italy.

KEY RECOGNITION FEATURES

- Large flat-sided turret mounted centre of hull with 155mm howitzer and double baffle muzzle brake and fume extractor

- When travelling, turret is normally traversed to rear and 155mm howitzer held in position by travelling lock at hull rear

- Driver at front, turret centre, engine and transmission rear. Suspension either side has seven road wheels, idler front, drive sprocket rear, track-return rollers. Upper part of suspension covered by skirts

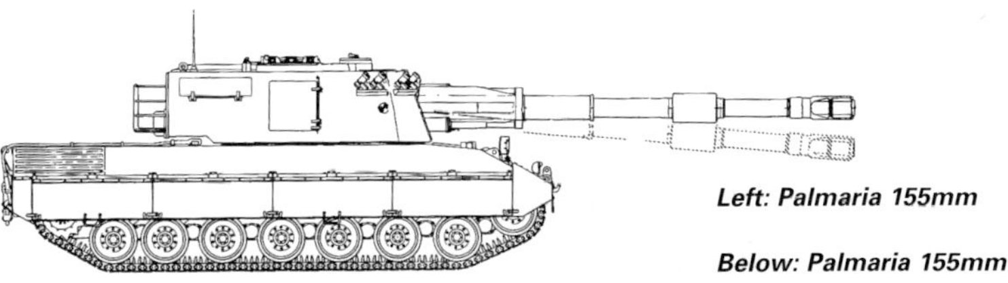

***Left:* Palmaria 155mm**

***Below:* Palmaria 155mm**

Mitsubishi Type 75 155mm self-propelled gun (Japan)

SPECIFICATIONS

Crew:	6
Armament:	1 x 155mm howitzer, 1 x 12.7mm AA MG
Ammunition:	28 x 155mm, 1,000 x 12.7mm
Length gun forwards:	7.79m
Length hull:	6.64m
Width:	3.09m
Height to turret roof:	2.545m
Ground clearance:	0.4m
Weight, combat:	25,300kg
Power-to-weight ratio:	17.78hp/tonne
Ground pressure:	0.64kg/cm^2
Engine:	Mitsubishi 6ZF 2-cycle 6-cylinder alr-cooled diesel developing 450hp at 2,200rpm
Maximum road speed:	47km/hr
Maximum road range:	300km
Fuel capacity:	650 lit
Fording:	1.3m
Vertical obstacle:	0.7m
Trench:	2.5m
Gradient:	60%
Side slope:	30%
Armour:	Classified
Armour type:	Aluminium
NBC system:	Yes
Night vision equipment:	Yes (driver only)

DEVELOPMENT

Developed from 1969 to meet requirements of Japanese Ground Self Defence Force with first prototypes completed in 1971–72 and accepted for service as 155mm Type 75 self-propelled howitzer in October 1975. A total of 201 production systems was built for the Japanese Ground Self Defence Force with flnal deliveries taking place in 1968.

Layout and appearance is similar to US 155mm M109A1/M109A2 with driver and engine compartment front and fully enclosed turret rear. The 155mm howitzer has powered elevation from -5° to +65°, turret traverse through 360°, and fires US HE projectile to range of 15,000m or Japanese HE projectile to maximum range of 19,000m. Other types of projectile include

illuminating and smoke. Semi-automatic loading system mounted in rear of turret allows 18 rounds to be fired in three minutes.

VARIANTS

There are no variants of the Type 75 155mm SPG. Japan also uses a small number of 105mm Type 74 SPH. The latest Japanese SPG is the 155mm Type 99 which has a 155mm/39 calibre ordnance based on that used in the towed FH-70 used in large numbers by the Japanese Ground Self Defence Force.

STATUS

Production complete. In service with Japanese Ground Self Defence Force.

MANUFACTURER

Mitsubishi Heavy Industries (hull and final assembly), Japan Iron Works/Nihon Seiko Jyo (gun and turret), Japan.

***Left:* Type 75 155mm (K Nogi)**

KEY RECOGNITION FEATURES

- Fully enclosed turret at far rear of hull with vertical sides and rear with chamfer between sides and turret roof

- 155mm howitzer has double baffle muzzle brake and fume extractor almost halfway down ordnance

- Suspension either side has six large road wheels with last road wheel acting as idler, drive sprocket front but no track-return rollers

***Below:* Type 75 155mm showing roof-mounted 12.7mm (M2) HB AA MG (Paul Beaver)**

HSW Krab 155mm self-propelled howitzer (Poland)

SPECIFICATIONS

Crew:	5
Armament:	1 x 155mm 1 x 12.7mm AA MG
Ammunition:	60 x 155mm
Length gun forward:	11.717m
Length hull:	Not available
Width:	3.48m
Height:	3.412m
Ground clearance:	0.44m
Weight, combat:	49,680kg
Weight, empty:	Not available
Ground pressure:	0.55kg/cm^2
Power-to-weight ratio:	16.86hp/tonne
Engine:	838hp diesel
Max road speed:	60km/h
Max road range:	650km
Fuel capacity:	Not available
Fording:	1m
Vertical obstacle:	0.80m
Trench:	2.8m
Gradient:	60%
Side slope:	40%
Armour:	Classified
Armour type:	Steel
NBC system:	Yes
Night vision equipment:	Yes

Above: Krab 155mm/52 calibre SPG (HSW)

DEVELOPMENT

The Krab 155mm self-propelled artillery system was developed to meet the operational requirements of the Polish Army. The system consists of a full tracked chassis developed in Poland by OBRUM and built by HSW (Huta Stalowa Wola).

To this has been fitted a BAE Systems Land Systems turret which is almost identical to that installed on the BAE Systems Land Systems AS90 self-propelled artillery system. This has been in service with the British Army for some years fitted with a 155mm/39 calibre ordnance.

The layout is conventional with the driver being seated front left with a single piece hatch cover above his position and the powerpack to the right. The latter has the air inlet and outlet louvres in the roof with the exhaust outlet on the right side of the hull at the front.

The large turret is mounted at the rear with the crew normally entering and leaving via a large door in the hull rear. Turret traverse is through a full 360° with weapon elevation from -3.5° to +70°. Elevation and traverse is powered

with manual controls for emergency use. A direct fire sight is provided as is a laser rangefinder.

Maximum range when firing enhanced ammunition is 40km while minimum range is 4.7km. A burst rate of fire of three rounds in 10 seconds can be achieved while sustained rate of fire is 18 rounds in three minutes.

A 12.7mm machine gun is mounted on the roof for air defence purposes and a bank of four electrically operated 81mm smoke grenades are mounted either side of the turret firing forwards. The latter can be used in conjunction with the laser warning system.

The Krab is fitted with an integrated command, control, communication and computer intelligence system and a digital map display. An auxiliary power unit allows the key systems to be operated with the main diesel engine shut down.

VARIANTS

None at present time although chassis could be be adapted for a wide range of roles such as command post and as a platform for other weapon systems.

STATUS

Trials with Polish Army. Not yet in quantity production.

MANUFACTURER

HSW, Stalowa Wola, Poland.

KEY RECOGNITION FEATURES

- Large chassis with well-sloped glacis plate that leads up to horizontal roof, which extends to rear of vehicle. Nose slopes back under front of vehicle with entrenching blade attached to lower part of hull front

- Large turret at rear with sides sloping inwards and with large external stowage boxes on either side. Long 155mm/52 calibre ordnance has a double baffle muzzle brake that extends over the front of the hull and is held in position by a travelling lock that is pivoted at the front of the hull. 12.7mm MG on left side of turret roof

- Hull sides are vertical with exhaust outlet on right side of hull above forward wheel stations. Suspension either side consists of seven road wheels with drive sprocket at front, idler at rear and track-return rollers. Latter are covered by side skirt with irregular shaped lower part.

Right: Krab 155mm/52 calibre SPG (HSW)

Model 89 122mm SPH (Romania)

Above: Model 89 SPH

SPECIFICATIONS

Crew:	5
Armament:	1 x 122mm howitzer
Ammunition:	40 x 122mm (estimate)
Length gun forwards:	7.305m
Length hull:	7.305m
Width:	3.15m
Height:	2.665m
Ground clearance:	Not available
Weight, combat:	17,500kg
Weight, unloaded:	15,500kg (estimate)
Power-to-weight ratio:	20.5hp/t
Ground pressure:	Not available
Engine:	1240 V8DTS supercharged V-8 diesel developing 360hp
Maximum road speed:	65km/h
Maximum road range:	500km
Fuel capacity:	600 lit
Fording:	Amphibious
Vertical obstacle:	0.80m
Trench:	2.50m
Gradient:	60%
Side slope:	40%
Night vision equipment:	Yes
Armour:	Classified
Armour type:	Steel (see text)
NBC system:	Yes

DEVELOPMENT

The Model 89 122mm self-propelled howitzer was developed in the 1980s to meet the requirements of the Romanian Army and essentially consists of a locally designed chassis that incorporates some parts of the MLI-84 infantry combat vehicle which is in turn based on the Russian BMP-1 infantry combat vehicle.

The new chassis has been fitted with the complete turret of the Russian 122mm 2S1 self-propelled howitzer which is covered in detail in a separate entry. The chassis has the driver and engine compartment at the front with the

remainder of the space being taken up by the fighting compartment.

These turrets were imported from Russia and are armed with a 122mm 2A31 howitzer which can be elevated from -3° to +70° with turret traverse a full 360°. Maximum range firing a standard HE projectile is 15,300m or 21,900m firing a rocket assisted projectile.

The vehicle is fully amphibious being propelled in the water by two waterjets mounted at the rear of the hull. The original Russian 2S1 is also fully amphibious but is propelled in the water by its tracks only.

VARIANTS

There are no known variants.

STATUS

Production complete. In service only with Romania.

KEY RECOGNITION FEATURES

- Low profile turret with curved front mounted at rear of long hull which has a pointed front
- Well-sloped glacis plate, horizontal hull top, vertical hull rear with door
- Vertical hull sides with seven road wheels, drive sprocket front, idler rear and three track-return rollers

MANUFACTURER

Romanian state factories (chassis); Russian state factories (turret).

Below: Model 89 SPH

240mm SPM M1975 (2S4) (Russia)

Above: 240mm SPM M1975 (SM-240) (2S4) in travelling configuration (Steven Zaloga)

SPECIFICATIONS

Crew:	4 + 5
Armament:	1 x 240mm mortar, 1 x 12.7mm MG (anti-aircraft)
Length:	7.94m
Width:	3.25m
Height:	3.225m
Ground clearance:	0.4m
Weight, combat:	27,500kg
Power-to-weight ratio:	18.9hp/tonne
Ground pressure:	0.6kg/cm²
Engine:	V-59 V-12 diesel developing 520hp
Maximum road speed:	60km/hr
Maximum road range:	500km
Fuel capacity:	850 lit
Fording:	1m
Vertical obstacle:	1.10m
Trench:	2.79m
Gradient:	60%
Side slope:	30%
Armour:	20mm (max) (estimate)
Armour type:	Steel
NBC system:	Yes
Night vision equipment:	Yes (IR for driver)

DEVELOPMENT

This system was first identified in service with the then Soviet Army in 1975 and was therefore given the designation M1975 by NATO. Its correct designation is the SM-240 (2S4) and within the Russian Army it is commonly called the Tyulpan, or Tulip Tree. The system is normally accompanied by another vehicle that carries the remainder of

the crew and additional ammunition. The chassis of the GMZ full tracked minelayer is used as the basis for the 2S4 system with the actual mortar being based on the towed 240mm M240 breech loaded mortar that was first fielded in the 1950s.

The powerpack is at the front of the vehicle on the right side with the commander and driver to the left and a crew/ammunition compartment at the rear. The 240mm mortar is mounted at the rear of the vehicle and fires an HE mortar bomb to a maximum range of 9,650m. Other types of projectile include chemical and possibly concrete piercing. It is believed that an extended range mortar projectile with a maximum range of 18,000m is also available.

The mortar has an elevation of +50° to +80° with a limited traverse of 10° left and right with the mortar projectile being loaded with the aid of a crane that is positioned at the rear of the vehicle on the left side. The mortar is breech loaded.

The system has been used in Chechnya in conjunction with the Smel'chak laser guided projectile.

KEY RECOGNITION FEATURES

- 240mm mortar is pivoted at rear of hull
- When travelling 240mm mortar barrel is in horizontal position above hull top pointing forwards with large spade at rear
- Suspension either side has six road wheels with drive sprocket front, idler at rear and four track-return rollers supporting inside of track only, with gap between first/second, second/third, third/fourth and fourth/fifth road wheels

STATUS

Production complete. Held in reserve in Russia.

MANUFACTURER

Russian state factories.

Below: 240mm SPM M1975 (SM-240) (2S4)

203mm self-propelled gun M1975 (2S7) (Russia)

Above: 203mm SPG M1975 (2S7) in travelling order (T J Gander)

SPECIFICATIONS

Crew:	7
Armament:	1 x 203.2mm gun
Ammunition:	4 x 203.2mm
Length gun forwards:	13.12m
Length hull:	10.50m
Width:	3.38m
Height:	3.00m
Ground clearance:	0.40m
Weight, combat:	46,500kg
Power-to-weight ratio:	18.06hp/tonne
Ground pressure:	0.80kg/cm²
Engine:	V-46-I V-12 liquid cooled diesel developing 840hp
Maximum road speed:	50km/hr
Maximum road range:	650km
Fuel capacity:	Not available
Fording:	1.2m
Vertical obstacle:	0.70m
Trench:	2.6m
Gradient:	40%
Side slope:	20%
Armour:	10mm (max) (estimate)
Armour type:	Steel
NBC system:	Yes
Night vision equipment:	Yes (driver)

DEVELOPMENT

The 203mm self-propelled gun is designated M1975 by US Army although its correct Russian designation is SO-203 and industrial number is 2S7. It entered service with Russian Army in the late 1970s and is largest full tracked self-propelled gun in the world. Within the Russian Army it is also known as the Pion (Peony).

The chassis is a new design with fully enclosed armoured cab front, engine to immediate rear and 203mm gun mounted on top at far rear of hull. No protection for gun crew from small arms fire, shell splinters or NBC agents. When in firing position a large hydraulically operated spade is lowered at rear for more stable firing platform. Separate loading ammunition consisting of projectile and charge, load assist device on right side of chassis. In action it is accompanied by another vehicle carrying remainder of gun crew and ammunition.

The 203mm ordnance has a traverse of 15° left and right with elevation from 0° to +60°. Maximum range firing an unassisted projectile is 37.5km while firing a rocket assisted projectile a maximum range of 47km can be achieved.

VARIANTS
Late production vehicles are designated the 2S7N and have minor modifications.

STATUS
Production complete. In service with Belarus, Georgia, Poland, Russia, Ukraine and Uzbekistan.

MANUFACTURER
Russian state arsenals.

KEY RECOGNITION FEATURES

- Fully enclosed cab at far front, well forward of front drive sprockets
- 203mm gun in unprotected mount at far rear, overhangs front of vehicle when in travelling lock
- Large spade at rear with ammunition handling system right

Right: 203mm SPG M1975 (2S7) in travelling order (Richard Stickland)

Below: 203mm SPG M1975 (2S7) in travelling order (Richard Stickland)

120mm NONA-SVK 2S23 self-propelled gun mortar (Russia)

Above: 120mm NONA-SVK 2S23 self-propelled gun/mortar system with thermal screens (Christopher F Foss)

SPECIFICATIONS

Crew:	4
Configuration:	8 x 8
Armament:	1 x 120mm mortar, 1 x 7.62mm MG (anti-aircraft), 2 x 3 smoke grenade dischargers
Ammunition:	30 x 120mm, 500 x 7.62mm
Length:	7.40m
Width:	2.90m
Height:	2.495m
Ground clearance:	0.475m
Weight, combat:	14,500kg
Power-to-weight ratio:	17.93hp/tonne
Engine:	Four stroke V-8 water-cooled diesel developing 260hp
Maximum road speed:	80km/hr
Maximum water speed:	10km/hr
Maximum road range:	600km
Fuel capacity:	290 lit
Fording:	Amphibious
Vertical obstacle:	0.5m
Trench:	2m
Gradient:	60%
Side slope:	30%
Armour:	15mm
Armour type:	Steel
NBC system:	Yes
Night vision equipment:	Yes (infra-red for driver)

DEVELOPMENT

The 120mm NONA-SVK 2S23 (this being its industrial number) is essentially the BTR-80 armoured personnel carrier (qv) fitted with a 120mm breech loaded mortar in a turret. The mortar is related to the 120mm weapon of the 2B16 towed combination gun which is also known as the NONA-K. The 2S23 is also referred to as the NONA-SVK while the tracked 2S9 (qv) is referred to as the NONA-S.

The standard BTR-80 hull has been modified in a number of areas including removal of the firing ports and associated vision devices, modified door between second and third road wheels and

modified roof hatches.

The turret is armed with a 120mm breech-loaded 2A 60 ordnance that fires a variety of projectiles to a maximum range of 8,850m, turret traverse is 35° left and right with weapon elevation from -4° to +80°. A rocket assisted projectile has a maximum range of 12,850m. In addition to firing projectiles of Russian design, it can also fire French TDA 120mm mortar projectiles.

The 2S23 is fully amphibious being propelled in the water by a single waterjet at the hull rear. Before entering the water a trim vane is erected at the front of the hull.

KEY RECOGNITION FEATURES

- Based on BTR-80 (8 x 8) APC chassis with four road wheels each side with larger gap between second/third road wheel

- Large turret mounted in centre of hull roof, with 120mm ordnance mounted in sloping turret front, turret sides curve to rear with three smoke grenade dischargers either side

VARIANTS

There are no known variants of this system.
Some 2S23 systems have however been observed fitted with thermal screens to the hulls and turrets.

STATUS

Production. In service with China and Russia.

MANUFACTURER

Motovilkikha Plants Corporation, Perm, Russia (Prime Contractor).

Right: 120mm NONA-SVK 2S23 self-propelled gun/mortar system (Christopher F Foss)

Right: 120mm NONA-SVK 2S23 self-propelled gun/mortar system

152mm 2S19 self-propelled gun (Russia)

Above: 152mm 2S19 self-propelled gun (Christopher F Foss)

SPECIFICATIONS

Crew:	5
Armament:	1 x 152mm, 1 x 12.7mm MG (AA)
Ammunition:	50 x 152mm, 300 x 12.7mm
Length overall:	11.917m
Width:	3.38m
Height to turret roof:	2.985m
Weight:	42,000kg
Power-to-weight ratio:	20hp/tonne
Engine:	V-12 Type V-84A diesel developing 780hp (or 840hp diesel)
Maximum road speed:	60km/hr
Maximum road range:	500km
Fording:	1.2m
Vertical obstacle:	0.5m
Trench:	2.8m
Gradient:	47%
Side slope:	36%
Armour:	Classified
Armour type:	Steel/advanced
NBC system:	Yes
Night vision equipment:	Yes (passive)

DEVELOPMENT

The 152mm 2S19 was first revealed in 1990 and at that time was said to be in service in small numbers as the replacement for the older 152mm 2S3 self-propelled gun/howitzer. The 2S19 uses the same ordnance as the towed MSTA-A 2A65 152mm gun/howitzer which is referred to by NATO as the M1986, this being the year that it was first observed.

The 152mm 2S19 is based on a T-80 chassis that incorporates some components of the T-72 MBT, with the driver being seated at the front, fully enclosed turret in the centre and powerpack at the rear.

The 152mm ordnance is fitted with a muzzle brake and fume extractor and when travelling is held in position by a travel lock that is mounted on the glacis plate. The 152mm ordnance will fire an HE-FRAG projectile to a maximum range of 24,700m although using an extended range projectile a range of almost 40,000m can be achieved. The 152mm 2S19 can also fire the Krasnopol laser guided artillery projectile. Turret traverse is a full 360° with weapon elevation from -3° to +68°. An automatic loading system is fitted which enables a maximum rate of fire of eight rounds a minute to be achieved. A bustle-mounted APU is fitted to the turret to allow it to be used with the main engine switched off.

VARIANTS

Russian sources have stated that a 155mm version is under development for export market. This is reffered to as the 155mm/52 calibre 2S19M1.

STATUS

Production. In service with Belarus, Russia and Ukraine.

MANUFACTURERS

Russian state factories.

KEY RECOGNITION FEATURES

- Well-sloped glacis plate with turret in centre and powerpack at the rear
- Turret has vertical front, sides and rear with upper part curving inwards to flat roof on which a 12.7mm MG is mounted
- Chassis has six road wheels either side, idler front, drive sprocket at rear and track-return rollers, upper part of suspension is covered by skirt

Right: 152mm 2S19 self-propelled gun (Christopher F Foss)

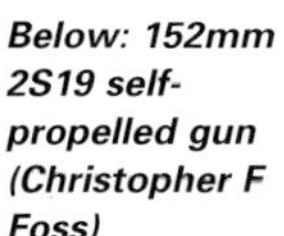

Below: 152mm 2S19 self-propelled gun (Christopher F Foss)

152mm self-propelled gun (2S5) (Russia)

SPECIFICATIONS

Crew:	5
Armament:	1 x 152mm gun
Ammunition:	30 x 152mm
Length gun forwards:	8.33m
Length hull:	7.3m
Width:	3.25m
Height:	2.76m
Ground clearance:	0.45m
Weight, combat:	28,200kg
Power-to-weight ratio:	19hp/tonne
Maximum road speed:	63km/hr
Maximum road range:	500km
Fuel capacity:	850 lit
Fording:	1.05m
Vertical obstacle:	0.7m
Trench:	2.5m
Gradient:	58%
Side slope:	47%
Armour:	15mm max (estimate)
Armour type:	Steel
NBC system:	Probable
Night vision equipment:	Yes (IR for driver)

***Above:* 152mm self-propelled gun 2S5**

***Right:* 152mm self-propelled gun 2S5 in travelling position (Richard Stickland)**

DEVELOPMENT

The 152mm self-propelled gun 2S5 was developed in the 1970s and is believed to have entered Soviet service in 1980. It has the same ordnance as the 152mm 2A36 towed artillery system.
It is believed that the chassis of the 2S5 is also related to that of the GMZ full tracked minelaying system. The 152mm ordnance of the 2S5 is mounted at the rear of the hull with no protection provided for the crew. It has a traverse of 15° left and right and can be elevated from -2.5° to +57°. Maximum range using standard ammunition is 28,400m, or 40,000m with a rocket assisted projectile.

The layer is seated on the left side of the system at the rear with the ordnance being provided with a projectile and charge ramming system to enable a rate of fire of 15 rounds a minute to be attained.

A total of 30 projectiles and charges are carried with the projectiles being stowed vertically in a carousel device in the left side of the rear compartment. The 30 charges are stowed to the right in three rows of ten. Each row is on a conveyor belt under the floor of the vehicle.

KEY RECOGNITION FEATURES

- 152mm gun in unprotected mount at far rear of hull, pepperpot muzzle brake, no fume extractor

- Large spade at hull rear swings upwards when travelling

- Suspension either side has six road wheels, drive sprocket front, idler rear, track-return rollers, larger gap between first/second, second/third and third/fourth road wheels

STATUS

Production complete. In service with Belarus, Eritrea, Finland, Georgia, Russia, Ukraine and Uzbekistan.

MANUFACTURER

Uraltransmash Works, Ekaterinburg, Russia.

152mm self-propelled gun M1973 (2S3) (Russia)

Above: 152mm self-propelled gun/self-propelled gun M1973 (2S3) with ordnance in travelling lock

SPECIFICATIONS

Crew:	6 (4 + 2)
Armament:	1 x 152mm howitzer, 1 x 7.62mm AA MG
Ammunition:	46 x 152mm, 1500 x 7.62mm
Length gun forwards:	8.4m
Length hull:	7.765m
Width:	3.25m
Height:	3.05m
Ground clearance:	0.45m
Weight, combat:	27,500kg
Power-to-weight ratio:	17.33hp/tonne
Ground pressure:	0.59kg/cm²
Engine:	V-59 V-12 water-cooled diesel developing 520hp
Maximum road speed:	60km/hr
Maximum road range:	500km
Fuel capacity:	830 lit
Fording:	1.0m
Vertical obstacle:	0.7m
Trench:	3.0m
Gradient:	60%
Side slope:	30%
Armour:	15mm (maximum turret), 20mm (maximum hull)
Armour type:	Steel
NBC system:	Yes
Night vision equipment:	Yes (infra-red for driver and commander)

DEVELOPMENT

The 152mm self-propelled gun/self-propelled gun M1973 (US Army designation) entered service with Russian Army in the early 1970s and is similar to American 155mm M109 self-propelled gun. Its correct Russian designation is SO-152 but in Russian Army it is commonly known as Akatsiya (Acacia); its industrial number is 2S3. M1973 is based on chassis of SA-4 Ganef SAM system but has six rather than seven road wheels. Driver's and engine compartment at front with fully enclosed power-operated turret at far rear. 152.4mm gun/howitzer is based on towed D-20 gun/howitzer and mounted in power-operated turret with traverse of 360°, elevation from -4° to +60°.

The 152.4mm howitzer fires HE-FRAG projectile to maximum range of 18,500m or rocket-assisted projectile to maximum range of 24,000m, other types of projectile including HEAT-FS, AP-T, illuminating and smoke. Of the

six-man crew, two are normally deployed as ammunition handlers at hull rear when in firing position. They feed projectiles and charges to the turret crew via the two circular hatches in the hull rear.

Late production versions, with some modifications, are designated the 2S3M and 2S3M1. The 152mm 2S3M2 has a 152mm/39 calibre barrel while the 155mm 2S3M3 has been developed for the export market.

VARIANTS

Chassis shares a number of components with SA-4 Ganef, 240mm self-propelled mortar M1975, and 152mm self-propelled gun 2S5.

STATUS

Production complete. In service with Algeria, Armenia, Belarus, Cuba, Georgia, Kazakhstan, Libya, Russia, Syria, Turkmenistan, Ukraine, Uzbekistan and Vietnam.

KEY RECOGNITION FEATURES

- Large turret with curved front mounted rear of hull, commander's cupola offset to left

- 152mm barrel overhangs chassis and has double baffle muzzle brake and fume extractor

- Suspension either side has six road wheels, drive sprocket front, idler rear, four track-return rollers. Distinct gap between first/second and second/third road wheels

MANUFACTURERS

Russian state arsenals.

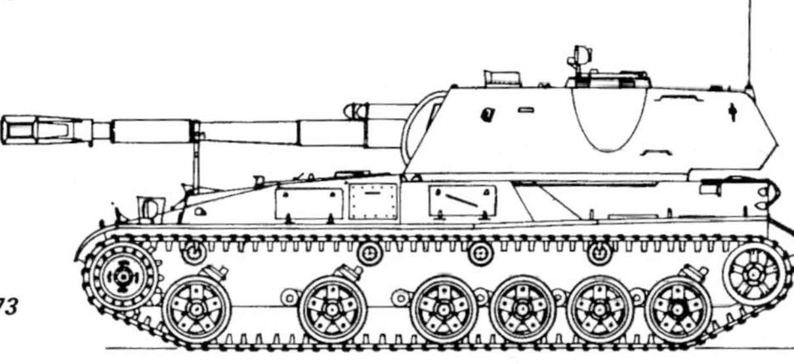

Right: 152mm self-propelled gun M1973 (2S3)

Right: 152mm self-propelled gun M1973 (2S3)

122mm self-propelled gun M1974 (2S1) (Russia)

Above: 122mm M1974 (2S1)

SPECIFICATIONS

Crew:	4
Armament:	1 x 122mm howitzer
Ammunition:	40 x 122mm
Length:	7.26m
Width:	2.85m
Height:	2.732m
Ground clearance:	0.40m
Weight, combat:	15,700kg
Power-to-weight ratio:	19.1hp/tonne
Ground pressure:	0.49kg/cm^2
Engine:	YaMZ-238N, V-8 water-cooled diesel developing 300hp at 2,100rpm
Maximum road speed:	61.5km/hr
Maximum water speed:	4.5km/hr
Maximum road range:	500km
Fuel capacity:	550 lit
Fording:	Amphibious
Vertical obstacle:	0.70m
Trench:	2.2m
Gradient:	77%
Side slope:	55%
Armour:	20mm (max) (estimate)
Armour type:	Steel
NBC system:	Yes
Night vision equipment:	Yes (infra-red for driver and commander)

DEVELOPMENT

The 122mm self-propelled gun M1974 (US Army designation) entered service with Russian Army in the early 1970s and was first seen in public during Polish Army parade in 1974. Correct Russian designation is SO-122 but in Russian Army is commonly known as Gvozdika (Carnation); its industrial number is 2S1.

Driver's and engine compartment is at front left with fully enclosed power-operated turret towards rear. 122mm howitzer is modified version of ordnance used in D-30 towed howitzer and fires HE projectile to maximum range of 15,300m or HE rocket-assisted projectile to maximum range of 21,900m. Other 122mm projectiles fired by M1974 include HEAT-FS, illuminating and smoke. Turret traverses through 360° and 122mm howitzer elevates from -3° to +70°.

The M1974 is fully amphibious with very little preparation and once afloat is propelled by its tracks. An unusual feature is that its suspension can be adjusted to give different heights. Normal tracks are 400mm wide but 670mm wide tracks can be fitted for snow or swamp.

VARIANTS

Artillery Command and Reconnaissance Vehicles. These are known as the MT-LBus (1V12 series) by the Russian Army and are based on the MT-LB chassis.
1V13 is called M1974-1 by NATO and is deputy battery commander's vehicle.
1V14 is called M1974-2A by NATO and is the battery commander's vehicle.
1V15 is called M1974-2B by NATO and is the battalion commander's vehicle.
1V16 is called the M1974-3 by NATO and is the deputy battalion commander's vehicle.
1V21/22/23/24 and 25 are air defence management vehicles.
MT-LBus is a jamming vehicle on M1974 chassis.
Dog Ear radar vehicle used by air defence units is on M1974 series chassis.
M1979 mine-clearing vehicle has turret-like superstructure with three rockets fired across minefield towing hose filled with explosive which detonates on ground.
RKhM chemical reconnaissance vehicle has raised superstructure on which is mounted 7.62mm MG cupola with boxes for dispensing pennants showing path through contaminated areas.
Da1 NBC Reconnaissance Vehicle.
Zoopark-1 artillery locating radar system.

KEY RECOGNITION FEATURES

- Low profile turret mounted at rear of long hull
- Suspension either side has seven large road wheels, drive sprocket front, idler rear, no track-return rollers
- 122mm howitzer does not overhang front of chassis, has double baffle muzzle brake and fume extractor

STATUS

Production complete. In service with Algeria, Angola, Armenia, Azerbaijan, Belarus, Bosnia, Bulgaria, Croatia, Cuba, Czech Republic, Eritrea, Ethiopia, Finland, Hungary, Iran, Kazakhstan, Kyrgyzstan, Libya, Poland, Romania, Russia, Serbia and Montenegro, Slovakia, Slovenia, Syria, Toga, Turkmenistan, Ukraine, Uruguay, Uzbekistan and Yemen.

MANUFACTURERS

Bulgarian, Polish and Russian state factories.

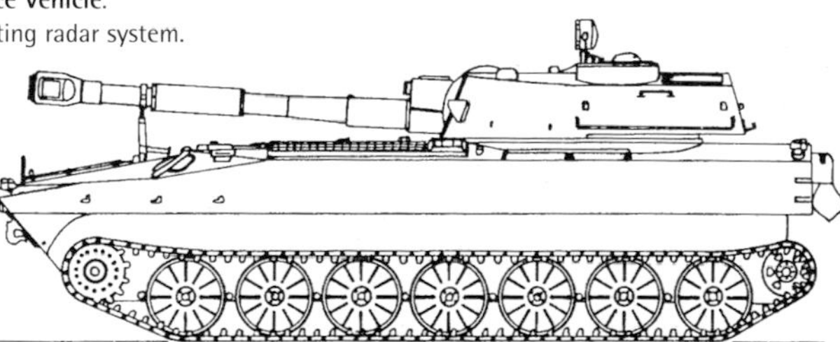

Right: 122mm M1974 (2S1)

Right: 122mm M1974 (2S1)

STK Primus 155mm self-propelled gun (Singapore)

Above: Primus 155mm SPG

SPECIFICATIONS

Crew:	4
Armament:	1 x 155mm, 1 x 7.62mm MG (anti-aircraft), 2 x 3 smoke grenade launchers
Ammunition:	(main) 26 x 155mm
Length (with armament):	10.21m
Length (chassis):	6.6m
Width:	3m
Height:	3.15m
Ground clearance:	0.45m
Weight, combat:	28,300kg
Power-to-weight ratio:	19.43hp/tonne
Engine:	Detroit Diesel Model 6V-92TIA developing 550hp
Maximum road speed:	50km/h
Maximum road range:	350km
Fuel capacity:	Not available
Fording:	1.1m
Vertical obstacle:	0.6m
Trench:	1.65m
Gradient:	60%
Side slope:	30%
Armour:	Classified
Armour type:	Steel and aluminium
NBC system:	Optional
Night vision equipment:	Optional

DEVELOPMENT

The Primus 155mm/39 calibre self-propelled gun was developed from 1996 by Singapore Technologies Kinetics in cooperation with the Singapore Armed Forces (SAF) and the Defense Science and Technology Agency.

It was first revealed in late 2003 by which time it was already operational and within the SAF its official designation is the Singapore Self Propelled Howitzer 1 (SPPH 1).

The Primus 155mm self-propelled artillery system is very similar in appearance to the American United Defense M109 155mm self-propelled artillery system.

The chassis of Primus is based on a modified M109 chassis which is supplied to Singapore Technologies Kinetics by United Defense STK who build the turret and then integrate this with the chassis. The powerpack, however, is new and similar to that installed in the Singapore

Technologies Kinetics Bionix IFV.

The driver is seated front left with the power pack to the right which leaves the remainder of the chassis free for the crew compartment and large fully enclosed turret.

Turret traverse is 360° under full power control with manual controls being provided as a back up. Maximum range of the 155mm/39 calibre ordnance depends on the projectile and charge combination but this can be up to 30km with an Extended Range Full Bore – Base Bleed projectile.

A semi-automatic loading system is fitted as standard to reduce crew fatigue and increase rate of fire to six rounds a minute. The projectiles are loaded automatically, with the charges, which can be of the bagged or modular type, being loaded manually. A total of 22 ready use projectiles are carried in the turret bustle mounted magazine.

A digital fire control is fitted as standard and this can lay the 155mm/39 calibre ordnance onto the target automatically. In addition, there is a direct fire sight.

VARIANTS

Under development is a command post vehicle and an ammunition resupply vehicle.

STATUS

Production. In service with Singapore.

KEY RECOGNITION FEATURES

- Well-sloped glacis plate leads up to horizontal hull that extends to rear. Large turret mounted on hull rear with vertical sides and rear and forward part of turret roof sloped to the rear

- Mounted in forward part of turret is 155mm ordnance which is fitted with a double baffle muzzle brake and a fume extractor with distinctive covering to ordnance forward of turret. When travelling 155mm ordnance is held in travel lock positioned at front of hull. Bank of three smoke grenade launchers mounted either side of turret

- Hull sides vertical with suspension either side consisting of seven dual rubber tyred road wheels with drive sprocket front and idler rear. There are no track-return rollers and upper part of track is covered by a skirt

MANUFACTURER

Singapore Technologies Kinetics, Singapore.

Below: Primus 155mm SPG

Denel G6 155mm self-propelled gun (South Africa)

Above: Denel Ordnance 155mm G6 (Christopher F Foss)

SPECIFICATIONS

Crew:	6
Configuration:	6 x 6
Armament:	1 x 155mm, 1 x 12.7mm MG (AA), 2 x 4 smoke grenade dischargers
Ammunition:	45 x 155mm, 1,000 x 12.7mm
Length gun forwards:	10.335m
Length hull:	9.2m
Width:	3.4m
Height:	3.8m (including MG), 3.3m (turret top)
Ground clearance:	0.45m
Weight, combat:	47,000kg
Weight, empty:	42,500kg
Power-to-weight ratio:	11.17hp/tonne
Engine:	Air-cooled diesel developing 518hp
Maximum road speed:	90km/hr
Maximum road range:	700km
Fuel capacity:	700 lit
Fording:	1m
Vertical obstacle:	0.5m
Trench:	1m
Gradient:	40%
Side slope:	30%
Armour:	23mm (maximum)
Armour type:	Steel
NBC system:	Yes (BC only)
Night vision equipment:	Yes (passive)

DEVELOPMENT

The 155mm G6 self-propelled howitzer was developed by Denel Ordnance to meet the requirements of the South African Artillery Corps for a highly mobile artillery system capable of operating over very rough terrain. The first prototype completed in 1981 was followed by a series of additional prototype and pre-production vehicles with the first production vehicles being completed in 1988. Prime contractor for the G6 is Denel Ordnance, part of the Denel Group which also manufactures the 155mm G5 towed artillery system which has identical ballistic characteristics to the G6 as they both have a 155mm/45 calibre ordnance. Chassis of the G6 is manufactured by OMC.

The driver is seated at the very front of the vehicle in the centre, to his rear is the powerpack with the turret being mounted at the very rear. Turret traverse is 180°, although only 90° is used with weapon elevation being from -5° to +75°. Firing Extended Range Full Bore - Base Bleed

(ERFB-BB) projectiles a maximum range of 39,000m can be achieved. A flick rammer is provided to obtain higher rates of fire. The G6 is normally supported in action by another vehicle which carries additional projectiles and charges. When deployed in the firing position, four stabilisers are lowered to the ground, one either side of the hull between the first and second road wheels and two at the rear.

Standard equipment includes an APU, air conditioning system, fire detection and suppression system, computerised fire control system, powered steering and a central tyre pressure regulation system.

VARIANTS

Latest version is G6-52 which has a new turret armed with a 155mm/52 calibre weapon. This is the same turret as fitted to Indian Arjun tank chassis.

KEY RECOGNITION FEATURES

- Three large road wheels each side with distinctive gap between first and second road wheel, driver's compartment at very front of hull in centre with windscreens to his front and sides

- Large turret at rear with raised commander's cupola on right side, front and sides of turret slope slightly inwards, 155mm ordnance has long barrel with large single baffle muzzle brake and fume extractor. When travelling ordnance is horizontal and held in travel lock

- Hull front is pointed and hull rear vertical, louvres in upper sides of hull between first and second road wheel station

STATUS

Production as required. In service with Oman, South Africa and the United Arab Emirates.

MANUFACTURER

Denel Ordnance, Pretoria, South Africa (but see text).

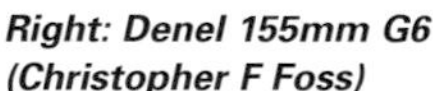

Right: Denel 155mm G6 (Christopher F Foss)

Above & Left: Denel 155mm G6

Samsung Techwin K9 Thunder self-propelled gun (South Korea)

Above: 155mm K9 Thunder self-propelled gun in the travelling configuration (Samsung Techwin)

SPECIFICATIONS

Crew:	5
Armament:	1 x 155mm 1 x 12.7mm AA MG
Ammunition:	48 x 155mm, 500 x 12.7mm
Length gun forward:	12m
Length hull:	7.44m
Width:	3.40m
Height:	2.73m (turret roof), 3.5m (with 12.7mm M2 MG)
Ground clearance:	0.41m
Weight,combat:	46,300kg
Weight,empty:	Not available
Power-to-weight ratio:	21.6hp/tonne
Engine:	MTU MT 881 Ka-500 water-cooled diesel developing 1,000hp at 2,750rpm
Max road speed:	67km/h
Max road range:	360km
Fuel capacity:	850 lit
Fording:	1.5m
Vertical obstacle:	0.75m
Trench:	2.80m
Gradient:	60%
Side slope:	30%
Armour:	19mm (maximum)
Armour type:	Steel
NBC system:	Yes
Night vision equipment:	Yes

DEVELOPMENT

The 155mm/52 calibre K9 Thunder self-propelled artillery system was developed by Samsung Techwin, Defense Program Division, to meet the operational requirements of the Republic of Korea Army for a new system to supplement its large fleet of locally assembled 155mm United Defense M109A2 series self-propelled howitzers.

The first prototypes of the system were completed in 1994 which were followed by pre-production vehicles. It was subsequently type classified as the K9 Thunder in 1999 and is now in quantity production.

The driver is seated front left with the powerpack to his right and the fully enclosed turret at the rear. Main armament comprises a 155mm/52 calibre barrel which is fitted with a slotted muzzle brake and a fume extractor. Turret traverse is a full 360° with weapon elevation from -2.5° to +70°. Maximum range when firing a locally developed K307 high explosive projectile is 40km. Projectiles are loaded automatically with the modular charges being loaded manually.

A computerised on board fire control system is fitted as standard and this enables it to carry out Time On Target (TOT) procedures and put three rounds on target at once. Maximum rate of fire is six to eight rounds a minute and sustained rate of fire is two to three rounds a minute. It can open fire within 60 seconds of coming into action.

A muzzle velocity radar is mounted over the rear part of the ordnance and this feeds information into the on-board fire control computer.

KEY RECOGNITION FEATURES

- Large chassis with vertical hull front, almost horizontal hull top with vertical hull sides and rear. Large turret mounted at hull rear with turret sides sloping slightly inwards and vertical turret rear with stowage cage. Large door in hull rear

- Mounted in forward part of turret is 155mm/52 calibre barrel which overhangs front of vehicle and is fitted with distinctive muzzle brake and fume extractor. When travelling ordnance is held in travel lock pivoted at front of hull

- Suspension either side consists of six large road wheels with drive sprocket at front, idler at rear and three track-return rollers that support inside of track. At present no side skirts are fitted to the K9 Thunder

VARIANTS

An ammunition resupply vehicle is under development under the designation of the K10 and a slightly different version has been developed for Turkey under the name of the Firtina (Storm) with first deliveries in 2002. These are being assembled in Turkey with some sub-systems being imported.

STATUS

Production. In service with South Korea and Turkey.

MANUFACTURER

Samsung Techwin Company Limited, Seoul, Korea.

Below: Turkey's Firtina (Storm) SPG is essentially the K9 Thunder (Christopher F Foss)

155mm AS90 self-propelled gun (UK)

Above: AS90 155mm self-propelled gun

SPECIFICATIONS

Crew:	5
Armament:	1 x 155mm, 1 x 12.7mm MG (AA), 2 x 5 smoke grenade dischargers
Ammunition:	48 x 155mm, 1,000 x 12.7mm
Length gun forwards:	9.90m
Length hull:	7.20m
Width:	3.40m
Height overall:	3m
Ground clearance:	0.41m
Weight, combat:	45,000kg
Power-to-weight ratio:	14.66hp/tonne
Ground pressure:	0.90kg/cm²
Engine:	Cummins VTA 903T 660T-660 V-8 diesel developing 660bhp at 2,800rpm
Maximum road speed:	55km/hr
Maximum road range:	370km
Fuel capacity:	750 lit
Fording:	1.5m
Vertical obstacle:	0.88m
Trench:	2.8m
Gradient:	60%
Side slope:	25%
Armour:	17mm (max)
Armour type:	Steel
NBC system:	Yes
Night vision equipment:	Yes (passive)

DEVELOPMENT

In 1981 Vickers Shipbuilding and Engineering (VSEL) (today BAE Systems Land Systems) built the prototype of a 155mm artillery turret called the GBT 155. The company then started development work, as a private venture, on a brand new complete 155mm self-propelled artillery system which was called the AS90, the first of two prototypes of this were completed in 1986. The AS90 was subsequently entered in the British Army's Abbot Replacement Competition and in

1989 AS90 was selected and a contract placed for 179 systems, with final deliveries being made to the British Army early in 1995. AS90 has replaced all other self-propelled guns in the British Army.

The driver is seated at the front left with the powerpack to his right, and the turret at the rear. Access to the turret is via a large door in the chassis rear. Turret traverse is a full 360° with weapon elevation from -5° to +70°. The 155mm 39 calibre ordnance has a maximum range of 24,700m using standard ammunition or over 30,000m using extended range full bore ammunition. Of the 48 projectiles carried, 31 are stowed in the turret bustle magazine. A burst rate of three rounds in ten seconds can be achieved with sustained rate of fire being two rounds a minute.

The suspension of the AS90 is of the hydropneumatic type and standard equipment on British Army systems includes muzzle velocity measuring equipment, land navigation system and a fully automatic gun laying capability.

VARIANTS

There are no variants of the 155mm AS90 although the company proposed the chassis for a wide range of other systems including recovery, maintenance and flatbed. British Army AS90s have a 39 calibre barrel but part of the fleet may be fitted with 155mm/52 calibre barrel. AS90 turret has also been fitted onto T-72 MBT chassis for trials in India. The turret of AS90 is installed on the Polish 155mm self-propelled artillery system Krab (qv).

KEY RECOGNITION FEATURES

- Well-sloped glacis plate with driver on left and raised engine compartment to his right. Turret at very rear of chassis with sloped front, sloped sides and vertical rear

- 155mm ordnance has double baffle muzzle brake and when in travelling lock projects over front of hull. Travel lock is pivoted at very front of hull and lays back on glacis plate when not required

- Chassis has vertical sides and rear with each side having six dual rubber tyred road wheels, drive sprocket at front, idler at rear and three track-return rollers

STATUS

Production complete but can be resumed. In service with British Army.

MANUFACTURER

BAE Systems Land Systems, Barrow-in-Furness, UK.

Above right: AS90 155mm self-propelled gun (Christopher F Foss)

Right: AS90 155mm self-propelled gun (Christopher F Foss)

M110 203mm self-propelled gun (USA)

SPECIFICATIONS

Crew (on gun):	5
Armament:	1 x 203mm howitzer
Ammunition:	2 x 203mm
Length gun forwards:	7.467m (spade up)
Length hull:	5.72m (without gun or spade)
Width:	3.149m
Height:	2.93m (top of barrel travelling), 2.809m (top of mount), 1.475m (hull top)
Ground clearance:	0.44m
Weight, combat:	26,534kg
Weight, unloaded:	24,312kg
Power-to-weight ratio:	15.26hp/tonne
Ground pressure:	0.76kg/cm²
Engine:	Detroit Diesel Model 8V-71T, turbocharged, 2-stroke liquid cooled, 8-cylinder diesel developing 405bhp at 2,300rpm
Maximum road speed:	56km/hr
Maximum road range:	725km

Above: 203mm M110A2 SPG (Steven Zaloga)

Fuel capacity:	1,137 lit
Fording:	1.066m
Vertical obstacle:	1.016m
Trench:	2.362m
Gradient:	60%
Side slope:	30%
Armour:	Classified
Armour type:	Steel
NBC system:	No
Night vision equipment:	Yes (driver only)

DEVELOPMENT

The 203mm (8-inch) M110 was designed in the 1950s at the same time as M107 175mm which has identical chassis and mount. First production vehicles completed by Pacific Car and Foundry in 1962 with later production by FMC and finally BMY. The M110 was followed in production by the improved M110A1 and M110A2, some of which were conversions of the original vehicle.

The M110 has a total crew of 13 of whom five (commander, driver and three gunners) are carried

on the actual M110 and remainder in the M548 tracked cargo carrier or truck which also carries projectiles, charges and fuses.

The 203mm howitzer has powered elevation from -2° to +65°, powered traverse of 30° left and right. Maximum range is 21,300m with standard HE projectile, but other projectiles can be fired. When in firing position a large hydraulically operated spade is lowered at rear of hull to provide more stable firing platform. The gun crew has no protection from elements, NBC contamination, small arms fire or shell splinters.

The M110 series of self-propelled howitzers has been phased out of service with a number of countries, for example the United Kingdom and the United States, and replaced by the American Lockheed Martin Missile and Fire Control 227mm Multiple Launch Rocket System.

VARIANTS

M110A1 is M110 with new, much longer barrel and therefore longer range.
M110A2 is same as M110A1 but barrel has muzzle brake.
M578 ARV used almost same chassis as M107/M110.

STATUS

Production complete. In service with Bahrain, Greece, Iran, Israel, Japan (built under licence), Jordan, Morocco, Pakistan, South Korea, Spain, Taiwan and Turkey. In most cases M110s have been converted to M110A2 standard.

KEY RECOGNITION FEATURES

- Short stubby barrel, no fume extractor or muzzle brake
- Howitzer is in unprotected mount towards rear of hull with large spade at far rear
- Chassis same as M107 175mm self-propelled gun (qv) with either side five large road wheels, front drive sprocket, no track-return rollers

MANUFACTURER

Pacific Car and Foundry Company, Renton, Washington; FMC Corporation, San José, California; and BMY, York, Pennsylvania, US.

Below: 203mm M110A2 SPG (Kensuke Ebata)

M107 175mm self-propelled gun (USA)

Above: M107 175mm self-propelled gun in travelling configuration

SPECIFICATIONS

Crew (on gun):	5
Armament:	1 x 175mm gun
Ammunition:	2 x 175mm
Length gun forwards:	11.256m (spade up)
Length hull:	5.72m (without gun or spade)
Width:	3.149m
Height:	3.679m (top of barrel travelling), 2.809m (top of mount), 1.475m (hull top)
Ground clearance:	0.46m
Weight, combat:	28,168kg
Weight, unloaded:	25,915kg
Power-to-weight ratio:	14.37hp/tonne
Ground pressure:	0.81kg/cm²
Engine:	Detroit Diesel Model 8V-71T, turbocharged, 2-stroke liquid cooled, 8-cylinder diesel developing 405bhp at 2,300rpm
Maximum road speed:	56km/hr
Maximum road range:	725km
Fuel capacity:	1,137 lit
Fording:	1.066m
Vertical obstacle:	1.016m
Trench:	2.362m
Gradient:	60%
Side slope:	30%
Armour:	Classified
Armour type:	Steel
NBC system:	No
Night vision equipment:	Yes (driver only, passive)

DEVELOPMENT

The 175mm M107 was designed in the 1950s at the same time as the M110 203mm (8-inch) self-propelled howitzer (qv) which has the same chassis and gun mount. First production vehicles were completed by Pacific Car and Foundry in 1962 with later production by FMC and finally BMY. A total of 524 M107s were built by BMY by the time production was completed in May 1980, but it has now been phased out of service with many armies including Germany, Italy, Netherlands, Spain, the United Kingdom and the United States.

The M107 has a total crew of 13 of whom five

(commander, driver and three gunners) are carried on the actual vehicle and the remainder in the M548 tracked cargo carrier (or truck) which also carries the projectiles, charges and fuses.

The 175mm gun has powered elevation of -2° to +65°, powered traverse of 30° left and right. The 175mm gun is mounted at the rear of the hull with no protection being provided for the gun crew. A load assist device is mounted at the left rear to assist in loading projectiles into the breech of the weapon. In US Army service, the 175mm M107 only fired one combat projectile, the M437 high explosive which had a maximum range of 32,700m. In addition, the former Space Research Corporation developed a special projectile which could achieve a maximum range of around 40,000m. Israel was the only customer for this.

VARIANTS

There are no variants of the M107 although the M110 self-propelled howitzer and M578 ARV use the same chassis.

STATUS

Production complete. In service with Greece, Iran, Israel, South Korea and Turkey.

KEY RECOGNITION FEATURES

- Long thin barrel, no fume extractor or muzzle brake
- Gun is in unprotected mount towards rear of hull with large spade at rear that is raised for travelling
- Chassis is same as M110 203mm self-propelled howitzer with either side five large road wheels, drive sprocket front, no track-return rollers

MANUFACTURER

Pacific Car and Foundry Company, Renton, Washington; FMC Corporation, San José, California; and BMY, York, Pennsylvania, US.

Below: M107 175mm self-propelled gun in travelling configuration

United Defense, LP, M109A2 155mm self-propelled gun (USA)

Above: M109A6 Paladin

SPECIFICATIONS

Crew:	6
Armament:	1 x 155mm howitzer, 1 x 12.7mm MG
Ammunition:	36 x 155mm, 500 x 12.7mm
Length gun forwards:	9.12m
Length hull:	6.19m
Width:	3.15m
Height:	3.28m (including AA MG)
Height:	2.8m (reduced)
Ground clearance:	0.46m
Weight, combat:	24,948kg
Weight, empty:	21,110kg
Power-to-weight ratio:	16.23hp/tonne
Ground pressure:	0.85kg/cm²
Engine:	Detroit Diesel Model 8V-71T, turbocharged, liquid-cooled 8-cylinder diesel developing 405bhp at 2,300rpm
Maximum road speed:	56.3km/hr
Maximum road range:	349km
Fuel capacity:	511 lit
Fording:	1.07m
Vertical obstacle:	0.53m
Trench:	1.83m
Gradient:	60%
Side slope:	40%
Armour:	Classified
Armour type:	Aluminium
NBC system:	Optional
Night vision equipment:	Optional (infra-red or passive for driver)

DEVELOPMENT

M109 series was developed in the 1950s and shares common chassis with M108 105mm self-propelled howitzer. First production vehicles were completed in 1962 with over 4,000 built so far.

The driver sits front left, engine compartment to his right and large turret at hull rear. Turret traverses through 360° and 155mm howitzer elevates from -3° to +75°. Ammunition is separate loading type with 34 projectiles and charges carried, plus two Copperhead Cannon Launched Guided Projectiles. Following types of projectile fired by M109A2: HE (maximum range 18,100m), Improved Conventional Munition, Remote Anti-Armor Mine system (RAAMS), Area Denial Artillery Munition (ADAM), High Explosive Rocket Assist (HERA), illuminating, smoke, high explosive (grenade) and numerous other types.

VARIANTS

M109, first model to enter service has very short barrel, double baffle muzzle brake and large fume extractor to immediate rear, maximum range 14,600m.
M109A1 is M109 with new and longer barrel and other improvements, maximum range (standard HE) 18,100m, as with **M109A2** which was built with these and other improvements.
M109A3 is an upgraded M109A1 with a number of modifications including new gun mount and improved RAM-D.
M109A4 is an upgraded M109A2 or M109A3 with improvements to NBC system etc.
M109A5 is upgraded M109A4.
M109A6 is the latest production model for US Army and is also referred to as the Paladin with first production vehicles completed in 1992. Many improvements including new turret with longer barrel ordnance, automatic fire control system, upgraded suspension and improved armour.
M109A3G is German Army M109G with many improvements including new ordnance.
M109L, Italy has fitted its M109s with ordnance of FH-70, these are known as M109L.
M109AL is Israeli version of M109.
M109 Taiwan uses M108/M109 chassis but without turret and has 155mm weapon in open mount. Short barrel version uses ordnance of towed M114 and more recent version has new and much longer ordnance.
M109L47, modified M109 for UAE with 47 calibre barrel; Swiss M109s are getting 47 calibre barrel.
M992 Field Artillery Ammunition Support Vehicle, in service with Saudi Arabia, Spain, Thailand and the United States is M109 chassis with fully enclosed rear hull to carry 155mm ammunition and feeds this to M109 self-propelled gun when in firing position.
FDC, Fire Detection Centre or Fire Control Centre, uses same chassis and hull as M992. Greece and Taiwan.

KEY RECOGNITION FEATURES

- Hull has vertical sides with glacis plate sloping up to horizontal hull top which extends to rear. Spade mounted each side of rear hull door

- Large turret-mounted rear with curved front, vertical sides and rear. Long barrel with fume extractor and double baffle muzzle brake that overhangs front of vehicle when travelling. Roof-mounted 12.7mm AA MG

- Suspension either side has seven small road wheels, drive sprocket front, idler rear, no track-return rollers

STATUS

Production as required. In service with Austria, Belgium, Canada, Denmark, Egypt, Ethiopia, Germany, Greece, Iran, Israel, Italy, Jordan, South Korea, Kuwait, Morocco, Netherlands, Norway, Pakistan, Peru, Portugal, Saudi Arabia, Spain, Switzerland, Taiwan, Tunisia, United Arab Emirates, US and Venezuela.

MANUFACTURER

United Defense, LP, York, Pennsylvania, US.

Right: M109A2 of US Army

M44 155mm self-propelled gun (USA)

Above: M52T 155mm/39 calibre self-propelled gun in service with Turkey (Christopher F Foss)

SPECIFICATIONS

Crew:	5
Armament:	1 x 155mm howitzer, 1 x 12.7mm AA MG
Ammunition:	24 x 155mm, 900 x 12.7mm
Length:	6.159m (spade up)
Width:	3.238m
Height:	3.11m (with tarpaulin)
Ground clearance:	0.48m
Weight, combat:	28,350kg
Weight, empty:	26,308kg
Power-to-weight ratio:	17.63hp/tonne
Ground pressure:	0.66kg/cm^2
Engine:	Continental AOS-895-3, 6-cylinder, air-cooled, supercharged petrol developing 500hp at 2,800rpm
Maximum road speed:	56km/hr
Maximum road range:	122km
Fuel capacity:	568 lit
Fording:	1.066m
Vertical obstacle:	0.762m
Trench:	1.828m
Gradient:	60%
Side slope:	30%
Armour:	12.7mm
Armour type:	Steel
NBC system:	No
Night vision equipment:	None

DEVELOPMENT

The M44 155mm was developed after the Second World War with production by Massey Harris. The M44 was followed in production by the M44A1 which has a Continental AOSI-895-5 engine with fuel injection. The M44 was replaced from 1962 in US Army by the 155mm M109 self-propelled howitzer.

The 155mm howitzer has manual elevation from -5° to +65° with traverse 30° left and right. It fires standard HE projectile to maximum range of 14,600m, although other types of projectile can be fired including illuminating and smoke. When in firing position a large spade is lowered at rear to provide more stable firing platform. The open-topped gun compartment can be covered by tarpaulin and canvas. 12.7mm MG is mounted on ring mount at rear of gun compartment on left side, with driver seated to immediate front.

VARIANTS

The M44T was developed by a German consortium to meet the requirements of Turkey. It has many improvements including the longer 155mm/39 calibre barrel of the 155mm FH-70 towed artillery system, new MTU diesel engine, new fuel tanks and new electrical system. It is in service with Turkish Army with conversions being carried out in Turkey. The Turkish Army has also upgraded its fleet of 105mm and M52 self-propelled howitzers which have a similar chassis to the M44. The upgraded Turkish M52 is designated the M52T has a fully enclosed turret at the rear in which is mounted the same 155mm/39 calibre barrel as fitted to the M44T and has a large spade which is lowered at the rear. The upper part of the suspension is covered by a skirt.

STATUS

Production complete. In service with Jordan, Taiwan (some upgraded) and Turkey (upgraded systems designated M44T).

MANUFACTURER

Massey Harris, US.

KEY RECOGNITION FEATURES

- 155mm howitzer with no muzzle brake or fume extractor is mounted in open-topped gun compartment rear and does not overhang front of vehicle
- Suspension either side has five road wheels, drive sprocket front, idler rear, four track-return rollers
- Chassis is almost identical to M52 105mm self-propelled howitzer's

Below: 155mm SPG (US Army)

M108 105mm self-propelled gun (USA)

Above: Belgian Army VBCL command post vehicle (Pierre Touzin)

SPECIFICATIONS

Crew:	5
Armament:	1 x 105mm howitzer, 1 x 12.7mm AA MG
Ammunition:	87 x 105mm, 500 x 12.7mm
Length:	6.114m
Width:	3.295m, 3.149m (reduced)
Height:	3.155m (including AA MG), 2.794m (reduced)
Ground clearance:	0.451m
Weight, combat:	22,452kg
Weight, empty:	18,436kg
Power-to-weight ratio:	18.038bhp/tonne
Ground pressure:	0.71kg/cm2
Engine:	Detroit Diesel Model 8V-71T, turbocharged, 2-stroke liquid-cooled, 8-cylinder diesel developing 405bhp at 2,300rpm
Maximum road speed:	56km/hr
Maximum water speed:	6.43km/hr
Maximum road range:	390km
Fuel capacity:	511 lit
Fording:	1.828m, amphibious with preparation
Vertical obstacle:	0.533m
Trench:	1.828m
Gradient:	60%
Side slope:	30%
Armour:	Classified
Armour type:	Aluminium
NBC system:	No
Night vision equipment:	Yes (driver only)

DEVELOPMENT

The M108 105mm was developed in the 1950s at the same time as M109 155mm which has same chassis and turret with modifications. Production

of M108 was by Cadillac Gage Motor Car Division of General Motors Corporation in 1962/63. In US Army it replaced M52 105mm self-propelled howitzer but M108 itself was soon replaced in US Army by M109.

The 105mm M103 howitzer has manual elevation from -4° to +74°, manual turret traverse through 360°. Maximum range firing HE round is 11,500m, other projectiles including rocket-assisted, illuminating and smoke.

Amphibious kit was developed for M108 which enabled vehicle to propel itself across rivers and streams by its tracks. As far as it is known this amphibious kit has not been deployed with any of the current users of the M108 system.

VARIANTS

Belgian Army has replaced its M108s with M109A2 155mm system and some M108s have been converted to command post vehicles designated VBCL.

KEY RECOGNITION FEATURES

- Large turret with curved front mounted at rear of hull which is identical to M109 155mm self-propelled howitzer
- Very short barrel with fume extractor
- Chassis has seven small road wheels, either side drive sprocket front, idler rear, no track-return rollers

STATUS

Production complete. In service with Brazil, Spain, Taiwan and Turkey.

MANUFACTURER

Cadillac Motor Car Division, General Motors, US.

Below: 105mm M108 SPG (C R Zwart)

Glossary

AA	anti-aircraft
AAAV	armoured amphibious assault vehicle
ACRV	armoured command and reconnaissance vehicle
ADAM	Area Denial Artillery Munition
ADATS	Air Defence Anti-tank System
AEV	armoured engineer vehicle
AFSV	Armoured Fire Support Vehicle
AIFV	Armoured Infantry Fighting Vehicle
AML	Automitrailleuse Legere (light armoured car)
AMX	Atelier de Construction d'Issy-les-Moulineaux
AP	armour piercing
APC	armoured personnel carrier
APC-T	armour-piercing capped - tracer
APDS	armour-piercing discarding sabot
APDS-T	armour-piercing discarding sabot - tracer
APERS-T	anti-personnel - tracer
APFSDS	armour-piercing fin-stabilised discarding sabot
APFSDS-T	armour-piercing fin-stabilised discarding sabot - tracer
APHE	armour-piercing high explosive
APSE-T	armour piercing secondary effect - tracer
API-T	armour piercing incendiary - tracer
AP-T	armour piercing - tracer
ARE	Atelier de Construction Rôanne
ARRV	Armoured Repair and Recovery Vehicle
ATR	automotive test rig
ATGW	anti-tank guided weapon
ATTS	air-transportable towed system
AVGP	Armoured Vehicle General Purpose
AVLB	armoured vehicle launched bridge
AVRE	Armoured Vehicle Royal Engineers
BARV	Beach Armoured Recovery Vehicle
bhp	brake horsepower
BLR	Blindado Lingero de Ruedas
BMR	Blindado Medio de Ruedas
CAF	Canadian Armed Forces
CEV	combat engineer vehicle
CFE	Conventional Forces Europe
CFV	Cavalry Fighting Vehicle
CLGP	Cannon Launched Guided Projectile
COV	Counter Obstacle Vehicle
CVR(T)	Combat Vehicle Reconnaissance (Tracked)
CVR(W)	Combat Vehicle Reconnaissance (Wheeled)
EBG	Engin Blindé Genie
EBR	Engin Blindé de Reconnaissance
EOD	Explosive Ordnance Disposal
ERA	Explosive Reactive Armour
ERC	Engin de Reconnaissance Cannon
FAASV	Field Artillery Ammunition Support Vehicle
FCC	Fire Command Centre
FCS	Fire Control System
FDC	Fire Direction Centre
FISTV	Fire Support Team Vehicle
FLIR	Forward Looking Infra-red
GLLD	Ground Laser Locator Designator
HAV	heavy assault bridge
HB	heavy barrel
HCT	HOT Compact Turret
HE	high explosive
HE-T	high explosive - tracer
HEAT	high explosive anti-tank
HEAT-FS	high explosive anti-tank fin-stabilised
HEAT-T-MP	high explosive anti-tank - tracer - multi-purpose
HE-FS	high explosive - fin stabilised
HE-FRAG	high explosive fragmentation
HE-FRAG FS	high explosive fragmentation - fin stabilised
HEI-T	high explosive incendiary - tracer
HESH	high explosive squash head
HEP	high explosive plastic
HE-T	high explosive - tracer
HERA	high explosive rocket assist
hp	horsepower
HVAP-DS-T	high velocity armour-piercing discarding sabot - tracer
HVAP-T	high velocity armour-piercing tracer
IAFV	infantry armoured fighting vehicle
ICM	improved conventional munition
ICV	infantry combat vehicle
IDF	Israel Defence Forces
IFV	infantry fighting vehicle
IR	infra-red
IS	internal security
ITV	Improved TOW Vehicle
KIFV	Korean Infantry Fighting Vehicle

kg/cm²	kilogram per centimetre square
km/hr	kilometre per hour
LAV	Light Armoured Vehicle
lit	litres
LLLTV	low-light level television
LVT	landing vehicle tracked
LVTP	landing vehicle tracked personnel
LVTR	landing vehicle tracked recovery
m	metre
mm	millimetre
MBT	main battle tank
MEWS	mobile electronic warfare system
MG	machine gun
MICV	mechanised infantry combat vehicle
MILAN	Missile d'Infanterie Léger Antichar
MLRS	Multiple Launch Rocket System
NBC	nuclear, biological, chemical
NVE	Night Vision Equipment
pto	power take-off
RP	rocket propelled
RAAMS	Remote Anti-armor Mine System
RMG	ranging machine gun
ROKIT	Republic of Korea Indigenous Tank
RO	Royal Ordnance
rpm	rounds per minute or revolutions per minute
SAM	Surface-to-Air Missile
SANTAL	Système Anti-aérien Léger
SATCP	Système Anti-aérien a Très Courtée
shp	shaft horse power
SPAAG	Self-propelled anti-aircraft gun
SPAAM	self-propelled anti-aircraft missile
SPATG	self-propelled anti-tank gun
SLEP	service life extension programme
SP	self-propelled
SPG	self-propelled gun
SPH	self-propelled howitzer
SPM	self-propelled mortar
TADDS	Target Alert Display Data Set
TAM	Tanque Argentino Mediano
TD	tank destroyer
TEL	transporter, erector, launcher
TELAR	transporter, erector, launcher and radar
TLS	Tank Laser Sight
TOGS	Thermal Observation and Gunnery System
TOW	Tube-launched, Optically-tracked, Wire-guided
VAB	Vehicule de l'Avant Blindé (front armoured car)
VBC	Véhicule Blindé Combat
VBL	Véhicule Blindé Léger
VCI	Véhicule de Combat d'Infanterie; Vehiculo combate infantria (infantry combat vehicle)
VCR	variable compression ratio
VCR	Véhicule de Combat à Roues
VCTP	Véhiculo de Combate Transporte de Personal
VCG	Véhicule de Combat du Génie
VDA	Véhicule de Defense Anti-aerienne
VEC	Véhiculo de Exploracion de Caballerie
WAPC	Wheeled Armoured Personnel Carrier
WFSV	Wheeled Fire Support Vehicle
WMRV	Wheeled Maintenance Recovery Vehicle